AMERICAN FREEDOM AND CATHOLIC POWER

Paul Blanshard has had a varied career as lawyer, public official, journalist, and author. Under Mayor Fiorello La Guardia he was head of New York City's Department of Investigations and Accounts. During World War II he was a State Department official in Washington and the Caribbean. Among his books are *Communism, Democracy, and Catholic Power* (1951), *The Irish and Catholic Power: An American Interpretation* (1953), and *The Right to Read: The Battle Against Censorship* (1955).

The first edition of *American Freedom and Catholic Power,* published in 1949, went into twenty-six printings for a total of 240,000 copies.

AMERICAN FREEDOM
AND
CATHOLIC POWER

by Paul Blanshard

Second edition, revised and enlarged

BEACON PRESS *Beacon Hill* **Boston**

Contents

Preface to the Revised Edition

It is almost ten years since *American Freedom and Catholic Power* was published as a book, and somewhat more than a decade since major portions of this work appeared in magazine form. It seems appropriate, therefore, that I should regard this occasion as a kind of tenth birthday celebration—without Roman candles—and that I should express my appreciation to those American and foreign readers—estimated by the Catholic press at several millions—who have made possible the rather miraculous passage of this book through the vicissitudes of twenty-six printings in this country and abroad.

I am not unaware that there may be as many mourners as celebrants at this anniversary occasion. No book in recent years has drawn a heavier barrage from ecclesiastical batteries. The work is often called "controversial," a description which in this age of conformity has come to be used as a term of obloquy. It has even earned its author the undeserved title in one newspaper of "the dean of American controversy." I do not care to repudiate this title, since I regard controversy in a good cause as entirely honorable, but I have no intention of making this revised edition into a controversy about controversies, or a rebuttal of the Catholic counterattack. (I have covered some of that ground in a fifty-three-page pamphlet, *My Catholic Critics*.[1]) This is an up-dated book about the central issues, a factual manual designed to inform the general reader about a great undiscussed area of American social life which must be freely discussed if our liberties are to be preserved. The book has been partially rewritten and entirely reset.

It is my purpose here to bring all factual statements up to date, to cover the most dramatic and significant events in the battle of Catholic power during the past decade, and to add to the narrative more abundant documentation so that every controversial assertion may be supported by the latest items of evidence from Catholic sources. The Bibliography and the Notes at the end of the volume contain hundreds of new titles and new items of factual ammunition. In addition I have added a Calendar of

Significant Events of the last ten years, which, I hope, will serve a useful purpose for research students in this field.

My fundamental theses remain unchanged. The arsenal of factual weapons has simply been augmented and modernized to meet changing conditions.

This last decade has been a stormy and significant one for all Americans who are interested in preserving the separation of church and state. The conflict between Catholic hierarchical power and American institutions has never been more obvious. The battle has broken out on many fronts in the areas of censorship, education, marriage, medicine, birth control, and science. The traditional American and the traditional Catholic conceptions of church-state separation have been revealed as completely contradictory in several areas. In many states our citizens have been compelled simultaneously to defend their intellectual freedom against Catholic censorship, their school system against clerical sabotage, and their public treasuries against financial raids. Millions of Americans who had never been aware of the issues involved in the struggle have now come to realize that the battle is one of the irrepressible conflicts of our time.

What have been the most important events of that decade? Where do we stand at the end of it? Many detailed answers to these questions will be offered in the text. Here certain things can be mentioned by way of an advance summary, with chapter references for the details.

The nominally Catholic population of the United States has increased faster than the general population because of superior Catholic fertility, until today more than 20 per cent of the American people are officially in the Church. Catholic authorities claim that one baby in every four born in the nation is baptized a Catholic. (Chapter 2)

Simultaneously Protestantism has gained on the general population in about the same ratio as Catholicism, and the resistance movement against Catholic power (Protestant, Jewish, and unchurched) has probably gained more rapidly than any of these other phenomena. (Chapter 2)

Catholic schools are temporarily gaining in numbers a little faster than public schools, but their financial plight is desperate because of the increasingly acute shortage of nun-teachers. Because of this difficulty, the next decade may see their *relative* decline. (Chapter 4)

At the national capital and in most of the states the Catholic drive for public money for parochial schools has been stopped both by Supreme Court decisions and by well-organized popular opposition. The turning point in the general battle came in 1949 when Cardinal Spellman's bitter attack on Mrs. Roosevelt revealed the temper and scope of the hierarchy's educational ambitions. Locally the Church is making some gains in winning bus funds. (Chapter 5)

Catholic censorship has been repeatedly challenged and resoundingly defeated in the areas of literature, motion pictures, and the stage until today it is more thoroughly discredited than any other feature of clerical policy. (Chapter 9)

In the racial struggle in the South the hierarchy's liberal stand against segregation has won new non-Catholic support, and very limited Negro affiliation. Simultaneously the Catholic schools in the South have been placed in a position to gain by a possible break-up of the public-school system in that region. (Chapter 11)

Two very minor changes have been made in Catholic medical rules. A Catholic nurse in a Catholic hospital is now officially permitted to summon a Protestant or Jewish clergyman to a dying Protestant or Jewish patient. Also, a Catholic doctor, in treating a patient who is dying of cancer, is now permitted to shorten the patient's life a little with drugs, so long as the last rites of the Church are not interfered with, and so long as the drugs have some hypothetical therapeutic result in addition to their life-shortening effect. (Chapter 6)

Catholic hospitals, with their strictly sectarian medical code, are increasing rapidly with the help of federal money. In fact, this area of hospital development is the only one in which the hierarchy has been distinctly successful in the general drive for public funds. (Chapter 6)

Catholic punitive boycotts of welfare federations which include birth-control clinics have been successful in many cities because of the timidity of financial contributors and of the press. Because of organized Catholic political power, Massachusetts and Connecticut continue to ban birth-control activity. (Chapter 7)

A small movement has begun within the American Catholic Church to modernize its censorship policy, to repudiate its pro-Franco propaganda, and to adapt its theory of church and state to the American concept, but it is still very feeble and fearful. It is not to be regarded with much confidence so long as it is led by the agile and authoritarian-minded Jesuits. (Chapter 13)

In the case of the Hierarchy versus Mixed Marriage, the plaintiffs are losing on all counts. More Catholics are marrying outside the Church; more Catholics are refusing to force their non-Catholic partners to sign the discriminatory mixed-marriage pledges; more Catholics as well as non-Catholics are defying such pledges after they have been signed; and probably much more than half of the children of such marriages are permanently lost to the Church. (Chapter 8)

Several appeasement movements, operating in the name of "brotherhood" and tolerance, have grown rapidly in the last decade, with the aid of large contributions from wealthy industrialists, and have weakened the resistance to the intolerant and separatist policies of the Catholic Church. They are based upon the sincere and misguided notion that "good personal relations" must be maintained between faiths even when one faith is destroying the national foundations of tolerance and freedom. (Chapter 13)

The 1951 attempt to give a new political status to the Catholic Church by sending an American ambassador to the Vatican was promptly defeated by the pressure of adverse public opinion. A revival of the proposal remains a possibility. (Chapter 3)

The hierarchy's chief financial hope for the coming decade is pinned on a new national scheme, patterned after the G.I. educational bills, to get federal grants and "scholarships" for individual students in Catholic schools and so support those schools out of the public treasury without violating the Constitution. (Chapter 5)

The central power-structure of Catholic dictatorship has not been changed by one iota in the past decade, nor has there been any major change in Canon Law or Papal policy. Neither the Catholic bishops nor the Catholic people of the United States have been permitted to hold any plenary council during this period. Pius XII has moved to the right theologically with his new doctrine of the Assumption of the Virgin Mary bodily into heaven. (Chapters 3 and 10)

Looking back, I believe that my three most serious mistakes in the first edition were all errors of omission. I failed to discuss the Al Smith campaign at all—and Lewis Gannett rightly chided me on this omission;[2] I skipped over too briefly our past diplomatic relations with the Vatican; and I did not even mention the Catholic-Biblical defense of the Church's form of government contained in Matthew 16:18: "Thou art Peter and upon this rock I will build my church. . . ." I tried to remedy the Al Smith omission in Chapter 10 of *Communism, Democracy and Catholic Power* by showing how Smith was allowed to evade or gloss over the most important, controversial items of Catholic policy in his *Atlantic Monthly* exchange with Charles C. Marshall. The fact that three-fourths of the objections raised against a Catholic president in the 1928 campaign were based on prejudice or misinformation did not excuse honest men from facing the other fourth. It *is* important, as I shall point out in Chapter 13, that a president of the United States should not be an uncritical and obedient member of an organization which advocates a boycott of the public school, which demands support for its schools from the public treasury, and which attempts to deny birth-control rights even to non-Catholic citizens.

The third omission deserves some comment. Can a writer who discusses Catholic social and political power logically avoid a discussion of the heart of Catholic faith? I made the attempt. At least I tried to write a book which centered upon the encroachments of the Catholic hierarchy upon American freedom, while avoiding unnecessary comment upon Catholic faith as such. As I say in the Personal Prologue: "It is a book not about the Catholic faith but about the cultural, political, and economic policies of the rulers of the Catholic Church."

But it must be admitted that no honest critic can describe the machinery of Church power comprehensively without bringing in and criticizing adversely certain factors which *Catholics themselves* rate as organic parts of their own faith. The reason for this is that the Church's hierarchy has incorporated its own exclusive and undemocratic system of control into the "faith" of the Catholic believer. In the Catholic lexicon of good and evil—written entirely by the bishops—disbelief in that system is as much a mortal sin as disbelief in God, Jesus Christ, and the sacraments.

That is the reason why many Catholics become very angry when non-Catholics, in the process of assailing clerical dictatorship, separatism, and intolerance, innocently insist that they are not attacking "the Catholic faith." The phrase "the Catholic faith" is far more comprehensive to Catholics than, let us say, the phrase "the Methodist faith" is to most Methodists. A Methodist can condemn his denomination's system of authority to his heart's content and advocate a complete revolution in Methodist machinery without impinging upon his own conception of the Methodist faith.

The Pope, as Catholic dictator, has seen to it that no corresponding freedom is permitted to Catholics. His own personal and absolute supremacy is "of faith." Who says so? Why, the Pope, of course. And where did he get the right to confer such power upon himself? From the Bible, of course, via almost nineteen centuries of "tradition" which lie between the death of Christ and Pius IX's declaration of infallibility. And it all goes back to Matthew 16:18, of course—"Thou art Peter. . . ."

It is obvious, therefore, that no one can squarely challenge Catholic clerical absolutism without indirectly challenging *what Catholic priests consider* the Biblical basis of that absolutism. In this edition I accept the responsibility of that challenge. While still believing that the alleged derivation of Catholic absolutism has no necessary connection with any genuine faith because it is both irrelevant and fraudulent, I cannot ignore it so long as the Catholic hierarchy uses it to justify a dictatorial society within America's democratic society. Hence, in this volume I discuss, in a few paragraphs, the tiny Biblical fragment which the Papacy has inflated into a sacred historical foundation for its system of priestly control.

P. B.

1

Personal Prologue: The Duty to Speak

PROBABLY NO PHASE of our life is in greater need of candid discussion than the relationship of the Roman Catholic Church to American institutions, and certainly no important factor in our life has been more consistently neglected by responsible writers. The Catholic issue is not an easy subject to discuss objectively; most Americans have automatically accepted their attitudes on the subject from their parents, and they do not want those attitudes disturbed. They are Catholic* or they are not Catholic. If they are Catholic, they tend to view their own Church with favor, and its critics with suspicion. If they are not Catholic, they tend to reverse the process and view all distinctively Catholic policies with doubt. Both American Catholics and American non-Catholics tend to leave the discussion of religious differences to denominational bigots; and many Americans have never had an opportunity to hear a reasoned and temperate discussion of the place of Catholic power in our national life.

The policy of mutual silence about religious differences is a reasonable policy in matters of personal faith; but when it comes to matters of political, medical, and educational principle, silence may be directly contrary to public welfare. When a church enters the arena of controversial social policy and attempts to control the judgment of its own people (and of other people) on foreign affairs, social hygiene, public education, and modern science, it must be reckoned with as an organ of political and cultural power. It is in that sense that I shall discuss Catholic power in this book. The Catholic problem as I see it is not primarily a religious problem: it is an institutional and political problem. It is a matter of the use

---

* I have used the word "Catholic" to describe the Roman Catholic Church in this volume, and I have capitalized "Church" when referring to the Roman Catholic Church as a courtesy to the Catholic people, who adopt this mode of expression. I am well aware that other churches have a claim to the word "Catholic," but I prefer the ordinary colloquial usage.

1

and abuse of power by an organization that is not only a church but a state within a state, a state above a state, and a foreign-controlled society within American society.

There is no doubt that the American Catholic hierarchy has entered the political arena, and that it is becoming more and more aggressive in extending the frontiers of Catholic authority into the fields of medicine, education, and foreign policy. In the name of religion, the hierarchy fights birth-control and divorce laws in all states. It tells Catholic doctors, nurses, judges, teachers, and legislators what they can and cannot do in many of the controversial phases of their professional conduct. It segregates Catholic children from the rest of the community in a separate school system and censors the cultural diet of these children. It uses the political power of some thirty-five million official American Catholics to bring American foreign policy into line with Vatican temporal interests.

These things should be talked about freely because they are too important to be ignored. Yet it must be admitted that millions of Americans are afraid to talk about them frankly and openly. Part of the reluctance to speak comes from fear, fear of Catholic reprisals. As we shall see in this book, the Catholic hierarchy in this country has great power as a pressure group, and no editor, politician, publisher, merchant, or motion-picture producer can express defiance openly—or publicize documented facts—without risking his future.

But fear will not entirely explain the current silence on the Catholic issue. Some of the reluctance of Americans to speak is due to a misunderstanding of the nature of tolerance. Tolerance should mean complete charity toward men of all races and creeds, complete open-mindedness toward all ideas, and complete willingness to allow peaceful expression of conflicting views. This is what most Americans think they mean when they say that they believe in tolerance.

When they come to apply tolerance to the world of religion, however, they often forget its affirmative implications and fall back on the negative cliché, "You should never criticize another man's religion." Now, that innocent-sounding doctrine, born of the noblest sentiments, is full of danger to the democratic way of life. It ignores the duty of every good citizen to stand for the truth in every field of thought. It fails to take account of the fact that a large part of what men call religion is also politics, social hygiene, and economics. Silence about "another man's religion" may mean acquiescence in second-rate medicine, inferior education, and anti-democratic government.

I believe that every American—Catholic and non-Catholic— has a duty to speak on the Catholic question, because the issues involved go to the heart of our culture and our citizenship. Plain speaking on this question involves many risks of bitterness, mis-understanding, and even fanaticism, but the risks of silence are even greater. Any critic of the policies of the Catholic hierarchy must steel himself to being called "anti-Catholic," because it is part of the hierarchy's strategy of defense to place that brand upon all its opponents; and any critic must also reconcile himself to being called an enemy of the Catholic people, because the hierarchy constantly identifies its clerical ambitions with the supposed wishes of its people.

It is important, therefore, to distinguish between the American Catholic people and their Roman-controlled priests. The Catholic people of the United States fight and die for the same concept of freedom as do other true Americans; they believe in the same fun-damental ideals of democracy. Their record of loyal service to our country in time of war is second to none. If they controlled their own Church, the Catholic problem would soon disappear because, in the atmosphere of American freedom, they would adjust their Church's policies to American realities.

Unfortunately, the Catholic people of the United States are not citizens but *subjects* in their own religious commonwealth. The secular as well as the religious policies of their Church are made in Rome by an organization that is alien in spirit and control. The American Catholic people themselves have no representatives of their own choosing either in their own local hierarchy or in the Roman high command; and they are compelled by the very nature of their Church's authoritarian structure to accept nonreligious as well as religious policies that have been imposed upon them from abroad.

It is for this reason that I am addressing Catholics fully as much as non-Catholics in this book. American freedom is your freedom, and any curtailment of that freedom by clerical power is an even more serious matter for you than it is for non-Catholics. I know that many Catholics are as deeply disturbed as I am about the social policies of their Church's rulers; and they are finding it increasingly difficult to reconcile their convictions as American democrats with the philosophy of their priests, their hierarchy, and their Pope.

It is scarcely necessary to say that no man has a right to discuss the Catholic issue if he is incapable of appreciating the mighty achievements of the Church in the past. No fair-minded man can fail to render homage to the Church's lofty moral purpose and to the heroic sacrifices of its devoted servants in all ages. I do not question the sincerity of that purpose or belittle the devotion it has inspired in the hearts of men. I only hope that some day the institution that has inspired such supreme devotion will be divorced from an antidemocratic and an alien system of control, and that its hierarchy can be induced or compelled by its own people to abandon its separatist and intolerant policies.

Some readers who accept every fact that I have recorded in these pages may still question the wisdom of discussing these matters in public at the present time, because of the critical international situation which finds the United States pitted against Communist power. These critics would keep silent about the antidemocratic program of the Vatican until the present crisis is resolved, because they regard the Catholic Church, with all its faults, as a necessary bulwark against militant Communism. I respect the sincerity of this view, and I share with most Americans the conviction that Communist aggression must be met with determined resistance. But I do not believe that fear of one authoritarian power justifies compromise with another, especially when the compromise may be used to strengthen clerical fascism in many countries. Certainly in this country the acceptance of *any* form of authoritarian control weakens the democratic spirit; and one encroachment upon the democratic way of life may be used as a precedent for others. In the long run, the capacity to defend American democracy against a Communist dictatorship must be based upon a free culture, and I believe that the facts that I have marshaled in these pages demonstrate the impossibility of reconciling a free culture with the present policies of the Vatican.

I have tried in this book to put down plain facts about the Catholic question, facts that every American should know. The method of treatment is self-evident. It is not a history but a contemporary review. It is a book not about the Catholic faith but about the cultural, political, and economic policies of the rulers of the Catholic Church. Wherever possible I have let Catholicism speak for itself. There is a Catholic source for almost every major fact in this book, and the documents, dates, publishers, and official Imprimaturs are all listed, with due acknowledgments, in the Notes in the Appendix.

I have seen many of the things that I describe here, because I am not unfamiliar with Catholic machinations in big-city politics, and because I have lived in Rome and Mexico, and studied Catholic policy first hand in most of the nations of western Europe. But this is not a personal narrative, and I have tried to make it primarily a documentary study.

Many readers have asked me how I came to be interested in the Catholic issue. As a libertarian I had always been concerned with any threat of cultural or political autocracy, but my special introduction to Catholic policy came through my interest in birth control and the population problem. After much study in the field of sociology, I had come to regard overpopulation as the most basic and formidable threat to the future happiness of the human race. And, simultaneously, I had come to feel that organized clerical fanaticism was the most serious obstacle to constructive remedies in this field.

One day while browsing in the stacks of the Baker Library at Dartmouth I accidentally stumbled upon a Catholic moral manual for priests which set forth the Catholic rule of the equality of mother and fetus in childbirth. I had never heard of the doctrine before. I was startled and horrified to realize that, in spite of the camouflaging verbiage, the policy which was arbitrarily imposed upon American Catholic doctors and mothers amounted in practice to a kind of murder by negligence. A celibate priest was instructed by his celibate hierarchy to tell Catholic doctors and nurses, on pain of mortal sin, that they must permit a Catholic mother to die rather than resort to direct interruption of pregnancy *even when the unborn child could not survive in any case.* I was astonished no less by the brutality and unrealism of the policy than by the bland evasions which the priests were circulating in this country to create the illusion that by this policy they were merely preserving life and saving souls. (Later the Jesuit magazine *America* was to publish an article in reply to my analysis in which the Jesuit author did not once mention the key fact that under the childbirth doctrine a mother is allowed to die *even when the fetus cannot survive anyway.*[1]) I reasoned that a priesthood which could stoop to such tactics should be carefully studied. I began to explore the whole field of Catholic Canon Law in the areas of education, medicine, marriage, divorce, annulment, and censorship; and what I found there is summarized in these pages.

It seemed to me that the only sound approach to the subject was documentary. Personal investigations of Catholic policy in Catholic institutions by a non-Catholic are not practical unless the investigator is prepared to accept what is offered to him without question—although I later discovered that I could directly observe quite a few facts in Catholic institutions in Italy and Ireland. It seemed to me also that a sectarian religious approach to the problem would be undesirable, since I would soon be bogged down in denominational rivalries and my disclosures would be branded as proselyting propaganda. (I am not wholly unqualified to make the religious approach, since I studied theology in my youth and was ordained a minister, but my life has been spent in other professions which have conditioned me for a more nontheological treatment.) Having specialized as a government official and lawyer in the investigation of political corruption, I decided that Catholic clerical policy (not the Catholic religion as such) might profitably be submitted to an equally rigorous factual probe. I was moved to make this decision partly by something which I soon discovered, an astonishing public ignorance of the actual priestly policies and rules which govern the Church, behind its elaborate façade of modern Americanism. I found that many Catholics as well as non-Catholics were abysmally ignorant about the social policy and governmental mechanism of their own authoritarian Church. Here, it seemed to me, was a great and relatively unexplored underworld of medieval policy and practice which had been prettified and camouflaged by clerical window dressing. It was time for candor. I began my ten years of research.

My first findings saw the light of day in *The Nation*,[2] under the gallant editorship of Freda Kirchwey, where they provoked such a fiery response from Catholic critics that the magazine was banned from the high-school libraries of New York City in June 1948, as "offensive" to the followers of a certain faith. This ban not only provided national publicity but also produced a strong counterattack by free-speech advocates of national prominence. They wanted no suppression of free discussion even when they personally disagreed with my conclusions. The Ad Hoc Committee to Lift the Ban on *The Nation* was headed by Archibald Mac-Leish, and it included Mrs. Eleanor Roosevelt and scores of other famous Americans.

Then, while *The Nation* controversy was still raging, Cardinal Spellman attacked Mrs. Roosevelt, only a few weeks after the publication of this book.[3] In the indignant counterattack on the cardinal, *American Freedom and Catholic Power* was seized upon as the most readily available verbal hand grenade. It soared to the best-seller lists and remained there for about six months. The momentum lasted for several years, carrying the successor volume, *Communism, Democracy and Catholic Power,* to the best-seller lists for many months, and producing a steady demand to this day for the 26 printings of the original volume, here and abroad.

But before these events, the book had been obliged to run a fearful gauntlet in the world of publishing, advertising, and reviewing. Ten leading publishers refused the manuscript, and several of them admitted quite frankly that the sole reason for rejection was the fear of Catholic reprisals against their other publications. America's first newspaper, *The New York Times,* refused to carry advertising for the book on the ground that it was an attack on the Roman Catholic Church and its clergy, and because its chapter on "Sex, Birth Control, and Eugenics" was "particularly objectionable since it involved highly controversial matter of a religious nature." [4] * In New York, Macy's refused for a time to sell the book across the counter, then yielded in the face of public indignation and lifted the ban. (Altman's still preserves the ban on counter sales, as do a few other stores.)

Across the country countless booksellers and librarians were confronted with organized Catholic demands to reject the book, or remove it from display, or stop its circulation after sales had begun. Most of the booksellers and nearly all the public librarians stood firm, and the book soon climbed to the top list of works in library circulation. But it was the fear of organized Catholic boycotts against small newsdealers and booksellers that prevented the publisher and author from issuing a 50-cent paperback edition, which would undoubtedly have added several millions to its circulation. The great distributors of paperback books have warned the publisher that newsstand and drug-store paperback sales are impractical because of potential priestly reprisals against small merchants.

Throughout this fight, Melvin Arnold, then editor and director of the Beacon Press, played a leading role. He welcomed the manuscript when other publishers dared not handle it; he personally supplied invaluable factual additions; and he led the fight in the publishing world for the author's right to be heard. The vigor-

* We gratefully acknowledge that the *New York Times* lifted its advertising ban on this book just after it had been set up in plates.

ous promotion of the book by Edward Darling of the Beacon Press was also an important factor in its success. The judgment of these two men was confirmed when the Beacon Press, partly as a result of its new fighting reputation, assumed a more important place in the publishing industry.

The Catholic counterattack on the book was vigorous and bitter. A leading Catholic columnist headed his reply: "Blanshard the Fascist." The author was called everything in the calendar of contumely except a Communist—*that* would have cost any financially responsible accuser a heavy assessment in court damages. *America,* the Jesuit weekly, ran seven articles by Father George Dunne, S.J., which were later published in pamphlet form. *The Commonweal,* organ of liberal Catholic intellectuals, chimed in with an attack which approximated the tone and accuracy of the yellow diocesan press.[5] *America* discovered that the author operated "on the lowest level of bigotry." *The Commonweal* found that "the book is of no importance." But neither magazine could deny that the author's lifetime record as a liberal crusader and opponent of bigotry, prejudice, and the Ku Klux Klan was as consistent as that of any editor on either masthead.

Both *America* and *The Commonweal,* after listing my sins in great detail over a period of many months, refused point blank to carry even the simplest factual advertisement for the book: "You've read Father Dunne's reply to Blanshard; now read the book itself." *The Nation,* of course, gladly carried advertisements for opposing literary works, and Beacon Press, with my warm approval, mailed free of charge to thousands of purchasers, along with the book itself, the Jesuit "exposure." On two occasions the Jesuit critics consented to public debates, and I met them before capacity audiences at the Harvard and Yale Law Schools. Then, suddenly, no priests were "available" for similar platform appearances.

Altogether at least seven books and pamphlets were written by Catholic authors in reply to *American Freedom and Catholic Power*—the titles and names of publishers are contained in the Appendix so that readers may secure them more readily.[6] Unfortunately, no priest or member of the hierarchy has attempted a definitive or complete reply. The most voluminous counterattack, *Catholicism and American Freedom,* which I have analyzed in *My Catholic Critics,* was written without an Imprimatur by a layman and former professor of public speaking at Brooklyn College,

James O'Neill. It avoided the most important facts concerning ecclesiastical dictatorship and reaction, and it "liberalized" Catholic law in such an amateurish manner that O'Neill was later severely rebuked for "misleading" and "confused" interpretations of the teachings of his own Church by the most authoritative priestly journal in this country, *The American Ecclesiastical Review,* published by the Catholic University of America.[7]

I regret to say that most of the Catholic analyses of this book, even in the scholarly Catholic journals, were completely unscrupulous. Many of the analysts deliberately withheld from their Catholic readers the most significant portions of my reasoning and of my documented evidence, and then charged me with "quoting out of context." In one sense, of course, every author who quotes briefly from any work must quote "out of context"; that is to say, he must take out a limited portion of a document unless he intends to reprint the whole. The sole question which involves his integrity is whether the quoted portion is truly representative of the whole in respect to the point which he is making. On this score the scholarly Catholic critics could find little material to argue about. They resorted often to vague general charges that I represented a materialist or atheist point of view, or they asserted that I stood for an all-powerful state that would destroy Catholic rights, all of which maundering is too absurd to dignify with an answer here.

For the first few months most of the great newspapers and magazines refused to review the book—or gave it for literary assassination to professional Catholic reviewers. However, the tide turned as the circulation soared, and indignant letters poured in to newspaper and magazine offices, protesting against the mysterious silence concerning a best-seller. Before the first year had ended, many summaries of the book's contents had appeared in magazines and newspapers. Usually they were cautious, noncommittal, or slyly vindictive. But they were better than silence. It was Samuel Johnson who said once: "I would rather be attacked than unnoticed; for the worst thing you can do to an author is to be silent as to his works."

The thousands of letters I have received from interested readers in this last decade have been overwhelmingly favorable, and the most encouraging fact is that many of them have come from Catholics. It was the late Thomas Sugrue, courageous author of *Strangers in the Earth* and *A Catholic Speaks His Mind,* who assured me that *American Freedom and Catholic Power* told the truth, and that no man needed to apologize for truth. Some of the world's greatest philosophers and scientists stepped forward to render favorable public testimony at critical moments in the campaign of vilification. The book, said John Dewey, was done "with exemplary scholarship, judgment and tact."

One night in 1951, at the end of a crowded meeting in Princeton, a frail old gentleman with towering brow and white, bushy hair stood up in the audience and said: "I wish to express my gratitude to a man who is fighting the abuses of a powerful organization. We are grateful to him for his efforts." For that one brief comment, Albert Einstein was hounded continuously in the Catholic press until his death. He did not waver in his view. In reply to a letter of violent protest from a Catholic devotee, he wrote:

> I am convinced that some political and social activities and practices of the Catholic organizations are detrimental and even dangerous for the community as a whole, here and everywhere. I mention here only the fight against birth control at a time when overpopulation in various countries has become a serious threat to the health of people and a grave obstacle to any attempt to organize peace on this planet. . . .
>
> Reading your letter, I cannot help to doubt whether you have really studied Mr. Blanshard's publications.

Einstein's doubt has been verified in my own experience in hundreds of other instances. Probably nine-tenths of the hostile criticism I have received from Catholic correspondents has revealed by internal evidence that the writers had never read a line of this book.

It is impossible adequately to acknowledge the great debt I owe to many distinguished scholars and specialists who helped me in the preparation of the first edition of this book. Among them the most important was George La Piana, Professor Emeritus of Church History at Harvard, an outstanding authority on Catholic policy. Giovanni Pioli of Milan, former vice-rector of the Propaganda Pontifical College, Rome, was also most helpful. The two chapters on "The Church and Medicine" and "Sex, Birth Control and Eugenics" were reviewed by the dean of American gynecologists, Robert Latou Dickinson, former president of the American Gynecological Society.

2

How the Hierarchy Works

1

IN TWO HUNDRED YEARS the Roman Catholic Church in the United States has increased from the smallest to the largest church in the nation, claiming in 1957 the allegiance of some thirty-five million Americans.[1] The American branch of the Roman faith is now almost three times as large as the largest single Protestant denomination in the United States, the Methodist Church, and it constitutes about one-fifth of the total population. It contributes more money to the hierarchy at Rome than all the other national branches of the Catholic Church put together. Nominally the United States has become the fourth Catholic country in the world—below Brazil, Italy, and France—but there are many ways in which it is the first Catholic country. Catholicism in the United States is more secure and more prosperous than it is in any other major nation of the world.

This substantial position is something quite recent for the American Catholic Church. As late as 1908 it was a missionary branch within the Roman system, supported partly by contributions from abroad, and treated with conspicuous condescension by the European hierarchy. It was so unimportant in the total scheme of world Catholicism before 1875 that until that date not a single American cardinal had been appointed.

For the first 150 years of our history the Roman Church in America was on the defensive. All except one of the original thirteen colonies were settled by Protestants, and most of them were militant Protestants. Even Maryland's Catholics were not in a majority in that colony, and they soon lost control to non-Catholics. At the time of the Revolution less than one per cent of the people of the American colonies were Catholic. Father John Tracy Ellis points out in his *American Catholicism* that there were

11

"scarcely more than 25,000 Catholics" in a population of nearly 4,000,000 in the United States in 1785.[2] The greatest political leaders, writers, and reformers of our early national history were all non-Catholics, and all the early centers of higher learning were dominated by Protestant influence.

In such an atmosphere the colonial Catholics were treated as outsiders by the other colonists, and when the new nation broke away from European control, the Romanists, as they were often called, were doubly suspect because of their continued allegiance to a European ruler. The Roman Church was the only church which did not sever its European controls and become an American church. Although its hierarchy accepted in America the new policy of disestablishment for all churches, its world policy remained unaltered. The suspicion increased rather than diminished as a great flood of Catholic immigrants poured into the country from Europe. Clustered together in little colonies in our great cities, these immigrants seemed to live a life apart. They were the poorest and the least assimilated members of the American community, and their presence increased the feeling among non-Catholics that the Roman Catholic Church did not "belong" in America.

During this stage the Catholic churches gained by the alienation of their people from the rest of America. Hostility drove the immigrant communities back upon themselves. The newcomers turned to their priests for leadership as well as comfort, and the priests became chieftains in the war against prejudice. It is not surprising that in this period of immigrant influx the Catholic Church in America gained strength more rapidly than it has ever gained before or since. Although the Irish immigrants, who became the most powerful group in the American Church, found more freedom here than in Ireland, they also found much personal hostility.

In many parts of America this feeling of hostility broke out into open persecution. Anti-Catholic fanatics in the forties and fifties of the last century caricatured priests, burned a few convents, and spread wild rumors that Catholics were plotting to capture the country by armed rebellion. The A.P.A. (American Protective Association) in the nineties became one of the most noisy and effective pressure groups in the country, and "no Popery" was adopted as one of the most popular political slogans. Millions of otherwise sensible Americans were persuaded that Catholic convents were little better than brothels, and that few priests observed their oaths of celibacy. The great cultural and humanitarian achievements of the Church were almost forgotten.[3] Anti-Catholic political parties appeared in several states and even anti-Catholic candidates for President.

Although the attack on the Catholic Church was bitter, it should not be supposed that all groups that criticized Catholic policy were unbalanced or irrational in their views. The nativist movement against Catholic power was not confined to religious fanatics. William Ellery Channing distinguished carefully between the autocracy of Roman power and the great moral achievements of the Catholic people, attacking one with bitter irony and praising the other with a sincere tribute. Theodore Parker, nineteenth-century Unitarian, centered his attack on the political and educational policies of the hierarchy. Declaring that the Catholic Church "hates our free churches, free press, and, above all, our free schools," he said:

The Roman Catholic Church claims infallibility for itself, and denies spiritual freedom, liberty of mind or conscience, to its members. It is therefore the foe to all progress; it is deadly hostile to democracy. To mankind this is its first command— Submit to an external authority; subordinate your human nature to an element foreign and abhorrent thereto! It aims at absolute domination over the body and spirit of man. The Catholic Church can never escape from the consequences of her first principle. She is the natural ally of tyrants, and the irreconcilable enemy of freedom.[4]

Because of the fundamental tolerance of the American majority, the most fantical anti-Catholic movements of pre-Civil War days, and of the nineties, flowered briefly and then died down. Finally common sense was restored and fanaticism discredited. The Irish and other immigrants were rapidly assimilated and soon gained important posts in political life. By the time of World War I the Catholics, Protestants, and Jews in this country approximated one nation indivisible, even if that nation did not provide justice for all.

But the Catholic problem is still with us. Primarily it is not the problem of the assimilation of the Catholic *people;* they have been absorbed into the American community as completely as could be expected in view of the attitude of their priests. Essentially the Catholic problem in America is what to do with the hierarchy of the Roman Church. The American Catholic *people* have done their best to join the rest of America, but the American Catholic hierarchy, as we shall see in the course of this survey, has never been assimilated. It is still fundamentally Roman in its spirit and directives. It is an autocratic moral monarchy in a liberal democracy.

But we are getting ahead of our story. Before we start to discuss the political and ecclesiastical philosophy of the hierarchy we should describe the hierarchy itself and its basic methods of operation. And before we discuss these methods of operation, we should say a few words about certain special facts which make it difficult to judge just how large and powerful the Catholic Church actually is in this country.

2

I have said that the Catholic Church claims thirty-five million people in this country and that it has grown from the smallest to the largest American church in the course of about two hundred years. Such a statement might give the impression that Catholicism is a great and spontaneous mass movement of thirty-five million Americans, and that it is increasing very rapidly *proportionately* in the population. It *is* increasing in numbers, but there are many special factors in that alleged increase which need to be studied before Catholic claims can be assessed.

The Catholic Church in America is growing in *power*—there is no doubt about that—but it is not growing in numbers as fast as it appears to be growing. In the first place, the hierarchy includes in its figures infants and children under thirteen. Most other churches do not do that. That one factor alone adds about 27 per cent to the adult Catholic population in this country.[5]

In the second place, the Catholic Church does not drop people from its rolls except under the most extraordinary circumstances. In general, "once a Catholic always a Catholic." Some of the most determined opponents of the Church are still counted as part of the thirty-five million "Catholics" in this country. The Church admits quite frankly that it continues to count "occult heretics" so long as they are "ostensibly Catholics." [6] The system of recruiting and discipline used by the priests calls for almost no obligatory affirmative action by an adult to remain a "Catholic." The practicing Catholic is directed to attend Mass on Sundays and confess his sins to a priest at least once a year, under pain of definite penalties, but nothing outwardly happens to him if he neglects these duties, because it is a spiritual dereliction, remedied when he again confesses and attends Mass regularly. He is baptized as an infant, is confirmed and receives communion as a child. Thereafter he is counted in the totals of the Catholic Church.

It is doubtful that the Church is increasing any more rapidly than Protestantism when equivalent tests are applied to membership figures. (Of course, all religious statistics are inaccurate because we do not have a national religious census.) Almost all churches in the United States have gained substantially in the last decade, until the membership proportion in the population reached an all-time high of 62 per cent in 1957.[7] According to the *Yearbook of American Churches* for 1957, the Roman Catholic proportion in the population jumped from 16 per cent in 1926 to 20.3 per cent in 1955, an increase in proportion of 27 per cent; but the Protestant proportion in the population jumped from 27 per cent in 1926 to 35.5 per cent in 1955, an increase in proportion of 31 per cent.

If Protestant churches counted their adherents as generously as Catholic statisticians count theirs, it is likely that Protestantism could claim almost three times as many adherents as the Catholic Church claims. By Catholic standards of measurement there are twelve states which have more Catholics than Protestants—all the New England states, New York, New Jersey, California, Arizona, New Mexico, and Louisiana;[8] but there are millions of uncounted citizens in these states who are nearer to the Protestant outlook than to the Catholic outlook. They are not counted as Protestants because Protestant churches usually require some adult act of affirmation to continue names on membership rolls. The 1956 estimate of *Presbyterian Life* that for every two official Protestant members in the United States there is one "church-related" Protestant, either child or adult, seems conservative.[9] By this method of counting there were about 84,000,000 Protestants and 33,000,000 Catholics in the United States in 1956.

How many of the thirty-five million people in America claimed by the Church are really loyal to the Church? Nobody knows, but one index of loyalty is some kind of support. Almost any "good" Catholic can give a dollar or two if he is loyal to the institution. By that test probably about half of our thirty-five million "Catholics" are real Catholics. Catholic writers who ought to know the field thoroughly have estimated that about half of the

Catholic people in the United States give some kind of support to the Church.[10] That would make at most eighteen million Catholics in the country, less than 11 per cent of the population. The *Osservatore Romano* itself, the newspaper of the Vatican, has admitted that only about half of the world's alleged Catholics are practicing Catholics.[11] (One difficulty in describing the status of their belief accurately is that the majority of the world's Catholics are almost certainly illiterate, but no one can prove this fact statistically.) A similar admission concerning the lapsed and dormant Catholics in the United States has been made by Father Thomas J. Harte, assistant professor of sociology at the Catholic University: "One would estimate as high as fifty per cent of parish populations can be called practising Catholics in any sense of the word." [12]

But even an 11 per cent bloc in the American population can make a tremendous impression if its controlling hierarchy is closely knit and well disciplined. The Protestant and Jewish "opposition" appears to be weaker than it is because it is so fragmented.

The concentration of the Catholic population in certain large cities gives the Church unusual political and civic power in those regions—two-thirds of all Catholics in the United States live in one-seventh of the national territory,[13] and in the total population of our fifty largest cities they outnumber Protestants by a considerable margin. The concentration is especially marked in the northeastern part of the United States, where two states, Massachusetts and Rhode Island, have, by Catholic methods of computation, Catholic majorities.

The Roman Church in America has a great gift for showmanship, and its ceremonials and costumes lend themselves naturally to pageantry in the grand manner. Ten thousand Quakers can live in an American community all their lives and not attract half the attention that ten thousand Catholics do, especially if the Catholics have an energetic bishop who understands modern publicity methods.

It is doubtful if the face of any nonofficial personage in America is more familiar to American readers than that of Cardinal Spellman, the American hierarchy's chief leader. Publicity worth millions of dollars in revenue and good will is given to the Catholic hierarchy every week by the newspapers and magazines of the country, all glamorous and respectful, with never a critical tone. Protestant leaders and Jewish rabbis are accorded kindly treatment also, but not quite such pronounced reverence, and they are relatively drab and prosaic figures compared to the colorful, costumed leaders of Catholic spectacles.

To many non-Catholics from abroad the power of the Catholic hierarchy to gain and hold public attention in America is one of the most striking phenomena of our life. Cecil Northcott, British correspondent of the *Christian Century,* has remarked on what Harold Laski called "the immense and arrogant authority assumed by the Roman Catholic hierarchy" in American life. He said:

I would put this fact first among the vital maneuvers now going on in the U.S.A. It seems to condition nearly every phase of American thought. Rome has not captured America, but she has very nearly captured the machinery of American life. What the great roads were to the missionary expansion of the faith in the ancient Mediterranean world, the press, the radio, the public relations machines are to the Vatican in the New World. The hierarchy is marching down them with the ordered tramp of Roman legions.[14]

The Catholic parish buildings are also important items in the technique of denominational display. The Catholic church is usually a *big* church, and often an oversized church. Frequently the priests go to great extremes in their campaigns for building funds, even in the parishes of the poor. In 1936 the Catholic Church edifices of the State of New York had forty-one millions in debt, an *average* of $23,000 for every edifice, old and new, in the state.[15] The big church in the American community is the Catholic hierarchy's Exhibit A of ecclesiastical power, and the Catholic people have accepted it as their symbol of success even when it is heavily mortgaged. To raise the money for such a structure the parish priest often imposes a levy upon the Catholic community which burdens every one of its members for many years.

The resistance to these money-raising drives for huge buildings is sometimes very strong in the Catholic lay community. In spite of continuing pressure and the emotional appeal of Mother's Day collections, the National Shrine of the Immaculate Conception in Washington, planned as a multi-million-dollar rival of St. Peter's, Notre Dame, and Chartres, has been in the process of planning and construction since the 1920's and is not yet completed. When it is completed, it will be the greatest denominational show piece in the United States.

It will belong, of course, to the bishops and not to the Catholic people of the United States, who will have paid for it. This rule of complete clerical ownership is an organic and vital part of Catholic world policy. Under Canon 1518, "The Roman Pontiff is the supreme administrator and dispenser of all ecclesiastical goods." The bishops, as the Pope's representatives, sometimes admit lay trustees to controlling boards of local churches but these laymen do not have any real ownership power. In order to keep laymen in their place in such matters, the Sacred Congregation of the Council has instructed American bishops to favor the mechanism of Catholic ownership now prevailing in New York under which: "No act or proceeding of the trustees of any such incorporated church shall be valid without the sanction of the Archbishop or Bishop of the diocese. . . ." [16] Catholic laymen have been accustomed to this financial autocracy for a long time. Local churches and dioceses sometimes make public the financial facts concerning building drives and local costs, but the Vatican itself never renders a financial report even to its own people concerning its own vast financial holding and enterprises. The Catholic Information Society has issued figures indicating that American Catholics gave about $365,000,000 a year to their Church in 1953, an average of $11.21 per member.[17] This is far below the average contribution per member of many Protestant churches.

In many states Catholic Church property is owned outright by the bishop under the device called corporation sole. I was a little startled to receive some years ago a prospectus from a broker in Wisconsin offering me investment opportunities in these words:

$370,000. The Roman Catholic Archbishop of Santa Fe, 3-3½% serial notes, due 1950-59.

$50,000. The Roman Catholic Bishop of Pueblo, Colorado, 3½% notes due 1958.

$150,000. Catholic Bishop of Corpus Christi, 3-3¼% bonds due serially, 1950-1961.

3

The special factors of favorable publicity and traditionally showy edifices must be weighed carefully in assessing the real hold of the Catholic hierarchy upon the American people. Another practice which must be taken into account is the gigantic religious spectacle. The American people take delight in big shows, and the hierarchy in recent years has learned to give them the kind of displays they want.

Americans were given their first demonstration of what the Church could do in the way of an international spectacle at the Eucharistic Congress in Chicago in 1926 when, according to Catholic estimates, 400,000 men gathered under the auspices of the Holy Name Society at Soldier Field in what one Catholic writer called "the most impressive demonstration of religious faith and loyalty ever staged in the Western Hemisphere." When darkness came and the arclights were extinguished over the field, 400,000 men lighted candles, held them aloft, and repeated in unison their oath of religious loyalty with "an upsurging roar of voices that could be heard great distances through the streets of Chicago." Since then the Church has staged a number of spectacles almost as impressive, and the American press has described them with admiration.

What Protestant or Jewish organization could parallel the pageantry of the great international Marian Congress in June, 1947, in Ottawa's baseball park, where sixty-six special trains and countless autos brought a quarter of a million Catholics headed by nine cardinals to pay homage to the Virgin Mary as the Mother of God?

For the Catholic Church [said *Life*], which has put on spectacles for fifteen centuries in all manner of places, it was no trick at all to turn the ballpark into an impressive open-air cathedral. Making their recurrent symbol the letter "M" (for Mary), church architects built a dais 515 feet long. Along its back wall four blue and white angels raised their golden trumpets toward a statue of the Virgin, leaning forward a little toward the worshippers, which stood on a globe atop a 115-foot tower. In the center of the enormous dais was the stage and altar, used interchangeably for pageants and High Masses. In the flanking grandstands sat the clergy on long lines of prayer benches. Along the bottom of the dais, on the level of the field, stretched a row of confessional booths.

Twenty plaster effigies of the Virgin Mary on floats were pulled through the streets by horses, and one of her images was kissed on the foot so often by kneeling nuns that the paint was worn off before the five-day Congress had ended.[18]

It is not surprising that one American journal said in 1937: "No other church on earth has the taste for pomp of the Roman Catholic Church, or possesses such a world-wide organization geared to deck a city with yellow and white flags, and provide a week-long demonstration by happy enthusiastic masses. The Committees of the International Eucharistic Congress included even a Committee on Bells and Whistles." [19]

It is hard for an outsider to believe that a Church that can produce such enormously successful spectacles is not increasing rapidly in its proportionate share in the population. Actually the Church's slight proportionate increase in the national population appears to be wholly a matter of a superior birth rate—although no scientific statistics are available to prove this superiority. The present Catholic claim is that at least one child in every four born in the United States is Catholic, while only one person in every five in the general population is Catholic.[20] This claim seems to be conservative. There is a trifling transfer of Americans to Catholicism from other faiths, and there is a considerable unrecorded transfer in the opposite direction. The Church's claim of more than 100,000 "converts" a year includes as "converts" all adult baptisms. Father Paul Rust, writing in the *Homiletic and Pastoral Review* for April, 1957, complained that the Church was winning only one convert annually for each 240 Catholics, which is certainly a very low proselyting rate when the success of Protestantism in recruiting Catholic members is considered. Father Rust said mournfully that "neither we nor our parishioners are contributing any really constructive part to the Catholic apostolate of making America Catholic."

Here and there a conspicuous conversion takes place and is given due acknowledgment by the press, but the annual losses far exceed the conversions, and the annual losses are not recorded in the Church books or in the press. It is only in the journals written by priests for priests that one can discover the extent of the erosion that is going on in the Catholic system.

Father Felix M. Kirsch, instructor in religion at the Catholic University of America, has complained that "all thoughtful observers of the American scene are alarmed over the frightful leakage from the Church in the United States—some going so far as to estimate the annual loss to the Church to be half a million. . . ." [21] Father Kirsch thinks that estimate of half a million is too high, but even if it is only 150,000, it still balances the conversions. We shall see later in chapter 8, that from one-fourth to one-half of the marriages of American Catholics are mixed marriages, that at least one-fifth of the Catholics involved give up the faith, and that the majority of the children of such marriages are probably lost to the Church. All these losses and leakages are so de-emphasized in Catholic propaganda that one has to be a sociological detective to discover them.

This does not mean that the American Catholic Church is losing its commanding place in the Catholic world system. Far from it. The European branches of the Church have lost proportionately for the past one hundred years. The Church still dominates Spain, Ireland, Portugal, and some of the South American countries, but it is on the defensive in most of Europe. It lost the whole Rumanian Uniate church in 1948 when that body of more than one million members returned to the Rumanian Orthodox Church, and it had already lost two or three million Ruthenian Catholics of the Slavic rite. Yugoslavia will sooner or later be lost to the Roman hierarchy if present trends continue, and the Church's position is a question mark in Italy, East Germany, Poland, and Hungary. Not one of the five greatest powers in the world today is a genuinely Catholic state. The French people are nominally Catholic but the Church's followers are in a minority politically, and only about 20 per cent of the French people are practicing Catholics. The Vatican claims more than 484,000,000 souls throughout the world, but to reach this optimistic estimate the hierarchy includes millions of people who no longer pay even lip-service to the Pope, and millions of non-white Asians and Africans who will undoubtedly repudiate "the white man's religion" when they have achieved their cultural independence. The Church's statistics on world growth are produced by a propaganda organization, the Catholic Students Mission Crusade, whose estimates may safely be described as charitable. Its figures apparently include at least 100,000,000 in membership padding. For example, it credits Latin America with a 93 per cent Catholic population, whereas the same *Catholic Almanac* which publishes this estimate also includes the results of a detailed priestly survey showing that "the great body of people of Latin America live outside the Church . . . only about 10 per cent actually practice the faith." [22] Its world statistics in 1955 still claimed 67,000,000 alleged Catholics in countries under Communist control, including 3,000,000 in China, although Catholicism in that country has been almost wiped out, and its 5,700 foreign missionaries reduced to sixteen—eight in prison and eight free.

4

The observer of any great Catholic spectacle in the United States is impressed with one thing—the evidence of the absolute rule of the clergy. The public adulation given to clerical leaders is without parallel in the Protestant churches. The great masses of Catholic people who line the streets during a Catholic spectacle may kneel before the Host or a statue of the Virgin Mary or the relic of a saint, but the actual focus of their worshipful attention is more likely to be a gorgeously appareled cardinal with a red cloak three yards long. The genuflections of the faithful before the so-called princes of the Church, and even before simple bishops, annoy and disturb non-Catholic Americans, who are likely to ask: "Is not such servility utterly contrary to the American tradition?" "What good American ever kneels to any man?" "How did this medieval posturing ever get to the United States?"

This reaction to conspicuous medievalism is quite natural and justified. The framework of the power of the Catholic Church *is* medieval. The clerical caste, on the whole, corresponds to the nobility, and the Pope corresponds to the king. In the total authoritarian scheme the people are subjects, as they were in the Middle Ages, not participants in the government.

In a very real sense the Catholic Church *is* the clergy. Certainly the Catholic Church is not a church in the same sense that a congregational body is a church. In a congregational church the members can buy and sell the church's buildings as they choose, "call" or dismiss the pastor, and even determine the institution's creed. They do all these things by majority vote if any issue is raised which shows a difference of opinion.

In the Catholic system the people have none of these powers. The central structure of the Church is completely authoritarian, and the role of laymen is completely passive. The priest and his priestly superiors dominate the whole ecclesiastical, educational, and financial machinery. Priests are called to their vocation without any lay approval and assigned to parish or institutional posts by order of a bishop without any by-your-leave from the congregations they serve. A priest can be suspended summarily by his bishop without even a hearing if the reasons seem sufficient to his bishop, and the bishop is not even required to inform the priest of his reasons.[23] The priest can be promoted also for reasons which seem sufficient to his bishop alone.

The beliefs of the Church are controlled in an equally arbitrary manner. They are crystallized in a long list of dogmatic utterances of councils and Popes that do not admit of modification or change by the Catholic people. The maintenance of these dogmas against error and heresy is the task of the Congregation of the Holy Office. Accordingly, the Pope himself heads this Congregation, and it is composed entirely of cardinals and minor prelates; there are also advisers, but no adviser may even be present at a meeting of the Congregation when a vote is being taken on any doctrinal matter.[24] A solemn oath binds the eleven cardinals of the Congregation and the staff not to disclose any discussion which goes on behind the closed doors concerning the activities of the Congregation, and the penalty for violating this oath is excommunication.

The word "congregation" evokes in the minds of most Americans something democratic in nature, a group of people who meet together as members of some organization to decide something on their own authority. The twelve Congregations which surround the Pope in the government of the Roman Church are not congregations in that sense. They are not committees of Catholic people chosen by the members of the local churches in various nations. They are appointed committees of appointed cardinals, with a few minor prelates and advisers who are also appointed by the Pope directly or indirectly. They make important decisions but those decisions are subject to approval by the Pope and not by the Catholic people. The Congregations are entirely clerical and unanimously male. They are, in effect, departments of the central government of the Roman Church, and they form a great network of ecclesiastical power which reaches to every corner of the world.

The bureaucracy of the Roman Church at the capital is huge, centralized, and tightly controlled. The Roman Curia[25] consists of the Pope, the Sacred College of Cardinals (maximum number seventy), twelve Congregations, three Tribunals, and five Offices. It is, as one Catholic writer has said, "the most conservative of all governments," and it rules its subjects with the pomp and pageantry of the Middle Ages.

The Sacred College chooses the Pope, and that Pope chooses the cardinals of the Sacred College as vacancies occur. A Pope can change the whole character of the Sacred College overnight if he wishes to make a flood of new appointments. Pius XII appointed thirty-two cardinals on one day, December 23, 1945.

The College of Cardinals has virtually no power independent of the Pope, except to appoint a new Pope when one has died. Having exercised its elective function, it becomes merely a subordinate Papal committee, without even the power to change or dispense from Papal laws during the interim between popes.[26] It is quite significant that every cardinal, at the time of his ceremonial appointment, must kiss the Pontiff's foot before receiving his red hat and his red *cappa magna*.

The Congregation of the Holy Office controls the faith of the Church and includes in its scope indulgences, heresies, miracles, medical practice, and the banning of books. The Congregation for the Propagation of the Faith supervises missionary effort; the Congregation for Seminaries and Universities controls the teaching and discipline in all Catholic seminaries and religious universities in the world; the Congregation of Rites controls worship, ceremonies and liturgy, and so on. I shall discuss the Roman political machinery later.

One Congregation, the Congregation of the Religious, deserves special mention. Its existence is a reminder that the ecclesiastical caste of the Church is divided into two sections, secular and regular. The secular clergy includes the ordinary priests, who live under the jurisdiction of their bishops. The regular clergy belong to monastic, mendicant, and other religious Congregations or orders, each having its own special rules approved by Rome. In the United States religious-order priests are gaining rapidly on secular priests in numbers. The secular priests have the advantage of being able to keep the money which they receive by gift or inheritance—and some of them die quite wealthy—but the religious-order priests have the even greater advantage of living in housing quarters with other priests, where they are able to combat the celibate's most dreaded enemy, the psychological disintegration that comes from loneliness.

Secular priests are bound by their oaths to live celibate and obedient lives; but their discipline is not so strict as that of the orders, and they take no vows of poverty. The members of orders observe a double discipline, that of the Church and that of their own orders. Such orders as the Benedictines, Carthusians, Trappists, Franciscans, and Dominicans have gained world-wide fame. Most famous of all are the Jesuits of the Society of Jesus, often considered the intellectual leaders of the Western Church. They have the largest and most powerful religious order in the United States.

More important in the total scheme are the feminine orders, for the Church in the United States is based largely on its nuns. The women's orders also come under the control of the all-male Congregation of the Religious. Although there are three times more nuns than priests in the Catholic system in the United States, the Religious women of America are completely subordinate to the men and have no voice in ecclesiastical affairs. Catholic nuns may vote in American political elections but not in their own Church. Altogether in the United States there are about 163,000 Sisters, garbed in the special dress of their orders, pledged to obedience, chastity, and poverty, living a community life in 275 religious organizations. They do the teaching and nursing and some of the social-service work of the Church.[27]

The women's orders shield their members from the pitfalls and temptations of the world, and foster a certain amount of institutional pride. They adopt medieval names and medieval practices of living. Many of them are very small, and there is frequent overlapping and jurisdictional conflict among them.

Most established religious orders are partially independent of the authority of local bishops and are governed by the Roman Congregation of the Religious directly, unless they have a local parochial responsibility. Their importance in the total Roman scheme is recognized by the fact that outstanding members of the greatest orders are often given key posts in the Congregations at Rome.

Discipline, poverty, chastity, and obedience are the watchwords of the Religious, as they are called. Not many of them in the United States in these modern days are completely cloistered, for usefulness is now more highly regarded than flight from the world. But many of the Religious practice personal mortification to repress the desires of the flesh, and all of them adopt a manner of living that is narrow, ascetic, and deeply devotional.

One of the latest guide-books for nuns, by Father Winfred Herbst, recommends "abandonment" and "dying to self" in terms of the following illustrations:

A clean sheet of paper on which God may write what He pleases.
A liquid, which has no shape of its own, but assumes the shape of the vessel in which it is put.

A ball of wax in the hands of God, which He can shape as He pleases.

A beast of burden (e.g., a pack horse) that is loaded by its master as the master wishes, having nothing to decide about the quality or quantity of its burden, and that goes or stops at the will of the master.[28]

In the struggle for Roman power the Religious form the front line of Catholic expansion, the idealists and zealots of Catholic faith. Their spirit of extreme loyalty is well expressed in the mandate of the constitution of the Jesuits: ". . . let those who live in obedience allow themselves to be disposed of at the will of their superior like a corpse which permits one to turn and handle it any way one pleases." [29]

In practice the members of the orders are sometimes far too lively to be classed with corpses and pack-horses, and it is no mean task for the Congregation of the Religious to regulate and co-ordinate them. Each order has its governing hierarchy, its convents or monasteries, and its systems of discipline. Each Mother Superior of a female order is likely to be especially anxious to recruit more members for her order and to promote the welfare and prosperity of her community. There are many reasons, as we shall see later, for competition among the orders. Recruiting is becoming more and more difficult in a nation where women are emancipated and independent. Obligatory chastity is losing some of its appeal as knowledge of sex spreads even to those adolescents who would normally be considered prospective recruits.

Although the regulation of the religious orders is difficult business, it is not impossible because the whole Roman system is strongly centralized in the Roman Curia, headed by the Pope. He is the absolute monarch of the Catholic world. He is the One Voice of God speaking through the Vatican. Every bishop in the world, after selection by the Congregation of the Consistory, must receive his appointment from the Pope and report personally to the Vatican at five to ten year intervals.

The mechanism for the screening of potential bishops is so thorough that there is virtually no possibility of the appointment of any bishop who is not completely subservient to his own bishop and to the hierarchy.[30] Obedience is an essential qualification for securing or holding office. The system of control is essentially imperial, and in the total Catholic picture the United States is still a colony, with each American bishop appointed by a foreign monarch. Since he is responsible for his future to that monarch, the bishop has no more American independence in his professional life than a colonial governor in the days of George III.

Every two years every bishop in every nation must forward to his metropolitan a list of priests he considers worthy of episcopacy; after the nominees have been investigated, the names are sent on to the Apostolic Delegate of the Pope in that country, and then to the Congregation of the Consistory for further sifting. The Pope and the Pope only has the final right of approval, and the Pope can and does at times select bishops without going through the Congregation of the Consistory. The Pope, in fact, is the Commander-in-Chief of the Catholic army, and more than a million clerical soldiers throughout the world—priests, nuns, and brothers —follow him with unquestioning obedience.

5

It is no reflection upon the Pope as a human being to say that, as he is presented to the American public, he is a glorified synthetic personage, exalted by competent photographers, efficient publicity men, and devout officials. Americans are told all the good things about him, and there are plenty of good things to tell. The Pope is said to work and pray about seventeen hours a day, and to sleep six. He is photographed frequently in democratic poses, speaking benevolently to little children and common laborers. All his speeches, even when flat and platitudinous, are given lengthy and respectful treatment in the press.

The Pope, as one of the few remaining absolute monarchs in the world, lives in an atmosphere of continuous adulation. His Vatican palace has 1,400 rooms. His 500 dial telephones do not work for incoming calls. Because he is considered too exalted to eat a meal with any other human, he eats alone at a little table covered by red silk, sitting under a red *baldachino*. When Catholic visitors are admitted to his presence, they remain kneeling unless he invites them to stand up or take a seat. When they quit his presence they genuflect three times and leave the room backward. The men visitors commonly wear formal suits, and the women long black dresses. No legs or arms may be uncovered during a Papal audience.

To kiss the Pope's ring is, for devout Catholics, the event of a lifetime, and to kneel in the streets as his golden chair is carried past is a duty and a privilege. When a Pope is to be elected by the

Sacred College of Cardinals, the cardinals are locked up in the Conclave and the windows blinded and sealed with lead. Each cardinal sits on a little special throne covered with a violet *baldachino* and when the Papal vote is called for walks solemnly from that throne to cast his written ballot in a large chalice; he also kneels in prayer and repeats a special oath. The whole ceremony is surrounded with the self-consciousness of creative history. A new epoch is being born. Great crowds gather for blocks in St. Peter's Square to watch for the special smoke which signals the election of a new Pope. When the two-thirds-plus-one vote necessary for election has finally been achieved, there is wild rejoicing.

When the Pope proceeds to his coronation he is weighted down heavily with ceremonial robes and carried through worshipful crowds from the Sistine Chapel to St. Peter's in a gold sedan borne by twelve servants clad in crimson damask. Underneath five layers of garments he wears special Papal stockings heavily embroidered with gold. When the senior cardinal-deacon finally puts the triple tiara on his head, he says: "Receive the three-fold Crown of the Tiara, and know that Thou art the Father of Princes and Kings, the Ruler of the round Earth, and here below the Viceroy of Jesus Christ, to Whom be honor and glory forever. Amen." [31]

In contemplating this figure of imperial and priestly splendor one is reminded of the comment addressed by St. Bernard to Pope Eugenius II in his *De Consideratione* in the twelfth century: "I do not find that St. Peter ever appeared in public loaded with gold and jewels, clad in silk, mounted on a white mule, surrounded by soldiers and followed by a brilliant retinue. In the glitter that environs thee, rather wouldst thou be taken for the successor of Constantine than for the successor of Peter."

It is one of the ironies of history that this figure of imperial splendor has been evolved from the teachings of an impecunious prophet of Galilee who had no worldly possessions and no ecclesiastical rank. Certainly the immediate followers of Jesus gave no sign that they ever contemplated anything like this when they began to spread the tidings of their leader. According to the greatest authorities on Christian history the early Christians knew nothing about the primacy of Roman bishops. That primacy, in fact, emerged in the doctrinal conflicts which rent the Church in later centuries. For three or four centuries after the death of Jesus the authority of the Roman bishops was by no means universal in the Church, and even in the western part of Europe as late as the fourth century the Roman Church played quite a minor role. The notion of Rome's primacy developed after this, and Rome's universal jurisdiction began only in the ninth century.

Although it is not the function of this book to discuss theological issues, it must be pointed out that the Vatican's alleged basis and justification for Papal dictatorship in both the religious and political fields is purely Biblical, and when challenged in the political field, the priests always fall back on a religious formula, one passage in one book of the New Testament, the sixteenth chapter of Matthew, as a complete answer to all critics who accuse the Church of betraying democracy. The form as well as the substance of Church government, the priests claim, is prescribed automatically by this delegation of authority to the Pope as successor to St. Peter. "And I say unto thee, thou art Peter, and upon this rock I will build my church; and the gates of hell shall not prevail against it. And I will give thee the keys of the kingdom of heaven; and whatsover thou shalt bind on earth shall be bound in heaven; and whatsoever thou shalt loose on earth shall be loosed in heaven."

To deny this delegation of authority, the priests assert, is to deny the will of God. And it must be conceded that if this passage is all that the priests claim, the argument for orthodox Christians is ended. A moment's reflection, however, will convince any independent critic that, even if the statement was actually made by Jesus, it gives no carte-blanche sanction for Roman dictatorship. (I discuss this passage in Chapter 3 of *Communism, Democracy and Catholic Power.*) It is ambiguous and very general. Jesus said nothing about popes, bishops, or centralized ecclesiastical power. And the passage itself, written long after Jesus's death by a writer who relied chiefly on earlier manuscripts, has often been under suspicion as a possible interpolation.

Even when Roman supremacy began to take shape in the western part of Europe, the Roman bishops and Popes were not absolute rulers of the Church in the sense that they are today. There was even a little democracy in the hierarchy for a few centuries, since laymen took part with the lower and higher clergy in choosing Popes. *Qui omnibus praeest ab omnibus eligatur*—he who is above all must be chosen by all—was a statement endorsed by several Popes, and, in theory, this principle lasted for several centuries. The election of Popes by appointed cardinals began only in the eleventh century. Princes took part in Papal elections in early days and for a time the Papal position was a political football kicked about by various sovereigns. It is not surprising that under such circumstances some Popes were elected who were guilty of simony and nepotism, and who sometimes lived scandalous lives. Lewis Browne in his *Since Calvary* has written a vivid account of the individual robberies, murders, and adulteries of the worst Popes. Benedict IX, a twelve-year-old Pope of the tenth century "ruled like a captain of banditti, committing murders and adulteries in open daylight. . . . Finally in 1045, after emptying the treasury, he put up the Apostolic See at auction and sold it to a presbyter for a thousand pounds silver." [32] For forty-one years in the fourteenth and fifteenth centuries there were two competing Popes with competing sets of cardinals and competing capitals. For a short time there were even three Popes to add to the confusion. Driven from Rome, the Papacy almost perished before it finally came back to greater glory than before.

If Catholic theologians were compelled to base their claims of Papal infallibility on the *character* of their Popes, they would be gravely embarrassed. Some of the Popes have belonged so obviously in a rogues' gallery that Catholic historians have frankly admitted their imperfections.[33] To reconcile their villainies with an exalted concept of papal character, the Church's theologians have developed the doctrine that an imperfect man may yet be a perfect conduit for divine grace.

Thomas F. Woodlock puts it this way: "A Pope may be a wicked man with a load of deadly sins on his soul, which would damn him forever if he died under it unshriven and unrepentant, yet he will not define untruth. If he define, he will define truth—or else he will not define." [34] "The Pope can't sin, but the man who is pope can sin," says another Church writer.[35]

6

The American Catholic Church was founded in the days when the Pope had less authority than he has today. In the eighteenth century absolute kings disputed his rule over various national churches; then the French Revolution and the rise of liberalism left him free to control his own ecclesiastical world but greatly reduced his sphere of influence.

In the middle of the nineteenth century Pius IX came to the papal throne and served for more than thirty years. At the beginning of his pontificate, Pius adopted some liberal measures in the government of the Pontifical States, but he soon learned that people were beginning to think for themselves and to repudiate absolute sovereigns. From then on he tried desperately to stem the liberal tide. He made common cause with kings and urged the union of throne and altar, but thrones were toppling and parliaments rising to power. The new science which culminated in Darwin's *Origin of Species* was beginning to challenge established beliefs. The Church, which had been the exclusive custodian of culture in the Middle Ages, saw the intellectual as well as the political leaders of the period drifting away from its power. Should the Papacy adjust its doctrines to the new attitudes and institutions? Pius IX decided not. The Church was unchanging and unchangeable. As Cardinal Gibbons put it later, ". . . the Church is not susceptible of being reformed in her doctrines. . . . Is it not the height of presumption for men to attempt to improve upon the work of God?"

So the Papacy decided that it must defy the whole trend of modern thought in Europe. Pius IX issued what is probably the most famous document ever issued by a Pope, the *Syllabus of Errors* of 1864, which branded as false many of the basic beliefs of democracy and liberalism. It attacked public education, the separation of church and state, and the right of men to choose their own religion.

Here are some of the propositions upon which Pius IX pronounced anathema as among "the principal errors of our time."

Every man is free to embrace and profess the religion he shall believe true, guided by the light of reason.

The Church ought to be separated from the State, and the State from the Church.

The Roman Pontiff can and ought to reconcile himself to, and agree with, progress, liberalism and civilization as lately introduced.

In the present day, it is no longer expedient that the Catholic religion shall be held as the only religion of the State, to the exclusion of all other modes of worship.[36]

Naturally this antidemocratic philippic caused an indignant reaction in the intellectual world of Europe and America. It was, as the *Encyclopedia Britannica* says, "a declaration of war against the modern political and social order, which in its day provoked the unanimous condemnation of public opinion."

Pius made his anathemas "infallible" by sending them out with an important encyclical, *Quanta Cura,* in which he reiterated and underlined the reactionary doctrines in the *Syllabus.*

Four years later he committed himself to the greatest intellectual blunder of Papal history—matched only by the social blunder of his namesake, Pius XI, in banning birth control—by declaring himself virtually divine and errorless in his role as Pastor of the Human Race. While the political world was moving toward liberty and democracy, the Church went to the other extreme and proclaimed the dogma of Papal infallibility. That this dogma could be promulgated in the year 1870 without a complete split in the Church was a demonstration of the supreme discipline of Catholic world organization.

As it was, the doctrine of infallibility of the Vatican Council of 1870, even though it was restricted to matters of faith and morals, was a cause of profound embarrassment to American Catholics. The American bishops opposed it as either unfounded or untimely, and some of them threatened to walk out of the Council if they were not given more time to consider it. They had good reason to believe that the proclamation of such a dogma would make their position in America more untenable than ever in a period of militant anti-Catholic agitation. There is little doubt that if the whole question could have been discussed freely and voted on by the Catholic *people* of the world, they would have repudiated the doctrine, and possibly the Papacy along with it. Certainly the doctrine was repugnant to contemporary American ways of thinking—and still is. Professor Geddes MacGregor of Bryn Mawr in his new book, *The Vatican Revolution,* has proved to the hilt the thesis that the doctrine of infallibility had no sound basis in the history of the Christian Church.

The hierarchy, under the usages of the Church, could not give the American Catholic people or even the lower clergy of this country any opportunity to take part in the Council which proclaimed infallibility. Only bishops and high prelates were eligible to echo or challenge the Pope's design.[37] Pope Pius IX feared French and German reactions, and he would have feared American reaction if the United States had had a large episcopate. As it was, an elaborate technique for smothering the opposition was worked out by the Vatican before the Council began.

Although the Popes had long claimed that their decisions in matters of faith and morals were final, British and American bishops had been careful not to emphasize Papal infallibility. The Catholic Church as a minority group was on its good behavior in England and the United States. A Catholic catechism in England had spread the theory that the doctrine of infallibility was a libelous Protestant invention circulated by anti-Catholics. American and English bishops were especially fearful of the possible reaction against claims of infallibility because of the hostility to any kind of absolute rule among their people.

In this critical situation Pius IX convoked the *last* ecumenical council of the Church. It proved to be a Council that made any later sessions unnecessary. In preparing his Bull of Convocation for the session, Pius was deliberately vague. He left it to the Jesuit-controlled periodical, *Civiltà Cattolica,* to mention casually the fact that Papal infallibility was on the agenda. The reaction was immediate and bitter. Many leading Catholic theologians denounced the doctrine, and Lord Acton, the foremost British Catholic, calling the dogma a "soul-destroying error," expressed the hostility of his people in a letter which said of the proposed reform: "It makes civil legislation on all points of contract, marriage, education, clerical immunities, mortmain, even on many questions of taxation and Common Law, subject to the legislation of the Church, which would be simply the arbitrary will of the Pope. Most assuredly no man accepting such a code could be a loyal subject, or fit for the enjoyment of political privileges." [38] Acton regarded the whole doctrine of infallibility as contrary to Christian tradition and remarked that he could see no reason to change his religion because the Pope changed his. He escaped excommunication by an eyelash, because his expulsion would have created almost as much scandal as the promulgation of the doctrine itself.

Pius IX went ahead with calm determination. He had arranged to have the question of infallibility brought up in the form of a humble prayer to himself, and the hope was entertained that the proposal might pass quickly by acclamation. He determined the general scope of discussion at the meeting and he controlled in one way or another not only the committee chairmen but the working majority of the bishops. He had the support of the Jesuits, who had served as a pro-dictatorship party in working up sentiment for the proposed reform.

In spite of all the advantages, it took Pius two months to persuade the Council of his own infallibility, and then he won out in the first test vote by a margin of only 451 to 150. That may seem like a wide margin, but it must be remembered that the bishops who opposed Pius IX were risking their whole careers. They were living and working inside a tightly controlled, absolute monarchy, and it took unusual courage to oppose the monarch. Among the negative voters were the bishops of St. Louis, Pittsburgh, Rochester, and Louisville. According to Dom Cuthbert Butler, the American bishops in attendance at the Council were opposed to the declaration of infallibility by a count of about 22 to 8. When the effort was made to make the vote unanimous, Bishop Fitzgerald of Little Rock was one of the two who held out to the bitter end. Fitzgerald knew what reception an American would get in Arkansas who voted for the proposition that a Pope could not make a mistake in matters of faith and morals.

The new doctrine, of course, did not claim that the Pope was *always* infallible, or that he could not make a mistake in political matters. It said that "the Roman Pontiff, when he speaks *ex cathedra,* that is, when, in discharge of the office of pastor and teacher of all Christians, by virtue of his supreme Apostolic authority he defines a doctrine regarding faith and morals to be held by the Universal Church, is, by divine assistance promised him in Blessed Peter, possessed of that infallibility with which the divine Redeemer willed that His Church should be endowed in defining doctrine regarding faith and morals . . ." [39]

American and British Catholics, faced with a storm of criticism in their own countries, stressed the fact that the Pope's infallibility was strictly limited and that he could, in the fields of politics and economics, make mistakes with which a Catholic could safely disagree. Cardinal Gibbons jokingly pointed out that the Pope had pronounced his name "Jibbons," so he could not be infallible in everything.

But who determines what subjects come within the sweep of infallible power? The Pope, of course! The power to define jurisdiction makes authority almost limitless. The word "morals" is so broad that it invites indefinite expansion; similarly the word "faith." If faith deals with ideas and morals deals with behavior, is not the whole range of human experience encompassed within the Papal claim?

The Popes, although they have persisted in describing themselves as infallible, have had the good sense to be vague about specific utterances. It is impossible for the inquiring student to discover a list of alleged infallible statements. Some Catholic writers claim that there have been scores of infallible utterances by the Holy Pastor; others contend that the infallible pronouncements of the Popes can be counted on the fingers of one hand. According to Bishop Wright of Worcester, "The first solemn exercise of infallibility of the Roman Pontiff since the definition of that prerogative in the Vatican Council" was the declaration of Pius XII on November 1, 1950, that the body of the Virgin Mary had been miraculously taken up to heaven—the dogma of the Assumption of the Blessed Virgin.[40] Certainly the declaration of this dogma was the most spectacular event in recent Papal history, the crowning show of the Holy Year, but there is no reason to believe that it was more genuinely *ex cathedra,* more binding or more significant, than, let us say, the 1929 and 1930 encyclicals of Pius XI on education, marriage, and birth control.

The Holy See never issues statements with labels attached; it never says *this* paragraph on birth control in this encyclical is everlastingly sacred because it is in the field of morals and the Pope addressed it to all Christians simultaneously, and *that* paragraph on school control is fallible discipline. In general, Papal encyclicals addressed to the whole Church on moral and spiritual subjects are rated as having the highest authority but are not necessarily infallible. Statements made to an individual may be rated on a lower level, and casual speeches of the Popes may be treated simply as casual speeches.

However, all Catholic authorities are agreed on the infallibility of one type of Papal utterance. The Pope is always and indisputably infallible when he declares a certain person to be a saint. (By good fortune I stood within a few yards of Pius XII and heard such infallible pronouncements on two occasions during the 1950 Holy Year in Rome.)

The difference between an infallible and a fallible statement by the Pope, as far as practical results are concerned, may be important for theologians; but it is not important for the public at large, because the Pope is the Vicar of God in any case, and it is a Catholic's duty to follow his teaching and directives in all things that affect religious life. And the definition of "religious life" belongs to the Pope. For all practical purposes there is no appeal from a Pope's judgment, since Canon 2332, promulgated in 1918, provides excommunication for any Catholic "of whatever state, rank, or condition, even though he be king, Bishop, or Cardinal, who appeals from the laws, decrees, or mandates of the reigning

Roman Pontiff to a universal Council . . ." [41] "There is no distinction made here," says Father Ayrinhac in his standard work on Canon Law, "between legitimate and illegitimate decisions, as all are presumed to be legitimate . . ." [42]

Catholic dialectitians like to describe the infallibility of the Pope as something which resembles the power of the United States Supreme Court. "See," they argue, "you have a supreme authority in the United States to act as final arbiter under your constitution, and we have a supreme authority under our constitution. It is natural and fitting that such authority should exist." [43] The analogy is not accurate. The power of the United States Supreme Court is derived from the people, and the people could abolish the Court if they wished by constitutional amendment. The members of the Court are chosen by an elected official and confirmed by an elected Senate. They are subject to impeachment and trial by an elected body. They have never claimed divine or even juridical infallibility in anything. The Catholic doctrine of the infallibility of the Pope does not provide for any of these democratic safeguards.

The most embarrassing aspect of the doctrine of infallibility is that it must be retroactive or it is nothing. Infallibility was not created or discovered in 1870; it was only promulgated and stamped with official approval at that time. It is a "tradition received from the beginning of the Christian faith," as Pius IX put it. Since it came from St. Peter down through the long line of Popes, every solemn declaration by all the Popes in the field of morals and faith *must* be true. This is an ambitious claim, and it has taken all of the skill of the Catholic historians to adjust history to it. To answer some of the embarrassing questions with some show of consistency, the Jesuits have created several grades in Papal utterance. The most embarrassing Papal blunders are classified in one of the minor grades for which infallibility is not claimed.

7

The Popes have been apprehensive about American Catholicism for many years, and they have watched its growth in power with great anxiety, being fully aware of the dangerous influence of liberalism under religious freedom. This fear reached its climax with the transmission by Leo XIII in 1899 of a special letter to Cardinal Gibbons condemning the "heresy" of Americanism. This "heresy" of Americanism was not American patriotism as such but "the pretext . . . that in matters of faith and of Christian life each one should be free to follow his own bent in the spirit of the large measure of civil liberty recognized in these days. . . ." The Pope was horrified by the prospect of the growth of such independence in the United States, and declared that "it raises the suspicion that there are some among you who conceive and desire a Church in America different from that which is in the rest of the world." [44] Since then there has not been a visible glimmer of defiance of Papal autocracy among the American bishops. Nor has there been any American movement toward Church democracy among laymen to correspond to the anticlerical movements of Europe. The most eloquent American Catholic advocates of democracy do not dare to apply that gospel to the structure of their Church's goverment.

Every move by the American Church toward self-government has been scrutinized and double-checked to avoid the possibility of a drift toward national independence. While the American Church has had its provincial and national councils, the acts of those councils have always been subjected to Roman veto or approval, and Rome has always been careful not to elevate any bishopric in the United States to a position of primacy. For a time the bishops of Baltimore enjoyed a kind of primacy of honor, but even this has now disappeared. Leo XIII, instead of creating an American primate whose viewpoint and background might be fundamentally American, created an Apostolic Delegacy at Washington, and each succeeding Pope has sent his own representative to occupy the spacious building in Washington which, in effect, is the general Roman headquarters of American Catholicism. Since the Pope's appointee is always an Italian, whose line of promotion runs toward Rome instead of the United States, there is little danger that he will become infected with the "heresy" of Americanism.

For a long time American Catholicism was in considerable confusion because of the lack of a central administrative authority in this country. The confusion was accentuated in the beginning by the fact that many immigrant branches of the Church spoke different languages and represented competing national interests. As late as 1912, 43 of the 231 churches in Boston, 84 out of 200 in Chicago, and 40 out of 156 in New York were national.[45] Even to this day there is no love lost between the dominant Irish- and the German-, Polish-, or Italian-American Catholics. The rivalry between them is natural because in many sections of America the

Church is virtually an Irish church operating under Irish priests and cardinals. All but one of the ten native-born cardinals of American history have been sons of Irish immigrant workers.[46]

This Irish dominance explains many of the characteristics of American Catholicism. The Irish hierarchy which rules the American Church is a "becoming" class. It represents the Irish people struggling upward in a hostile environment, using the Roman system of authoritative power to compensate for an inner sense of insecurity which still seems to survive from the days when the Irish Catholics were a despised immigrant minority. Boston is aggressively Catholic largely because it is aggressively Irish, and it is aggressively Irish because its people have not quite overcome their sense of being strangers in a hostile land. Jealousy between the Irish and the Italians is only one phase of the competition among all immigrant groups to make good in the American environment. The growth of Catholic power in America is part of the Irish success story. Perhaps the Italians find compensation in the thought that the government of the universal Church is in Italian hands, that all the Popes for four hundred years have been Italians, and that all the Apostolic Delegates have been fellow countrymen.

After the establishment of the Apostolic Delegacy at Washington, it was the war (World War I) which gave the American bishops a chance to create a closer unity in American Catholicism. Some agency had to speak for all American Catholics in dealing with the government during the war, and out of the National Catholic War Council, created for this purpose, grew the National Catholic Welfare Conference.[47] At first it was called the National Catholic Welfare Council, but to a Vatican which could remember other defiant councils that word "council" smacked too much of national authority. So the word "council" was changed to "conference" the following year, and even then the whole idea of a conference of American bishops encountered much skepticism at Rome. Periodic conferences of American bishops were approved by the Holy See only after it was made perfectly clear that they were not to be legislative, canonical councils but merely private meetings for the exchange of ideas.

The N.C.W.C. is still careful to call itself merely "a voluntary association of the bishops of the United States." In 1922, just after the death of Benedict XV, it was announced that Benedict had signed a decree dissolving the National Catholic Welfare Conference shortly before his death. Pius XI, out of respect for his predecessor, declared that he would promulgate the law. Later it was alleged that some enemy of "Americanism" had slipped the decree in among the late Pope's papers after his death. So Pius XI allowed the National Catholic Welfare Conference to continue, but he hedged it about with a set of special regulations.[48]

American laymen were completely excluded from all places of power in the new American organization. It was provided that even the chairman of the "laymen's" division in the N.C.W.C. was to be a bishop or archbishop. The more than 20,000,000 members of Catholic lay organizations are without any power in the Church, except advisory power. The Vatican wants everyone to be sure that the N.C.W.C. is an organization of the hierarchy and not an organization of the American Catholic people. Pius XII went out of his way, in a 1954 allocution at the time Pius X was canonized, to rebuke any lay independence and "lay theology" in the Catholic Church.[49]

Once a year all the Catholic bishops in the United States— 200 more or less—meet in Washington to discuss American Church activities. They profess their utmost devotion to the Pope, and then proceed to promote American Catholicism with characteristic American energy. In spite of the restrictions, they have built up during the last forty years an efficient and aggressive organization that is the envy of many other American religious groups. An administrative board of archbishops and bishops supervises all operations, and eight departments send out propaganda and advice to all Catholic organizations in the United States. The organization is especially useful in co-ordinating the vast money-raising activities of American Catholicism. It is a gigantic and successful public relations office.

The bureaus of the N.C.W.C. are full of busy young priests, lobbyists, pamphleteers, journalists, and lawyers who attempt to co-ordinate the Catholic population of the country as one great pressure group when any "Catholic issue" arises. The Press Department sends out myriad news releases and feature articles to some 500 Catholic papers in this country and abroad with a circulation of more than 20,000,000. That is one reason the front pages of the diocesan newspapers in this country look so much alike.

Whenever any issue arises in Congress which may or might affect Catholic interests, a seasoned lobbyist in priestly garb is likely to appear in a congressman's office, reminding the legislator that 35,000,000 Catholics in America feel such and so about this matter. Even when the legislator knows perfectly well that the opinion is actually that of a handful of top-ranking bishops, acting on orders from Rome, he may swallow his convictions and say "Yes, yes," because he knows that in American Catholicism the bishops speak for Catholic power. He knows also that Catholic pressure can be mortally effective in swinging any close election against him.

The theory on which the National Catholic Welfare Conference is organized is that the Catholic people of the United States should function primarily as Catholics in every branch of their activities. The keynote of the Church's strategy in a non-Catholic country is denominational separatism, described as "the preservation and expansion of the faith." (It is in many ways the direct opposite of the strategy recommended in Catholic countries like Spain.) Catholic advertising promoters boast that "37,800 Catholic institutions of all types are operated and maintained by Catholic organizations" in the United States, and that for these institutions alone "an estimated billion dollars will be spent each year from now through 1965 in new construction, remodeling, equipment, furnishings, decorations and maintenance." [50] The national strategy is based upon the assumption that American Catholics should not only worship and work together but also buy together, read together, play together, boycott together, and (ultimately) vote together when any issue of direct interest to the Church arises.

There are no Catholic regiments in the army, but there is a Catholic organization for almost every other aspect of American life.

In the educational and scientific field there are the National Catholic Educational Association, the American Catholic Sociological Society, the Catholic Anthropological Conference, the American Catholic Psychological Association, the American Catholic Philosophical Association, the National Federation of Catholic College Students, the Catholic School Press Association, etc. There is even an American *Catholic Who's Who*.

In the literary, book, and dramatic world there are the Catholic Library Association, the Catholic Dramatic Movement, the Legion of Decency, the National Office for Decent Literature, the Catholic Book Club, the Newman Book Club, the Catholic Children's Book Club, the Catholic Actors Guild, the Catholic Writers' Guild, etc.

In the field of journalism and communications there are the

Catholic Press Association, the Catholic Broadcasters Association, the Catholic Film and Radio Guild, the Catholic Information Society, etc.

In the field of youth activity and sports there are the Catholic Boy Scouts, the Catholic Girl Scouts, the Newman Club Federation, the All-Catholic All-American Football Team, the Junior Catholic Daughters of America, etc.

In music and art there are the National Catholic Music Educators' Association, the Catholic Cadet Choir of the United States Military Academy, the Catholic Art Association, etc.

In the field of government, law, and military service there are the Catholic War Veterans, the Catholic Postal Employees' Eucharistic League, the Catholic Court Attaches' Guild, the Guild of Catholic Lawyers, etc.

In the economic and labor world there are the Catholic Economic Association, the Catholic Conference on Industrial Problems, the Association of Catholic Trade Unionists, the Young Christian Workers, etc.

In medicine there are the Catholic Hospital Association, the Federation of Catholic Physicians' Guilds, the National Council of Catholic Nurses, the Hospital Social Service Association, etc.

In addition there are the Knights of Columbus, the Holy Name Society, the National Council of Catholic Men, the National Council of Catholic Women, Catholic Action, the Catholic Daughters of America, the Catholic Total Abstinence Union, the Catholic Airmen of America, the National Catholic Rural Life Conference, the National Catholic Interracial Council, etc.

Of these organizations the best known is the Knights of Columbus—although its 1,000,000 membership is smaller than the 3,500,000 membership of the Holy Name Society. The K. of C. allows its name (and funds) to be used for a gigantic and continuing religious propaganda campaign of advertising designed to convert non-Catholics. (See Chapter 13.) Under the guidance of specially trained priests and public-relations advisers, the Knights issue a great amount of literature protesting the one-hundred-percent American loyalty of all Catholics and asserting the imperative necessity of uniting to fight Communism. The organization's strength comes not only from its social activity but also from its 700-million-dollar, low-cost life insurance program. It controls what *Life* magazine calls a "billion-dollar financial empire," and its monthly magazine, *Columbia,* claims the largest Catholic circulation in the world.[51] It can produce a wave of "public opinion" on almost any subject on twenty-four hours' notice from the Catholic hierarchy. In 1956, by producing a flood of angry letters, telegrams, and editorials, addressed to the federal government, it brought about the cancellation of a visit to the United States of Marshal Tito of Yugoslavia, as an enemy of the Catholic people. Its propaganda for Franco as a friend of the Catholic people has been equally effective.

The K. of C. has been the particular target of anti-Catholic sentiment in the South during its seventy-five years of existence, and an alleged "secret oath" of the organization has been widely circulated through the Southwest, in which the Knights are pictured as promising to tear out the bowels of their opponents and effect similar and sundry changes in American life. Unhappily, this type of anti-Catholic fanaticism—the oath is purely imaginary and has been proved so in court on a number of occasions—has produced counter-fanaticism in the K. of C. Its propaganda persists in the illusion that critics of Catholic autocracy are somehow attempting to revive the Ku Klux Klan and destroy the liberties of the Church. The priests encourage this illusion, since it is a valuable stimulant to partisan spirit. Aside from this partisan spirit, and the uses to which the order is put by the hierarchy, the K. of C. is simply one more American fraternal order, composed of men who love plumes, their country, and a good time.

8

These multiple and expanding organizations are an important part of the Catholic system of power, and they have a serious purpose in the Catholic plan for America. I shall discuss some of their operations in detail in later chapters, particularly the operations of the over-all organization known as Catholic Action, which describes itself as "an army engaged in a holy war for religion." Catholic Action creates in many non-Catholic as well as Catholic organizations cells of devotees which function in a manner strikingly similar to Communist cells.

The Catholic organizations in America are not merely fellowships of genial and like-minded Catholic people. They contain many genial and broad-minded Catholic laymen, but in the hands of the hierarchy they become instruments for the development of a militant and exclusive faith. The lay members are carefully guided by the hierarchy into ways of separatism and monopoly. They are segregated from the rest of American cultural and social life as much as possible in order to preserve their faith unsullied. The Church tries to parallel every activity of non-Catholics with a specialized activity under Catholic auspices.

The hierarchy is not satisfied with an American Mother of the Year. It must celebrate the maternal instinct with someone who is distinctly Catholic. So we must have a Catholic Mother of the Year, with all the fanfare of a national Mother of the Year. A mere American mother might be a Methodist, a Jew or an agnostic. She might practice birth control and have only two or three children. So the hierarchy boldly appropriates the idea of the Mother of the Year for its own purposes, and all over America priests take advantage of the selection of this Catholic mother to deliver little sermons on the superiority of the Catholic home and the high devotion of the mother who worships only at a Catholic altar.

A similar method has been used in developing the Catholic Boy Scouts in the United States. One of the chief purposes in creating the original Boy Scout movement was to build national solidarity among all classes of boys by getting them to associate together as loyal and honest Americans regardless of creed. The Catholic hierarchy has taken over this concept for its own purpose and developed a segregated Boy Scout movement for Catholic boys to promote its own brand of denominational loyalty. In 1956 the Catholic Committee on Scouting served 520,000 Catholic Boy Scouts in 8,776 troops, almost 14 per cent of the total membership.

The various Catholic organizations all have priestly "advisers" whose purpose, as *The Catholic Action Manual* says, is officially to serve merely as "a safeguard of the orthodoxy of the associations," but actually they serve as a supreme authority in many cases. Intolerance of all other faiths is cultivated and emphasized by these priestly advisers because such intolerance is part of the Catholic philosophy of religion.

"Protestantism," says Bishop Fulton J. Sheen, the favorite prophet of American Catholicism, "in great part has ceased to be Christian." [52] Under Canon 1325, all Protestants are branded as heretics, and the very name of "faith" is denied to Protestant and Jewish organizations. The *Homiletic and Pastoral Review* of February, 1947, in answering a question for priests as to whether it is right to use the word "faith" to describe other religious groups, said: "For, if there is anything in Catholic teaching, it is the doctrine that the Son of God established only one religion and imposed on all men the obligation of embracing it; consequently no other religion has a real objective right to exist and to function, and no individual has an objective right to embrace any non-Catholic religion."

This narrowness of outlook should not surprise anybody who has studied Church history. The attitude has been traditional with the Popes for centuries, and the doctrine is still official that: "Out of the Church there is no salvation."

This is the doctrine that is taught to Catholic school children in the standard text, *Manual of Christian Doctrine,* when it says:

> For whom is there no salvation outside the Church?
>
> For whoever wilfully remains outside the Church, refusing to profess the faith taught by the Church, to partake of her sacraments, and to obey her laws.[53]

Any honest interpretation of these words leads to the conclusion that under this rule a Protestant or Jew who studies Catholicism and then rejects it is damned. In the famous controversy in Cambridge, Massachusetts, in 1949, the Jesuit leader Father Leonard Feeney insisted on a literal interpretation of this principle and was finally expelled from the Jesuit order and excommunicated for defying Archbishop Cushing of Boston. Feeney was a fanatic, but his interpretation of Catholic dogma was far more honest and accurate than the liberal make-believe adopted by Archbishop Cushing. The official letter of the Holy Office on this subject, withheld from publication by the Boston hierarchy for three years, condemns Feeney's intransigence but reaffirms the basically exclusive doctrine of salvation which the Church has taught for centuries.

Now, among those things which the Church has always preached and will never cease to preach is contained also that infallible statement by which we are taught that there is no salvation outside the Church. However, this dogma must be understood in that sense in which the Church herself understands it . . . that one may obtain eternal salvation, it is not always required that he be incorporated into the Church *actually* as a member, but it is necessary that at least he be united to her by *desire* and *longing* . . . this desire need not always be explicit . . . when a person is involved in invincible ignorance, God accepts also an *implicit* desire . . .[54]

For the sake of appearances the Vatican nominally stood by its archbishop and his synthetic liberalism in the Feeney case. Then, when Archbishop Cushing was due to receive a red hat at a Papal consistory, he was conspicuously passed over.

The hierarchy is particularly concerned about protecting Catholic youth against association with non-Catholics who accept "indifferentism." Indifferentism is the form of broad-mindedness which permits men to view other religions with calm detachment and to search for a common denominator of agreement. Nothing enrages Catholic theologians more than "common denominator" talk. "It is sheer nonsense to talk of a common religion for all American children or a common denominator for the hundreds of religious beliefs that we have in America," [55] said the Most Reverend John T. McNicholas, late general president of the National Catholic Educational Association. To be safeguarded against indifferentism young Catholics are forbidden in their various organizations to discuss *any* subject connected with their faith with non-Catholics without the consent of their priest.[56] Every Catholic is forbidden, in general, to explain or defend the truths of his faith publicly, or to attend Protestant services regularly, or to read any book which takes a critical attitude toward the fundamentals of Catholic faith. The prohibition was extended in the summer of 1957 to the New York revival meetings of Billy Graham.

The chief diocesan Catholic newspaper in the United States, *The Register,* carried in its religious information column on May 12, 1957, the following question and answer by Father Robert Kekeisen:

If a Catholic attends a social affair in a Protestant church hall, should he bow his head along with the others present when the Protestant minister says the blessing?

No. A Catholic who is present at a public Protestant service (and this seems to be the case here, though the service is most brief) must give no signs whatever of participation in the rites. To give visible signs of taking part in non-Catholic prayer services is a manifestation of religious indifference and also a possible source of scandal to others in this matter.

If a Catholic eats dinner privately in the home of a Protestant family, he may bow his head as the meal prayer is said, as this does not take on the nature of a public religious service.

The Church's most noted British authority on morals, Father Henry Davis, in his *Moral and Pastoral Theology* summarizes some of the protective rules that Catholics are bound to observe in their organizations in order to avoid doctrinal contagion:

1. It is wrong to play the organ in a non-Catholic church as a help to the religious service, or to be a member of the choir during religious services.

2. In Protestant marriages in a Protestant church, a Catholic should, in general, not take part as witness. . . .

3. [Catholic servants who must accompany masters and children to a Protestant service must not] take any part in the service.

4. It would be sinful and scandalous for Catholics to contribute specially to the upkeep of . . . Salvation Army shelters. . . .[57]

The very alarm with which the hierarchy combats all forms of "indifferentism" among its various organizations is proof that it is having a difficult time in holding young Catholics to a restricted, denominational point of view. The intellectual climate of America is not congenial to narrow zealots, and the hierarchy must struggle constantly to keep its people from drifting to that most dangerous condition which the nineteenth-century Popes branded as "liberalism."

One device for maintaining an exclusive spirit among the faithful is to punish swiftly and severely any priest who proposes mercy for heretics. One of America's most noted priests, Father John A. O'Brien, in 1934 and 1935, wrote a series of articles in the magazine for priests, the *Homiletic and Pastoral Review,* in which he suggested that a heretic in hell might some day, after centuries of torture, cease burning and sink into welcome oblivion. He pointed out that fire is often used in the Bible in a metaphorical sense, and asked: "What good would it do to torture souls without end in another life for sins, however numerous and grave, committed during a few years on earth?" The hierarchy was horrified, and both Father O'Brien and the editors of the magazine were compelled to print an abject and craven apology. On June 22, 1935, they signed a retraction which was printed in the August issue of the magazine, repudiating without mental reservation the heresy that "Catholics should not be forced to believe in the *eternal torment* of the damned," and accepting the dogma that such unfortunates never lose consciousness while suffering in *real* fire.

The sufferers, according to official Catholic teaching, include every faithful Protestant and Jew who "deliberately remains outside the pale of the said Catholic Church through his own fault . . . should he continue in this state to the end." [58]

9

The whole Catholic system of global discipline rests fundamentally on its great army of priests. The parish priest is the contact man between the hierarchy and the people, and the agent for Roman spiritual and political goods. Although he is never allowed to forget that he is subordinate to the hierarchy, he must be a man of versatility, initiative, and independent judgment to operate a modern parish successfully.

The priest's role is varied and often difficult. He is a comforter for the dying, an adviser for the troubled, a friend of the lonely, and a teacher of those who thirst after knowledge. His success depends partly upon his intimate personal knowledge of his people. He must be an able administrator and businessman because he carries the whole burden for the parish school as well as the parish church upon his shoulders. In general, he must live a personally exemplary life in order to hold the respect of his parishioners. He must be a reasonably vigorous preacher, but not necessarily a brilliant or original one. The preaching in a Catholic pulpit is more authoritative and less original than in a Protestant church or Jewish synagogue, because the limits of variation in belief are so much more precisely drawn.

In general, the hierarchy tells its American priests what to believe in great detail. Usually the parish priest has no strong inclination toward heretical belief because he has been conditioned and indoctrinated systematically in the Catholic educational system from the kindergarten through the seminary. A glance at any biographical list of prominent Catholic prelates will show how few of them ever stray from the Catholic educational system. Most of the priests are conditioned for the priesthood in a Catholic parochial school, then in a Catholic high school, then in an American Catholic college and seminary, and finally, perhaps, in the North American College at Rome, which has been made "the United States national seminary in the Eternal City." Auxiliary Bishop John J. Wright of Boston declared in 1948 that not a single Roman

Catholic prelate in the United States is the son of a college graduate.[59]

One reason for the limited culture of these bishops is that after they have finally arrived at episcopal status they are too busy with problems of administrative supervision to fill in the gaps in their sectarian education. It was H. G. Wells who said:

> These Catholic prelates, so imposing in their triple crowns and mitres and epicene garments, are in fact extremely ignorant men, not only by virtue of the narrow specialization of their initial education, but also by the incessant activities of service and ceremony that have occupied them since. They can have read few books, they can have had no opportunities of thinking freely.[60]

Inside the closed cultural system the priest is supplied at second hand with all the arguments against Catholicism, and the stereotyped answers. He takes his religion from others above him as a matter of duty because he has always been taught that submission to Church authority is the essence of "freedom." In the diocesan synod the priest does not even have the right to vote against any law or rule promulgated by the bishop. Likewise, the members of the parish church are taught to take religion in turn from the priest, with what has been described by one Catholic writer as "the apron-string mentality which leaves the clergy to do all thinking for the faithful."

No one has stated this systematic subjection of the Catholic mind to clerical guidance more frankly than the noted British Catholic writer Hilaire Belloc:

> Harnack uttered a profound truth in what he intended to be a sneer, when he said that men had their own religion or somebody else's religion. The religion of the Catholic is not a mood induced by isolated personal introspection coupled with an isolated personal attempt to discover all things and the Maker of all things. It is essentially *an acceptation of the religion of others;* which others are the Apostolic College, the Conciliar decisions, and all that proceeds from the authoritative voice of the Church. For the Catholic, it is not he himself, it is the Church which can alone discover, decide and affirm.[61]

With such an attitude toward his own personal doubts and toward any independent thinking in his own congregation, the parish priest becomes primarily the Voice of Authority. He is not a man among men. He is a member of a special caste. He follows a routine which is almost military in its severity, and he must obey his superiors with military precision. He wears special uniforms and does not marry. He is called "Father" to emphasize his paternal supervision over his people. He has certain special powers that distinguish him from his fellows, and by using those powers he becomes a purveyor of certain supernatural benefits to all believers.

The Catholic priest is also armed with several special and effective devices of control over his people. The people are told that under certain circumstances he is able to forgive sin and grant absolution, and he performs these operations with impressive dignity. As an instrument of divine power he performs the exclusively Catholic miracle of transubstantiation, transforming bread into flesh and wine into blood, actually, not figuratively. He blesses certain articles, and thereupon they take on some of the mysterious qualities of a primitive charm. He makes certain motions and repeats certain words, and the souls of struggling penitents in purgatory are presumably moved up one step on the long stair that leads through the valley of the shadow.

I shall discuss some of the abuses of priestly practice in the chapter on "Science, Scholarship, and Superstition." Not all the abuses are due to any shortcoming in the priests themselves. To a certain extent the priests are the victims of the medievalism of their own Church, imprisoned by ancient beliefs and forced into the role of a "good" magician.

One unfortunate result of tradition is the survival of certain commercial practices in connection with prayer, forgiveness, and indulgences which shock non-Catholics. Although Catholics resent the suggestion that prayers for the dead and indulgences for the punishment of sins are bought and sold, there is no doubt that the ceremonial accompaniments of prayer and indulgences are paid for in cash at standard prices, and sometimes at competitive prices.

Many of the financial policies of the hierarchy seem to the outsider to be dangerously near commercialism, or worse. The gambling game of bingo is one of the great sources of revenue for Catholic churches in the United States, and the game is openly encouraged on church premises in many parts of the United States. Even Mayor LaGuardia was not powerful enough to eliminate it from New York City Catholic institutions. One parish in New

England has maintained five Catholic missionaries in the foreign field from the profits of gambling alone. The spiritual territory of the late Archbishop McNicholas (Cincinnati), administrative leader of American Catholicism, made a profit of almost $1,500,-000 for some thirty Catholic churches in 1939 out of bingo as played by 2,500,000 players, after the Archbishop had valiantly defended the practice against threats of legal suppression.[62] In 1948 Catholic groups in New Jersey spear-headed the successful drive for a state-wide law permitting gambling for religious organizations, after the state supreme court had ended a predominantly Catholic gambling enterprise that had yielded an annual "take" of almost $4,000,000 in the political territory of Frank Hague. "Gambling in itself," says the Church, "is not sinful. It may become sinful however by reason of certain circumstances often related to it." [63]

It should be added that the gambling enterprises of the Church disturb the consciences of many priests. "While we would not tolerate any insinuation that our schools have come under the influence of money changers," says Father John A. O'Brien, "or that they are vestibules to gambling dens, as a Catholic jokingly said to me some time ago, we can scarcely escape the accusation that with lotteries, raffles, chance books, and punch boards in the hands of the children, we are developing the gambling instinct that may lead them to the pool rooms and the gambling dens in the not too distant future." [64]

Every Catholic diocese has its schedule of fees for the various grades of prayer and the various types of religious ceremony. It is difficult for a non-Catholic to read one of these fee schedules without arriving at the conclusion that the priest is, in some ways, a salesman for magic. The inferential commercial tags are not pleasing. The most profitable activity of priests during the year is the offering of special prayers for the dead, appealing for their rapid progress through purgatory. On All Soul's Day in November a popular priest is likely to receive several hundred dollars extra for the performance of his functions.

The lowest Mass takes about twenty-five minutes of the time of one priest; the High Mass with three priests, for which a fee of $35 to $40 is collected, consumes perhaps an hour. Priests are not allowed to argue over rates and they are told not to turn away the indigent, but few Catholics dare ask the favor of intercession for themselves or their departed relatives without paying both the minimum stipend for the parish and the extra gift for the priest. Under certain circumstances bishops and pastors may keep part of the Mass stipend or the extra emolument and farm out the actual praying to their assistants or to smaller churches whose priests are not overwhelmed with requests, where the fee for Masses is lower. The bishops receive a portion of parish income and the bishops themselves determine their own percentage. Incidentally, the bishops render a financial accounting for such revenues only to Rome. The ordinary priest is not a rich man, and, especially in country districts, he is likely to be a very poor man.

In all of these spiritual transactions, the suggestion is painfully apparent that there is a relationship between money payments and the favors granted by a Catholic Providence. Forgiveness for the violation of Church regulations is especially tied up with the payment of standard fees, since dispensations and indulgences call for specific contributions or acts. Frequently the only external fact which distinguishes a priestly devotional proceeding from a sales transaction is that a poor petitioner may be granted this service free of charge.

Rome shares directly in many of these transactions of American prelates. If, for example, a bishop grants a faithful Catholic permission for a mixed marriage, the bishop asks for a fee for the dispensation, and the fee is divided between himself and Rome. Appeals for Church funds are coupled with promises of spiritual rewards. Missionary funds controlled by Rome are raised with the definite written pledge in official advertisements that all contributors will "gain all indulgences now granted members of the Confraternity of the Propagation of the Faith." Purgatorian Societies and Mass Leagues are popular in the United States; they solicit funds in the Catholic press for blanket Masses recited for beneficiaries *en bloc,* and every Catholic who contributes $10 to such a league can have a specified name of a departed soul included in the blessings of "eleven High Masses celebrated daily . . . in perpetuity." [65] American priestly organizations which advertise for contributions in the Catholic press have accepted cash from me at various times to pray for (1) a new family car; (2) the removal of a nonexistent wart on my left hand; (3) the termination of a nonexistent alcoholism in my wife. This commercialization of a spiritual faith horrifies many Catholic mystics, but it also guarantees the maintenance of the priesthood.

In a sense the survivals of magic in the Catholic system give the priest an enormous advantage over his Protestant and Jewish confreres in controlling a congregation. In times of crisis and bewilderment human beings crave authority and definiteness. Also in times of crisis and bewilderment most human beings want some definite thing to *do,* some act that will serve as a token of inner hopes and longings, some physical gesture toward the mysterious Power which rules the universe. The Catholic priesthood satisfies that craving in the ministrations of the comprehensive ritual for birth, illness, marriage, confession, death, and burial.

Most important of the devices of priestly control is that of the confessional. Every good Catholic is supposed to kneel down at least once a year before the dark screen in the Church where, in a confession box, a priest is posted unseen to hear him confess his innermost thoughts. Particularly when the penitent is a woman, her mind in the process of unburdening her regrets and worries is delivered, so to speak, wide open to the priest. The joy of release for pent-up emotion and the comfort of communion are mingled with personal submission and the yearning of the grown-up child for a substitute father.

It is a tribute to the high moral standards of American priests that a device which is so intimate and inviting is rarely abused to the point of scandal. In Latin countries this is not the case; there, under the severe penalties of Canons 904 and 2368, action must frequently be taken against priests who are guilty of sexual solicitation in the confessional. In 12 years of intensive study of the Catholic problem in the United States, I have heard of almost no sexual scandals among priests and nuns involving members of the opposite sex. There are a few, of course, and they are dutifully hushed up by the newspapers under pressure, but the remarkable fact is that there is so little justification for scandal. I am convinced that nearly all American priests and nuns strictly observe their oaths of chastity. The most fundamental objection to the confessional is not its obvious sexual temptation but its elevation of sexual amateurs and unscientific dogmatists to the role of family advisers.

The priest is trained to supply promptly in the confessional a definite answer for every situation, a Catholic formula approved by the Holy See and given out as the law. The latest devotional manuals even tell the priest precisely how to take a confession in an airplane. As we shall see in our chapters on medical and sexual matters, the young celibate priest has only one Catholic answer for the mature married woman inquiring about birth control, or for the experienced surgeon on therapeutic abortion. In each case the priest delivers the answer confidently, declaring that he speaks the word of God in the field of religion and morals.

Is it surprising that, with such a perfect instrument for the control of conduct, the priest does not hesitate to extend the directive power of the confessional into the regions of politics, sociology, and economics? Who could resist the temptation to mold character at its most malleable moment, when a consciousness of imperfection makes the mind receptive to priestly guidance? At any rate, the record shows that in many parts of the world the confessional is used not only to keep Catholic girls pure and Catholic boys honest but also to defeat British control in Malta, birth-control reform in Massachusetts, and democratic government in Spain. The priests would be more than human if they did not use this remarkable instrument for the attainment of the *whole* Catholic program. And the whole Catholic program, as we shall see in our next chapter, is almost as much political as spiritual.

3

Church, State, and Democracy

1

THUS FAR I HAVE spoken of the Roman Catholic Church in its religious aspects. As an institution in this world the Church is also a political organization. When the word "Church" is used in Catholic literature, it may refer to the political entity or the religious one, or both, and the uninformed reader may be completely deceived by the double and triple meanings of ordinary terms.

The thinking of the average American about church and state is based upon the settled American tradition of the separation of church and state by law. "Congress shall make no law respecting an establishment of religion, or prohibiting the free exercise thereof," says the First Amendment to the United States Constitution. Throughout American history, with the help of Supreme Court interpretations, that amendment has come to stand for certain basic policies: complete freedom for all faiths, complete equality of all churches before the law, and freedom of the taxpayer from all general assessments to support a church which he does not endorse. State constitutions and statutes have made the "separation" interpretations even more clear and definite.

All three of these basic interpretations of religious liberty and the policy of church-state separation are in fundamental conflict with the world policy of the Catholic Church. As we shall see later, the Church frequently unites with Catholic governments to destroy freedom of religion for non-Catholics; it secures special status for itself as the state church, by means of concordats, wherever possible; and it charges part of its expenses, as a matter of right, to the public treasury when it has the power to do so.

How can such policies be reconciled with the American conception of church and state? The honest answer is that they cannot be reconciled, but this is an answer that the Catholic hierarchy

54

is very reluctant to make in a nation where the Church does not include more than one-fifth of the population. Accordingly, the hierarchy seeks temporarily to impose its own philosophy of church and state upon the American concept without emphasizing differences, pretending that there is no fundamental conflict. It is a little like a child who, being unable to find the appropriate piece to insert in a picture puzzle, jams in the wrong piece loosely, hoping that somehow the puzzle will come out right in the long run in spite of the misfit.

For the time being the Catholic hierarchy must disguise the misfit by semantic artifice. It uses familiar words with private meanings. The word "church," the word "state," and the word "democracy" all have special meanings in Catholic dialectics. In general, the concept "church" includes a much larger sphere of power than the same concept when used by a non-Catholic; the concept "state" is comparatively shrunken and dwarfed; and the concept "democracy" is hedged about by a whole group of conditions precedent which make political rights dependent upon clerical approval. It was Humpty-Dumpty in *Through the Looking Glass* who said: "When I use a word it means just what I want it to mean, neither more nor less."

Some of the confusion in church-state discussions is due to the deliberately evasive technique which the Catholic hierarchy employs in political arguments. Catholic priests frequently parry an attack upon the Church's political policy by shifting the defense to the field of religion. Many of the purely religious terms used by the priests have a latent political meaning that is not apparent on the surface. To understand the political position of the Church it is necessary to go behind its religious terminology and examine the dual structure of the institution.

The problem of the Catholic Church and the modern state is so vast and complex that any brief discussion of it can easily lead to confusion. I can offer here only enough of the major facts to give the average reader a basis for a tentative judgment. Probably the easiest way to introduce the subject is to run through a brief check list of elementary questions:

Is the Catholic Church a sovereign power? According to Catholic theologians, yes. It has the three requisites of a sovereign power, legislative, executive and judicial, including the power of coercion. The ruler of the Church, the Pope, claims sovereignty by divine right, and he is also the head of a small state, the Vatican State, created by the Lateran Treaty of 1929 with Mussolini. This Vatican State is ruled by the same machinery that rules the religious aspect of the Church.[1] "The Holy Father is not alone the supreme head of the Catholic Church. He is also the head of a sovereign State. Thirty-eight countries have representatives at the Holy See." [2] This statement was made by Cardinal Spellman on March 12, 1940, when President Roosevelt's 1939 appointment of Myron C. Taylor as personal representative to the Vatican was under fire. At that time nearly all the important countries of the world except the United States and the Soviet Union had official diplomats at the Vatican. By 1956, forty-four nations had representatives at the Vatican, and the Vatican in turn had nuncios or lesser diplomats at the capitals of these powers. In addition, the Vatican had fifty-eight religious representatives serving as Apostolic Delegates in as many capitals, appointed by the same sovereign who appointed the nuncios.

How far does the Church as a sovereign power extend its jurisdiction? Everywhere where there are Catholics. It claims that it is a supernatural institution with complete territorial jurisdiction.

What is the Pope's temporal state? For about seven hundred years it consisted chiefly of the nation in central Italy called the Papal States, a district about the size of Switzerland, running from the Adriatic to the Tyrrhenian, which was finally lost to the Vatican in 1870 when Italy captured it. (Macaulay called this state "the worst governed in the civilized world.") Now, by the Vatican-Mussolini Concordat of 1929, the Roman Catholic state has been revived as a 108-acre section of Rome, with some extraterritorial rights outside of Rome.[3] Its existence was confirmed after World War II by the Italian constitutional assembly, which inserted the Lateran Treaties in the new Italian constitution.

Does this Vatican State have a government of its own? Yes, it has a full civil government with a flag, a police force, courts, and postage stamps. It even issues currency in the form of gold and silver coins bearing an effigy of the Pope, and it has some 500 to 1,000 national citizens who use Vatican passports when they wish to travel. It has armed guards and before 1870 it had a full-blown military establishment.

Is the government of this state democratic? No. According to the first article of its constitution, it is a complete autocracy in which "the plenitude of legislative, executive and judicial power" is vested in the Pope.[4]

Does this state have a diplomatic corps? Yes, a large and active diplomatic corps, headed by a Secretary of State, with ambassadors called nuncios.

Do these diplomatic representatives of the Vatican State have equality of status with the ambassadors of other powers? Yes and no. They have *superior* status in most cases, and the Vatican expects them to take precedence over other ambassadors. In most capitals they outrank the representatives of the United States government. In Berlin an American bishop, as Papal nuncio, outranks another American, the United States ambassador.

Do the constitution and courts of the Vatican State provide any check upon the absolute power of the Pope? No. Nominally the Church is ruled by Canon Law, which can be rewritten by the Pope at any time.

Does the Pope maintain a court and confer titles of nobility? Yes, he maintains a court in the largest palace in the world, and he appoints Papal nobles who are entitled to wear uniforms and swords. Incidentally, the grant of these orders of Papal nobility is a substantial source of income for the Papal treasury.

This is enough for the Vatican State. We have never recognized the present Vatican State officially, although we have dealt with it in a style of such flaccid friendliness that our relationship might fairly be described as semi-recognition. Our leading politicians like to be photographed in respectful attitudes in the vicinity of the Pope, and our State Department representatives in the chief capitals of Europe meekly acknowledge the Vatican's Papal nuncios as deans of the diplomatic corps without so much as a murmur of protest against the partial union of church and state which this procedure implies.

Our government actually did recognize the old Papal States to the extent of sending a string of consuls to its capital in the early years of the last century, and from 1848 to 1868 the United

States had either a chargé d'affaires or a resident minister at the Papal capital. However, President Buchanan, in commissioning the first chargé, was careful to lay down the rule for him and for later representatives that the United States occupied an "entirely different position" from the governments which were "connected with the Pope as the head of the Catholic Church." Our representatives were instructed to keep away from "ecclesiastical questions" and devote themselves exclusively to "civil relations." [5] Even this limited recognition of the old Papal States was allowed to lapse in 1868 when Pius IX became known as a reactionary, when some Presbyterians were refused permission to meet in Rome, and when the American minister narrowly averted the burning of 2,000 Italian Protestant Bibles in Rome. Anti-Catholic feeling was especially strong after *The New York Times* inaccurately reported that the Papal government was "the only Government in the world that recognized the rebel Confederacy."

From 1868 to 1939, our relationship with the Papacy as a temporal power was extra-diplomatic. Then, in 1939, President Roosevelt began a questionable era in personal diplomacy by sending the Episcopal steel magnate Myron C. Taylor to the new Vatican State (formed in 1929) as his "personal representative." The maneuver permitted the President to by-pass Congress and establish a new wartime diplomatic policy without ratification by the Senate. Taylor was called a personal representative but he was recognized by the Vatican itself as a *de facto* ambassador from the United States. The State Department furnished him with free quarters and a staff of assistants on the United States payroll, who did most of his work. It is not surprising that when Congress reasserted its authority over the situation after the war—and after the 1950 resignation of Taylor—our representatives inserted a provision in an appropriation bill that funds for desultory diplomatic missions could not be spent in the future without the specific approval of Congress.[6]

Meanwhile, in 1951, when President Truman attempted to send General Mark W. Clark to the Vatican as a full ambassador, his proposal was met with an overwhelming and unmistakably genuine wave of popular opposition. Spearheaded by a new and militant organization, Protestants and Other Americans United for Separation of Church and State, the Protestant churches of the country united on the issue as they have rarely united on any policy in our history. In the *Atlantic Monthly,* in a two-part discussion with Professor Arthur Schlesinger, Jr., of Harvard, I pointed out that if General Clark were confirmed he would be the only full ambassador at the Vatican from a non-Catholic power. America did not want such a unique distinction. Obviously President Truman had misjudged the American temper. Mark Clark withdrew his name when it became evident that his appointment faced certain defeat. I think that my comment on the victory in the *Atlantic* still holds good:

> It was a spontaneous and amazingly powerful reaction in defense of the American tradition of the separation of church and state. It was opposition to any move that might entangle America in any church-state alliance. The force of the protest was so overwhelming that I doubt whether *any* ambassador to the Holy See will be confirmed at Washington during this generation.[7]

Many non-Catholics learned for the first time during this Vatican-ambassador controversy that the Catholic conception of the separation of church and state is quite distinct from the ordinary American conception. In the Catholic scheme of development, political power may theoretically be added to sectarian religious power without tainting the religious institution in any way with political significance.

For American Catholics there is nothing anomalous in venerating a religious leader who is both a priest and a statesman. The concepts of the sovereignty of the Catholic Church and the sovereignty of the Pope are welded together so closely that the average Catholic can scarcely make a distinction between political and religious programs. It is an understatement to say that the Roman Catholic Church is *in* politics. It *is* political. "Separation of church and state" is described by Father John Courtney Murray, the leading current writer on this theme in the American hierarchy, as "that negative, ill-defined, basically un-American formula, with all its overtones of religious prejudice." [8]

Father Murray later became the most advanced of the "liberal" Jesuit leaders in advocating accommodation of Catholic policy to American principles. But his voice is still, in the final analysis, the voice of the controlled hierarchy. In making such a statement Father Murray is simply echoing the official teachings of many Popes. Pius IX in Section 6 of his *Syllabus* denounced as one of "the principal errors of our time" the statement: "The Church ought to be separated from the State, and the State from the Church." In practice that means that the Catholic state and the Catholic Church function as one entity under one sovereign.

The funds for the world-wide network of political diplomacy are all controlled by the same absolute autocracy that controls the creation of saints and the administration of Catholic schools. The religious and political reports from bishops and nuncios all go to the same headquarters. So does the money; and the bishops render no accounting to their people for the expenditure of either religious or political funds. When Mary O'Brien of Montana puts a dollar in the collection plate for Peter's Pence, it may go toward the expense of the Papal nuncio in Paris, or the political drive for the Christian Democratic Party in Italy, or the cost of medical supplies for Dutch-Negro lepers in Paramaribo, or the living expenses of the Pope himself. American Catholic generosity in these matters is munificent and undiscriminating. In a normal year, according to Thomas Sugrue, the Archdiocese of New York "contributes more money to the support of the Church of Rome than all of Europe." [9]

Nobody knows how much of the Pope's funds go to religious and how much to political purposes—the distinction would be futile in any case because political and religious activities in the Roman system are inextricably mixed. The Church does not contribute as such to its string of Catholic political parties in Italy, France, Belgium, Holland, etc., but it accomplishes the same purpose by supporting Catholic Action groups which serve as the phalanxes of these parties. Official figures about the ownership of property and income are kept secret, so that nobody can speak with certainty about the Church's wealth and the proportion of that wealth which is used for political activities. A Catholic writer has estimated that the Papal court alone cost at least $2,000,000 a year before World War II.[10] That money, of course, was primarily American money.

2

The Church's philosophy of church and state is far more important than the continued existence of a bit of acreage which has its own postage stamps and flag. In fact, the philosophy of church and state espoused by the Vatican is the most important thing in the whole Catholic system because it determines the political and social policies which the bishops and priests will pursue throughout the world.

Underneath all its ponderous verbiage the Catholic theory of church and state is quite simple. It is essentially a variation of the doctrine of the divine right of rulers. "The origin of public power," said Leo XIII in his *Christian Constitution of States,* "is to be sought for in God, Himself, and not in the multitude. . . ." The divine authority of the Church is paramount in its own sphere because the Church is God's vicegerent on earth. The authority of the state comes next and is decidedly secondary. "In the [Italian] Concordat," said Pius XI in his famous rebuke to Mussolini contained in a letter to Cardinal Gasparri, "there are face to face, if not two States, most certainly two Sovereignties in the full significance of that word, each perfect in every sense in its own sphere, which sphere is necessarily determined by the end which each pursues, and to this it is scarcely necessary to add that the objective dignity of the ends pursued determines, no less objectively and necessarily, the absolute superiority of the Church." [11]

In particular areas the authority of the Church is superior to that of the United States government and of all governments, and no government is conceded the moral right to deny this. The Pope is a kind of special world monarch who rules a synthetic moral empire that overlaps and penetrates the sovereignty of all earthly governments. His special territory is religion, education, and family life, but he also has supreme power over a vaguely defined area known as "morals." Also he has special and exclusive jurisdiction over any matter which may affect the life of the Church either directly or indirectly. The Roman Catholic Church concedes that the state has supreme power in military matters, the punishment of crime (except that of priests), the collection of taxes, and the preservation of public order. Because of this doctrine priests tell their people to obey their governments in time of war even when Catholics are fighting Catholics, and even when the Vatican itself is committed to one side.

Leo XIII expressed the ancient and basic doctrine of church and state when he said in *Christian Constitution of States:*

The Almighty, therefore, has appointed the charge of the human race between two powers, the ecclesiastical and the civil, the one being set over divine, and the other over human things. Each in its kind is supreme, each has fixed limits within which it is contained, limits which are defined by the nature and special object of the province of each, so that there is, we may say, an orbit traced out within which the action of each is brought into play by its own native right.[12]

The snare in this innocent-sounding proclamation is that if there is a dispute between the Catholic Church and the state over the right to rule any specific area, the Church and the Church alone has the right to decide who wins. And "the Church" means Rome, not the American Catholic people or even the American Catholic bishops. "In cases of direct contradiction," says the *Catholic Encyclopedia,* "making it impossible for both jurisdictions to be exercised, the jurisdiction of the Church prevails, and that of the State is excluded." In Catholic theory the Church and the state are parts of a single temple with movable interior walls, and the Pope has the power to say where the separating partitions will stand.

In order to make sure that the scope of the Church's claims would not be curtailed by the modern welfare state, Pius XI in his *Reconstructing the Social Order* declared that "it is Our right and Our duty to deal authoritatively with social and economic problems. . . . For the deposit of truth entrusted to Us by God, and Our weighty office of propagating, interpreting and urging in season and out of season the entire moral law, demand that both social and economic questions be brought within Our supreme jurisdiction, in so far as they refer to moral issues." Hence, cremation, the Odd Fellows, socialism, Kant's *Critique of Pure Reason,* therapeutic abortion, and *Baby Doll* are all brought within the scope of the primary authority of the Church—and they are all condemned. More important, as we shall see later, the whole field of domestic-relations law is brought within the scope of Church authority by the establishment of competing Catholic marriage courts which claim superiority over America's own courts in matters of marriage, divorce, separation, and annulment.

While the hierarchy does not openly challenge American law in non-Catholic forums, the teachings of the Church's leaders in official publications make the challenge quite unmistakable. America's leading Catholic philosopher, Jacques Maritain, concedes to the Pope unlimited and supreme authority to intervene in any field of government he chooses, since his "sphere of activity does not admit of any predetermined limits and the extent of the application of which it is for the Pope alone to determine in any particular case. It is sufficient that the Pope should consider that a sufficiently spiritual interest is involved in any temporal arrangement for an intervention by him in regard thereto to be legitimate." [13]

A study, *The Judicial Power of the Church,* issued by the Catholic University of America in 1953, declares: "Since there is no superior with whom appeal can be lodged when the Church and State have become involved in controversy as to their relative competence, the decision is to be made by the Church." [14]

In its official documents the American hierarchy is quite frank about its teaching concerning the limited rights of civil government. The *Catholic Almanac* of 1948 says (italics supplied):

The Catholic citizen is in conscience bound to respect and obey the duly constituted authority *provided faith and morals are thereby not endangered. Under no circumstances may the Church be subjugated by the State. Whatever their form may be, states are not conceded the right to force the observance of immoral or irreligious laws upon a people.*[15]

In practice, as we shall see, "immoral and irreligious laws" are sometimes laws that non-Catholics consider supremely moral.

Under the theory of two powers, divine and civil, democracy is simply one of a number of acceptable types of civil government which may exist side by side with the divine kingdom of the Church. As far as the hierarchy is concerned, the acceptability of a form of government depends upon its attitude toward the Church. As Leo XIII said in his encyclical on *Human Liberty,* "it is not of itself wrong to prefer a democratic form of government, if only the Catholic doctrine be maintained as to the origin and exercise of power." If a democracy favors the Church, then the hierarchy tolerates it; if it opposes the Church, then that proves that the government is godless and lacks the necessary divine authority. If a democracy in Spain controlled by baptized Catholics expels the Jesuits and seizes Church property, then it is a murderous outlaw. If a democracy in the Netherlands controlled by Protestants supports all the Catholic schools with taxpayers' money and pays the salaries of the priests, its divine right to govern is recognized as authentic.

Behind the Catholic theory of church and state is the assumption that the state is something *over against* the people. It is not the people themselves and it does not express the genuine aspirations of the people as well as the Church does. The Church developed its philosophy of church and state when governments consisted of minority groups of nobles, warriors, and gentry. The Church was then one of the privileged classes ruling over the peo-

ple and sharing control with other privileged classes. Because of
its medieval traditions the Church still acts in the United States
today as if it were protecting the Catholic people from their own
government. It refuses to admit that the state expresses the will
of the people as a whole, the people of all religions.

  ⌐   There is a certain understandable shrewdness in this attitude
toward the democratic welfare state. If the hierarchy once conceded that ultimate sovereignty lies wholly in the people, anything
might follow. The state might then rightfully expand its jurisdiction over many fields of authority now claimed by the Church.
Because of this danger, the American Catholic bishops who praise
democracy always utter their praises with an important mental
reservation, that the real source of the authority of the American
government and of all governments is God and not the people.
And when the bishops use the name of God in this connection,
they do not mean a genial or undenominational Deity of all the
people; they mean the particular Catholic Deity who established
Roman primacy through St. Peter, whose Vicar on earth is the
Pope.

  You cannot find in the entire literature of Catholicism a single
unequivocal endorsement by any Pope of democracy as a superior
form of government. The Popes frequently speak in favorable
terms about certain aspects of democratic rule, but they cannot
afford to say anything which might be used to sanction a democratic government in its campaign for public schools or for the
disestablishment of religion. Nor can they afford to oppose political dictatorship as such when their favorite political ruler is
dictator Franco of Spain. The Popes frequently denounce "tyranny" and "mob rule" and "totalitarian methods" in government,
but this is perfectly safe politically because it does not commit
them to oppose any specific Catholic dictator. Fundamentally, as
The Catholic Action Manual says, "the church declares herself
indifferent in face of an absolute or of a democratic form of government." [16]

  Historically, in both Catholic and non-Catholic countries, the
Church has never ceased to be an aggressive state within a state,
claiming as much of the area of community life as it can safely
capture. It has yielded to the welfare state very grudgingly those
areas of cultural and charitable service which it once monopolized.
Its leaders, in full retreat before the expanding conception of the
democratic state, have kept repeating the unrealistic thesis of Leo

XIII, that there is a natural "orbit" for both church and state and that there are "fixed limits" between the orbits. No independent political scientist has ever been able to discover those fixed limits.[17]

3

Some American Catholics will not accept the foregoing paragraphs as a true picture of the Catholic position on church and state, in spite of the detailed quotations from Papal documents. They have heard progressive American bishops praise democracy so often that they honestly believe that their Church stands unequivocally for *complete* democracy in government. They have been taught to believe in their schools that there can be no real conflict between the Roman Church and democratic government because the two operate in different, non-competing fields. They have been reassured by such sweeping (and astounding) claims as that of President George N. Shuster of Hunter College, one of the more liberal of the Catholic apologists, that American Catholics "have never once attempted to use governmental power for their own ends, and they have zealously refrained from all attempts to write one of their special moral principles into federal or state law." [18] As we shall see later, the Catholic hierarchy is now engaged in a great national campaign to write into state and federal laws the principle that the state owes the Church financial support for its schools.

Much of the confusion in Catholic discussions of church and state is semantic. The Catholic bishop who discusses church and state uses words in a special sense. He draws his definitions from a ready-made world, and the words "church and state" do not mean to him the same things that they mean to a non-Catholic, or even to many Catholics. The bishop begins by including in the concept "church" large areas of political, social, and educational life which the non-Catholic regards as part of the normal sphere of democratic government. The bishop, *after* he has included these special ecclesiastical preserves in the picture of his Church, can honestly say that he believes in some separation of church and state *from that point forward.*

This conditional and provisional endorsement of the principle of church-state separation was expressed very frankly by Monsignor George B. O'Toole, professor of philosophy at the Catholic University of America, in 1939:

It is clear, then, that no Catholic *may positively and unconditionally approve* of the policy of separation of church and state. But given a country like the United States, where religious denominations abound and the population is largely non-Catholic, it is clear that the policy of treating all religions alike becomes, all things considered, a practical necessity, the only way of avoiding a deadlock. Under such circumstances, separation of Church and State is to be accepted, not indeed as the ideal arrangement, but as a *modus vivendi.*[19]

Usually American leaders of the Church are not so revealing about the equivocal meaning of their "endorsements" of church-state separation. The administrative leader of American Catholicism, the late Archbishop McNicholas of Cincinnati, said in January, 1948, in a ringing attack on the new organization Protestants and Other Americans United for Separation of Church and State: "We deny absolutely and without any qualification that the Catholic bishops of the United States are seeking a union of church and state by any endeavors whatsoever, either proximate or remote." [20] This famous sentence, which has been widely used in Catholic propaganda, when carefully analyzed, reveals no commitment whatever to support the American conception of the separation of church and state as set forth by the Supreme Court. It contains enough loopholes to permit government tax support for both sectarian schools and other Catholic institutions, in the manner developed in the Netherlands, which was described by a 1951 pamphlet, *American Separation of Church and State,* by Father Jeffrey Keefe, as "separation of Church and State in the form of impartial cooperation between government and the various sects." [21] In fact, in the very same statement by Archbishop McNicholas which I have quoted he indicated his belief in government support for Catholic parochial schools, and described the Pope as "the ruler of a sovereign state."

In the mind of Archbishop McNicholas this was not ecclesiastical double-talk, although it conveyed the false impression that the Catholic Church actually believes in the separation of church and state. When the Archbishop spoke of a "union of church and state," he meant a *complete* union, and he was correct in saying that American bishops do not favor such a union. Nobody, in fact, favors such a union. What the Catholic bishops of the United States favor is a *partial* union in which the Roman Catholic Church will have a privileged position as the recognized sovereign of the nation's moral and religious life. The editor of the leading diocesan paper in the United States, Monsignor Matthew Smith, made this quite clear in discussing Archbishop McNicholas's statement when he said: "Where the Catholics are in overwhelming majority, it is theoretically better to have an official union of Church and State, with the state participating from time to time in public worship and using the machinery of government, when needed, to help the Church." [22]

How large must "the overwhelming majority" of Catholics be in order to bring "an official union of Church and State" into being? The Church admits that it has not attained that goal yet in the United States. In the words of a recent comprehensive and approved study, *The State in Catholic Thought* by Heinrich A. Rommen, the situation of the Church in the United States is now "fully satisfactory" (p. 591). But when "the people of the state are in great majority Catholics," the following program is "possible as a practical policy" (p. 593):

It would mean the acknowledgement of the canon law in matters that are admittedly of spiritual nature (e.g. matrimony, hierarchy, clerical education, and legal exemption of the clergy from the secular jurisdiction in certain matters); the recognition of the Catholic religion as the religion of the people with these consequences: privilege of exclusive public cult, recognition of Church holydays, Catholic public schools, protection of the Church, her institutions, sacraments, and doctrine against libel, contempt, etc., in the penal law, membership of higher state officials in the Church, and financial support by the state for the ecclesiastical institutions so far as they cannot fulfill their functions on their own resources.

This approximately Spanish solution of the church-state problem is not described by Dr. Rommen as "a union between Church and State." It is merely "cooperation in concord and unity of both," with "mutual respect for the independence of each."

The full significance of this double standard in the Catholic theory of church and state cannot be appreciated by studying the American experience alone. The Catholic Church in the United States has always been a minority church, and it was so distinctly on the defensive during the first century and a half of our history that its leaders seldom asserted the full doctrine of Catholic rights in government.

Now the hierarchy is becoming more confident. Occasionally it allows the publication of some expression of fact or sentiment that illuminates the whole clerical landscape like a flash of summer lightning. Here is an item from Puerto Rico published in the *Catholic Almanac* of 1954, among the "Events of Catholic Interest" for January, 1953.

Anna Collazo, an employee of the Puerto Rican Department of Education, refused to swear allegiance to the entire constitution. She would defend all the laws of the commonwealth, she said, except those opposed to divine law. Father Arroyo, director of the Confraternity of Christian Doctrine, defended her action, declaring it the duty of all Catholics to make a mental or written reservation against birth control, sterilization and the secularistic school laws when pledging to defend the Puerto Rican commonwealth laws.[23]

Such frank speaking is not usually encouraged in the United States, although nominally American Catholics are instructed by their hierarchy to defy the laws of the American people when these laws differ from the rulings of the Church. The word "defy" is not contained in the Papal encyclicals, but the word "resist" is there, and its meaning is unmistakable. As Leo XIII said in his encyclical on the *Chief Duties of Christian Citizens:*

If the laws of the state are manifestly at variance with the divine law, containing enactments hurtful to the Church or conveying injunctions adverse to the duty imposed by religion, or if they violate in the person of the Supreme Pontiff the authority of Jesus Christ, then truly, to resist becomes a positive duty, to obey, a crime.[24]

This doctrine in practice means that American Catholics are instructed to accept the privileges of American democracy and work to bring the lives of *all* the people, Catholic and non-Catholic, into the pattern laid down in Rome. Here, for example, are seven matters of social policy in contemporary America in which the Catholic hierarchy seeks to impose one position on both Catholics and non-Catholics, while the people, through their federal or state governments, take an opposite position. I shall not attempt to discuss these Church policies in detail here, since they will be treated in later chapters, with ample references to the Catholic documents involved.

Official religion: The Church teaches that in the perfect state the Catholic religion should be established and supported by public taxation. The First Amendment to the Constitution of the United States forbids the establishment of any religion.

Divorce: The Catholic Church says: "The State has no right to grant divorces since it has no authority to annul a valid marriage." The federal and state governments disagree. The American people now permit divorce in every state.

Marriage: The Church refuses to recognize marriages as valid when non-Catholic clergymen or public officials perform marriage ceremonies for Catholics. The people, through the United States government and state governments, recognize the validity of civil as well as religious marriages, and refuse to discriminate against marriages of Catholics by non-Catholic clergymen.

Birth control: The Church says that all use of contraceptives by Catholics or non-Catholics is illegal under Church law. The people in all but two of the states of the United States permit doctors to give contraceptive advice to patients.

Education: The Church teaches that Catholic schools should be supported by public (non-Catholic and Catholic) taxpayers and that the priests should have the right to censor public-school textbooks. The people have enacted both state and federal laws to make *direct* contributions to Catholic schools illegal, and nominally they reject Catholic censorship in public schools.

Sterilization: The people in twenty-seven states, permit some eugenic sterilization of certain insane, feeble-minded, and criminal citizens, under specific safeguards. The Church says this is illegal and immoral, except as a specific penalty for a crime.

Therapeutic abortion: The Church says that therapeutic abortion is murder even if it is absolutely necessary to save the life of a mother. The people in all states permit therapeutic abortion when it is indicated to save the life or health of a mother.

Unquestionably Catholics have a moral right to oppose any law in a democracy so long as they believe in submission to law. But the freedom to disagree is not the freedom to defy; and the attitude of the hierarchy concerning many American laws goes far beyond the limit of mere disagreement. In some cases the alien-controlled hierarchy demands defiance of existing American law; in other cases it notifies the government that it *would* defy certain laws if they were passed; in still other cases it urges temporary submission without conceding the state's moral right to enforce a law; and in almost all cases in which the Church and the American people disagree the hierarchy uses ecclesiastical penalties to punish its members for making their own choice in good conscience between Church policy and public policy.

Let us look at one illustration of each one of these anti-democratic attitudes.

1. Flat defiance of an existing law: American Catholic judges, in spite of their official oaths to enforce all laws impartially, are directed by the hierarchy in official documents not to carry out, with Catholics or non-Catholics, the sterilization laws which exist in twenty-seven states. Father Francis J. Connell, dean of the School of Sacred Theology at the Catholic University of America, in his *Morals in Politics and Professions,* says that "in those states which now prescribe or permit eugenic sterilization for certain types of defectives and criminals, no circumstances can justify a judge in giving a decision that the law should be put in operation." [25]

2. Threatened defiance of a proposed law: Leading Catholics have repeatedly declared that if the United States ever adopted a law compelling all children to attend public schools, they would defy the law, as they have done in Mexico. Pope Pius XI in his encyclical on *Christian Marriage* declared that "unjust and unlawful is any monopoly, educational or scholastic, which physically or morally, forces families to make use of government schools." [26] By using the word "unlawful," he asserted his right to overrule such a law with his own divine authority.

Only one American state, Oregon, has passed such a law, and it was declared unconstitutional partly because of special circumstances existing at the time. (Probably it was an unwise law, but we do not need to discuss its merits here.) Presumably if the Constitution were amended to permit such a law, or if a milder form of the Oregon law were declared acceptable by the Supreme Court, the Catholic Church would make good its threat of defiance.

The noted Catholic Hilaire Belloc stated Catholic intentions on this point very bluntly when compulsory public education was being debated after World War I (italics supplied):

It has already been proposed, and may at any time become law, in certain parts of the United States, that a parent should be forbidden to send his child to any but one particular type of school agreeable to the State, and shall be compelled to send his child to that school. The State here affirms the doctrine and practice that a certain religious atmosphere is, or should be, universal to the human race; or, at any rate, to all its citizens; which religious atmosphere is other than Catholic. *Such a law no Catholic would obey;* for, by Catholic definition, it is the parent who should decide upon the education of the child, not the state.[27]

We shall see later that in practice the Catholic parent is given no independent right to "decide upon the education of the child."

3. Conditional and temporary acceptance of a law: The Church teaches that the American practice of treating all religions on an equal plane is temporarily acceptable but ultimately wrong, since the state should give a preferred position to the Catholic faith. Accordingly, Catholics are taught to offer no resistance to the American policy of freedom *at the present time* but to take advantage of this freedom while working to destroy it—through the setting up of a state which will prevent the dissemination of non-Catholic views and limit the public activities of non-Catholic sects. As we shall see, this is now the system of clerical rule in Spain. "Should such persons [non-Catholics] be permitted to practice their own form of worship?" is the question asked by two great Catholic writers, Monsignor John A. Ryan and Father Moorhouse F. X. Millar in their standard work, *The State and the Church.* They answer:

If these are carried on within the family, or in such inconspicuous manner as to be an occasion neither of scandal nor of perversion to the faithful, they may properly be tolerated by the State. . . . Quite distinct from the performance of false religious worship and preaching to the members of the erring sect, is the propagation of the false doctrine among Catholics. This could become a source of injury, a positive menace, to the religious welfare of true believers. Against such an evil they have a right of protection by the Catholic State. . . . If there is only one true religion, and if its possession is the most important good in life for States as well as individuals, then the public profession, protection, and promotion of this religion and the legal prohibition of all direct assaults upon it, becomes one of the most obvious and fundamental duties of the State.[28]

We shall see later that American Jesuits are trying desperately to have this doctrine modified, since they recognize its damaging effects upon their claim that Catholicism accepts democracy.

4. Ecclesiastical penalties for disagreement: When Church law says one thing and American law another, the hierarchy punishes its people with *religious* penalties for following American law. Of the many illustrations of this practice, perhaps the clearest is the rule about clerical immunity from actions in American courts. Under American law, all men are equal in legal rights whether they wear religious garb or not, but under Catholic law priests may not be sued by Catholics in American courts without permission of their Church superiors. If they do resort to American courts for the redress of grievances against a priest, they are subject to excommunication under Canon 2341. As Father Stanislaus Woywod puts it:

God has provided two supreme organizations of human society, Church and State, each supreme and independent in its own sphere of jurisdiction committed to it by God. . . . Offenses which violate the civil law only are subject to the civil authority, with the exception that the Church claims for the clergy and the religious the so-called *privilegium fori,* which means that these persons are to be tried by an ecclesiastical court, and may only with the consent of the competent ecclesiastical authority be tried by the courts of the State. In the United States and other countries which have no Concordat with the Holy See, this claim of the Church is ignored. That fact, however, does not free Catholics from this rule of the Church. They may not sue the exempt persons [priests or nuns] either in civil or criminal cases in the courts of the State.[29]

In 1928 the Holy See officially excommunicated a whole group of American Catholics of Rhode Island who went to an American court to sue their bishop over the question of the language to be used in "their" parochial schools.[30]

These four instances which I have cited of basic conflict between the Roman Church and the American government are not incidental or exceptional. Some Catholic authorities are frank enough to admit that the conflict goes back to an irreconcilable difference between the Church and American democracy in their attitudes toward governmental power. Hilaire Belloc called it a "necessary conflict between the Civil State and the Catholic Church where the two are not identified." Then he went on to say:

The Catholic Church is in its root principle at issue with the Civic definition both of freedom and authority. For the purpose of the State, religion is either a universally admitted system, or a matter of individual choice. But by the definition which is the very soul of Catholicism, religion must be for the Catholic *First,* a supreme authority superior to any claims of the State; *Secondly,* a corporate thing, and not an individual thing; *Thirdly,* a thing dependent upon Authority, and not upon a personal mood; *Fourthly,* a guarantee of individual freedom in all that is not of Faith.[31]

Belloc admits that these principles are in fundamental conflict with the American outlook, and he predicts that a struggle that "will seem monstrous" may develop because: "On the one side you have a plain affirmation that the law is the law and must be obeyed, and indignant surprise on the rejection of what seems so obvious and universal a rule. On the other, you will have, as you have had throughout history, resistance to and denial of that rule." For once, I think Mr. Belloc was a good prophet. The signs of the "monstrous" conflict which he predicted are all about us.

4

Having glanced at Catholic political philosophy in action, we come now to an important question: Is the Roman Catholic Church a foreign power? That question was asked in November, 1946, by a group of American Protestant editors in a letter to the Attorney General of the United States. The editors asked for a grand-jury investigation by the Department of Justice into the activities of the representatives of the Vatican State in the United States in order to determine whether these activities were in violation of the Foreign Agents Registration Law.

The purpose of the Foreign Agents Registration Law, as modified and amended during World War II, is to identify agents of foreign principals and compel them to make a public record of the nature of their employment. The law does not attempt to suppress foreign propaganda or foreign organizations; it merely compels agents of foreign governments to disclose the nature of their connections so that Americans who deal with them may know their background.

The law (Title 22, Chap. 11, U.S. Code) provides that any person, not a diplomatic or consular official, who deliberately and willfully acts in the United States as agent of a foreign government without registering, or who makes a false statement of a material fact in registering, may, upon conviction in our courts, be punished by a fine of $10,000 and five years' imprisonment. Section 1 of this law includes in the definition of "agent of a foreign principal" any person who "collects information for or reports information to a foreign principal" or any person "who, within the United States, solicits, disburses, dispenses or collects compensation, contributions, loans, money, or anything of value, directly or indirectly, for a foreign principal." Another paragraph says: "The term 'government of a foreign country' includes any person or groups of persons exercising sovereign *de facto* or *de jure* political jurisdiction over any country, other than the United States, or over any part of such country. . . ." One of the provisions of the law compels foreign propagandists to label their propaganda plainly, showing the nature of its manufacture by an agent of a foreign power.

There is an exemption in the law for purely religious agents of a church. The law does not apply to any "person engaging or agreeing to engage only in activities in furtherance of bona fide religious, scholastic, academic, or scientific pursuits or of the fine arts. . . ." On the surface, this provision indicates that any Catholic bishop might gain exemption from the law by *agreeing* to confine himself to purely religious pursuits. In fact, this appears to be the only possible loophole for Catholic bishops in the law. There is no doubt that the Roman Catholic Church is itself a political power whose seat of government is located outside the United States, and the hierarchy boasts of this fact. It has all the necessary appurtenances of a foreign monarchy, by its own admission.

Is this a foreign power? Probably the apologists for the Vatican would say that, although its capital is located in Rome, it is an *international* rather than a foreign power, drawing its authority from God and its sanction from Catholics of all nations, including the United States. This contention will not stand analysis. The "internationalism" of the Church is not structural, since the hierarchy does not represent the people of any nation in the world, nor the government of any nation in the world. Its machinery is completely authoritarian, and the people of the United States do not have any more voting right in controlling it than the Catholic priests of the United States have. Its administrative personnel is almost wholly Italian. Professor D. A. Binchy, leading Catholic scholar, has pointed out that "the central administration of the universal Church is for all practical purposes confined to members of the Italian clergy." [32]

To what extent are the bishops of the hierarchy in the United States agents of the Pope as the sovereign of the Vatican State? Their elaborate oath of allegiance is taken to the Pope;[33] their political, sociological, and religious reports are commingled and sent to the same central headquarters; their instructions to oppose certain types of American legislation come to them in the same type of encyclicals that cover matters of mysticism and ritual. In all that they do, they obey the Pope not only as a spiritual pastor but also as head of a sovereign state, and the money which they raise and send to the Vatican is used indiscriminately for both religious and political activities. It is undoubtedly true that Catholic bishops appointed by the Pope engage in "activities in furtherance of bona fide religious . . . pursuits." But can the Attorney General of the United States say honestly that they are engaged *"only"* in such pursuits?

The federal government is quite embarrassed by the fact that the Vatican is simultaneously both a church and a state, a foreign power in some of its aspects and a domestic church in others. In general, federal officials have adopted toward this two-headed phenomenon a policy which might be described as genial ambivalence. Wherever possible the government permits the Catholic Church in any particular situation to decide for itself which it will be, a church or a state. This enables the Papacy to gain the advantages of both classifications and the complete responsibilities of neither. Four illustrations of the grand confusion which results from this ambivalent policy may be cited:

1. Proposed federal tax regulations permit every Catholic religious order to consider itself an "integral" part of a domestic church and thus eligible to come under the tax umbrella of the

word "church." This permits a Catholic organization to escape all taxes on unrelated business income even for such unchurch-like activities as manufacturing Christian Brothers' brandy or selling commercial time for a Jesuit radio station.* American taxpayers probably suffer to the extent of several million dollars a year by this discriminatory special privilege—it is not granted to the corresponding peripheral organizations of Protestantism because of the looser organization of the Protestant world—but the secrecy which surrounds individual tax returns makes it impossible to publish an accurate estimate of the total loss. (My Washington testimony on this subject before a House subcommittee on taxation is published in the hearings of November 19, 1956.)

2. When the Vatican claimed damages to the Pope's summer home at Castel Gandolfo, in four American bomber raids of 1944, it could not lawfully recover direct damages from the United States treasury as a "church," since war damages to churches were paid out of the treasuries of enemy countries where the war was fought. Nor could we pay the damages to the Vatican as a neutral power, since we do not recognize the Vatican officially. So the State Department evolved a linguistic compromise: cheerfully disclaimed all legal responsibility to pay any damages for Castel Gandolfo; firmly declared that payment "cannot be regarded as a precedent"; and then cautiously suggested the possibility of payment "as a matter of grace" of $964,199.35 with the comment that "papal domains were not territory of a neutral state but had the status of a neutral diplomatic mission located in the territory of a belligerent (just as, for example, the Swiss Embassy in Berlin)." [34] The appropriation was passed unanimously in an election year, and no member of Congress raised the embarrassing question: How could the Roman Catholic Church escape taxes as a domestic church in one section of the Treasury Department while collecting a tax gift from another door as an embassy of a neutral nation?

3. The government is in even greater confusion concerning an American public officer's right to accept a title from the Vatican. Under Article 1, Section 9, of the Constitution, and a Congressional act of January 31, 1881, a member of Congress may not accept any title or present from a foreign state without special permission of Congress, and even then no decoration may be "publicly shown or exposed upon the person." In April, 1957, John W. McCormack, majority leader of the House and for many years the chief Catholic spokesman in Congress, and Representa-

* The Christian Brothers have now paid up back taxes, sued for a $490,000 refund, and, in March 1958 the government has denied their application. The suit is pending.

tive John J. Rooney of New York, an equally faithful servant of Vatican interests, were awarded by the Pope the rank of Knight Commander of the Order of St. Gregory with Star. "The award," said *The New York Times,* "is one of the highest the Papacy may bestow on a layman."

The honor is not an ecclesiastical honor but a political one, and is so classified by the *Catholic Almanac,*[35] which separates it from "Significant Ecclesiastical Honors" and describes it as one of the chief "Pontifical Orders of Knighthood," established "to reward the civil and military virtues of the subjects of the Papal States." When the illegality of the award was mentioned in the press, McCormack had a bill introduced quietly into the House and run through by unanimous vote without debate, authorizing the award for himself and Mr. Rooney, describing the award erroneously as "ecclesiastical." [36]

Does this constitute a recognition by the United States that the Vatican is a foreign power? Certainly it constitutes an acknowledgement Congress in passing the law acted on the assumption that it was dealing with a sovereign nation. Otherwise no law would have been necessary. But neither Congress nor the State Department will accept the implications of that assumption and subject Rome-appointed Catholic officials in this country to the disabilities of foreign agents.

4. Even when a federal statute is indisputably specific, the government agencies do not enforce it against Catholic organizations if it involves the admission that they are controlled by an alien power. The federal radio and television law (Communications Act, Section 310) outlaws the ownership of any broadcasting station by an "alien or the representative of an alien" because aliens and the representatives of aliens are not properly amenable to American democratic control. Although the Jesuit order (Society of Jesus) is completely controlled by the Pope, its Belgian Superior General, and the overwhelmingly alien majority of its members, it has been permitted to own American radio stations and is now attempting to establish a chain of television stations. Protestants and Other Americans United for Separation of Church and State pointed out in a letter of protest to the Federal Communications Commission on this subject in 1957 that "local ownership" in the case of the Jesuits is a mere artifice.[37] Loyola University of New Orleans and St. Louis University, Jesuit applicants for stations in a Catholic television chain, are controlled by boards

of directors made up wholly of Jesuit priests who are subject to removal or transfer at any time by an alien Superior General for purely ecclesiastical reasons. They are true subjects of the Pope, a status which they freely acknowledge when applying for tax exemption. The F.C.C. is so strict in enforcing the "alien" provisions of the law in dealing with non-Catholics that it recently denied a television license to a small Mormon sect because its controlling board had one alien member, a Canadian. But it granted a television channel in New Orleans to a Jesuit organization in July, 1957. (It is likely that the F.C.C. policy on Jesuit stations will be challenged in court before this book goes to press.)

4

Education and the Catholic Mind

1

"BIGOTRY ONCE AGAIN is eating its way into the vital organs of the greatest nation on the face of the earth, our own beloved America," said Francis Cardinal Spellman at a Fordham University commencement. "Once again a crusade is being preached against the Catholic Church in the United States . . . now it is the growth and expansion of Catholic education which is claimed to be a constant threat to the supremacy of public education in the United States."

It is true that a tremendous revival of anti-Catholic feeling is taking place in the United States and that its focal point is the educational policy of the Church. But the new anti-Catholic sentiment is not an offensive against the Church so much as a broad defensive movement against a new educational aggressiveness on the part of the hierarchy. The new opposition is not based upon the type of personal bigotry which disgraced the country during the Al Smith campaign. It is strongest among the liberals who have always stood most courageously for personal tolerance.

What has caused this new opposition to Catholic educational policy? The immediate occasion has been the extension of some bus transportation at public expense to the parochial-school children of twenty states, and the fight of various Catholic lobbies before Congressional committees in Washington against any federal aid to education except that in which parochial schools share. The financial issue was dramatized and advertised by Cardinal Spellman in 1949 when he launched a bitter and insulting attack on Mrs. Roosevelt because she stood for the traditional American principle that public money should be expended for public schools only. As we shall see later, the proposed financial program of the Catholic hierarchy for its schools would cost the American taxpayers more than one billion dollars a year, and most taxpayers are emphatically opposed to subsidizing any faith to that extent. But the financial cost of endowing Catholic schools is not the only obstacle in the hierarchy's campaign to enlist sympathy and support. The quality and nature of Catholic education is also involved. The federal-aid fight, particularly, has raised certain basic questions about Catholic education which most Americans have never faced before. Are the Catholic schools worthy of public financial support? Are they democratic? Do they teach responsible freedom? Do they teach tolerance and national solidarity? Non-Catholics have a right to ask these questions, not only because the Catholic schools are training nearly 5,000,000 [1] future citizens in more than 12,000 tax-exempt institutions, but also because the people have accepted the Catholic schools as substitutes for public education under the state compulsory-education laws.

Until recently, most Americans had never stopped to think about the significance of a dual school system. Perhaps they had imagined that Catholic schools were simply "American public schools with a little religion added." Probably they felt a certain sympathy with Catholic parents who pay taxes for public schools that they do not use, and also support their own schools. Few non-Catholics have appreciated how large the parochial-school system has become or how completely it now serves as an instrument of the Catholic hierarchy.

Today there are some American communities in which the Catholic schools are actually larger than the public schools, and there are a great many communities in which the Catholic schools drain off from the public schools at least one-quarter of the community's children. Often the parochial and public schools are on opposite sides of the same street, dividing the children into competing and even hostile groups, conscious of their own differences and suspicious of each other's way of life. Even when both schools emphasize patriotism and community spirit, the fact that they exist as separate establishments tends to divide the community emotionally and culturally. The separatism is particularly harmful when, as so often happens, the Catholic group is largely an immigrant group that needs assimilation and Americanization more than any other part of the community.

This divisive pattern is most noticeable in the great Eastern and Midwestern centers of the country, where Catholicism is strongest. New York State alone has more than 640,000 children in its Catholic schools, and in New York City the attendance at parochial schools is rapidly approaching the attendance at public schools. Boston has 136,000 parochial-school children; Chicago about 285,000. A Catholic authority has estimated that in one year before World War II the total Catholic-school enrollment in the eight states where the Catholic population is most heavily concentrated exceeded the total enrollment in the public schools of fourteen of the less populous states. In 1934 the total Catholic enrollment was equivalent to the public-school population of seventeen states.[2]

The Catholic educational system does not stop with elementary schools. It includes over 250 colleges and universities with 260,000 students, 2,385 parish and diocesan high schools, and 500 seminaries. Before the last war many Catholic children had to attend public high schools because there were not enough Catholic high schools to accommodate them. That deficiency is now being remedied by a great high-school building campaign. It is the announced ambition of the hierarchy to have within a few years enough full-term high schools to accommodate every child who graduates from a parochial elementary school, and enough colleges to accommodate every Catholic high-school graduate who desires to continue his education beyond the secondary level.

All of these schools belong to the Catholic hierarchy or the religious orders, not to the American Catholic people. When American Catholic churches and schools were first established, the Catholic people wanted to control the physical property through trustees or boards of their own choosing, as public schools are controlled. In that respect American Catholics had absorbed the independent spirit of Americans, and they did not wish to spend their money and efforts in erecting buildings that would be owned by priests who, in turn, would be completely subject to European orders. But there was no place in the Catholic system for this kind of popular ownership. The hierarchy won its fight against American "trusteeism" after brief flurries of revolt in Philadelphia and other cities.[3]

Today, the American Catholic people do not own a single brick or board in "their" churches and schools. The system of priestly ownership in Chicago and Boston may be taken as typical. In those cities all Church buildings, including schools, are owned by a corporation of one man, called in law a corporation sole. He is the bishop (archbishop or cardinal) of the ecclesiastical territory, and no layman can challenge his authority over the Roman Catholic establishment. This incorporated bishop is tax-exempt, and he can issue notes with the Church and school buildings as collateral without consulting the Catholic people.

Americans would never tolerate such a system of ownership for their public schools. Such schools are controlled democratically by elected school boards, or by boards chosen by elected officials. Public-school buildings belong to the people of each district, and the people, as voters, have the final say as to their use. This system of democratic educational control is so well established in American tradition that no one thinks of questioning it.

The contrast between the methods of control of public and parochial schools is evident in every department of school activity. The Catholic people of a community do not decide for themselves whether a school is to be erected in their parish. The decision was made for them many years ago when the Third Plenary Council of Baltimore in 1884 laid down the flat rule that every parish priest must have a Catholic school attached to his church.[4] Every priest was ordered to raise the money for a school and to impose the burden of supporting it upon the people of his parish.

Today the tradition that the school is an organic part of the parish is so thoroughly accepted that the priests do not bother to separate the treasuries of the church and the school. The double and triple collections which they frequently take up in church on Sunday are for the "expenses of the Parish," and that includes repairs on the church roof and the priest's support, along with repairs on the school roof, the heating bill for both buildings, and the living expenses of the nuns who teach in the classrooms.

"The pastor," says the Right Reverend John R. Hagan in *Vital Problems of Catholic Education,* "is responsible by ecclesiastical law for the existence, maintenance, and conduct of the parish school. The religious superior [of the nuns and brothers] appoints the teaching staff and principal and exercises over them a supervision which is at once religious and educational. The Catholic school board, or the superintendent, represents a third authority, namely the bishop." [5] Frequently the priest himself is an auxiliary teacher in his parish school, and he can be the dominating influence in that school if he cares to exercise his power.

It is easy to imagine the financial strain that this support of both the school and the church puts upon the average, poor Catholic family. In order to support both ecclesiastical and educational establishments the priests must resort again and again to "money talks" in the pulpit and to persistent "money visits" to Catholic homes. "In most parishes," wrote a Catholic woman in the *Forum* of June, 1929, "it is a practice—and without which it would be futile to appeal to conscience—to publish at regular intervals the exact amount each member of the congregation has given to the support of church and school. Disgrace befalls a person whose name appears on the monthly list with contributions considered too small." Actually the average amount that Catholic families in the United States contribute for the elementary schools alone has been estimated at less than $2 per month per child, but this does not include the church contribution proper.

Non-Catholics who read about a Catholic school board may think it represents the people of a parish, since the school board in public education is always a democratically chosen institution. In the Catholic system it is composed of priests, and it is part of the tightly controlled hierarchy. "Diocesan control over schools," says the Right Reverend William R. McNally, "is usually exercised through the diocesan school board, composed of priests and presided over by the bishop. Its executive officer is the superintendent, a priest specially chosen and trained in the supervision of schools." [6] The bishop, if he chooses, can be a complete czar over the educational system of his diocese, for he has the power to remove any priest or nun, throw out any textbook or course of study, and overrule any school board of priests. The number of Catholic school boards has actually declined in recent years, leaving control more and more in the hands of superintendents who are personally responsible to bishops.[7]

There is no national head to the Catholic school system, no American superior to challenge the bishop's authority in education. In practice the drudgery of actual direction of each parochial school is performed by a Sister principal who, in the average school, supervises about ten teachers and five hundred pupils. She works under a Community Supervisor of her teaching order who supervises many schools and visits them only occasionally. Altogether there are more than two hundred teaching orders in the United States engaged in teaching in the Catholic elementary schools alone, each with its own buildings, supervisory hierarchy, and distinctive costume.

The same system of control exists in American Catholic colleges. They are chiefly the property of religious orders, and are controlled not by boards of laymen but by priests, bishops, and archbishops. The Jesuits, America's largest religious order, control a chain of colleges of their own, and exert great influence throughout the Catholic college world. Although Catholic colleges have a much larger percentage of lay teachers than high schools have, the entire Catholic educational system in the last analysis is completely dominated by priests and nuns. Any teacher who publicly turns against this hierarchical system of control is immediately deprived of his post and his livelihood.

2

How does it happen that in a nation in which the taxpayers provide free public schools for all children so many million people agree to support a separate school system at their own expense?

Part of the answer lies in the early American tradition. Our country did not formally establish separation of church and state in educational matters until the nineteenth century. Virtually all schools in colonial days were church schools, and until about 1825 the religious domination of elementary schools was taken for granted by the majority of Americans. Most schools before 1825 were Protestant, and the great Eastern universities like Harvard, Yale, and Columbia were almost as much theological as scientific in their emphasis. The Catholic schools were simply one part of the religiously dominated elementary-school system.

Then, as the movement for free public education gained headway,[8] various Protestant sects began to fight among themselves over the religious and moral teaching that should be given to children. It became apparent that the community would be split into warring factions unless the public school could be lifted above the battle. Most American Protestants recognized the necessity for compromise and agreed to support the public schools as secular institutions divorced from distinctively religious teaching. It was a decision in keeping with the spirit and letter of the Constitution, since the First Amendment had declared against any "establishment of religion."

But the Catholic hierarchy observed a "higher loyalty" in order to maintain its own enterprise. The Catholics in the United States were ordered to keep their children out of "neutral" schools. They have no choice in the matter since this rule is a part of the Canon Law of the Church. The boycott rule reads:

Catholic children must not attend non-Catholic, neutral or mixed schools, that is, such as are also open to non-Catholics. It is for the bishop of the place alone to decide, according to the instructions of the Apostolic See, in what circumstances and with what precautions attendance at such schools may be tolerated, without danger of perversion to the pupils.[9]

Not content with a mere prohibition or moral exhortation, the hierarchy in many American dioceses has written into the law of the Church a provision denying absolution to those Catholics who send their children to a public school when a Catholic school is available. This is now the Catholic moral law in the United States. The Statutes of the Diocese of Indianapolis are typical and are based squarely upon the instructions of the various Popes beginning with Pius IX:

Where a Catholic parochial school exists, parents ordinarily violate the general Canon Law of the Church (Canon 1374) if they send their children to public or non-Catholic schools. If they persist in this violation, they sin gravely and cannot be absolved until they make proper adjustment with the Ordinary through the Pastor (Statute 117).[10]

Behind this sweeping dictum lies a whole philosophy of education that is alien to the American outlook. Most Americans assume that education is primarily the business of the whole community, and that the people's government is the logical agency to educate the children of the people. The Catholic teaching on this point consists of two principles, that every "subject taught be permeated with Christian [Catholic] piety," [11] and that "the government has no primary right to educate at all." The first principle justifies the hierarchy in condemning all non-Catholic education as amoral or immoral. The second sustains the hierarchy in its claims to complete supremacy in education. The government, according to Catholic theory, is a sub-junior partner in education. It has an *interest* in education and a duty to provide the means for education because it wants children to be patriotic and obedient to law, but it has no primary right or capacity to teach children in the way they should go. That right has been given by God, the source of all governmental power, to the Roman Catholic Church.

I have already quoted enough statements from Hilaire Belloc and other Catholic authorities to indicate the official nature of this doctrine. Pope Pius IX enunciated the teaching for American Catholics in 1864, and later Popes have reiterated it again and again. In order to spare American feelings the American hierarchy has usually softened the wording of the full gospel as much as possible, but it has not dared to depart from the doctrine's fundamental exclusiveness. The gospel which was stated by Pius XI in his encyclical, *Christian Education of Youth,* in 1929, is the law of American Catholicism:

> And first of all education belongs pre-eminently to the Church, by reason of a double title in the supernatural order, conferred exclusively upon her by God Himself; absolutely superior therefore to any other title in the natural order . . . the Church is independent of any sort of earthly power as well in the origin as in exercise of her mission, as educator, not merely in regard to her proper end and object, but also in regard to the means necessary and suitable to attain that end. . . . Every form of instruction, no less than every human action, has a necessary connection with man's last end, and therefore cannot be withdrawn from the dictates of the divine law, of which the Church is guardian, interpreter and infallible mistress . . . it is the duty of the State to protect in its legislation the prior rights, already described, of the family as regards the Christian education of its offspring, and consequently also to respect the supernatural rights of the Church in this same realm of Christian education.[12]

It was in this same encyclical that Pius XI reiterated the Vatican doctrine that Catholic children may not go to non-Catholic schools, even when they receive their religious education separately, from Catholic teachers.

When this encyclical reached America, it produced a considerable shock. *The New York Times* said:

> The Pope's encyclical sounds a note that will startle Americans, for it assails an institution dearest to them—the public school—without which it is hardly conceivable that democracy should long exist. . . . If other churches were to make like claims—that is that "the educative mission belongs pre-eminently" to them for their children, and were to lay like inhibitions, the very foundations of this Republic would be disturbed.[13]

Pius's doctrine has been carried over into the American community in countless manifestations of separatism and intolerance. Any law based upon the accepted American theory that education is primarily the function of the people encounters the opposition of the hierarchy. In March, 1947, liberal political forces in New York appeared to be on the verge of success in their long fight for a bill that would prevent racial and religious discrimination in the state. Suddenly, Coadjutor Archbishop J. Francis McIntyre, now a Los Angeles cardinal, denounced the bill as one "formed after Communistic pattern," not acceptable to Catholics. In amazement the friends of the bill listened to the Archbishop give his reason. They were told that the Church would fight the measure because, to use the Archbishop's words as reported in *The New York Times:*

> The bill states that education is the function of the State. Education is not the function of the State. Education is the function of the parent. If the statement that education is a State function is written into the law, it will permit future encroachments on the parental function of education. That is what we mean by the infiltration of Communist ideas.[14]

As a whole the statement is not less amazing than the reiteration of the supposed doctrine that the Catholic Church believes in the primacy of parents in education. If there is anything that the hierarchy does *not* believe in in the field of education it is the primacy of parents. No Catholic parent, as we have seen, is allowed freely to choose a non-Catholic school for his children. In practice it is clear that the doctrine of the primacy of parents is simply a device for asserting the supremacy of the priest as against the power of a democratic government.

The priests have been only half successful in their efforts to get "every Catholic child into a Catholic school." Only a little more than 50 per cent of the Catholic children of school age in the United States are in the Church's schools and the defections to the public schools have been heaviest in great Catholic centers where parochial schools are available. Father Joseph Fichter, S.J., of Loyola University of the South predicted in 1957 that two-thirds of these Catholic children will be in public schools in the near future because of the shortage of teaching nuns and the superior building program of public schools.[15]

3

So much controversy has been created by the Catholic methods of educational control that the public has almost overlooked the chief participants in the educational scheme itself. They are the 95,000 teaching nuns who comprise about 90 per cent of the teaching force in American Catholic elementary schools.

In a sense these teaching nuns are the forgotten women of the educational world. When American newspapers talk about teachers' wages and teachers' incentives, these 95,000 nuns are not included. National labor unions make no attempt to organize them, although the Church favors unionization for almost everybody else. Non-Catholics never encounter them except as strange passing visions of flowing black, with maidenly white faces snugly bordered by white linen.

Some of their isolation and obscurity is self-imposed. They belong to an age when women allegedly enjoyed subjection and reveled in self-abasement. Their unhygienic costumes and their medieval rules of conduct establish a barrier between themselves and the outside world, a barrier that has been erected deliberately to protect them from worldly taint. Even the names of the 244 religious orders for women in the United States reflect a medieval attitude of piety and feminine subordination that seems utterly alien to the typically robust and independent spirit of American womanhood. The Sisters of Our Lady of Charity of the Good Shepherd is the most typical name I can think of; it sums up an atmosphere and an attitude.

All the money that these teaching nuns make must be turned over to the orders to which they belong, even the Christmas presents from their pupils. This rule applies even to those who have taken only simple vows and are teaching in public schools. When they draw full teaching salaries from the public schools they turn over all of their pay to the superiors of their orders—in fact, they are obliged to do this whether they want to or not. The Church rules concerning poverty apply with special force to all Religious.[16]

The cultural sequestration of these nuns goes so far that, even when they receive their teacher training in general Catholic colleges for women, the younger nuns are not allowed to study in the same classrooms with ordinary Catholic girls. "Mingling of young Sisters with young women of the world in all the intimacy of the classroom would be disruptive of their religious life," says Father John R. Hagan. "Hence classes are held for them separately." [17] Older nuns occasionally take special courses in non-Catholic universities, but this is usually after they have become seasoned devotees.

Most nuns are recruited as teen-age girls by the professional "vocation" promoters of the Church, often in the classrooms of the Catholic high schools. Then they are pledged to poverty, celibacy, and obedience for life. When they take the veil, they give up their own names, their families, and their old associates. (Ordinarily priests are allowed to keep their own names, but nuns are not.) Frequently they take male names which are used in curious combination with names of female saints. Among the nuns who are presidents of American women's colleges are women named Mary John, Mary Frederick, Mary Matthew, Mary Emmanuel, and Mary Thomas. In some religious communities every young woman who enters the novitiate takes the name of Mary as her first name, and adds to it a name as far removed as possible from her worldly name.

Nominally the young girls who are recruited into the Catholic religious orders have freedom to escape, and many of them actually do leave their orders before becoming full-fledged members, but the pressure upon them to remain is so systematic and powerful that few adolescents can resist it. The recent national best-seller, *The Nun's Story,* by Kathryn Hulme, makes it clear how difficult it is even for a mature and relatively sophisticated nun to escape from her profession (as she did) when her convent superiors care to use all the familiar devices of brain-washing and social pressure to restrain her.

The life of the nuns is in sharp contrast to the life of the public-school teacher. The American public-school teacher frequently complains of community censorship of her activities but she is reasonably free to marry and live a life of intellectual freedom. The celibate nuns of the Catholic system never know the meaning of this kind of freedom. They are completely surrounded by a cultural wall from the moment of their entrance into religious orders until the moment of death. Their activities and amusements are controlled by Superiors who, in turn, are cut off from full cultural contacts with the community by the rules of their orders.

Ordinarily the nuns are not free to read books, newspapers, or magazines of their own choice, to attend theaters or motion pictures, or to participate in any public amusements. In their personal and intellectual lives they are regimented almost as completely as convicts. Their courses of training are carefully guided, so far as possible, within the limits of the Catholic educational world. They are carefully segregated from free males and free thinkers. "The teaching nun," according to Father Paul E. Campbell, for thirteen years a diocesan school superintendent, "lives a life of exclusion, and the ideal teacher must be a person living apart from the world. . . . There are many worldly contacts that unfit a person for the work of teaching, that make him unworthy to guide and govern the young." [18]

No matter how competent and devoted the nuns may be—and no one questions their industry and devotion—they do not acquire occupational tenure within the school system. They can be removed instantly as teachers or as members of their religious orders for reasons which have no bearing on their competence as classroom teachers. Their superiors in the convents and the schools are usually the same persons, empowered to exercise complete discipline for any personal or intellectual insubordination. Nominally these nuns receive teacher-training courses either in their convents or in diocesan normal schools, but even the shorter courses consist largely of theological indoctrination. They are never allowed to forget that they are primarily religious missionaries whose chief mission is the inculcation of the Catholic faith.

Naturally, their techniques of teaching are authoritarian because they have never learned to use the intellectual freedom of the unshackled, inquiring mind. Memorizing and repetition are stressed; the respect for tradition is emphasized and re-emphasized, and Catholic tradition is exclusively taught. The catechetical method of moral instruction is stubbornly maintained in the face of the more modern techniques of progressive education. The late Archbishop McNicholas, general president of the National Catholic Educational Association, issued a special pastoral letter in June, 1948, in which he condemned as dangerous such expressions as: "The child, according to its years, should have a reasonable understanding of religion, and not be compelled to commit to memory formulae which it does not or perhaps cannot understand," and "Children should be made to realize that religion is something they live, not merely definitions or questions and answers committed to memory." [19]

The recruiting of young girls as nuns is permitted at the end of the fifteenth year by Canon Law.[20] The teaching orders in the United States do not call for final vows at such an early age, but the practice of the Church's recruiting agents is to recruit early before the desire for love and marriage has conquered the religious impulse. "In view of modern conditions," says Father Henry Davis, "it will be well to accept candidates at as early an age as possible, before the allurements of the world have cast their spell over them. The conflict in the youthful heart between grace and worldly attractions is often intense." The postulants, as they are called, are accepted on a temporary-pledge basis at an early age and then led gradually into complete religious membership after six months or more of concentrated attention. Perhaps the word to describe this concentrated attention should be "rushing," for the Catholic religious orders for women are essentially religious sororities that guide and shelter their members, and also attempt to instill in them a strong institutional pride. Unlike the sororities of normal life, they are anti-masculine and anti-marriage in their teachings. They attempt to cleanse the mind of each postulant of the desire for romantic relations and motherhood, and to sublimate the libido in passionate religious devotion.

In the all-female life of the convent very strict rules are enforced to prevent the ever-present peril of homosexual attachments. There must be no fondling among the Sisters, no touching, no concentrated personal friendship.

Many devices of prayer and exhortation are used to induce the young nuns to forsake worldly desires and sublimate their latent energy. They are kept prodigiously busy with devotional and manual work. If they feel strong sexual desire, they are encouraged to practice mortification by wearing hair shirts and even chains to overcome this "sin."

Father Winfrid Herbst in his 1956 guide-book for nuns, *The Sisters Are Asking,* warns that "chains and hair shirts should be worn for only comparatively brief periods of time" and not in the classroom. He even condones the wearing of hair shirts over the underwear instead of next to the skin, as a "compromise" penitential act, but he ridicules the wearing of chains next to the skin with the points turned *out,* since the whole purpose of the chain-wearing is to chasten the spirit by having the points turned *in.*[21] He declares that "it is refreshing to recall how in religious communities where the use of the discipline [scourge] is a regular practice, that a cat-o'-nine-tails, or less, is often found hanging on a nail in the room, back of the door or on the wardrobe cabinet, within handy reach, and is cheerfully referred to as 'the fire extinguisher.' This can be applied to the fires of concupiscence or of hell, or to both."

The nuns are indoctrinated with an imagery of sublimation that, at times, is almost painfully revealing. Here is a typical devotional series of exhortations taken from *The Interior Spirit of the Religious of the Visitation of Holy Mary,* published under the Imprimatur of the Archbishop of Baltimore:

> These souls are living holocausts, hosts and precious victims of perpetual sacrifice, who offer themselves to God on the altar of Cavalry to serve unceasingly Jesus Christ crucified, their only Spouse. . . .

The manual goes on to comment on the vow of chastity by saying that:

> On the Vow of Chastity . . . you ought to live, breathe and pant for your Celestial Spouse alone. . . . You should then, my dear Daughters, resolve to live on this sacred mount (Calvary), with your Spouse, dying among suffering and abandonment, saying with the Spouse in the Canticles: My beloved Jesus Crucified is to me a posy of myrrh: I will place Him tenderly on my bosom and I will say a hundred times a day, this is my hope. . . . How can anyone press Jesus Christ to his breast, and not be wounded by the nails and thorns that transpierce Him?

The manual then describes the climax of the experience:

> . . . a union with Him, so intimate, naked, simple, sweet, and so perfect that nothing can be added to it. . . . Oh holy inebriation, which in the holy commerce of prayer transports a soul into the cellars of divine love. . . . Drink and be inebriated, my beloved.[22]

This manual goes on to say: "A Religious of the Visitation should always remember that she is no longer permitted to live humanly, as at her profession it was announced to her that, by her vows she was dead to the world and to herself, to live no longer but for God." Along with this abandonment of worldly happiness the nun is taught to "consider that it is God Himself whom she obeys in her Superioress." The constitution of the order "forbids all kinds of games," and it boycotts "birds, little dogs and other animals which only serve for amusement," since even "those diversions which seem most innocent to persons of the world are not becoming to a Religious of the Blessed Virgin."

Catholic teaching nuns, of course, are not cloistered in the manner in which medieval monks were cloistered. Although they are compelled to live in convents, they may live and laugh with their pupils during the school day. In spite of this relatively useful life, with its compensations of respect and security to those who remain submissive, it has become increasingly difficult in recent years to persuade American girls to become nuns. The enrollment in Catholic elementary schools is growing almost four times as fast as the number of teaching Sisters, and the resulting teacher shortage is becoming more desperate year by year. The maintenance of these elementary schools is dependent almost entirely on teaching nuns who work without salary for a meager expense allowance.[23]

Many Church authorities have expressed grave alarm over the future of orders for women if the drift toward family life and normal social service continues, and the Church is taking many special measures to check the decline in the popularity of "vocations." Little girls in Catholic congregations are frequently dressed up in religious costumes during festivals and taught to dramatize themselves as religious devotees. Parents are constantly reminded of their duty to furnish good Catholic sons and daughters to the Church. Catholic high-school teachers are obligated as part of their work to plead tactfully for more vocations. In the larger schools a vocational director is appointed who speaks in the classrooms about industrial and other employments that students may pursue, and then leads tactfully to the highest of all callings, that of the Religious.

In public propaganda the nuns are often pictured as gay, laughing, and buxom young ladies, sometimes wielding a tennis racket or a baseball bat. Their somber and restrained life is described as "holy freedom."

The recruiting agent who enlists young girls for the convents is often a priest, and his primary interest is in the Church. A priest in Maywood, Illinois, was commended in the 1946 *Bulletin of the National Catholic Educational Association* for adding a new fillip to recruiting techniques. He not only organized processions of children dressed in costumes of various nuns' orders but also established the system of putting up Honor Plaques for each recruit, listing the names of the *parents,* and calling for the issuance of Church certificates to these *parents,* which they could hang on their walls, conferring on them the titles of Knight and Lady of a Community.

The movement toward cloistered—entirely isolated—convents for nuns has almost collapsed in the United States, and it has sharply declined even in Spain, Italy, and France as modern science has learned to appraise the mentally abnormal types of individuals to whom this manner of life appeals. In order to save the remnants of these convents from disappearance, Pius XII in November, 1950, issued a new apostolic constitution for them, and in March, 1956, he issued another set of new rules which had the effect of bringing many nuns of solemn vows out of their self-imposed prisons into the world of useful work in hospitals and schools. But, nominally, the United States still has more than 100 convents of cloistered nuns, usually small, isolated houses occupied by withered older women who are called "cloistered contemplatives." *St. Joseph's Magazine* published in 1956 that rarest of disclosures, a series of photographs taken inside such a convent, showing the "revolving half-cylinder" in the wall through which all objects must be passed, without any personal contact with the outside world. These nuns are not allowed to use carpets, curtains, or cushions; no games of any kind are permitted; they are wakened each morning in the dark, and they spend a large part of each day in prayer and fasting.[24]

4

One reason the nuns of the Catholic schools are forgotten women is that the Catholic school system itself is a no-man's-land in American education. Very few non-Catholics know anything about it, and Catholic laymen get their over-all picture from the self-serving declarations of their hierarchy.

The Catholic schools tend to follow the pattern of public education in respect to subject matter, not because the priests have any admiration for the public schools but because there is a constant interflow of students between the public and Catholic systems and the smaller system must conform to the larger in order to win admission to state high schools and universities for parochial students. That necessary conformity has been the greatest single factor in keeping the Catholic schools as good as they are.

The Catholic schools offer the lowest-cost education in the United States, far lower than education in Mississippi, which has the cheapest public education in the American public-school system. The cheapness in the case of the Catholic schools is achieved at the expense of the teaching nuns.

In 1944 Mississippi spent $42.25 per pupil for its schools; in 1937 the Diocese of Indianapolis spent an average of $15.53 per pupil in five of its typical parochial schools, at a time when the corresponding expenditure in the public schools was $76.51.[25] The present average expenditure per pupil in American Catholic elementary schools is much more than $15, but the great disparity between parochial-school and public-school expenditures still continues.

The Catholic Church probably operates its elementary schools for less than one-third of the corresponding expenditures for public schools; that was the conclusion of a Catholic survey in Appleton, Wisconsin, in 1953, which reported a comparative expenditure of $78.88 per pupil as against $254 in the two systems.[26] A recent Catholic study of the operating costs of forty Catholic elementary schools in California showed an average tuition payment of only $22.15 per year;[27] another national study showed $26.54. Since no decent schools could function on such an annual allowance per pupil, the parish members must dig down in their pockets and supplement this tuition by contributions up to 60 per cent of the total cost. Even with this sacrifice, the Catholic parochial schools are far below the level of the public schools in respect to many of the most important items of teacher training, equipment, and space.

The Catholic schools are able to operate on this lower financial level partly because they permit gross overcrowding, but chiefly because their teaching nuns get a miserably inadequate living allowance in place of a salary. The California study revealed that public-school teachers were getting a median salary of $4,635 while the Sisters were far below their "necessary" $1,600. The average teaching nun probably does not get more than $500 or $600, paid in a lump sum to her religious order for her support. Even the few male lay teachers in the Catholic elementary system are paid far below the average for men in the public schools.

When Catholic writers discuss the virtues of the parochial-school system and point out that the taxpayers of the United States would have to pay more than one billion dollars a year in additional taxation if they assumed the burden of educating all of America's Catholic children in public schools,[28] they do not include in their reckoning any of the social gains that would accrue from better economic standards among Catholic teachers, nor do they include an estimate of the social value of superior public education.

One reason the public knows so little about the Catholic schools is that the public agencies of the various states which are supposed to exercise some supervision over Catholic education studiously neglect this function. Most state legislatures provide their educational departments with no funds for an inspection force. The public never hears of the enforcements of standards in these Catholic schools or of the deficiencies in the system.

There is a motive in this neglect. Politically speaking, any action that might offend the Catholic Church is a "hot potato." No governor or state board of education is anxious to grasp it. All the states have some kind of legislation on the matter of educational standards because the Catholic schools have been accepted as substitutes for public education under the state compulsory-education laws, but there is little attempt to enforce standards except in four states. "State approving agencies" give perfunctory approval to almost anything that the Catholic hierarchy cares to consider adequate. The only things that are checked carefully are attendance and the giving of certain required courses.

Three-fourths of the states declare officially in their statutes that education in parochial schools must be the "equivalent" of public-school education.[29] But what does "equivalent" mean? The law is very vague on this subject, and no one presses the embarrassing question. Some states require standard courses in American history and government, and many states require that teaching be done in English, but even this latter requirement is not always enforced. In Maine, for example, many parochial schools are still being taught in French in violation of the state law which requires that instruction should be in English. Maine Catholic schools are almost never checked by any state inspectors to see whether they are measuring up to state standards.

Only four[30] states in the Union require teachers in the Catholic schools to have the same certification as to training that is required of public-school teachers, and only one state, Alabama, requires anything like a complete picture of the parochial school in official reports. For the most part Catholic bishops and school superintendents go their own way and write their own requirements for the certification of their own teachers. Sometimes these self-imposed standards are fairly high; more often they are low. The National Catholic Welfare Conference made a survey of teacher training in Catholic schools in 1937 and discovered that only ten of forty-three dioceses that responded to a questionnaire demanded any diocesan certification of elementary teachers even on paper.[31] The most bizarre inequalities exist in teaching standards and requirements within the Catholic system, and the state authorities look the other way. There is no will to investigate, and no money for regular inspection in most of the states. The Catholic writer Richard J. Gabel said that in 1928 "direct state or local supervision was authorized in only four states and inspection in sixteen."

Sometimes the sketchy and dogmatic character of Catholic teacher training is compensated for by the fact that teaching nuns spend their whole lives in teaching, while public-school teachers often leave the profession for marriage. But none of the states questions the spirit or outlook of the segregated Catholic system. No one asks whether the system is producing Catholics first and Americans second, or whether the closed system develops real community spirit, or whether nuns who are shut off from the outside world are competent to teach children about that world.

Frequently young nuns are sent out into the Catholic school system with virtually no training at all because of the great demand for teachers. Also, the financial needs of the convents are sometimes so pressing that they cannot afford to support nuns who are not drawing an income. "The pressure on the various Religious teaching communities threatens at times to destroy all opportunity for effective teacher education," says Father Paul E. Campbell. "Superiors are often forced to send into the field laborers who have not been thoroughly fitted in advance for the work that lies before them.[32] Father John R. Hagan has cited a 1932 study of Catholic teacher training to show that, even when strict requirements are written into the rules of convents, those requirements are disregarded in practice. Only five of sixty-six Catholic communities of teaching nuns surveyed in 1932 held strictly to their training requirements before sending out young nuns into the schools.[33]

For the young nuns during the first years of membership in an order the short time given to teacher training is largely devoted to theology. In one typical teacher-training course for Religious teachers, lasting nominally two and one-half years, as described by Sister Francis Joseph, Community Supervisor of Schools for St. Mary-of-the-Woods, Indiana, all novitiates were required to take a full "canonical" year in which they studied virtually nothing but religion.[34] In their "normal" course they were required to include Christian Doctrine, twelve semester hours; Church History, four; Content Method, six; Ascetic Doctrine, 12G weeks, two hours, no credit; and Bible History, thirty weeks, one hour, no credit. "Training in the principles and practices of asceticism is daily given special attention during the two-and-one-half years of the Novitiate," said Sister Francis Joseph.

Connecticut, which has a large and politically powerful Catholic population, does not require anything at all in the way of a specified method for training parochial-school teachers. Thirty-three Religious communities of teaching nuns operate in the Hartford diocese alone, and the very extensive living quarters that they occupy are tax-exempt.

5

In these Catholic schools there is no academic freedom as non-Catholics understand the term, nor is there any teaching of genuine religious freedom. The word "freedom" is used constantly in textbooks and classrooms, but examination discloses it to be a semantic artifice meaning readiness to *receive* divine—that is, Catholic—revelation. Redden and Ryan in their standard Catholic work for teachers, *Freedom Through Education,* define the Catholic conception of freedom in unmistakable terms:

> Freedom to worship God implies in its correct meaning and application that every man should acknowledge God as his Creator, submit to His divine rule and will, and through the proper use of faith and reason, embrace the eternal truths which alone insure salvation. This is true freedom. It is opposed to that so-called "liberty of conscience" which a "seditious and rebellious mind" dominated by man's lower nature and blinded to truth and goodness, employs to undermine, overthrow or destroy the infallible authority of religion to guide and direct all the individual's conduct in terms of the moral law.[35]

Under this interpretation of "freedom" no teacher in a Catholic school is free to disagree with the hierarchy on any social or religious policy that the hierarchy cares to include in its modicum of "eternal truths." As Father Wilfred M. Mallon, S.J., phrased it in criticizing the American Association of University Professors before the National Catholic Educational Association in 1942:

> Freedom to teach what is true is without practical applicability unless we have a norm. . . . The Catholic college norm must be not only natural knowledge, but the deposit of divinely revealed truths

immeasurably more certain than any truth arrived at by mere human deduction or experiment because we have for them the guarantee of the infinite knowledge and veracity of God. . . . We reserve the right to dispense with the service of the staff member whose life or utterances on the campus or off of it undermines the purposes for which we exist. . . . In view of the very nature and fundamental purposes of Catholic education, violations of Catholic doctrine, or Catholic moral principles, or of the essential proprieties of Catholic life, on the campus or off the campus, render a man unfit for service in a Catholic college.[36]

What does this priestly control of education mean in terms of intellectual freedom? The question can be answered by listing samples of Catholic popular beliefs that no teachers in the Catholic school system dare to challenge publicly without danger of penalties. Many of these beliefs are specifically outlined in the heavily indoctrinated textbooks used in Catholic schools. Most of these principles have been or will be discussed in detail elsewhere in this book; the sources of all of them are listed in the Notes.[37]

1. The Pope is the infallible leader of mankind, and when he speaks for the Church in matters of faith and morals, he cannot make a mistake.
2. The Virgin Mary returned to the earth six times in 1917 and told three peasant children of Fatima, Portugal, what the Western world should do to avoid destruction by Soviet Russia.
3. It is a grave sin for an American Catholic deliberately to join the Masons or Odd Fellows.
4. No good Catholic may positively and unconditionally approve of the principle of separation of church and state.
5. Thomas Aquinas is the greatest philosopher of all time.
6. It is a sin to teach the evolution of man as a whole from animal life.
7. In general, no Catholic has a moral right to secure a divorce and remarry even if married to a syphilitic, insane, or adulterous murderer; and any Catholic who does remarry after such a divorce is guilty of adultery.
8. The Reformation was a backward step in human history, and many of the worst evils of fascism and communism flow from it.
9. It is a grave sin for a Catholic under ordinary circumstances knowingly to own or use a Protestant Bible.
10. The Pope is the head of a sovereign temporal state which has co-equal rights with that of the government of the United States.
11. The rights of the Church as educator are prior to and superior to

the rights of the state as educator, and no government has the legal right to infringe upon this divine prerogative.

The penalties imposed upon Catholic professors for departure from orthodox dogma almost never reach the level of public revelation because the dissident Catholic has no real forum for the discussion of grievances. College faculties are dominated by priests who are themselves dominated by bishops. Their lines of promotion are all within the hierarchy or the Catholic educational system. There is no reward for independence and there are very severe penalties for defiance. Priests and Religious teachers who leave the Church because of a change of views usually avoid publicity because, as "renegades," they expose themselves to vindictive reprisals.

It is only when some famous "liberal" like the late Monsignor John A. Ryan of the National Catholic Welfare Conference talks frankly about his past that the non-Catholic can appreciate the nature of Catholic academic freedom. Monsignor Ryan admitted in his autobiography that he resigned from the national board of the American Civil Liberties Union "simply and solely because the organization had gone into the field of academic freedom. I called attention to the absurdity, for example, of my membership in the national committee of an organization which might undertake to defend a professor at a Catholic University who has been discharged for teaching heresy." [38]

It is evident that academic freedom in the Catholic system is freedom to *receive* what the hierarchy considers truth. What the hierarchy considers heresy is another matter. There is no place in the entire Catholic school system for that. Textbooks in the elementary Catholic schools are watched with special care for any fragments of heresy and, if possible, only those books are used that are produced by Catholic authors. The work of cleaning out all undesirable books and substituting Catholic syllabi and textbooks in parochial schools has been undertaken by a priestly group from the Catholic University of America that uses the euphonious title, "The Commission on American Citizenship." Its attitude was expressed by Father Charles J. Mahoney, associate superintendent of Catholic schools of the Diocese of Rochester in the following cumbersome locution:

Adherence by Catholic schools to syllabi and use of textbooks the basic philosophy of which assumes human nature to be the result of the interaction of cultural and hereditary factors, and that have as their objectives democratic society as the sole end of education, is a policy difficult to reconcile. To assume that the thinking of Catholic pupils will not be misdirected by the use of such syllabi and texts is to impugn the efficacy of both in the educative process.[39]

It is not surprising that Pius XII warmly commended the Commission on American Citizenship after forty-eight of its volumes had been reviewed at the Vatican.[40] The Commission is attempting to remake American and world history in the Papal image for parochial schools; and state administrative public-school authorities are too busy or too timid or too understaffed to expose the process. The Commission's philosophy was illustrated in a statement in the *Catholic Almanac* of 1957, from which I quote typical fragments:

American democracy is Christian democracy. It is based upon the Constitution of the United States, a document written by men familiar with the concepts of moral philosophy taught in schools of their time. Two of these men, Thomas FitzSimons and Daniel Carroll, were Catholics. . . .

For a thousand years the Church held the power to put into effect the social ideals of Christianity. It had built, by the thirteenth century, a simple and satisfied Europe. All too soon the social system fell, overwhelmed by the Black Death which ravaged the cities, by new economic conditions, and by the heresies of Luther and Calvin. . . .

Someone has truly said that [St. Thomas] Aquinas discovered America politically 200 years before Columbus discovered it geographically. His philosophy, carried through generations of political thinkers, finally reached the minds of the men who wrote the American Declaration of Independence. . . .

The Constitution is more to Catholic Americans than the guarantee of our religious liberties. It is a restatement for our own nation of the Catholic basis of all human liberties.[41]

Brother George N. Shuster of St. Louis put the case for controlled textbooks in a less polite manner when he attacked the "domination of literature courses in Catholic schools by English Protestant classics" in an address before 1,100 Catholic teachers in Providence in October, 1947:

Protestant literature should be relegated to the periphery—since we need some sort of roughage in our diet, as children occasionally need a dose of sulphur and molasses. Better to disinherit its students from Oscar Wilde and Byron than to disinherit them from the Catholic classics. Literature taught now is insular, decadent, a literature based on ignorance and negation of the Catholic way of life. The real question for Catholic teachers to ask themselves is: Do we want to form a Catholic mind or not? [42]

In general, all Catholic schools answer that question with an emphatic affirmative. The Seton Series in Arithmetic, widely used in Catholic schools, forms "the Catholic mind" by inserting fifteen pictures of saints, priests, altars, and angels in its first-grade arithmetic in teaching children how to count.

5

Public Schools and Public Money

1

BECAUSE OF THE SPECIFIC ruling in Canon Law that Catholics must boycott public schools wherever possible, the first requirement in the hierarchy's policy on the public schools is that Catholics should be kept out of them. Usually this negative policy is not emphasized publicly before non-Catholic audiences, but it is stressed consistently for the faithful. When priests talk to their own people about education, they scold, admonish, threaten, and wheedle in their anxiety to hold every possible child out of a public school.

Naturally there has been much grumbling among American Catholics because of the separatism of a dual school system and its extra financial burden. Catholics do not like to pay for two school systems at once, and they are now compelled to pay their share of the public school's expenses as well as the total cost of parochial schools. The priests tell their people that they are compelled "in conscience" to maintain a separate school system. Many a Catholic parent has recognized that the "conscience" is the conscience of the priests and not of the parents themselves.

In order to keep their people loyal to the segregated Catholic school system the priests feel obliged to conduct a continuous campaign against the public school. "Godless" is one of the milder epithets that they use in belittling the public system. Here, for example, are some random quotations from a pamphlet issued by the America Press under the Imprimatur of the late Cardinal Hayes, *May an American Oppose the Public School?* by Father Paul L. Blakely, S.J. This tract has never been repudiated by the hierarchy, although I am sure that it does not represent the attitude of most American Catholic laymen. Blakely was one of the editors of the important Jesuit magazine, *America*.

103

Our first duty to the public school is not to pay taxes for its maintenance. We pay that tax under protest; not because we admit an obligation in justice. Justice cannot oblige the support of a system which we are forbidden in conscience to use, or a system which we conscientiously hold to be bad in principle and bad in its ultimate consequences. . . .

The first duty of every Catholic father to the public school is to keep his children out of it. . . . For the man who sends his children to the public school when he could obtain for them the blessings of a Catholic education is not a practicing Catholic, even though he goes to Mass every morning. . . .

Not a single American who signed the Declaration of Independence, or fought in the Revolution, or sat at Philadelphia to draw up the Constitution, had ever been in a public school. . . .

"Is a Catholic free to attend a non-Catholic college or university?" The answer is that he is not free, since the only school, whether it be a kindergarten or a university, which is fit for a Catholic, is the school that is Catholic in its principles, its aims, its programs, its teachers, and in its submission to the direction and supervision of the Church. . . .

"Every Catholic child in a Catholic school," is the command of the Church. . . . Discussion is at an end. The obligations imposed by obedience are alone to be considered.[1]

It is hard for non-Catholics to believe that this attitude toward America's most treasured institution represents the outlook of the Catholic hierarchy, even though Father Blakely's pamphlet bears the Imprimatur of the Church's leading American cardinal of the thirties. Actually, Father Blakely's attitude is quite typical of *priestly* attitudes toward the public school, and some priests draw even more fantastic inferences. American priests are allowed to jeer and sneer at the public school because it has been one of the favorite targets of the Popes.

"It would be absurd to say that the Pope approves of our public school system," says Father William J. McGucken, S.J., in *The Catholic Way in Education.* "No Catholic can approve of such a system where religious instruction is barred. The only system he could approve would be one where 'Catholics are free to follow their own system of teaching in schools that are *entirely* Catholic'; and where religious instruction would be provided for non-Catholics according to the legitimate demands of parents, and financial aid given to all schools that met with the reasonable demands of the State." [2] The quotations of Father McGucken are from Pius XI's *Christian Education of Youth,* the Bible of Catholic educational policy.

The favorite priestly inference in discussing government education is that any all-out advocate of the public school is somehow a disciple of Hitler, Mussolini, or Stalin because these gentlemen were also, at one time or another, advocates of government education. The late Archbishop John T. McNicholas, general president of the National Catholic Educational Association, in addressing its 1947 Boston meeting, said: "There must be no wall of separation between God and the child. The secularistic educators who raise this wall are, in reality, fascist educators, who, perhaps without realizing it, are planning to give our country millions of uncontrolled juvenile criminals." [3] This was strong language coming from the leader of a denomination that has the highest proportion of white criminals in our American prisons of any denomination.[4] When the speech of Archbishop McNicholas was distributed for general consumption in a pamphlet, the reference to juvenile criminals was omitted, and the Archbishop merely charged the public schools with sending out "millions of young people ignorant of moral principles." But he still called government monopoly of education "in reality Fascistic control of schools." [5]

Archbishop McNicholas had become an expert at combining Communism, fascism, and public education in one sentence, sometimes without any separating commas. In 1946, he said:

Our thinking must not be influenced by a Soviet system of education or by atheistic Communists or by those in our government who would take their pattern of education from a Fascist, atheistic Russia or from School Boards or lobbies that wish to impose a totally secularistic system of education on American parents.

The constitutions of many of our States are unfair, un-American, undemocratic, discriminatory in their school legislation.[6]

Father William McManus, assistant director of the Department of Education of the National Catholic Welfare Conference, and now superintendent of Chicago's 300,000-child Catholic school system, said before a Senate hearing in 1947:

The school, particularly the private school, is the battleground between the forces of totalitarianism and those of freedom and democracy. In the totalitarian nation, the Government is the teacher; the

Government controls all the schools which it uses for the mental enslavement of the people. In the free nation, the government refrains from direct educational activities.[7]

The special meaning of the word "free" should be noted. A "free" nation in priestly parlance appears to be a nation that permits priests to control education. The nation that operates its own schools through school boards elected by the people is, by inference, totalitarian. The idea "that education belongs to the state is of German origin," says Father Felix N. Pitt, secretary of Louisville's Catholic school board, and "this idea is almost universally accepted by public school educators." [8]

The late Bishop John F. Noll of Fort Wayne, founding editor of America's most noted Catholic family paper, *Our Sunday Visitor,* summed up the priestly apprehensions about the American public school by writing a pamphlet called *Our National Enemy No. 1—Education Without Religion.* It did not discuss war, prostitution, graft, or venereal disease. Its public enemy No. 1 was the American public school without Catholic religion. Bishop Noll echoed the sentiment of the Jesuit magazine *America,* which declared in an editorial: "That the Catholic and non-Catholic school systems are absolutely irreconcilable is an indisputable fact." [9]

Recently the hierarchy has realized that such frank remarks about the public school are particularly inappropriate at a moment when the Catholic Church is attempting to secure public funds for its schools. Accordingly it has developed techniques of conciliation, at least in public pronouncements. The same Archbishop McNicholas who delivered, before his own people, the attacks on public education which I have cited above appealed later to the National Education Association for co-operation in getting public money for parochial schools, saying that "the Catholic and public schools are partners in American education."

2

Although the Church forbids its children to attend public schools without special dispensation, it does not forbid Catholics to teach in those schools or to supervise them—provided they remain good Catholics. The sectarian function of the Catholic teacher in the public school is often emphasized in the Catholic press, partly because about half of all American Catholic children attend public schools and the future of Catholicism depends largely upon their continuing loyalty.

It is assumed that a good Catholic serving as a teacher in the public schools will promote and foster the interests of the Church in the "neutral" environment. So the hierarchy encourages Catholics to teach in public schools, become members of school boards in the public-school system, and in general act as guardians and protectors of the Church's interests. According to the theory laid down by Pius XI, these Catholic public-school teachers represent the Pope in censoring all public education.[10]

For the Catholic teachers in the public-school system the hierarchy lays down rules in the moral manuals almost as definite as the rules for parochial-school teachers. Such teachers must not forget that the Church school is superior to the public school, even while they are teaching in the public school. They must remember their moral responsibility to the Church and not become mere creatures of the state.

Father Francis J. Connell, dean of the School of Sacred Theology at the Catholic University of America, has outlined a whole code for Catholic teachers in public schools, and his book, *Morals in Politics and Professions,* published under the Imprimatur of the Archbishop of Baltimore-Washington, has been widely circulated among Catholic public-school teachers. He instructs the Catholic teacher in the public school to act as an unofficial religious guardian for the Catholic children in her classes, and says that "the Catholic teacher should take some action if she discovers or suspects that a Catholic child is missing Mass or failing otherwise in his or her religious duties." [11] She should avoid the Protestant Bible if possible and "bring her own Bible to class and read it to the pupils" when custom calls for the reading of the Bible in the public school. When the recitation of the Lord's Prayer is called for, neither the Catholic teacher nor the Catholic pupils should recite the phrase "For thine is the Kingdom, etc.," because "in practice these words have taken on a Protestant connotation, so their use would constitute an implicit approval of heresy."

The Catholic teacher, according to Father Connell, should be tactful, and she "should abstain from taking the initiative in bringing the arguments for Catholicism to the notice of those under her care," but she should never permit Catholicism to be the object of calumny in her classes, either in spoken words or in the textbooks used in the school.

At times, the textbook used in class may contain statements relative to the Catholic Church that are false or misleading, particularly in history class. The Catholic teacher should not hesitate to bring out the truth on such occasions. It would be deplorable if a Catholic teacher allowed a calumny on the Church to pass unrefuted because she feared for the security of her position or she dreaded being regarded as a "bigoted Catholic."

Neither should the Catholic teacher hesitate to give the solution taught by her religion to problems of a moral or social nature which may be discussed in class. Particularly in high school discussions on social or civic topics she may be expected to make a statement on such matters as divorce, euthanasia, birth control, the rights of the individual in relation to the State, the mutual obligations of employer and employee, the right of the parent to educate children as contrasted to the right of the civil authorities, etc.

The Catholic teacher in the public school is especially warned by Father Connell against taking an impartial atittude toward the religious faiths of her children. He says (italics supplied):

Neither in the classroom nor in her associations with teachers of other creeds may the Catholic teacher use expressions savoring of indifferentism. She may, indeed, explain and uphold the American system granting equal rights to all religions, but in lauding this system she should make it clear that she is limiting her praise to our own country, because of particular conditions prevailing here, and that she has no intention of condemning other lands in which a different procedure prevails. *She must not speak in such wise as to give the impression that all forms of religious belief possess a natural right to exist and to propagate. Only the true religion possesses such a natural right.*

The attempt by the Catholic hierarchy to control large areas of public education through Catholic teachers and administrators has met with very limited success except in those cities that are predominantly Catholic. In such cities both the city government and the schools are frequently controlled by the same Catholic machine. The state of Rhode Island, with a Catholic majority, comes nearest of all American states to being a Catholic cultural unit. Boston has become so Catholic a city that the word "Bostonized" is now accepted as describing a community under Papal control. Boston, Providence, Buffalo, Newark, and San Francisco have had Catholic superintendents of schools, and Massachusetts and Rhode Island have had Roman Catholic directors of state education. An authoritative private estimate, which cannot be proved statistically, has put the proportion of Catholic teachers in the public schools of Chicago at 75 per cent of the total. Wisconsin, once the stronghold of the progressive LaFollettes, has had powerful Catholic blocs on public school boards and also a Catholic majority of seven to two on the board of regents of the state university. Milwaukee has had a Catholic majority on its school board.

A well-organized Catholic bloc in the population can frequently capture a school board even when Catholics are in the minority in the community. Cambridge, Massachusetts, is a notorious example. Newark, with a 38 per cent Catholic population, is another. The priests of that city, not content with a thriving parochial-school system, decided in 1939 that the city should have a Catholic superintendent of public schools and a Catholic majority on the city's Board of Education. It took Catholic organizations only four years to get a Catholic superintendent, and by 1947 six of the nine members of the Board of Education were Catholics. When the Catholic superintendent of public schools was inaugurated in 1943, Father John L. McNulty boasted to a communion breakfast of the Sacred Heart Holy Name Society:

> When I spoke to you Lyndhurst men four years ago, I discussed nonsectarian education. I told you how the church was against it. I told how our large cities were against it. What we started here that day is now bearing fruit. Next Wednesday we are going to have our first superintendent of schools in Newark. You men are as much responsible for that as anyone.[12]

The capture of a public educational system may yield rich rewards to the Catholic hierarchy not only in jobs for Catholics but in cultural control of the community. It was the Catholic superintendent of the Newark public schools who first ordered the permanent banning of *The Nation* from public high-school libraries because certain portions of this book, published in part in *The Nation,* were "offensive" to the Catholic hierarchy. No effort was made by the Catholic superintendent of schools to specify a single false statement in the text or to challenge the authenticity of a single Catholic authority cited, and yet his arbitrary act, performed without consulting the Board of Education, was confirmed by that Catholic-dominated Board without dissent. Incidentally, during the public controversy over the superintendent's boycott, it was revealed that he had sent all four of his own children to parochial Catholic schools while acting as superintendent of the city's public schools!

In cities and states where the Catholic bloc in the population is large, the priests frequently challenge any professor or college president of a public institution who is allegedly hostile to Vatican teaching. It was Catholic power in New York that was chiefly responsible for forcing Bertrand Russell off the payroll of the College of the City of New York after he had been engaged to lecture at that institution, largely because of his opposition to the hierarchy's views on marriage and divorce. The Illinois hierarchy, spearheaded by the late Bishop James A. Griffin of Springfield, sought to prevent the appointment of the eminent Unitarian psychologist, George D. Stoddard, as president of the University of Illinois in 1945 because Dr. Stoddard had written a book, *The Meaning of Intelligence,* in which he had spoken of people "systematically drugged with the vapors of dogma, superstition and pseudo logic," and had cast aspersions on hell fire and original sin. The board of trustees of the University finally found that Dr. Stoddard was "an outstanding Christian," quite worthy of continuing as president of the institution. But Dr. Stoddard was later forced out of his post by a reactionary alliance in which Catholic interests played a leading role.[13]

Catholic pressure on the public educational system is not always open or specific. It is rarely capable of documentary proof, since bishops, archbishops, and cardinals have learned to act indirectly through political and religious "independents" who have something to gain by co-operation. Sometimes, as in New York City, there is a kind of unwritten political law that (1) Catholics must get a certain proportion of all political and educational posts that are filled by appointment, and (2) no person in public life must ever say anything directly hostile to the Catholic hierarchy. Most Protestant and Jewish politicians and educators obey this unwritten law even more faithfully than Catholics because they are filled with panic by the mere suggestion that they might be branded "anti-Catholic."

Sometimes the informal, balance-of-power traditions of city politics bring into high places in the field of public education Catholics who are fundamentally hostile to the public school. George N. Shuster, liberal Catholic editor, was made president of Hunter

College in New York, America's largest *public* college for women, after he had said flatly in his book, *The Catholic Spirit in America* (page 175): "Had it not been for the grotesque stupidity of Protestants, we would long since have built up in this country a system of denominational schools subsidized and to some extent supervised by the state."

Nationally the hierarchy has not been successful in its campaign to eliminate from the public schools leaders who might be considered as opposed to its dogmas. Its most signal defeats have come in the largest and most influential American educational organization, the National Education Association. In that organization the thousands of Catholic members have generally backed up the Association's policy of public funds for public schools only. These Catholic teachers in the N.E.A. represent the enlightened majority of American Catholics who have never accepted the hierarchy's doctrine of educational segregation.

The hierarchy has also failed miserably in its attempt to win public-school administrators, except in those few urban centers where it exercises political control. Only an insignificant minority of the nation's school administrators are even willing to support the Church's efforts to secure public money for school buses. Scarcely any of such administrators back the Church's demand for full support of parochial schools.

Probably one reason for the hostility of public-school administrators to parochial schools is that these schools send their failures to the public schools, and the public schools are obliged to accept these failures under the law. There are some public schools in the United States composed almost entirely of "rejects" from the classrooms of nuns. Conscientious Catholics are embarrassed by this fact; they would like to assume more responsibility for backward and unruly children, but their schools lack facilities, personnel, and money to handle the large "problem" population of Catholic children. *America* in a 1948 editorial deplored "the situation vigorously commented on by public-school people, that parochial schools commonly 'dump' their problem students upon the public school. The comment, supported by reliable facts, argues an educational failure. It argues a lack of guidance and remedial techniques for handling problem and retarded children in the parochial schools. This is an aspect of the training of Catholic personnel which needs much more emphasis and much more conscience." [14]

3

In view of the hierarchy's attitude toward government control of schools, it may seem surprising to many Americans that it is willing to beg for public money for Catholic education. There is nothing inconsistent in this attitude, however. The Church has never believed in the separation of church and state in education. As long as the state does not challenge the Church's superior power and wisdom in regard to educational policies, its money is welcomed eagerly. It is true that there has been some apprehension among Catholic bishops about federal money because they have feared that federal appropriations might bring federal control. But the postwar financial crisis, caused by the spiraling of prices and the shortage of nuns, induced the hierarchy to forget all its fears except the one overshadowing fear that the Catholic schools might perish altogether unless they secured public support.

On the whole, the hierarchy has found the United States a very unsatisfactory country in which to plead for public funds. The principle of the separation of church and state not only is one of the most fundamental principles of American life but expresses the determination of most Americans to avoid snobbishness and separatism in community affairs. The American people have no desire to prevent Catholics from having schools of their own— that right has been guaranteed by the Supreme Court since 1925 in the case of *Pierce vs. Society of Sisters*—but they doubt the wisdom of such separatism, and they think it unfair that they should be asked to pay for a competing school system.

The attitude of most non-Catholic Americans toward public support for Catholic schools might be summed up in this fashion: The Catholic people have been offered the same free, democratic schools that have been offered to everybody else. If they do not wish to join the rest of the American community, that is their affair. Methodists, Baptists, Jews, and nearly everybody else belong to the great fraternity of American public education. The Catholic people have not been blackballed; they have been elected to full membership, but their priests have persuaded them to stay away from the meeting. They should not pretend that they are being discriminated against. Methodists, Baptists, and Jews cannot collect public funds for their schools. Neither can Catholics. We must treat everybody alike.

It is this simple philosophy of equality of treatment which caused forty-six states, after 1825, when the public-school system was expanding rapidly, to protect their treasuries against denominational raids by writing into their constitutions or statutes prohibitions against the spending of public money for sectarian schools.[15] Catholic leaders are fond of pointing out that the founding fathers, when they drew up the federal Constitution, did not write in such a prohibition specifically. That is correct. The First Amendment to the United States Constitution forbade the establishment of any religion, but it did not in so many words mention the schools.

This omission was partly due to the fact that the public-school system had not been born when the Constitution was written. As soon as the public-school system became general in the United States, the people of the states, acting upon the theory of the First Amendment, applied the principle to expenditures for religious schools in nearly all the states. They wanted the public schools to be the only schools in the community which had a claim upon the public purse, and they said so in unmistakable language to the horror of the American hierarchy, which had hoped for the same special treatment in the United States that it had received for its schools in many nations of Europe.

Probably the whole question of public funds for Catholic schools would not have been reopened in our generation if it had not been for the depression of the 1930's, and two world wars. During war and depression a new philosophy of state aid was born. The state accepted as never before the responsibility of caring for its citizens in distress. Catholics as citizens came in for their share of school lunches, free textbooks, and, in some states, school buses. During the depression, also, Catholic youths were given scholarships at Catholic schools by the National Youth Administration, and after World War II Catholic veterans were financed at Catholic colleges. These grants, however, were made to young people and to veterans not as Catholics but as needy youths or as veterans of the armed forces.

The Catholic hierarchy seized upon these borderline cases, which lie between the fields of education and welfare, to argue that Catholic education itself is charged with a public interest and is therefore entitled to full public support. This contention, which had some merit in itself, was unfamiliar to most Americans. At first the non-Catholic public was inclined to be very charitable toward all Catholic pleas. The Catholic schools won several minor and incidental services at public expense without much public opposition.

But when the hierarchy began publicly, after World War II, to use these special and incidental concessions as precedents for pleas in behalf of direct support for parochial schools, the non-Catholic people of the country woke up with an unpleasant start. By that time nineteen states had provided some free bus transportation for parochial pupils at public expense, and five states had started to provide some nonreligious textbooks.[16] Already some Catholic leaders were arguing that such auxiliary services were traditional and that it would be a great moral wrong to discontinue them.

The Supreme Court had legalized public expenditures for nonreligious textbooks in parochial schools in a Louisiana case in 1930 (*Cochran vs. Board of Education,* 281 U. S. 370), but it had not legalized such expenditures for parochial-school buses. Catholic pressure on local school boards and state legislatures did not wait upon legal clearance. Massachusetts, in fact, gave Catholic pupils free bus transportation at public expense for ten years before the constitutional principles involved were finally tested in the United States Supreme Court.

There was a quick revulsion of feeling in many states when voters began to appreciate the full meaning of the step-by-step gains of the Catholic hierarchy. Late in 1946, Wisconsin, in spite of its large concentration of Catholic voters, defeated by a large majority a constitutional amendment to permit free bus transportation for Catholic school pupils. The whole issue of Catholic bus transportation at public expense came to a head in the famous Everson bus case, in which a New Jersey taxpayer charged that the state had no right under the First Amendment to the Constitution to charge the cost of transportation for Catholic pupils to general taxpayers. At last, after a generation of delay and uncertainty, the Supreme Court was compelled to face the question of the legal limits of aid to religious schools. It finally decided in February, 1947, by a vote of five to four, that the state of New Jersey, under its general welfare powers, could compel school districts under certain conditions to charge the cost of bus transportation of Catholic parochial schools to the taxpayers without violating the United States Constitution.[17]

The decision was at first hailed as a great victory for the Catholic Church, but an examination of the text of the decision proved that it was a boomerang. Instead of opening the door for further extensions of aid to Catholic schools, it appeared to slam the door shut with a bang. The majority and the minority of the Supreme Court in their opinions made a ringing declaration in favor of the separation of church and state. It was clear that the particular New Jersey law that charged transportation costs for parochial pupils to the taxpayers represented the extreme limit of concessions to Catholic financial appeals. Bus transportation might be acceptable by a narrow margin as a welfare service to children as children—even that was very doubtful in view of the strong case against its constitutionality built up by the four judges who voted in the minority—but the Court, accompanied this special concession with a general statement that may well serve as a kind of charter of religious neutrality for American education in our time:

The "establishment of religion" clause of the First Amendment means at least this: Neither a state nor the Federal Government can set up a church. Neither can pass laws which aid one religion, aid all religions, or prefer one religion over another. Neither can force nor influence a person to go to or remain away from church against his will or force him to profess a belief or disbelief in any religion. No person can be punished for entertaining or professing religious beliefs or disbeliefs, for church attendance or non-attendance. No tax in any amount, large or small, can be levied to support any religious activities or institutions, whatever they may be called, or whatever form they may adopt to teach or practice religion. Neither a state nor the Federal Government can, openly or secretly, participate in the affairs of any religious organizations or groups and *vice versa*. In the words of Jefferson, the clause against establishment of religion by law was intended to erect a "wall of separation between church and State."

Then, surprisingly enough after such an eloquent declaration of the philosophy of neutrality, the five majority judges ended their decision by saying:

The First Amendment has erected a wall between church and state. That wall must be kept high and impregnable. We could not approve the slightest breach. New Jersey has not breached it here.

Four justices believed that New Jersey *had* breached the Constitution, and they proceeded to back up their judgment with an opinion that was much more detailed and carefully documented than the majority judgment. Justice Jackson in his dissent quoted the Canon Law of the Catholic Church that compels Catholic parents to send their children to Catholic schools as part of their religious discipline, and said: "Catholic education is the rock on which the whole structure rests, and to render tax aid to its Church school is indistinguishable to me from rendering the same aid to the Church itself." Justice Rutledge made a thorough analysis of the history of the constitutional fight for separation of church and state, and showed by quoting the contemporary debates that the purpose of the First Amendment "was not to strike merely at the official establishment of a single sect, creed or religion, outlawing a formal relationship such as had prevailed in England and some of the colonies. Necessarily it was to uproot all such relationships. But the object was broader than separating church and state in this narrow sense. It was to create a complete and permanent separation of the sphere of religious activity and civil authority by comprehensively forbidding every form of public aid or support for religion. In proof the Amendment's wording and history unite with this Court's consistent utterances whenever attention has been fixed directly upon the question."

The worst apprehensions of the hierarchy were realized a year later in the famous McCollum case, which I shall discuss later. The hierarchy, in winning a temporary victory for its schools, had set in motion the forces that would defeat its greatest ambitions in education.

4

For at least twenty years the Catholic Church was the chief opponent in this country of federal aid to education. Its original opposition appeared to be based upon its distrust of strong central governments and their ambitions in the field of education, but it is worthy of note that the Church does not oppose strong central governments when loyal Catholic leaders like Franco are in power. The actual reason for Catholic opposition to federal educational aid is that nearly all the measures suggested at Washington have failed to provide for a pro rata allotment to parochial schools.

For many years the Catholic Church took a kind of dog-in-the-manger attitude toward federal aid; it refused to ask for such aid directly, but objected to other people's getting that aid. The hierarchy officially admitted its opposition to federal aid in 1943 when the director of the Department of Education of the National Catholic Welfare Conference said: "The Catholic position is one of opposition to any measure for Federal aid to education that would: (a) interfere with local control of the purposes and processes of education, and (b) fail to make mandatory the inclusion of Catholic schools in its benefits." [18] The first of these objections has never been a serious one because nobody has ever seriously proposed federal control of American education. The second objection, that federal aid should include parochial schools or no schools, is the core of the hierarchy's obstructive position.

The need for some federal aid for public schools is now recognized by the great majority of educational specialists. The "spread" between the educational expenditures of the poorest and the richest states is appalling, and children in the poorest states are permanently penalized through no fault of their own. In 1943-44 the current expenditures per pupil in the nation's public schools were $42.25 in Mississippi; $52.36 in Arkansas and $54.17 in Alabama; $185.12 in New York; $164.79 in California and $158.02 in Illinois. [19] This disparity was not the fault of the poorer states—since many of them actually spent a larger *proportion* of their income on their schools than the richer states; Mississippi, for example, spent a larger proportion than New York.

It is the whole nation that suffers from this denial of opportunity to the children of the poorer states, for, as James B. Conant, while President of Harvard, pointed out, we are a mobile people and because of the constant movement of inhabitants from one state to another "the future citizens of many of our wealthy cities are now being educated in our poorer states." Or miseducated!

For many years, as general measures for federal aid were presented in Washington, the Catholic lobbyists appeared to oppose them. The Catholic opposition was just strong enough, when united with that of states'-rights conservatives, to tip the scales against relief. Special services like school lunches and scholarships were adopted in Washington with Catholic approval; general aid was defeated largely by the Catholic lobby. [20]

Until 1947 there seemed little prospect of success for any general federal-aid programs. Then the grimly mounting teacher shortage and the incontrovertible facts about educational inequality began to make an impression upon the American people. In 1945, under the pressure of changing public sentiment and the new attitudes that grew out of the war, the Catholic hierarchy decided to swing over to the general principle of federal aid on the ground that such aid was "an indispensable means for equalizing educational opportunities among states." [21] But it continued to fight desperately for the allotment of some federal funds to its own schools as a condition of support for any general program. Since the priests did not wish to appear as the chief obstacle to help for the poorer states, the leaders of the American Church announced that they would go along with any program "which would give practically all the money to the public schools and would give a few dollars to non-public schools as a token recognition of what they are doing for the nation, and, even more important, as a safeguard for freedom of education in our democracy." [22]

One reason for the hierarchy's new eagerness to get token recognition of its demands for federal aid is that state grants for teachers' salaries and the regular expenses of school operation are outlawed by forty-five of the forty-eight states, either in their constitutions or in statutes. The task of changing these state laws and constitutions in the face of stiffening opposition seems now more than ever impossible except in the few Eastern states where the Catholic population is close to a majority.

Because of this state opposition to the use of public money for religious schools, the hierarchy saw only two ways to get new monetary support for its educational program: to secure federal aid for extensive *auxiliary* services like bus transportation and textbooks, and to create some legal device for by-passing state laws concerning aid. The hierarchy has already been successful in securing large sums from *the states* for bus transportation and textbooks, and it is now attempting to increase this type of appropriation from the federal treasury.

In the 79th Congress a bill was introduced by Senator Aiken of Vermont which warmed the hearts of the hierarchy. It proposed not only an annual appropriation of $60,000,000 of federal funds to private schools for such important "extras" as bus transportation and instructional supplies and equipment, but also a scheme for by-passing state legislatures in giving federal funds directly to parochial schools in those states where the voters had forbidden such expenditures in their state constitutions and statutes. The proposed law made state treasurers into mere conduits through whom federal funds would flow to Catholic schools, and it created state trustees for such funds who had no power to stop the flow. Thus the will of the voters in each state was to be successfully circumvented and a new era in public support for Catholic education was to be ushered in. The amounts appropriated, in anticipation, were not for teachers' salaries, but it was easy to see that if this scheme could once be adopted, it would open the door for complete support of parochial schools by the federal treasury. Catholic leaders began to hope that the history of Canada, England, and the Netherlands would be repeated in this country and that their schools would become established charges upon community budgets.

The defenders of the public school realized their danger. They realized that even the smallest "token" payment to Catholic schools under this scheme would set a precedent that might destroy the constitutional guaranties against the establishment of religious organizations. Even health measures had to be scrutinized carefully. A leaking roof might be repaired as a "health" measure and so establish a precedent for thousands of new roofs on Catholic schools. The American Federation of Labor at one time was actually recorded as favoring roof repairs as special "services" for Catholic school children. Some legislators, confronted with these possibilities of indirect support for Catholic enterprise, favored a new federal constitutional amendment, paralleling the provision in the Missouri constitution that forbids all aid to churches, church schools, or any "sectarian purpose whatever."

Fortunately, two events made a new constitutional amendment seem unnecessary. Spearheaded by the huge and powerful National Education Association, the drive against the Aiken bill soon swamped that measure in public protests: and the United States Supreme Court came forward with a decision in the McCollum case in March, 1948, that seemed to slam the door against any *direct* federal appropriations to Catholic schools in the future.[23] The plaintiff in the case was Vashti McCollum of Illinois, humanist and free thinker, who complained that her son was being indoctrinated with Christian dogma at public expense in a public classroom in violation of the First Amendment.

The McCollum case did not specifically treat of federal expenditures for Catholic schools. Ostensibly it decided only one narrow question: Can local American school boards use public classrooms for "released time" religious classes? The answer was in the negative by eight to one, but the reasoning of the judges was more important than the decision itself. The reasoning of the majority, in fact, followed the line of the reasoning of the *minority* in the New Jersey bus case, and reaffirmed the statement of the court: "The First Amendment has erected a wall between Church and State which must be kept high and impregnable." To the chagrin of the Catholic hierarchy and press, the only Catholic judge on the Supreme Court, Frank Murphy, united with his fellows in this interpretation of the American Constitution.

The Catholic bishops of the United States, in solemn assembly at Washington, denounced the highest American court for paying "scant attention to logic, history, or accepted norms of legal interpretation." They came out for an interpretation of the Constitution which would permit complete public financial support of sectarian schools of all denominations, and they declared that the First Amendment's prohibition against the establishment of religion meant merely "no official Church for the country as a whole, no preferment of one religion over another by the Federal Government." [24] A few independent legal scholars agreed with the bishops against the eight to one majority of the Supreme Court; and a few Protestant leaders at Union Seminary, including Reinhold Niebuhr, adopted a similar attitude.[25] But almost all the great Protestant and Jewish religious organizations of the country welcomed the Court's clear rejection of the demands of sectarian schools on the public treasury.

The bitter denunciations of this decision in the American Catholic press reinforced the conviction that it was one of the most important decisions in American legal history. When the Court called the use of any public classroom for released-time religious training unconstitutional, it seemed certain that it would never permit *direct* appropriations for the continuous indoctrination of the Catholic school system.

Later on, in 1952, the Supreme Court in another very important case, *Zorach vs. Clauson,* softened its attitude toward released-time religious education but reiterated its opposition to the expenditure of public funds for such a purpose. By a vote of six to three the justices permitted released-time religious-education classes, under carefully prescribed conditions, away from public school buildings. The Court declared:

> The government must be neutral when it comes to competition between sects. . . . It may not make a religious observance compulsory. It may not coerce anyone to . . . take religious instruction. But it can close its doors or suspend its operations as to those who want to repair to their religious sanctuary for worship or instruction.[26]

Justice Black, who had written the majority opinion in the McCollum case, vigorously dissented in this one, saying: "New York is manipulating its compulsory education laws to help religious sects get pupils. This is not separation but combination of Church and State."

In practice the released-time classes in religion which have developed in many states under the Supreme Court's permissive rule in the Zorach case have been largely Catholic classes. In 1956 the Church claimed 2,453,000 Catholic public-school children in its released-time classes.

Since 1948 the Catholic hierarchy's campaign for federal funds for the support of its schools has met defeat after defeat in Washington. One cause of repeated clerical failure has been the rise of a powerful new national group, Protestants and Other Americans United for the Separation of Church and State, which has rallied non-Catholic forces to preserve the Supreme Court's interpretation of the First Amendment. Another factor has been the obvious duplicity in Catholic propaganda for public funds.

When Cardinal Spellman attacked Mrs. Roosevelt in 1949, he announced that his Church asked only for "welfare" benefits from the public treasury, but any reader of the Catholic press knew that this claim was fraudulent. The Catholic Church has never ceased to make complete support of Catholic schools out of the public treasury a major demand in its social program wherever it has sufficient political power, as the history of Spain, Ireland, France, Belgium, West Germany, and many other Catholic and non-Catholic countries bears out. Such complete support is the first plank in the platform of every Catholic political party in Europe.[27]

Although American Catholic bishops have not delivered to the White House and Congress any formal, countersigned demand for the one to two billion dollars annually necessary to support their schools in the public style to which they are not accustomed, they are constantly preparing their people for such a formal demand when the time is ripe. They are as firmly opposed to the Supreme Court's "distributive injustice" in denying them public financial support as the Southern Dixiecrats are opposed to the Supreme Court's anti-segregation decision of 1954. Bishop John P. Cody of Kansas City echoed their conviction quite frankly in dedicating the St. Pius X High School in April, 1957:

When we hear about federal aid to education we wonder if we, too, are not deserving. The law of this land prohibits federal contributions to sectarian schools, but laws have been changed.[28]

Pius XII himself, about two years after the Spellman-Roosevelt controversy, declared that "we must expect" from legislators throughout the world "that determination for justice" in school legislation which would guarantee that Catholic schools "be not placed in a worse condition than the State schools." [29] The standard American book of Catholic Canon Law which was published one year before Spellman's historic attack calmly announced: "The system of taxation which burdens Catholic citizens with the support of so-called 'public' schools which Catholics may not in conscience attend, is an evident violation of fundamental justice." [30] The *National Catholic Almanac* frequently denounces American laws as "unjust and discriminatory because they arbitrarily deny tax aid to schools, which, like the public schools, prepare for the responsibilities of American citizenship." [31]

In 1953 a study, *The Moral Obligations of Catholic Civil Judges*,[32] was published at the Catholic University of America with the *Nihil Obstat* of the highest-ranking Catholic theologian in the United States, Francis J. Connell, dean of the university's School of Sacred Theology. (The Catholic University is operated by the Catholic bishops of the United States and is the chief pontifical university in the country.) In outlining a program of conduct for American Catholic judges, the book not only condemned American educational tax laws but placed upon Catholic judges the responsibility for co-operating in avoiding such laws. It said (pages 165-66):

An example in our land of what might be called an unjust law opposed to a human good insofar as it burdens a special group excessively is the legal tax arrangement whereby Catholics contribute a large amount in taxes for educational purposes but do not receive anything from these collected funds for the support of their own parochial schools. . . . Since these laws are unjust, Catholics could not be held bound in conscience, in light of the demands of legal justice, to pay the excessive taxation, except in order to avoid scandal or disturbance. . . .

If because of the injustice involved a particular Catholic should refuse to pay a portion of his taxes, his portion of that part set aside for schools, and as a result be brought before the court in contesting the law, the Catholic judge should do what he can to show the law's injustice and to avoid its application. . . . The most mitigated penalty possible should be inflicted.

In the 84th and 85th Congresses (1955-57), Catholic legislative spokesmen like John W. McCormack of Massachusetts, chief Vatican representative on Capitol Hill, had come to recognize the futility of any direct demand on the federal treasury for parochial school funds. As a result of McCormack's insistence, no bill for Catholic school aid was introduced in these sessions, although the *Catholic World* of April, 1955, had published an open letter to President Eisenhower asking for the inclusion of funds for Catholic school buildings in the administration's school-building bill, on the ground that such appropriations could be justified as "welfare" funds. Said the letter, ". . . in the matter of erecting new school buildings, it's obvious that American children are entitled to the benefits of public welfare legislation regardless of race, creed or color."

In 1956 the hierarchy's drive for federal funds for its schools took a new direction. Cardinal James Francis McIntyre of Los Angeles, in dedicating the Catholic institution known as the University of Dallas, on December 9, announced himself in favor of a national educational plan for Catholic financing that would parallel the G.I. educational bills of World War II and the Korean war, under which some fourteen billion dollars was granted by the United States to members of the armed services for college scholarships.[33] The cardinal drew a bizarre analogy between the members of the armed forces who had been awarded scholarships as a reward for national service and the students of Catholic schools, indicating that they were both entitled to federal money. Under the McIntyre plan federal funds would be siphoned off to Catholic parents as individuals, then given to the children, and finally turned over to the Catholic Church for "scholarships." This plan, similar to the plan developed in France recently with the support of the French cardinals, will probably be the favored plan of the hierarchy during the next decade for federal financing of its schools. It is being promoted in the Catholic press as a scheme for *individual* awards which can be classed as "welfare" awards, in distinction from the direct appropriations to sectarian schools that have been declared unconstitutional by the Supreme Court. In September, 1957, a Jesuit professor at Marquette University,

Father Virgil C. Blum, embroidered the plan with a suggestion that the government give to parents "certificates of money value or a tax credit" not for the denominational institution but for the child. This plan, Father Blum argued, would have the advantage that it would not raise any "constitutional questions."

5

While attention has been centered upon the dramatic struggle of the Catholic hierarchy for federal funds in Washington, many small but equally important skirmishes between church and state have been going on in local communities. These local skirmishes are essentially struggles between the communities and the priests for control of the children and the tax funds. Frequently local priests defeat a bond issue for public schools by suggestions to the effect that the "Godless" schools are extravagant and expensive.

Sometimes the priests in a small American community are able to weaken and even to destroy a public school by drawing off the majority of the children into a parochial school. Many country districts do not have enough children to support two schools. When the parochial school wins the struggle for survival, the public school may be forced to close down. Then non-Catholic children may have no alternative but to attend a Catholic school or travel to a distant public school.

Frequently, when the Catholic population of a district is quite large, the priests win the battle of the schools by moving the parochial school into the public-school system and forming a kind of hybrid school that is semi-public in nature. Its funds come from the public, but its controls and spirit are Catholic.

In order to graft a parochial school onto the public-school system in this way without violating the First Amendment too conspicuously, the Catholic Church must observe certain amenities. Nuns cannot teach religion *directly* during regular school hours. In semi-public schools Catholic catechism is, therefore, taught before or after regular hours, and the non-Catholic children are not officially obliged to attend. The nuns on the public payroll must teach the regular subjects prescribed by the state law, but they do not need to teach them in a neutral manner or to use neutral textbooks. Local school boards, within limits, have a right to choose their own textbooks. In Catholic-controlled public schools all textbooks offensive to the hierarchy are removed.

These semi-public schools, staffed by nuns and brothers, are scattered throughout the United States in those states that permit nuns to teach in costume. The courts have declared that teaching in costume is a question for local decision; the states can make it illegal if they wish. Twenty-five states permit costumed nuns to teach in public schools and twenty-three forbid it, but only about a dozen states have any considerable number of nuns teaching in public schools. Missouri in 1947 had 108 costumed nuns and priests as public-school teachers. New Mexico had 134 nuns and brothers in costume, and North Dakota had seventy-four nuns and eight priests. There were hundreds more scattered through the twenty-six states which then permitted this practice. Most of them were in schools that had once been parochial schools and had been moved into the public-school system for financial reasons. North Dakota put an end to the practice of permitting nuns to teach in costume in public schools by referendum in July, 1948, whereupon the state's two Catholic bishops announced that, where desirable, the nuns would be permitted to take off their regular costumes and teach in a "respectable secular dress, which in no way indicates the fact that the teacher is a member of or adherent of any religious order or denomination." [34]

In New Mexico the hierarchy has gone to extremes in capturing public schools because of the Church's poverty and the heavy infiltration of Mexican Catholics from across the border. In that state in 1947 there were 134 nuns and brothers drawing their salaries from the taxpayers, and semi-public schools in twenty districts were listed as public schools by the state, although they were simultaneously carried as parochial schools on the lists of the Catholic Church.

One Catholic authority, the Very Reverend John Doyle, calling this type of school the "so-called Catholic public school," declares that "by some it is regarded as an anomaly, a hybrid, that is bound in the long run to displease all parties concerned and to disappear from the scene, giving place to the dominant types." [35] But this prophecy has not yet been realized. Professor Doyle cites one authoritative study, made in 1926, which indicated that there were 340 such semi-public schools at that time in thirty American dioceses.

Several attempts were made by American Catholic leaders in the nineteenth century to develop semi-public schools as a substitute for the parochial school. Archbishop Ireland instituted semi-public schools in Faribault and Stillwater, Minnesota, and advocated the system as a substitute for parochial schools where the latter were not feasible, but the hierarchy raised its eyebrows. Since every American priest had received his orders to build a parochial school in his parish, it seemed dangerously unorthodox to permit some to avoid the Papal directives.

Archbishop Ireland's scheme as an official substitute for parochial schools was soon abandoned, but it continued in operation quietly in many local communities. Local priests and bishops now regard it as practical if there is no great scandal about it. Sometimes they are able to operate hybrid schools for years quietly without any protests from local taxpayers. There are several hundred such "captive" public schools, taught and directed exclusively by nuns, in Indiana, Kentucky, Kansas, Illinois, and Ohio. Usually the buildings are located next to a Catholic church. In Indiana the practice is so open that many schools are simultaneously listed in the *Indiana School Directory* as public schools and in the *Official Catholic Directory* as parochial schools. (I have visited fourteen such schools.) In Jasper, Indiana, two school systems, public and Catholic, are located only four blocks apart, while the Indiana taxpayers are charged with the salaries of both the legitimate public-school teachers and the nuns who teach in the semi-public school.

In the semi-public school the children are brought to school an hour early and herded across the school yard to the adjoining Catholic church for Mass. The operation of these schools with public funds is clearly unconstitutional under the federal Constitution, but state school officers are frequently afraid to enforce the Constitution against powerful Catholic population blocs.

The Supreme Court of Missouri has written the most perceptive decision concerning the conflict between this type of school and the American public school. In *Harfst vs. Hogan,* in 1942, the court pointed out that Catholic nuns are disqualified as public-school teachers because of the nature of their obedience to the superior power of their religious orders, and "by the very nature of the obligations of their oaths of obedience said nuns, and each of them, place themselves beyond the control of civil authorities (except where agreeable to their superiors) . . . that said nuns and each of them by their oaths cease to exist as free citizens . . . that because of the character of their obligations said nuns are disqualified from teaching in any public school in the State of Missouri." [36]

The state superintendent of education of Michigan discovered in 1946 that a number of parochial schools had been operated illegally in nineteen districts, in some cases for twenty-five years, while receiving money from the taxpayers as public schools. "The schoolrooms," according to State Superintendent Elliott, "were adorned with statues, icons, and pictures that particularly depicted the Catholic faith. It was found that the textbooks and other reading materials used were those having the approval of the Catholic order." [37] The teachers in these hybrid schools were nuns, and the schools were carried on the diocesan records of the Church as parochial schools. The practice has now been discontinued.

In general Catholic priests do not attempt to move a parochial school into the public-school system unless there is such a large preponderance of Catholics in the population that the maneuver can be executed without fear of repercussions. But occasionally the priests attempt the maneuver in communities where the non-Catholic population is large and determined. Such was the case in the famous battle of North College Hill, Ohio, a suburb of Cincinnati, in 1947, a battle that attracted national attention.

North College Hill's local board of education had been captured by the Catholic voters by a narrow margin after an organized migration of Catholics to the area. The Catholic-dominated board took over the local St. Margaret-Mary parochial school, changed its name to the Grace Avenue School, paid $6,000 rent to the Catholic Archbishop, hired all the eight teaching nuns of the parochial school with public funds, and continued Catholic teaching in classes that started half an hour earlier than the other classes in the public-school system. When the town's non-Catholic superintendent, Dr. William A. Cook, a former professor at the University of Cincinnati, refused to hire and fire teachers according to the directives of the Catholic board, the board announced that he would be dropped. Whereupon most of the town's high-school students and twenty-eight of the high school's thirty-three teachers quit the school system in protest.

The National Education Association for the first time in its history blacklisted a whole school system. Substitute teachers could not be secured. National magazines featured the fight as a struggle for American principles in education. The Cincinnati hierarchy, embarrassed by the uproar, recognized its mistake when the damage had been done. The Catholic school board finally resigned, and the local courts promptly rehired the old superintendent of schools for a new term.[38]

A similar struggle in 1947 and 1948 made the little town of Dixon, New Mexico, famous. There the regular public school was closed, and the non-Catholic children had no public school to attend except a semi-public school, operated by nuns, that had been absorbed into the public system by the techniques I have just described. School buses arrived thirty minutes early to permit Catholic children to go to Mass before regular classes. Franciscan refugee nuns from Europe, not particularly expert either in teaching or in the English language, took over the classes.

Early in 1948 non-Catholic residents of Dixon began a suit in the state courts to bar 145 costumed Catholic nuns, priests, and brothers from positions in the New Mexico public schools. The suit demanded that twenty-nine hybrid schools in the state be turned back to the Catholic Church, and that the money now spent in them be used for public schools. The evidence that Dixon residents and others had to present to the courts was startling. Catholic holy pictures and charts had been freely used in the "public" schools. According to the editor of the *Christian Herald*,[39] Catholic control of some public schools had gone so far that the salary checks of some nuns were made out not to themselves as individuals but directly to the religious orders that were to receive the money in any case. The non-Catholics of New Mexico won the first round in the state court, but the battle continues.

In Kentucky, the Catholic-dominated school board of Marion County so gerrymandered the "public" high-school districts in favor of two semi-public high schools taught by nuns that the high school in Bradfordsville (in the non-Catholic end of the county) was closed down. The embattled non-Catholic parents went on a school strike for a year, carried their case to Kentucky's highest court, and won a resounding victory in a 1956 court order which directed the establishment of one central high school for the children of all faiths in the county, and the removal of the nun-operated schools from the public payroll.[40]

Many of these bitter local battles over public money for Catholic schools have developed over parochial-school bus transportation in the twenty-eight states which do not provide for it. In such struggles the Catholic press usually twists the Supreme

Court's decision in the Everson case to pretend that the Court has ruled unconstitutional *any denial* of public funds for Catholic buses, whereas the Court specifically said in that purely permissive decision that "we do not mean to intimate that a state could not provide transportation only to children attending public schools."

Under such instigation, Catholic parents in Augusta, Maine, in March, 1957, threatened to "dump" 900 parochial students suddenly on the public schools unless their "right" to get public funds for transportation was acknowledged by a local appropriation.[41] Unperturbed, the local superintendent announced that the public schools would receive the Catholic pupils as best they could. The "strike" evaporated overnight; and when the question of a legal test appropriation for Catholic bus funds was carried to Maine's highest court, that court ruled that it was illegal. The Maine case is still in a state of bellicose litigation.

There is no evidence that the majority of the Catholic *people* of the United States favor the aggressive tactics used by some Catholic leaders in Kentucky, Maine, Ohio, and New Mexico. Many Catholics, in fact, have specifically disapproved of such tactics and declared that the Catholic priests, if they insist on maintaining schools of their own, should leave the public schools alone. The leader of the embattled public-school teachers in North College Hill, Ohio, was herself a Catholic. Her successful challenge to the Church's overlords should remind non-Catholics that the whole educational policy of the Church has been imposed upon Catholic people at the point of a theological gun.

6

Although America has the largest and finest public universities in the world, the Catholic hierarchy in the United States may not take advantage of these institutions. It has been instructed by the Popes to build up a Catholic system of higher learning in order that the faith of Catholic students may be guarded completely. While the leading Protestant and Jewish groups in this country have accepted public college education as a great moral and cultural advancement, American Catholicism is still compelled to follow the pattern of separatism.

In this area of higher education, however, the Church has not been very successful. Only a small minority of Catholic college students are in Catholic institutions. The rest, who attend public and private, non-Catholic institutions, are "supervised" by Catholic campus chaplains who attempt to guard their morals and faith by advising them against liberal courses in philosophy and religion. Sometimes these chaplains become leaders of reactionary thought on non-Catholic campuses. Father Hugh Halton has served that purpose as Catholic chaplain at Princeton, where he has denounced "some Princeton professors" for doing "more damage than Karl Marx" and attacked "professors' unions" for "destroying the minds, the souls, and the intellects of the students." [42] "Dogmatic belief in objective truth," he asserts, "is fundamental to the idea of a university." In 1957, when Princeton's new president, Dr. Robert F. Goheen, withdrew all campus privileges from Father Halton for "irresponsible attacks upon the intellectual integrity of faculty members," *The Commonweal,* organ of liberal Catholic laymen, applauded the ouster, and a Catholic Princetonian announced that Father Halton had "done more harm to the cause of the Catholic Church at Princeton than a Communist could ever hope to do." But many more tactful Father Haltons continue to "supervise" the life of Catholic students on non-Catholic campuses, quietly sabotaging the activities of liberal professors who venture to bring into their classes any direct criticism of Catholic policy.

The whole system of American Catholic colleges is almost as completely controlled by priests as the system of parochial schools. In some colleges the lay teachers outnumber the clerics, but it is the priests who control policies, and the institutions they control are almost as doctrinal and denominational as the elementary schools. Of the twenty-seven American Catholic universities whose presidents are listed in the 1948 *Catholic Almanac,* every one has a priest for a president. Every one of the fifty-two senior colleges for men in the United States has a priest or religious brother for president. Of the 104 senior colleges for women listed, all but four have nuns or priests as chief executives.

In practice Catholic colleges are adjuncts of a Catholic diocese or a religious order. When they are attached to the local diocese, they are subject to the local bishop, and they may be supported by the same bingo games that cover the costs of local charities. Priests or members of religious orders are moved to an administrative post in diocesan colleges almost as casually as they are moved from one parish to another.

More often the colleges are operated by religious orders. The orders frequently have a difficult time making up college deficits by soliciting contributions from the faithful. Scores of tiny and struggling Catholic institutions have been established in the United States with the title of "college" which, Catholic authorities admit, should never have been called anything but high schools. In 1952, only two Catholic colleges in the country could command enough academic recognition to award Phi Beta Kappa keys.[43]

Until quite recently many of these struggling, second-rate Catholic institutions of "higher learning" were fighting for their lives in all parts of the country, with inadequate faculties, inadequate equipment, and very small student bodies. The students were largely recruited by local priests and nuns from families quite unfamiliar with first-rate educational standards. Many of the institutions were little better than devotional finishing schools, or postgraduate sections of diocesan high schools. Local bishops, monsignors, and mothers-superior who were susceptible to flattery could nourish their egos with the title "college president," while the Catholic students suffered. Degrees from many Catholic colleges were privately jeered at and sometimes publicly scorned. The duplication and inadequacy became so notorious that several devout Catholic educators made open attacks upon the system and called for reform.

"Are we attempting to support too many colleges and universities?" asked Professor Jerome G. Kerwin, Catholic educator from the University of Chicago.[44] "In a single state scores of Catholic colleges will be doing in mediocre fashion what two or three could with sufficient support do well. . . . My own suggestion would be that sixty per cent of our present colleges should undertake no more than junior college work." The Very Reverend William J. Bergin of St. Viator College, Illinois, writing for Catholic educators in 1938, reprinted a stinging attack which he had made in 1917 upon the "excessive multiplication," "ruinous competition," and low standards of the whole Catholic college system, indicating that more than 80 per cent of American Catholic colleges were substandard even by Catholic minimum standards. Before reprinting the following statistical indictment from his 1917 study, he declared: "Conditions have not changed fundamentally in Catholic higher education since that time. . . . While numbers have changed, the proportions remain the same."

In Illinois we have fourteen colleges, thirteen of which are offering courses in college work. . . . There are not enough Catholic college students in the State of Illinois for more than one, or at most two, fair-sized colleges, and yet we have fourteen colleges to supply that need. . . . The vast majority of them have nowhere near seventy students. . . . Fancy such a college attempting to maintain at least seven distinct departments with seven professors giving their entire time to college work! . . . There are scores of colleges which have less than twenty-five students. We have colleges listed which have six or eight college students.[45]

Dr. Bergin was equally scathing in attacking the extreme autonomy and confusion of controls in Catholic colleges, pointing out that "there are at least seventy-two religious communities of men in Catholic college work" in the United States, and that "each one of these is absolutely independent of all the others. . . . Each bishop in his diocese may found colleges without reference to the existing educational facilities. . . ."

Undoubtedly the great majority of the Catholic colleges of the United States have improved since 1938 when Dr. Bergin's criticism was published. World War II, with its G.I. Bill of Rights, was like manna from heaven for understaffed Catholic "colleges," as for many other institutions. Nearly 100,000 student veterans flooded the Catholic institutions of higher learning in 1947-48 and brought welcome government money for tuition and equipment.[46] The federal government was extremely liberal in interpreting its money-giving powers to Catholic colleges. Many of these Catholic colleges gained valuable permanent equipment in the guise of emergency help for veterans.

Several candid critics of Catholic colleges have admitted that the present situation in Catholic higher education is still serious and quite amazing. Father John Tracy Ellis of the Catholic University, in his 1956 work, *American Catholics and the Intellectual Life,* mentions "the competition—amounting in certain places to internecine warfare—among the more than 200 Catholic colleges of the land," and criticizes very severely "the development within the last two decades of numerous and competing graduate schools, none of which is adequately endowed, and few of which have the trained personnel, the equipment in libraries and laboratories, and the professional wage scales to warrant their ambitious undertakings. The result is a perpetuation of mediocrity. . . ." [47]

Dr. John J. Meng, in an address at the 1956 annual meeting of the National Catholic Educational Association, declared: "I believe we should reduce the number of senior, four-year colleges by at least 50 per cent. . . ." [48]

When the influx of veterans has finally stopped, will these inadequate Catholic institutions be able to survive? Will Catholic parents consider it worth while to compete with larger and better public universities that cost the student less money and give him a wider contact with his generation? This last question will have special force if the recommendations of the President's Commission on Higher Education are carried out and public junior colleges are established in most American communities.

The situation in graduate departments in Catholic colleges is considerably worse than it is in undergraduate study. A Committee on Graduate Instruction of the American Council on Education in 1934 was not able to find in any of the leading Catholic universities of America a single graduate department of top rank.[49] The total endowment of the twenty-two American Catholic graduate schools in 1954-55 was about one-seventh that of Harvard.

For non-Catholic America the chief danger from Catholic higher education is that a Catholic college lobby may be able to sabotage and defeat an intelligent program of expansion for public colleges. Earlier Catholic lobbies blocked federal aid for elementary schools for a generation because of self-interest, and the nation may be treated to a repeat performance in the case of a national college program. When President Truman appointed a Commission on Higher Education in 1946, he put two Catholic members on the Commission. When twenty-four of the twenty-six members signed an epoch-making report calling for an expenditure of nearly a billion dollars a year for higher learning in the United States by 1960, so that 4,000,000 Americans could secure higher education in public colleges at nominal cost, the two Catholic members were the only dissenters.[50] They refused to sign the Commission's report on the ground that such appropriations should not be made for public colleges unless they were also made for Catholic schools of higher learning. Such contributions, of course, if made directly, would be in effect contributions to the Catholic Church, since Catholic colleges are carefully controlled units of the Church.

The Jesuit organ, *America*, simultaneously discovered that American free high schools had been a failure, and launched into the following attack:

To deprive private schools of their share of responsibility would seriously weaken our democratic structure just when it needs most to be strengthened. Nor has it been our traditional practice to adopt, without extensive public discussion, so sweeping a proposal as the totally free education of our youth through the 13th and 14th years. It was only after many years of debate that the people agreed on the principle of free education in public high schools. And very few will grant that the results of that experiment have as yet justified the cost to the public treasury. They decidedly did not justify a further experiment, at this time, with tuitionless education for all on the college level.[51]

Thus the Catholic hierarchy is holding out for its price: the inclusion of Catholic colleges in federal appropriations. It is easy to read the anxiety behind this opposition to the Commission's program. Catholic colleges must raise many millions a year in private contributions even to maintain their present level of operations, and when the number of war veterans drops sharply, the financial crisis will be acute. There must be hundreds of American bishops and priests who are weary of imposing upon their people the costs of a second-rate college system when better colleges at lower cost are available to them as American citizens. But the Pope has spoken, and segregated culture must be preserved. Meanwhile, as we shall see in a later chapter, these struggling Catholic colleges maintain the lowest standard of scientific output of any considerable group of colleges in the United States.

The ultimate moral issue in the national struggle, *The Catholic Hierarchy vs. the Public School,* was succinctly stated by one of America's great philosophers, John Dewey, in *The Nation's Schools:*

It is essential that this basic issue be seen for what it is—namely, as the encouragement of a powerful reactionary world organization in the most vital realm of democratic life with the resulting promulgation of principles inimical to democracy. We cannot deny that public education needs federal aid in order to equalize opportunity between state and state, and between individual and individual. But it would be a poor bargain indeed to gain material aid at the expense of losing our greatest intellectual and moral heritage.

6

The Church and Medicine[1]

1

MOST AMERICANS WOULD BE somewhat startled if they picked up
a medical journal and read a table of contents like this:

EPISCOPAL PRINCIPLES OF THERAPEUTIC ABORTION *by Bishop Sylvanus Bump, D.D.*

BAPTIST TECHNIQUE FOR STERILIZATION OF THE FEEBLE-MINDED *by James Q. McCutcheon, S.T.D.*

HOW A METHODIST NURSE SHOULD BEHAVE IN A PRESBYTERIAN HOSPITAL *by Deaconess Matilda Little, M.A.*

JEWISH IDEALS AND THE CAESARIAN OPERATION *by Rabbi Marcus Goldberg, Ph.D.*

Such a table of contents, of course, is purely imaginary, but
the actual titles of priestly articles on medicine in Catholic magazines are no less startling. Denominational excursions into the
field of practical medicine are almost unknown among Protestants
and Jews, but the homiletical and ecclesiastical journals of the
American priesthood treat many medical problems as a branch
of theology and discuss specific medical subjects with great authority.

Here, for example, are the titles of eight articles and discussions published in recent years in America's two leading magazines
for priests, the *American Ecclesiastical Review* and the *Homiletic
and Pastoral Review:* "May Circumcision by a Jewish Rabbi Be
Done in a Catholic Hospital?" "May a Catholic Nurse Summon
a Non-Catholic Minister?" "The Use of a Vaginal Douche."
"Sterility Tests and Their Morality." "The Use of Contraceptives
When the Wife Is Sterile." "May a Catholic Doctor Employed by
the State Perform Eugenic Sterilization?" "Irradiation of the
Ovaries."

The priests of the Church not only are spiritual advisers to the Catholic physician and nurse but exercise definite authority over the doctor and nurse in respect to many aspects of professional life. This is particularly true in the special areas of birth, death, and sexual conduct. "Priests who have doctors among the faithful committed to their pastoral care should be mindful of their obligation in conscience to provide these men (or women) with adequate instruction on their professional duties," says Father Francis J. Connell in his *Morals in Politics and Professions*.[2]

Catholic priests tell Catholic physicians when the life of a soul begins in the womb, what the surgeon can and cannot do concerning the ending of the life of the fetus, and what must be done to the newborn child immediately after birth. In the field of sexual conduct the priests not only lay down very definite and detailed instructions concerning courtship, marriage, and divorce but also proclaim rules concerning contraception, abortion, masturbation, artificial insemination, sterilization, sodomy, and the manners of the marriage bed. They believe that celibacy does not disqualify them from giving advice on such matters.

This priestly participation in medical practice is based upon two theses that are basic to Catholic medical philosophy, namely, that the soul is more important than the body, and that the Catholic priest is the divinely appointed guardian of the soul. It is more important to save a soul than to save a life, and if there is a necessary choice between the two, the soul must come first.

In this scheme of things the Catholic doctor is in perpetual subordination to the priest in many matters of life and death. The doctor is merely the guardian of the body. He has no right to challenge the authority of the priest in that area that has been assigned to the priest by moral theology, Canon Law, and Papal regulations. Accordingly, although there are Catholic physicians' guilds, these guilds do not determine medico-ethical policies for the physician. In the last analysis, the medical code for Catholic Americans is determined by ecclesiastical authorities in Rome.

The American priest is trained and authorized to intervene in the field of medicine and surgery at all those points where there is any chance that the interests of the soul may be subordinated to the interests of the body. The three areas of medical conduct that the priest claims particularly for himself are the delivery room where the soul arrives, the death bed where the soul departs, and the marriage bed where the soul is launched. The priestly code for the delivery room is even extended to all premature deliveries, whether they involve surgery or not.

The training of the priests for this supervision begins in the seminaries. Although no courses in scientific medicine are given in Catholic seminaries, the young ecclesiastical students have thick textbooks in moral theology and "pastoral medicine," elaborately illustrated with pictures and charts showing the female sexual organs, the intricacies of childbirth, etc. The pastoral medical books treat quite frankly of sexual problems such as masturbation, homosexuality, and contraception, and discuss techniques of love-play and sexual intercourse in married life. Although most of the facts contained in these textbooks are scientifically correct, the point of view is wholly theological. Pastoral medicine is holy, spiritual medicine, based almost entirely on medieval premises and theories, particularly the teachings of St. Thomas Aquinas. The criterion for evaluating any particular medical solution is: How does this solution square with the revealed doctrinal and moral premises of the Church? It is assumed throughout these treatises that the Catholic doctor is the moral subordinate of the Catholic priest and that both must rely primarily upon theological authority in determining medico-ethical standards.

The priestly code for the practice of medicine applies primarily to Catholic doctors and nurses, but it also affects non-Catholic doctors and patients. As we shall see in the next chapter, the Catholic hierarchy in Massachusetts and Connecticut not only controls the standards of the Catholic physicians who serve Church hospitals but also attempts to impose upon non-Catholic doctors attached to Catholic hospitals rules concerning their conduct as citizens in the support of legislation with which the hierarchy does not agree. The boycott even applies to sick non-Catholics in Catholic hospitals who, in the opinion of a non-Catholic physician, need some remedy that the hierarchy does not approve.

Father Charles J. McFadden, in his *Medical Ethics for Nurses,* with foreword by Bishop Fulton J. Sheen, instructs Catholic hospital authorities to remove ill patients from their hospitals under certain circumstances rather than permit them to violate the Catholic code, even when their own doctors wish them to stay and undergo a treatment that is entirely acceptable to non-Catholics. On page 154 of his work Father McFadden says, concerning a woman suffering from uncontrollable and exhausting vomiting in early pregnancy, whose physician has directed interruption to save her life: "When a case of this kind occurs in a Catholic hospital, and the authorities cannot shake the determination of the doctor or patient to procure abortion, the authorities must order the patient removed to another institution." Father McFadden does not discuss the possible effects of delay or of movement upon the patient or the possibility that no other suitable place may be available for her.

If such a policy seems incredibly narrow to non-Catholics, they should remember that the priest who orders a sick woman out of a Catholic hospital at such a moment looks upon himself as a savior of the soul of an unborn child, and in risking the life of the mother for this soul of the unborn child, he is performing a highly "moral" act. The theological dogma upon which this reasoning is based is that the soul begins, as it were, *ab initio,* immediately after the fructifying sexual contact. For centuries the Church accepted the theories of Augustine and Thomas Aquinas that the male embryo acquired an immortal soul about forty days after conception, and the female about eighty days.[3] This doctrine was gradually abandoned, and by the time the Church promulgated the doctrine of the Immaculate Conception of the Virgin Mary in 1854—not to be confused with the doctrine of the Virgin Birth of Christ—it was generally agreed by Catholic theologians that the soul starts as soon as the male sperm and ovum unite.

Most present-day Catholic works on medical problems do not even mention the fact that for centuries the Church made a distinction between the embryo of the first few weeks and the more mature fetus. "Human life, and therefore the soul, is present at the first moment of conception," says the Jesuit writer, Father William S. Bowdern, in *The Catholic Nurse and the Dying.* "For this reason an embryo, even in very early miscarriage, has an immortal soul. If the embryo can be recognized, take it in your fingers, break the membranes, and dip it under the water and lift it out again while you pronounce the words of baptism. In case you cannot recognize the embryo at all, pour water on the blood clot in the miscarriage, and pronounce the words of baptism." [4]

Under Canon 747 the soul of the unborn child must be saved by baptism of the evidences of life even though exit in spontaneous abortion does not occur until two weeks or more after death of the fetus, and the fetus is expelled, particle by particle, over a period of two days. If there is doubt of life in the remains, the baptism is conditional. "This precept," says Father Robert Kekei-sen, "is based on the Church's strict practice of taking no chances where there is a question of a soul's entrance into heaven." [5]

This doctrine explains many of the most extreme rules of the hierarchy for physicians and nurses. If the embryo with a tail and no face is not baptized, its soul will be denied access to heaven for all eternity. Baptism guarantees reception into heaven. For this reason Catholic students in medical colleges are instructed that when they handle childbirth cases and a mother dies in childbirth, they should attempt to get the consent of the family in all cases at once to open up the dead body of the mother, remove the fetus and baptize it, even when they know that the fetus is almost surely dead or is so immature an embryo that it cannot live for more than a few minutes. "Even when the fetus is quite immature," says Father Francis J. Connell in his *Morals in Politics and Professions,* "Catholic principles call for a Caesarian section of the dead mother, so that the sacrament of baptism may be adminis-tered to the child." [6]

This attempt to indoctrinate Catholic physicians with the hierarchy's medical code begins in Catholic medical colleges. There are five full-term Catholic medical colleges in the United States, all operated by Jesuits, and in each of them there is a compulsory course in medical ethics conducted in part by a Jesuit priest who impresses upon his students the fact that any departure from the priestly medical code may lead to Catholic boycott and excommunication. A similar, and more successful, attempt is made to impress the principles of the Catholic code upon all nurses in the 340 Catholic nursing schools in the country.

2

One of the most important doctrines in the Catholic medical code is the doctrine of the equality of mother and fetus. This doctrine is of special interest to every potential mother who has a Catholic physician.

When the average American woman approaches the ordeal of childbearing, she takes it for granted that her physician will do everything possible to save her life in the event of complications. I feel sure that 99 per cent of all American husbands would con-sider themselves murderers if, confronted with the choice between the life of a wife and the life of her unborn child, they chose the life of the fetus. This is particularly true in the early months of pregnancy when such risks most frequently develop. Most of our citizens assume without discussion that every possible effort should be made to save the life of both mother and child, but that if a choice is forced upon the physician the mother should be given first consideration.

The Catholic hierarchy does not endorse this choice, nor can a good Catholic physician leave such a choice to the husband and father and be true to the dogmas of his Church. "The life of each is equally sacred," said Pope Pius XI in his encyclical, *Casti Connubii,* "and no one has the power, not even the public authority, to destroy it." [7]

The Jesuit scholar Father Henry Davis, in his *Moral and Pastoral Theology,* says:

> One of the most distressing problems which surgeons have to face is that of saving the lives of both mother and child in difficult cases of parturition. Each has a right to life and neither has a better right than the other. . . . Where induced abortion, *abortus provocatus,* is the procedure indicated, he [the Catholic doctor] will disregard his textbook and save the mother in some other way, and if there is no other way, he will abandon the case. In the last resort, where nothing whatever can be done to save the mother except abortion, he may not destroy a nascent life directly.[8]

Father Davis assumes here that the unborn child *might* live. That assumption is not contained in the statement of the dogma by a noted priest, Father Patrick A. Finney. Father Finney states the doctrine in all its naked brutality in his *Moral Problems in Hospital Practice,* reprinted by Herder in 1947 under the Imprimatur of the Archbishop of St. Louis. (The language is almost identical in the 1956 edition of this work by Finney and O'Brien.) He states the doctrine in terms of a question and an answer:

> If it is morally certain that a pregnant mother and her unborn child will both die, if the pregnancy is allowed to take its course, but at the same time, the attending physician is morally certain that he can save the mother's life by removing the inviable fetus, is it lawful for him to do so?
>
> *Answer.* No, it is not. Such a removal of the fetus would be direct abortion.

It should be noted that under this statement of the complete doctrine, *both* mother and child must be allowed to die rather than allow a life-saving abortion that is contrary to the code of the priests. There is no choice here between one life and another; it is a choice between two deaths and one. The priests choose the two deaths, presumably in order to save the souls of both mother and child from a sin that would send the mother's soul to hell and the child's to the twilight hereafter known as limbo. The fetus in Father Finney's question would die anyway. It is described as "inviable," which means incapable of life. It may be a six-week embryo about the size of a small marble, without a face. Nevertheless, the life of the mother must be sacrificed for this embryo that, by definition, is dying or will die.

This doctrine is not a matter of opinion that priests or doctors are free to reject. It has been repeated over and over by Catholic authorities and incorporated in positive Church law. Pope Pius XII reiterated the doctrine before the International College of Surgeons in Rome in May, 1948, when he declared that in spite of "the understandable anguish of husbandly love" it is "illicit—even in order to save the mother—to cause directly the death of the small being that is called, if not for life here below, then at least for the future life, to a high and sublime destiny. . . ." [10]

Catholic theorists are at great pains to defend this doctrine with elaborate theological reasoning. Dr. Austin O'Malley, in *The Ethics of Medical Homicide and Mutilation,* published under the Imprimatur of the late Cardinal Farley, stated the philosophy in some detail:

The assertion that an undeveloped fetus in the womb is not as valuable as the mother of a family is beside the question, and in certain vital distinctions it is untrue. Any human life as such, whether in a fetus or an adult, is as valuable as another, inasmuch as no one but God has any authority to destroy it, except when it has lost its right to exist through culpable action. Secondly, the quality of motherhood is an accidental addition to a mother's life, not substantial as is the life itself. This quality of motherhood does not create any juridic imbalance of values which justifies the destruction of the rights inherent in the fetus. That the fetus may not be able to enjoy these rights if the mother dies is, again, an irrelevant consideration. . . . An innocent fetus an hour old may not be directly killed to save the lives of all the mothers in the world. [11]

The corollary to this doctrine of the equality of mother and fetus is that a fetal monster with only part of a brain possesses a soul equal to that of the mother in value and must therefore be given equal treatment with that of the mother. "Medicus," author of a famous textbook, *Medical Essays,* used in Catholic seminaries, says:

> Human life is not subject to comparison of values. A living human fetus, even though a monster, may not be sacrificed to save all the human lives in the world. . . . If you say: Why should a useful mother suffer the hazard and the ills of the Caesarian section to save a monster whose hours are numbered, and who never could be a useful member of society? I answer because the monster is a human individual with the inalienable right of life. A beggar idiot may not be directly sacrificed to save the life of the most useful member of society; nay not to save the lives of all the members of society.[12]

Is it surprising that young American Catholic women are reacting against this whole priestly doctrine with considerable horror? As for American Catholic physicians, they are good Americans and decent husbands, and in practice, even in dealing with Catholic mothers, they are able to use a loophole that has been developed in the mother-fetus rule by Jesuit casuists. This loophole permits an *indirect* killing of a fetus by an operation if the operation is necessary in the process of saving the mother. If an operation has a "double effect," the surgeon may pretend that the less sinful effect is the controlling one. An acutely inflamed appendix, for example, may be removed from a pregnant Catholic mother even if the operation indirectly causes miscarriage. This exception to the general rule is extended to any operation that is necessary to remedy "an acute diseased condition." What Catholic physician is so stupid that he cannot find an "acute diseased condition" in the right case? If Catholic gynecologists did not have a moral code superior to that of their priests, they would lose a large proportion of their patients.

But officially, the Catholic physicians of America must go on obeying the dicta of the priests on all subjects that the Pope cares to bring within the scope of his moral authority. They must observe the rigid rule, embodied in Canon 2350, that even very early interruption to save life, called therapeutic abortion, is a sin serious enough to result in excommunication. Few Catholic doctors are willing to risk clerical boycott by violating such a rule officially even to save the life of the most useful Catholic mother. They know that in taking this course they disagree with perhaps 90 per cent of American doctors, who recognize that, at times, therapeutic abortion to save life or health is a moral obligation.

This moral obligation to perform therapeutic abortion in order to save the life of a mother has been recognized by the courts of every state in the United States, and is so vital a part of American legal tradition that it needs no special legislation to sanctify it. As the highest court of Maine declared in the case of *State vs. Rudman:*

It is well known that occasion arises where, in the exercise of proper surgical advice and care, it becomes necessary, in order to save the mother's life, to remove the unborn fetus. To such highly honorable and proper acts, in accord with the highest ethics of the medical profession, the dictates of humanity, and all legal precepts, the statute [concerning criminal abortion] has, and can have, no application.[13]

All religious faiths condemn illegal abortion, which is abortion performed when not necessary to save the life or health of the mother. Catholic propagandists do not always make the distinction clear between therapeutic and illegal abortion. They lump the two phenomena together as "murder," regardless of the physician's motive in saving the life of the mother by the only means known to medical science. According to Father Charles McFadden, "there is no essential moral difference between therapeutic and criminal abortion." [14]

Father Davis, in condemning craniotomy when it is recommended to save the life of a mother, says: "If craniotomy is absolutely indicated, a Catholic doctor must give up the case, but he is not thereby precluded from telling those whom it may concern that other medical advice must be got, or rather may be got." [15] To most non-Catholics the abandonment of a case by suggesting that a Protestant or Jewish physician should do what it is the plain duty of a Catholic physician to do is sheer evasion of the physician's medical oath.

Similarly, most non-Catholics would describe as misfeasance the technique recommended for handling one of the most serious diseases for pregnant women, nephritis, which involves kidney inflammation or stoppage. This technique is described in Father McFadden's *Medical Ethics for Nurses.* It should be noted that

Father McFadden admits that his theory is contrary to most medical texts, but this does not alter his dogmatic rule. In this quotation "prompt termination" of pregnancy means therapeutic abortion:

Nephritis is regarded as a serious complication of pregnancy. It sometimes accompanies eclampsia [convulsions and stupor] in the late months of gestation; but it may either develop during pregnancy, or pregnancy may occur in a woman who already has nephritis. Maternal and fetal mortality rates are very high in nephritis. De Lee gives an estimate of thirty per cent maternal mortality and seventy per cent fetal mortality. Medical texts usually state that, if the disease is discovered early in pregnancy, prompt termination offers the best prognosis [outlook] for the mother. *Such a procedure would constitute direct abortion and is, therefore, never morally permissible.*[16]

In practice this priestly rule, when applied in cases of acute nephritis, means that no doctor may save the life of a mother by loosening and withdrawing the contents of the womb even when the total to be removed is less than a level teaspoonful, or not large enough to cover a thumbnail. Father McFadden, incidentally, although he writes with great authority on medical matters, does not carry an M.D. after his name. He is a member of the Order of Hermits of St. Augustine.

How many Catholic mothers in the United States die each year because of the doctrine of the equality of mother and fetus? Catholic protagonists usually evade this unpleasant question by drawing their statistics from Catholic-dominated hospitals where therapeutic abortion is forbidden. When I originally published some description of this problem in *The Nation* of November 1, 1947, a Catholic physician, Dr. Joseph L. McGoldrick of Brooklyn, published a reply that was widely quoted in the Catholic press in which, without denying the authenticity of the doctrine, he contended that "the mother-or-child dilemma is a relic of the early days of obstetrics," and that therapeutic abortions for kidney, lung and heart conditions are now very rare as well as unnecessary.[17]

It is true that the number of such abortions is declining rapidly with improvements in medical science, but an analysis of non-Catholic hospital statistics shows that the problem is by no means a historical relic. The only documented statistics that Dr. McGoldrick cited to support his contention were presented by a physician from the Catholic-dominated Margaret Hague Maternity Hospital in Jersey City, and published in the *American Journal of Obstetrics and Gynecology* of September, 1944. In the Margaret Hague Hospital only four therapeutic abortions occurred in 67,000 deliveries from 1931 to 1943, or 1 in 16,750. The physician from the Hague hospital also cited figures from six other hospitals that showed a completely different picture of the problem, since the therapeutic abortions in these other hospitals ranged from 1 in 200 to almost 3 in 100 deliveries. Obviously, the statistics from a Catholic hospital in Jersey City where therapeutic abortion is frowned upon are no more useful in determining the incidence of the problem than the number of vaccinations in a home for Christian Scientists would be in determining the need of vaccination.

Dr. Nicholas J. Eastman of Johns Hopkins Hospital, replying to the physician from the Hague Hospital in the *American Journal of Obstetrics and Gynecology,* pointed out that at Johns Hopkins the physicians had found 1 therapeutic abortion necessary in 65 deliveries, and that there were special circumstances which made the Hague Hospital statistics untypical.[18] If the Johns Hopkins ratio of therapeutic abortions is accepted as reasonable and applied to the estimated 703,800 Catholic births in the United States in 1947, then 10,827 Catholic mothers in the United States needed therapeutic abortion to save their lives or their health in that year. If only one Catholic mother in ten died because a Catholic physician refused to perform the life-saving operation, there were 1,082 Catholic victims of this priestly doctrine of the equality of mother and fetus in the United States in 1947. This would seem to be an extremely conservative estimate, since the Johns Hopkins Hospital is one of the finest in the world, with a most conservative policy, and therapeutic abortions are not performed there except for the most serious reasons.

3

The most important field for the application of the Catholic medical code in the United States is the Catholic hospital. Bishops regard the building of Catholic hospitals as next in importance to the building of churches and schools, not only because of the general social value of hospitals but also because they serve a useful purpose in winning and holding Church members.

"A Catholic hospital," says Monsignor Matthew Smith, America's most noted Catholic editor, "is a constant mission enterprise."

There are 934 Catholic hospitals in the United States controlled by the Catholic hierarchy, and the Church is building many more. These hospitals operate entirely under the Catholic medical code and treat more than 4,000,000 patients a year, a very large proportion of whom are non-Catholics. In addition to the strictly Catholic hospitals there are many technically non-Catholic institutions that have enough Catholic members on their boards of directors to exercise a veto power in some matters of medical policy. Nearly all of the Catholic hospitals make general appeals to non-Catholics for financial aid, and many of them are built largely with non-Catholic funds.

The control of Catholic hospitals by the hierarchy is exercised more through chaplains and nurses than through doctors. Perhaps one-third of the nurses in Catholic hospitals are nuns, bound by the same vows of obedience, poverty, and chastity that bind the teaching nuns in educational orders. Even when only a few of the nurses in a Catholic hospital are members of a religious order, the order usually operates the institution and hires the staff, preserving a strong pro-Catholic atmosphere. In that atmosphere the Catholic priest and his ministrations receive the place of honor.

It is easy to see why, from the point of view of the hierarchy, the nurse in a Catholic hospital may be more important than the doctor. She is in more constant contact with the patients. She is able to suggest the sacraments of baptism and extreme unction at propitious moments. If she is zealous, she may add many souls to the Church. The nurse's duty, says Father William S. Bowdern in the tract I have already cited, "does not stop with the care of the body. Since the soul is far more important than the body—the eternal salvation of a man depending upon the state of his soul at death—the nurse should regard it as her duty to take care in a prudent and tactful manner of the far more important ills and ailments of the soul." "Our Blessed Saviour," says Father Francis J. Connell in his exhortation to nurses, "made it very clear that health of soul is far more important than health of body."

How much attention do Catholic nurses give to these moral mandates of the priests? Probably it is fair to say that the nursing nuns, working under the tight discipline of their orders, follow the lead of the priests quite faithfully. But priestly control in a modern hospital operates under many handicaps. The nursing nuns are not segregated in their daily life from adult non-Catholics as completely as they are segregated in the Catholic school system. They are outnumbered about two to one in the nursing staff by women who have an opportunity to live normal lives in normal clothing. The facts of the outside world cannot be wholly avoided. Whatever may be the cause, the Catholic hospitals are having a desperate time persuading young Catholic women to become nursing nuns and to remain faithful to the stern denominational features of the priestly medical code. The famous best-seller, *The Nun's Story,* reveals many of the small cruelties, intellectual restrictions, and petty jealousies that make the life of a nursing Sister in a Catholic hospital almost intolerable for any woman of mature mind and independent spirit. In fact, it was the cumulative weight of these irritations which finally resulted in the famous nun's resignation from her nursing order. Emmett McLoughlin, former priest and still superintendent of a great hospital, has given the public an even more thorough exposure of clerical oppression in the Catholic hospital system in his "silent best-seller," *People's Padre.*

One reason for the difficulty in recruiting nursing nuns is that the Catholic code for nurses attempts to make each nurse into a tactful missionary for her Church—and many nurses deeply resent this emphasis upon proselytism, particularly in hospitals that have been erected with the help of non-Catholic contributors. Here are some of the points in Catholic discipline for nurses that have created resentment. They are all official, drawn from four standard Catholic guides for nurses and one pamphlet on the nurse's conduct in handling dying patients. I have mentioned these works already, and the full titles, dates, and publishers are in the Bibliography under the names of their authors. These authoritative Catholic works have all been published in the United States since 1945, and approved by the Church.

Perhaps I should say that the quoted descriptions include some items that are physically revolting and some readers may prefer to skip this section. I feel justified in using them because these items help to show how the Catholic medical code is imposed upon Catholic hospitals and even, where possible, upon non-Catholic hospitals and their patients.

1. *Baptism by stealth:* Since, as McFadden says, "the unbaptized child can never enter the kingdom of heaven," Catholic nurses have a duty to save the soul of a dying Protestant or Jewish child by Catholic baptism even if the parents are unwilling. According to McFadden, "If a certain medicine were absolutely needed to save the physical life of a child, a doctor or nurse would give it, even though the parents were unwilling. The attitude of such parents would be unreasonable. . . . When the unreasonable attitude of the parents is evident, the nurse should quietly baptize the dying child without the knowledge of the parents." [19]

Father Bowdern, in *The Catholic Nurse and the Dying,* carries this thought a little farther by saying:

A nurse could baptize a person quietly, by squeezing a wet rag over the forehead of the person to be baptized and at the same time saying the words in a very low voice. Do not just rub the rag on the forehead; but squeeze it so that some water, even though a little, actually flows.[20]

According to Catholic doctrine, a child so baptized should be brought up in the Catholic religion and his marriage should be regulated by the Church.[21] This doctrine was applied to Jews in Italy as long as the Church had the power to enforce it.

2. *The nurse and the ritual of baptism:* The directives of McFadden and Bowdern suggest the importance that the hierarchy attaches to every detail of the ritual of baptism. The Catholic nurse is held responsible for the ritual and, when a priest is not present, she is instructed in great detail how to substitute for him. The nurse is told that the soul of the infant is tainted with original sin, and that that sin can be washed away only by full and regular baptism. If the baptism is a failure, the infant will never reach heaven. If the baptism is performed according to Catholic rules, the future is gauranteed, since, as Father Bowdern tells nurses: "Baptized infants go to heaven as soon as they die, where they will give unending praise to God, and where they will intercede for you, their benefactor."

The ritual required of the Catholic nurse is most specific. The only liquid that is valid for valid baptism is water. Nothing else will do, and if it is not available the child will never reach heaven. "If water is not available, Baptism cannot be administered," says Sister Mary Berenice Beck in her *The Nurse: Hand-maid of the Divine Physician,* Imprimatur Archbishop of St. Louis. "Not much water is needed, but there must be enough so that it can be said to flow. . . . Milk, juice of fruits, oil, excretions from the body as tears, saliva, perspiration, etc., are not considered water. . . . If certain that the substance could not be considered water, Baptism should not be administered, as it is undoubtedly invalid." [22] But the nurse may add, according to McFadden, one one-thousandth part of bichloride of mercury and still call it water.

"The water must be applied to the head . . . ," says Sister Beck. "There is question of the validity of Baptism administered to any other part of the body but the head." The water must also be applied to the infant's skin, not hair, and the same individual who pours the water must pronounce the words of baptism. "Furthermore," says McFadden, "the words should be pronounced *during* the pouring of the water."

If it appears that the fetus will die before delivery, the nurse is instructed to baptize "with a sterile bulb syringe or other irrigating instrument" in the womb, reaching in as best she can. A wet finger, according to McFadden, will not do, and exposes the soul of the fetus to the risk of hell or limbo. "Normally, one could have no confidence whatever in a baptism that depended on a hand or fingers retaining water from the time the vagina was entered until the head of the child was reached." [23]

Baptism is urged upon the Catholic nurse even after apparent death, since it may be effective at any time before bodily corruption has set in.

3. *Baptism of monstrosities:* Since monstrosities have souls equal to the souls of mothers, every Catholic nurse must baptize every monstrosity if possible. "Any living product of human conception, regardless of its deformity, must always be baptized," says McFadden.[24]

"If there are two or more heads and one body," says Sister Beck, "baptize one head absolutely and each of the chests conditionally. . . . If one being is distinct, the other, attached to it, indistinct, baptize the distinct being absolutely, the other conditionally." [25]

"When death is imminent in the case of multiple monstrosities," says McFadden, "it is permissible to baptize them simultaneously by pouring water on the head of *each* and pronouncing the baptismal form in the plural: 'I baptize *you* in the name of the Father, and the Son, and the Holy Ghost.' "

4. *How to behave at an immoral operation:* The Catholic medical code makes very careful distinctions between what can and cannot be done by a Catholic nurse in a non-Catholic hospital at an operation that is legal under public standards but immoral under Catholic standards. A supervising nurse who is a Catholic may ease her own conscience by assigning Protestant or Jewish nurses to "immoral" operations even if they perform acts that would be a mortal sin for a good Catholic. "It would appear to be a sound moral principle," says McFadden, "that one may legitimately designate persons to do that which it is morally permissible for them to do."

Since all non-Catholic surgeons are potentially immoral because they may practice sterilization, contraception, therapeutic abortion, and modified euthanasia, the Catholic nurse must render assistance to such surgeons with great caution. The Catholic medical code tends to apportion sin to a nurse according to her distance from the scalpel, but it does not absolutely prohibit her from rendering assistance in "immoral" operations, because the priests realize that such a prohibition would cause the discharge of Catholic nurses from nearly all non-Catholic hospitals. A Catholic nurse in the operating theater at an "immoral" operation may give "close proximate material aid" for "a very grave reason," says McFadden, but she may never render "formal or immediate material cooperation." [26] "Formal cooperation" is wrong because it involves approval of the operation, and "immediate material cooperation" is wrong because it involves actual participation in the operation. The nurse may prepare the patient for the "immoral" operation, hand the instruments to the surgeon, and give the anesthetics, if she would lose her position in the hospital by refusing. But she may never commit the mortal sin of advising anybody to have such an operation, or of praising the operation when once it has been performed.

5. *Rules for the dying:* The Catholic nurse has a sacred duty to make every dying patient a Catholic if it can be done tactfully without interference. She is supposed to co-operate with an organization, formed in Cincinnati in 1931, called the Apostolate to Aid the Dying, whose chief object is to "prepare well-meaning

non-Catholics for a happy death." She must be on the alert to transfer non-Catholic souls to the Church.

Until recently Catholic medical manuals instructed Catholic nurses to discriminate against non-Catholic clergymen, even in non-Catholic hospitals when non-Catholic patients were dying. McFadden, at page 333 of his work, in the 1946 edition declared flatly that a Catholic nurse "may not summon the official of any other religion for the express purpose of having him minister to members of his church." When I quoted this passage at page 119 of the first edition of this book, it made such a sensation in the non-Catholic medical world that, after many blustering denials in the Catholic press, the hierarchy quietly canceled the discriminatory rule. Without any fanfare, the following rule was incorporated in the "Ethical and Religious Directives for Catholic Hospitals," as published in a 1956 Jesuit manual:

> While avoiding odious proselytism, we must not be indifferent to the spiritual needs and desires of non-Catholics; and everything consonant with our principles must be done for them. In particular, when a non-Catholic patient asks to have his minister or rabbi called, this request should be honored.[27]

I have recited some gruesome particulars here primarily to show (1) how the Catholic hierarchy attempts to make Catholic nurses into diligent priestesses of the faith, (2) how Catholic hospitals are used as partisan and sectarian agencies in spite of public claims by the clergy that they are "community enterprises," and (3) how priests attempt to impose as much of their moral code as possible on non-Catholic hospitals.

4

The most serious defect in the Catholic system of control of medicine is its inelasticity, its resistance to innovation. The basis for this immovable conservatism is to be found in the alien and strictly theological machinery of supervision by Roman ecclesiastical authorities. No American doctor or woman sits on the control group of Catholic medicine, the Congregation of the Holy Office in Rome. It is slow-moving and completely doctrinaire. It takes many years to correct a medical blunder, and then the correction must be made in such a manner as to show that there has been no fundamental change in doctrine, but only inspired continuity.

I have pointed out how Catholic mothers are the victims of the medieval prejudices of this ecclesiastical system. These medieval prejudices are apparent in the handling of three other important problems of modern life, venereal disease, euthanasia, and the cremation of the dead. The Church's policies on all three of these questions are dictated by resistance to innovation.

The Church, of course, is "opposed" to venereal disease. Everybody is opposed to venereal disease. But the Church's techniques of opposing venereal disease are about fifty years out of date, and the whole American community suffers as a result. After World War I, the Committee of Special War Activities of the Catholic Church fought the presentation of special films against venereal disease prepared by the Department of Public Health of the federal government. Such films as *Fit to Fight* and *The End of the Road* were altered in deference to its criticism. The Church also campaigned successfully against the presentation of these pictures in public motion-picture houses after the Armistice of World War I. After World War II it continued its opposition through the ever-obedient Catholic War Veterans. When it was proposed in 1944 that a great educational campaign of advertising about venereal disease be conducted by the United States Public Health Service and other government agencies with the co-operation of business concerns, the national commander of the Catholic veterans declared that it was "poor taste and a direct affront to many millions of God-fearing Americans who avoid this filthy disease not because of man-made rules, but because they keep the laws of God." It might be pointed out that the Catholic commander was unduly optimistic. The director of the Army's venereal-disease program, answering him later in a speech, declared: "An eminent churchman, recently deceased, has contended that venereal disease is primarily a moral problem. One can only answer: If that be true, then the United States Army is twice as moral as it was in 1918, and six times as moral as it was during the Civil War period, for those are the relative venereal disease rates." [28] In June, 1946, the continued distribution by the Army of match-books containing printed information on the control of venereal disease was blocked by the Catholic War Veterans.

There are two primary reasons for this unwillingness to co-operate fully with public health agencies in fighting venereal disease. The priests wish to be the primary educators of the Catholic people on all matters of sex, and the Church wishes to

keep control of marriage regulations. The hierarchy fears that
compulsory health examinations before marriage will be the
natural outgrowth of wider knowledge of venereal disease, and
that such examinations will lead to the prohibition of marriage
for diseased persons. Several states already have passed laws prohibiting marriage for diseased persons, and the Church has opposed such laws. The Church does not officially oppose examinations but it denounces laws that prevent the marriage of the
diseased, as "unnecessary and imprudent legislation," "a trend
toward totalitarianism," and "intolerable tyranny." "The legal
obligation to obtain a certificate of good health before marriage
. . . implies a disguised form of the abuse of civil power, of its
intrusion into a territory of which it is not the sole arbiter," [29] says
Raoul de Guchteneere in his *Judgment on Birth Control,* which
was published under the Imprimatur of Cardinal Hayes.

Father Connell has gone so far as to say in *The Catholic
Mind:* "All the physical afflictions that can ensue from the marriage of a diseased person, both to the healthy consort and to the
offspring, are an immeasurably lesser evil than one mortal sin
which the marriage could avert." [30] What this ecclesiastical dictum
means in creating diseased American Catholic wives is made clear
in the November, 1946, *American Ecclesiastical Review* in the
following official question and answer for priests:

Question. Would a husband ever be justified in using a condom
when having relations with his wife—namely, if his only purpose is to
protect his wife from a disease with which he is afflicted, and there is
absolutely no possibility that she will ever again become pregnant?
Could he argue in such a case that what he is doing is no sin inasmuch
as he is not preventing conception?

Answer. . . . Even if his only purpose in performing the act in
this manner is to protect his wife from disease, he would still commit a
grave sin, for a good end does not justify the commission of an intrinsically evil act.

The Church's opposition to euthanasia, or mercy killing, is
historic, and is based partly upon the anxiety of the priests to keep
dying patients entirely conscious until they have received the last
rites. This opposition has become almost meaningless in recent
years because of improvements in pain prevention by modern
medicine. Even a cancer patient can now be greatly relieved with
drugs and the severance of nerves running to afflicted portions of

the body. The euthanasia movement, which was once a favorite target of the bishops, has gained most of its objectives indirectly.

In 1957 Pius XII himself made an important concession to those who had opposed the previous Catholic condemnation of any shortening of life in cases of incurable cancer. In an address to physicians and anaesthetists in Rome the Pope renewed his official condemnation of "mercy killing," but in describing the approved treatment for dying patients he climbed down quite gracefully from an impractical position:

> If there exists no direct causal link, either through the will of the interested parties or by the nature of things, between the induced unconsciousness and the shortening of life . . . and if, on the other hand, the actual administration of the drugs brings about two distinct effects, the one the relief of pain, the other the shortening of life, the action is lawful . . .[31]

The Catholic opposition to cremation remains unrealistic. Today when cremation is often the most hygienic and economical method of handling the problem of bodily dissolution in crowded modern cities, the American hierarchy is still forced to observe the Holy Office edict of May 19, 1886, that not only forbade Catholics to belong to societies which promoted cremation but also said that "the clergy must refuse public prayers and access to the church to the bodies of those who, while alive, ordered their bodies cremated." The Church permits cremation in time of plague and pestilence, but as long as the anti-cremation rule remains a part of the Canon Law, American priests must tell the faithful that this common-sense method of the disposal of the body is a mortal sin.[32]

5

In spite of official rigidity the dogmatists of the hierarchy have actually yielded one of their sacred medical principles, under the pressure of humane opposition, during the last decade. I refer to the Catholic doctrine on ectopic ("out of place") gestation or tubal pregnancy. In the total scheme of Catholic medical policy it is not very important—possibly not more than fifty American Catholic mothers die each year because of it—but the fact that it has been changed in spite of a decree of the Holy Office is tremendously significant.

In cases of tubal pregnancy—growth of the embryo outside the womb in the Fallopian tubes—the life of the mother is almost always gravely endangered. In fact, the abnormal condition is frequently not discovered even by the most alert specialist until the pregnant mother has already suffered some internal bleeding, and then immediate hospital operation to stop the hemorrhage usually is necessary to save her life. The one remedy that is universally accepted as essential in this condition is removal of the tiny embryo at the first possible moment, as soon as violent pain or hemorrhage has revealed the abnormal growth.

In such cases the tubal embryo cannot survive. To use the words of Dr. J. Clifton Edgar in his *The Practice of Obstetrics,* page 913, "the right of the child to be born alive does not enter into the question." When the growth of a human embryo begins in a Fallopian tube during its five-inch journey toward the uterus, the tube cannot distend beyond the size of a hen's egg, and the distention cannot continue for more than a few weeks. A common result of the abnormal swelling is the sudden bursting of the tube when menstruation is two or three weeks overdue.

The condition in such cases may be as grave as a burst appendix, and it is equally important to anticipate rupture if possible. If the ordinary expectant treatment is followed without any surgery, the mother's chances of survival may be less than one in three. The embryo at six weeks, when nature usually ends a tubal pregnancy, is a tiny and grotesque object with buds for arms and legs, a conspicuous tail, virtually no face, and no life prospect. This is the vague possibility of a being which, according to Papal doctrine, must not be directly removed even if a mother's life is sacrificed by refusal.

The application of the Catholic doctrine in such cases has disturbed many devoted doctors and priests. Can the sacrifice of a living mother be justified in order to rescue the soul of an embryo that cannot under any circumstances survive? For years the priests debated this subject in the American ecclesiastical journals, always approaching the subject from the authoritarian, theological angle, disputing the exactness of their opponents' quotations and the authenticity of sources. Apparently no priests cared to ask how a Catholic mother felt about it. The priests agreed graciously that an operation was permissible *after* a tube had burst, but their opinion was almost unanimous that it was more moral to sacrifice a mother than to excise a tube *before* it had burst. They sought to impose this doctrine on American Catholic doctors; in fact, they *did* impose it on the distressed doctors for at least a generation.

Father Patrick Finney, on page 135 of his approved *Moral Problems in Hospital Practice,* stated the doctrine:

> *Question 35.* In a case of ectopic pregnancy, which has been diagnosed as a case of unruptured tubal pregnancy, is it lawful, before the term of viability, to remove the unruptured tube with the living fetus, as a means of forestalling the danger to the mother's life, upon the rupture of the tube?
>
> *Answer.* No, it is not lawful. Such a removal is a direct killing of the fetus, and is therefore forbidden.

There is no doubt that Father Finney expressed the official Roman rule on the subject, and there is no doubt also that the doctrine had been made a matter of faith and morals in the Catholic Church. It was solemnly handed down on March 5, 1902, in almost the same words as used by Father Finney, by the Congregation of the Holy Office in Rome. And some Catholic medical manuals still cling to this archaic and unrealistic formula.

For once, however, American and British Catholics resisted a Roman priestly decree in the field of practical medicine. Perhaps some American Catholic doctors dared to ask themselves what an American jury might think about the problem. It is easy to imagine the struggle of conscience of a Catholic doctor in such a case. He could say: "If I sacrifice a mother for a *normal* unborn child, according to the directives of my priest, and the child survives, I can call that a reasonable Catholic choice even although many non-Catholics would not be so charitable. But if I sacrifice a mother for an embryo which has no prospect of life, what moral distinction is there between my Catholicism and homicide by neglect? What would an American jury say if the whole picture were fairly presented and I admitted that a patient of mine had died after I had refused to remove a swollen tube because my priest said that it was against the rules of the Church?"

Unfortunately, no clear-cut case of tubal-pregnancy homicide has ever come before an American jury, and now it will never come. The Catholic hierarchy has changed directives and begun a strategic retreat from an untenable moral position. The Jesuits are "re-interpreting" the Papal blunder of 1902 to fit the American conscience.

Father Henry Davis, in his *Moral and Pastoral Theology,* did not venture to defy the Holy See openly on this subject, but he gathered and published in his work the written opinions of scores of Catholic physicians to the effect that "tubal pregnancy is not only a pathological condition, but is far more dangerous than cancer of the uterus." [33] Then American priests began to quote this opinion cautiously. Finally, in the *Homiletic and Pastoral Review* of October 1, 1945, the Papal doctrine was thrown overboard gently:

> Medical men today are quite commonly agreed that tubal pregnancy constitutes a pathological condition and is as much a threat to the mother's health as cancerous uterus. The theologians of the past century who held that it was gravely sinful to remove an unruptured tube containing a living fetus, because such a procedure is direct killing, were right in their principle but wrong in their facts. . . . It is not direct but indirect killing.

It should be noted how tactfully the American priests corrected the Pope and the Holy Office. It was necessary for their own standing in the Church to save the hierarchy's face. They blamed the blunder on "theologians of the past century," and they softened the blow by saying that these theologians were "right in their principle." Actually the opinion that they corrected was not handed down by theologians of the past century but by the Pope and Holy Office in *this* century, and the principle of the decision was just as unscientific as the alleged facts.

A group of celibate cardinals in Rome, who had never studied medicine, had handed down a judgment that was too doctrinaire and inelastic for scientific medical practice. The enforcement of the rule was becoming a scandal in the practice of medicine in the United States and Great Britain. Something had to be done to protect the Catholic physician against the charge, which would ultimately have come before a jury, that the Catholic rule in effect prescribed homicide.

The priests justified the change in policy by saying that they had discovered that removing an unruptured tube was "indirect killing," which Catholic theology has always rated as permissible. This was a wholly fictitious piece of casuistry. The facts and principles of tubal pregnancy have not changed, and the removal of an unruptured tube is simply one kind of therapeutic abortion, no more justifiable than other kinds of abortion in cases where it is necessary to save the life of a mother. The truth is that the Church has begun to abandon an outworn dogma, but the priests dare not admit that the "unchanging" moral principles of the Holy See are ever modified. They must disguise the retreat from error skillfully.

In the latest Jesuit manual, *Medical Ethics,* Father Edwin F. Healy assures the reader quite cheerfully that "the Fallopian tube may be *removed* at once" by surgery when it is swollen, in order to save the life of a mother who is suffering from ectopic pregnancy; but if it is merely *slit open* and the wandering fetus *removed,* "this action would be gravely evil, for it would constitute a direct, unjust attack on the life of an innocent fetus. It would, in short, be murder." [34] Thus the more serious surgical operation, which permanently affects childbearing, is permitted because it conforms to the approved theology of the Holy Office, while the less drastic procedure is condemned.

Meanwhile the admiration of the observer for the skill of the Church's dialectitians in "adjusting" doctrine to a changing world is modified by the disturbing question: How many Catholic women died between 1902 and, let us say, 1945, while their priests were "right in their principle, but wrong in their facts"? It is certain that not as many died for this reason as for the Catholic refusal to perform therapeutic abortions. Only about one pregnancy in three hundred is ectopic,[35] and the choice between the life of the mother and the life of the embryo is not usually presented because the embryo is already dead when the condition is discovered. But the priests have realized at last that even one death in every fifty cases of ectopic pregnancy of American Catholic mothers—an estimated annual total of 92 deaths—would be in the long run too difficult to defend. So they have rejected an "infallible" moral judgment as adroitly and quietly as possible, and thus far there have been no excommunications.

Should sectarian hospitals which practice a distinctively denominational medical code receive public money? Should general taxpayers be assessed for any funds granted to hospitals that are owned and operated by churches? Are such grants in violation of the principle of church-state separation as enunciated in the First Amendment and interpreted by the Supreme Court?

These are questions on which many American churches differ. In general the Catholic Church welcomes public grants. It received more than $112,000,000 in federal money under the Hill-Burton Act in the first ten years of the operation of that act, about 80 per cent of the total granted to *religious* hospitals.[36] Some Protestant and Jewish religious organizations also accept such grants for their hospitals; but they do not have the exclusive and archaic rules of medical practice that separate Catholic hospitals from American public hospitals. In general, Protestant and Jewish hospitals have the same ethical rules for operation as public hospitals. Catholic hospitals, on the other hand, accept patients of all faiths freely—and therefore boast that they are essentially "public" institutions—but subject even non-Catholic doctors, nurses, and patients to the rigid limitations of the Catholic medical code.

Unhappily the legal and constitutional questions involved in the use of public money for such thoroughly denominational institutions has never been passed on by the Supreme Court in this century, since that Court ventured to discuss the modern applications of the First Amendment. Public funds have gone to Catholic (and other denominational) hospitals under an old (1899) case, *Bradfield vs. Roberts,*[37] which reached the fantastic conclusion that even all the monastic and other ecclesiastical rules of Catholic medicine, and the complete control of such institutions by religious orders, "do not in the least change the legal character of the hospital, or make a religious corporation out of a purely secular one. . . ." It is not surprising that Justice Rutledge, in his dissenting opinion in the Everson bus case, went out of his way to describe the reasoning of the Court in the *Bradfield vs. Roberts* hospital case as "highly artificial." Meanwhile, federal taxpayers are supporting Catholic hospitals very generously and these "mission enterprises" are expanding rapidly.

7

Sex, Birth Control, and Eugenics

1

NOBODY KNOWS EXACTLY WHERE the elaborate sexual code of the Catholic Church has come from. It has been developed by accretion over a period of nineteen centuries until, today, it is one of the most conspicuous parts of Catholic moral philosophy. Perhaps it ought to be called an anti-sexual code (even though the Church teaches that "a wife may not without sufficient reason deny herself to her husband") because the primary emphasis has always been upon the negative rather than upon the wholesome aspects.

Austerity was identified with virtue by many leaders of early Christianity. Two Popes, Clement VIII and Paul V, declared that anybody should be denounced to the Inquisitors of the Faith who declared that kissing, touching, and embracing for the sake of sexual pleasure were not grievous sins.[1] Father Henry Davis, in his *Moral and Pastoral Theology,* expresses a contemporary priestly view when he says that "sexual pleasure has no purpose at all except in reference to the sexual act between man and wife . . . it is grievously sinful in the unmarried deliberately to procure or to accept even the smallest degree of true venereal pleasure."

Freud's wisdom was not available to the Popes and theologians who first imposed celibacy upon a reluctant clergy, and they could scarcely be held responsible for failing to appreciate the gravity of the effects upon human nature of suppressing the basic human instincts. The usual attitude of American Catholic priests toward Freud is one of petulant anger. Bishop Fulton Sheen, according to the *Catholic Almanac* (1948, p. 790), described Freud and Karl Marx as the "two men who contributed most to the modern tragedy of the world."

The anti-sexual emphasis of early Christianity came partly from the Orient, where certain ascetic cults glorified celibacy, masochism, and dirt, and thus gave lazy men of that time a chance to escape from family responsibility without condemnation. The anti-sexual cults spread westward at the time when Paul and his associates were building the early church. Paul himself seemed to be distinctly anti-sexual, and some of his followers developed his teaching to such an extreme that by the third century Origen achieved victory over his lower nature by castrating himself. Leo XIII condemned castration early in its history, but for centuries choirboys were castrated in order to preserve their soprano voices for the choir of the Pope's private chapel. Following certain tendencies in Eastern religions and certain primitive taboos, early Christianity exalted virginity as a status of perfection, and the Church finally imposed celibacy by elaborate disciplinary measures upon almost all of its nuns and priests.[2]

Perhaps it would be more accurate to say that the Church attempted to impose celibacy upon almost all of its nuns and priests. The celibacy rule, embodied in Canon 132, is now recognized as binding on all Roman Catholic clerics except those of the Eastern rites. But for many centuries, particularly from the fourth to the thirteenth centuries, thousands of priests defied it by maintaining concubines. As late as 1332 a Spanish bishop, deploring the incontinence of the priests, exclaimed, "would that they had never promised continence, especially in Spain and Southern Italy in which provinces the sons of the laity are scarcely more numerous than those of the clergy." [3]

These weaknesses of the flesh, though still apparent in some Latin nations, have been quite generally overcome in the English-speaking countries by strict discipline and by constant propaganda in favor of the unmarried state. Pius XII gave that propaganda new emphasis in 1954 by issuing an encyclical, "The Preeminence of Evangelical Chastity," in which he rebuked those who "so exalt marriage as to rank it ahead of virginity and thus depreciate chastity consecrated to God and clerical celibacy." He followed this up in 1957 by a rather startling—and startlingly unrealistic—attack on the remarriage of widows. According to *The New York Times* of September 18, 1957, in an address on "The Greatness of Widowhood," he said: "Though the Church does not condemn a second marriage, she expresses her predilection for the souls who wish to remain faithful to their spouses and to a perfect symbolism of the sacrament of marriage."

Cardinal Gibbons went so far in his *Faith of Our Fathers* as to suggest that Jesus chose His closest disciples on the basis of their virginity, and that when He went to heaven He chose a special band of 140,000 virgin angels for the same reason. Today, Catholic theology, in pursuance of this theory of the exalted nature of virginity, represents the mother of Jesus as a *perpetual* virgin who had no other children except the miraculously conceived Christ Child, and Joseph also is represented as a perpetual virgin. It seems to be a constant source of regret to Catholic theologians that Peter, the putative founder of the Church, had a wife. Cardinal Gibbons interpreted an obscure and general passage in Matthew to mean that Peter "after his vocation did not continue with his wife." [4]

From primitive beginnings the celibate devotees of the Church have expanded and developed the Catholic sexual code until today it covers every aspect of sexual life from petting to homosexuality and rape. The Catholic moral manuals, in their specific descriptions of sexual matters, go far beyond any novel ever banned by government censors. One reason such frankness is permitted in print is that the most specific sexual descriptions are printed in Latin.

The authors of these manuals are sure that there is no sexual sin that a competent priest is not prepared to handle in a confession, and for every sexual situation they contend that there is a specific Catholic answer. "We need not be afraid, whatever we have to confess, of shocking the priest," says the Reverend John C. Heenan in *Priest and Penitent*. ". . . He [the priest] must plumb the lowest depths of human depravity, however unpleasant he may find the task, in order that, at no time, in his future ministry, can he be faced with a sinner whose particular difficulties he has not learned to solve. He must become in a sense hardened." [5]

The hardening is acquired by the modern priest by assuming wide authority as sexual expert in the confessional. If, for example, a Catholic girl is raped, the priest tells her that she may remove the offending male sperm by mechanical means within the first ten hours and still remain a good Catholic, but she may not, married or unmarried, perform such an act of cleansing under any other circumstances without definite risk of hell. If, after being raped, she fails in her efforts to remove the sperm, "once conception has taken place, nothing may be done." [6]

If a Catholic doctor is asked to test the potency of a husband who seeks medical advice in establishing a family, he may direct the man and wife to have intercourse and then remove the male sperm for testing immediately afterwards, but if the husband should secure such spermatazoa for the microscope slide by other means then both the doctor and the husband are guilty of mortal sin.[7]

One can imagine the astonishment and bewilderment of Jesus if He returned to this mortal sphere and heard members of the Catholic hierarchy expounding these tortuous and detailed sexual regulations as a necessary part of His teaching. The Biblical evidence is absolutely clear that Jesus never said anything specific about birth control, large families, sexual perversion, masturbation, or sterilization. He never established a celibate priesthood or directed believers not to marry unbelievers. His most celebrated comment on sexual ethics was a stinging rebuke to a group of Pharisees in the presence of the woman taken in adultery: "He that is without sin among you, let him first cast a stone at her."

The absence of divine authority in sexual matters has not greatly embarrassed the Catholic hierarchy because the Church has developed its own techniques for plucking selected precedents out of history. Today, as the hierarchy gains strength in the genial and tolerant climate of America, the Catholic sexual code is being asserted with increasing aggressiveness. Sometimes it is adorned with all the latest clichés of science by earnest young Ph.D.'s who write theses supporting the sexual views of St. Thomas Aquinas, himself a celibate. More often the code is imposed upon reluctant congregations by routinely schooled priests with a confidence that amazes Protestants and Jews. Non-Catholics can find no warrant for such doctrines in their own scriptures.

An important corollary to the Catholic sexual code is that all sexual education for Catholic children should be under celibate priestly control. The state is not competent to educate in such matters because it may disregard Catholic fundamentals. Hence sex education in public schools is denounced as inappropriate, and the priest is exalted as the most suitable director of sexual education for the child. "We protest in the strongest possible terms against the introduction of sex instruction into the schools," said the Catholic bishops of the United States in an official pronouncement on the subject in 1950.[8]

In general, the priests emphasize reticence and "modesty" in sex education and deplore frank speaking. They underscore the dangers of premature knowledge in the young, in spite of the fact that scientific studies of the subject indicate that children acquire information or misinformation very early. The Kinsey report on males was denounced vigorously by the National Council of Catholic Women in 1948 as "an insult to the American people." The second Kinsey report (on women) almost produced apoplexy among the priestly editors. Archbishop Paul Schulte of Indianapolis called his fellow Hoosier "a cheap charlatan." [9]

One of the most noted writers of the Paulist Press, Father Martin J. Scott, says in his *Marriage Problems:*

It has always been a problem with good people what policy to pursue with regard to sex instruction. Modesty is the guardian of purity. Modest people are ordinarily pure in thought and deed. Knowledge of evil does not keep people from evil. . . . Our predecessors got along without all the sex instruction that is now ruining so many under pretext of educating them. The purest and healthiest nations of the world have been those least acquainted with sex knowledge.

The Church opposition to co-education is entirely consistent with this attitude. Pope Pius XI declared that co-education was "false also and harmful," and that in general the rule against it must "be applied to all schools, particularly in the most delicate and decisive period of formation, that, namely, of adolescence." [10] The gospel is respected in most Catholic colleges, where men and women are carefully segregated, but the Church has found it too expensive to put in operation in all high schools. Two new Catholic high schools in Buffalo have recently created a "coinstitutional not coeducational" system, with separate classes for boys and girls, but with common use of libraries, lunch rooms, etc.

2

The Church's opposition to birth control has now become the most important part of its sexual code. Perhaps Catholicism's unrealistic attitude on this subject goes back in part to the negative attitude of celibate priests toward the enjoyment of married life. If sex is essentially sinful, then its enjoyment should be counterbalanced by certain obligations and penalties. In the Augustinian conception the sexual act was sinful in itself, and the essence of the original sin in the Garden of Eden was the concupiscence which accompanied the act of generation. For the priest the method of escape from this sin is perpetual virginity. Ordinary people compensate for their sin by fulfilling their obligation to create children. If this aim of producing children is not consciously held in the marriage bed, at least the possibility of procreation must be accepted as a divine blessing by the dutiful Catholic. The dutiful Catholic must not use medical or mechanical devices to avoid his duty. So runs the Catholic philosophy that lies behind the opposition to birth control.

Probably no policy in the history of the Church has excited more widespread opposition and defiance than the priestly prohibition of birth control. The priests frequently report that the enforcement of the anti-birth-control rule causes them more trouble than all other regulations of the Church combined. The present rigid policy seems to have been adopted with some hesitation because of conflicting views among Church leaders. As late as 1926 in Rome a high dignitary of the Church informed Dr. Robert L. Dickinson, noted American gynecologist, that opinion among officers of the Roman Curia was about evenly divided concerning recommendations to be made for or against birth control in general. "But I fear it will go reactionary," he said. Four years later Pius XI "discovered" that Christianity and birth control were incompatible.

The theologians had been reactionary on this subject for several centuries. In the thirteenth century St. Thomas Aquinas declared in his *Summa Theologica* that every carnal act from which generation cannot follow is "a vice against nature." [11] Like so many of the beliefs of St. Thomas, this doctrine on birth control was derived from dogmatic and theoretical speculation, not from any scientific observation of family life.

Apparently the few Catholic colonists who came to America in the early days did not establish any tradition that Catholics should take a leading part in fighting birth control. The first American laws on the subject were not produced or noticeably influenced by Catholic pressure. Of course, modern contraception was scarcely possible in the first part of the last century, since the vulcanization of rubber was not discovered until the forties and Pasteur did not lay the basis for modern antisepsis until the fifties. Respectable discussion about birth control was scarcely known until the twentieth century, and there was no organized movement in its behalf in the United States until 1914.

In the seventies and eighties of the last century contraception was classed by most people with illegal obscenity, partly because they did not quite understand what the concept meant. In the so-called Comstock law, a federal statute of 1873 that forbade the use of the mails for obscene, lewd, and lascivious literature, contraceptive information and devices were included almost by accident.

It was sixty-three years after the passage of the general obscenity statute by Congress before the federal courts in 1936 finally cleared up the interpretation of the law by permitting the shipment of birth-control supplies and contraceptive information in interstate commerce where needed for the "well-being of the patient." Many states put "little Comstock laws" on their statute books, repeating the ambiguous phrases of the federal law. After the federal courts had interpreted the federal law, it took a long time for state courts to bring their interpretations of state law into line with new knowledge, and some of them have not yet passed on the chief issues involved. Today several states still have ambiguous obscenity laws on their statute books which reactionary and Catholic-dominated courts could twist into prohibitions against contraceptive advice. Nineteen states do not mention contraception specifically in their laws; twenty-seven allow contraception as a legitimate feature of the practice of medicine either specifically or by necessary implication.

Law or no law, contraceptive material is sold almost everywhere in the United States today. Sometimes it is sold under the obvious camouflage label "For the prevention of disease only." The editors of *Fortune* estimated that the contraceptive industry did a prewar business of $250,000,000 a year in the United States and had 300,000 outlets for its products.[12]

Two states where Catholic politicians are very subservient, Massachusetts and Connecticut, still interpret their statutes as forbidding doctors to give birth-control counsel to their patients. In these states, however, as many contraceptive devices are sold proportionately as in other states. The only apparent effect of the adoption of the Catholic policy by the state governments is to deny accurate information to the poor and the uneducated.

Although the Catholic Church did not play an important part in the opposition to birth control in the United States before 1914, it took the lead against Margaret Sanger as soon as she had launched a formal birth-control movement, and in 1930 the hierarchy became the world's contraceptive enemy No. 1. Just why Pope Pius XI finally slammed the door on all kinds of contraception as late as 1930 is hard to understand. His pronouncement on the subject in December, 1930, was timed to collide directly with twentieth-century science at the moment of its greatest prestige. In one respect Pius XI's pronouncement was even more untimely than Pius IX's edict on Papal infallibility in 1870, since it invaded a field of practical medicine unfamiliar to celibate priests.

He announced in one section of his famous encyclical on *Christian Marriage* that birth control is "against nature" and that "any use whatsoever of matrimony exercised in such a way that the act is deliberately frustrated in its natural power to generate life is an offence against the law of God and nature, and those who indulge in such are branded with the guilt of grave sin." [13] He made an exception, however, in regard to periodic continence and intercourse during a "safe period," which he specifically permitted.

Pius XI could find no Biblical authority for his extreme position on contraception so he manufactured the "authority" out of an irrelevant story in the Old Testament, by overemphasis and distortion. He used the story of Onan in Genesis 38 that relates how Judah ordered Onan, his second son, to marry his brother's widow and "raise up seed" to him, and how Onan, not wishing to give his brother official credit for paternity under the system of Jewish law, spilled his seed on the ground, whereupon God "slew him also."

If this story has any moral, it is that all men who refuse to marry their brothers' widows should be killed. Indeed, that was the moral of the original story, since the Levirate law laid down the rule for the Jews that a man inheriting his brother's cattle and lands should also cohabit with his deceased brother's wife or wives and raise a direct heir for his brother's property. Onan's primary sin was defiance of a property law of the ancient Jews, a law that was abandoned at least two thousand years ago. This interpretation of the story is supported by the *Jewish Encyclopedia,* which points out that the law violated by Onan had a twofold purpose, "to perpetuate the husband's name and to prevent the alienation of the property. The widow is permitted to insult publicly an unwilling brother-in-law by loosing his shoe and spitting in his face." [14]

Catholic theologians have taken this ancient story of Onan, distorted its meaning by declaring that Jehovah slew Onan for his *coitus interruptus,* and inflated this "interpretation" into a whole system of social hygiene for the twentieth century. They have used their techniques of exegesis so skillfully that millions of American Catholics actually believe the statement that "God and Jesus Christ condemn birth control." During every campaign over a birth-control referendum in Massachusetts they blanket the countryside with billboards carrying the headline BIRTH CONTROL IS STILL AGAINST GOD'S LAW.

If some curious believers should ever question the dicta of their priests sufficiently to examine the whole story of Onan in Genesis 38, they would be sadly disillusioned. The unpublicized portion of the story tells how, after Onan had been killed for refusing to cohabit normally with his brother's widow, the widow covered herself with a veil, sat by the side of the road as a harlot, and seduced her father-in-law, Judah, bearing him twins. Judah, however, was not punished by Jehovah, since he had mistaken the lady for a professional. Catholic theologians have never explained why the ethical standards of the second part of this story should be any less binding upon the United States in the twentieth century than the moral deductions from the first part.

Recently the American Catholic press has added a new fillip to its anti-birth-control campaign by announcing that birth control is forbidden by the Ten Commandments. Father Raymond Neufeld, in the August 24, 1957, issue of the *Tablet,* official organ of the diocese of Brooklyn, published the following statements in his Question Box:

Q. Which of the Ten Commandments or the Precepts of the Church forbids the practice of Birth Control?

A. Artificial birth control in any form of contraception is forbidden all men by the Law of God in the Sixth Commandment of the Decalogue, not just Catholics in a disciplinary precept of the Church. . . . The Sixth Commandment "Thou shalt not commit adultery" safeguards the integrity of the person and of the marital union by forbidding the abuses of sex . . .

Adultery, according to Webster's Collegiate Dictionary, is "Voluntary sexual intercourse by a married man with another than his wife or by a married woman with another than her husband."

3

As soon as Pius XI gave the signal with an official pronouncement in 1930, the celibate theologians of the entire world increased the fervor of their attack on contraception. It would be hard to imagine a worse thing for the hierarchy to have done from the point of view of intelligent non-Catholics in the United States. From the sociological point of view it was the greatest blunder in the history of the Church. Since the early days of the birth-control movement when Margaret Sanger was sent to jail for her principles, birth control has won both acceptance and respectability in the United States. Almost all well-to-do people in the country practice it to some extent, including well-to-do Catholics. The Planned Parenthood Federation now lists more than five hundred clinics in the United States that give child-spacing services, of which many offer services to improve the fertility of married couples. Some six states include birth spacing in their public-health services. The right of married couples to receive birth-control counsel from their physicians has been endorsed by the Federal Council of Churches of Christ, the Central Conference of American Rabbis, the American Medical Association, and more than 96 per cent of American doctors who answered a questionnaire.[15]

It is now generally recognized that scientific birth control offers the best hope of reducing the enormous number of criminal abortions performed each year in the United States. "To fail to provide birth control is to foster abortion," says Dr. R. L. Dickinson in his *Control of Conception.* The *Cyclopedia of Medicine and Surgery* estimates that today more than one-third of all the pregnancies in the United States are "purposely interrupted," and it declares: "More women die from criminal abortion than from labor and its complications." [16]

Intelligent Catholics know these things and are rebelling against their hierarchy's medieval attitude on the subject of birth control. The Catholic author Harry Sylvester, in his novel *Moon Gaffney,* has a liberal Catholic say: "I think what I mind is the relish with which the clergy, many of whom do not understand the meaning of their own chastity, tell their people they must fill three-room flats with children on their twenty-eight dollars a week."

This attitude of Catholics is reflected in the independent

opinion polls on the subject of birth control, and in the use of birth-control clinics. In the clinics of the Planned Parenthood Federation, Catholic women use the facilities in about the same proportion to their numbers in the community as do non-Catholic women. National public-opinion polls have demonstrated that Catholic women do not follow their priests on birth control. When the *Ladies' Home Journal* asked its women readers in 1938 if they believed in the right to disseminate birth-control information to married couples, 51 per cent of the Catholic women answering the poll said "Yes." When *Fortune* posed a similar question in 1943, 69 per cent of the Catholic women said "Yes." The conclusion of an opinion poll published by the *Woman's Home Companion* in July, 1948, was that almost 80 per cent of American Catholic women have accepted the belief that "birth-control information should be made available to some extent; only one-fifth think it should be legally forbidden to everybody." Since the hierarchy will not permit a free vote on birth control within the Church, these unbiased polls constitute the only real index of Catholic sentiment on birth control; they show that the hierarchy is losing ground steadily in its extreme dogmatism.

The growing defiance by Catholic women, as well as men, has driven the priesthood into a corner. In self-defense the priests have resorted to systematic vilification of the birth-control movement. Sometimes they pretend, with assertions that have no medical backing, that birth control is likely to cause cancer, that it lowers or destroys the vitality and health of married women, and that it is a form of abortion. They frequently pretend that advocates of birth control do not want children, whereas their usual desire is for properly spaced children. They ignore the fact that the overcoming of infertility has now become one of the most important collateral services of the planned-parenthood movement.

One of the leading Jesuit writers of the United States, the late Father Daniel A. Lord, classed American wives who use contraceptives with prostitutes and called them "daughters of Joy" in his pamphlet, *Speaking of Birth Control,* which went into its twenty-second printing in March, 1946. "The advocates of birth control," he said, "are thorough materialists, to whom a child is just a little animal without any destiny beyond the grave or any relationship with the one whom Christ called our Father." [17] Father Dominic Pruemmer, in a widely circulated pamphlet published under the

Imprimatur of Cardinal Hayes, said: "Birth control is nothing else than mutual masturbation or unnatural lust." [18] Many similar frenzied expressions on this subject can be found in official Catholic literature.

Faced with increasing skepticism and revolt among their own people, the priests have turned to a Catholic birth-control formula of their own that is technically permissible under one interpretation of the general phrases of Pius XI's encyclical, *Casti Connubii*. Originally the formula was sponsored in this country by the very prelate, Cardinal Hayes, who had been responsible for directing New York Catholic police to break up a birth-control meeting arranged by Margaret Sanger. The new "discovery," published in official pamphlets,[19] is called the rhythm method. It is based upon the finding that conception takes place midway between menstrual cycles, about fourteen days before the next period. Catholics, according to this formula, may avoid pregnancy without sin by refraining from intercourse during a part of each month so long as they are submissively receptive to the arrival of an unwanted soul in case there is a miscalculation. The theologians call this rhythm method "natural" because it involves no medicine or contraceptive device.

Whether the rhythm method is "natural" or not, it is certainly a difficult and inferior method of birth control, as Dr. Robert L. Dickinson has pointed out in his authoritative work, *Techniques of Conception Control*. Any fright, slight illness, or journey may disturb the menstrual cycle enough to destroy a calculation. An attempt made in good faith by planned-parenthood leaders to educate the natives of India to use the rhythm method failed miserably. Four-fifths of all women vary five days or more in their cycles, and very precise handling of a calendar is required to make the rhythm method successful. Some specialists believe that the rhythm method allows only six or seven "safe" days a month for sexual relations without danger of conception, and they agree that abstinence during the balance of each month is one of the surest methods of destroying a marriage.[20]

The advocacy of the rhythm method puts Catholic theologians in a paradoxical position. For years the priests who discussed birth control attacked the conventional arguments for child spacing as morally mistaken. Now they are using many of those same arguments for the systematic regulation of planned intercourse in the Catholic pattern. The Catholic physician, Dr. Leo Latz, in his officially approved plea for the rhythm method, says:

> Burdens that test human endurance to the utmost limit, and to which all too many succumb, will be lightened. I speak of economic burdens, the burdens of poverty, of inadequate income, of unemployment, which makes it impossible for parents to give their children and themselves the food, the clothing, the housing, the education and the recreation they are entitled to as children of God. I speak of physiological burdens, the burdens of depleted energies and exhausted vitality resulting from a previous birth or miscarriage, the burden of chronically or temporarily adverse conditions of the heart, the kidneys, or other organs, or of conditions that threaten the life of the mother in case of pregnancy. I refer to psychic burdens, not infrequently more difficult to bear than any I have so far mentioned, burdens of uncontrollable fear, anxiety, irritability, of rebellion against God and His Church for seeming to make demands beyond human nature, beyond human power to endure.[21]

There is no doubt that by a strict interpretation of Papal prohibitions the constant use of the rhythm method may "deliberately frustrate" the conjugal act as truly as contraceptives. The priests accept this method as permissible only because they are fighting against such persistent and critical pressure for birth control among their own young married people that they must offer some compromise with reality. They advance the wholly specious distinction between "natural" and "unnatural" birth control to cover their slow retreat from dogmatism. If they were consistent, they would also oppose shaving, the removal of tonsils, and the straightening of teeth. Celibacy itself is far more "against nature" than contraception because it means the thwarting of one of man's most powerful instincts for the whole adolescent and adult life of an individual.

But reason and logic now play a decidedly secondary role in the Catholic war against birth control. The Pope has spoken and the doctrine against contraception must be defended as divine and eternal.

4

The front-line trenches in the birth-control battle are in Massachusetts and Connecticut because these are the only two

states in the Union that still make it illegal for a doctor to give
birth-control counsel to his patients. The people of Massachusetts
are about 51 per cent Catholics and the hierarchy is exceptionally
powerful as a political pressure group in that state. It has so ter-
rorized the state legislature by threats of pulpit boycotts that many
representatives are afraid to stand on their feet and fight for a
revision of the antiquated law.

Probably Catholic propaganda in Massachusetts has reached
the lowest level that it has ever attained in the United States. In
1940 the Reverend George S. L. Cannon, pastor of the Holy
Name Church of Springfield, Massachusetts, told his people that
"Margaret Sanger with her pail of filth . . . is coming to interfere
with the laws of our Commonwealth. She is coming to enlist the
aid of dog-loving women in changing the fundamental laws of our
state." In 1942, when the birth-control forces proposed a revision
of the law by a referendum that would permit doctors to give complete contraceptive advice to their patients, they were confronted
by one of the most fantastic campaigns of misrepresentation in
American political history. For many Sundays before the referendum election, priests fulminated against birth control as murder
from almost every Catholic pulpit in the state, and on the Sunday
morning before election, special circulars were distributed at
church doors saying that the proposed revision of the law would
legalize abortion. Catholics in Springfield were told that if they
voted for the revision bill they could not expect absolution. According to Professor Karl Sax of Harvard,

> Three of the major metropolitan Boston newspapers, and the only
> newspaper in Fall River, and the three major Boston radio stations,
> refused to accept advertising in favor of the amendment. At the same
> time three papers, *The Post, The Record* and *The American,* devoted
> columns of space to the vicious campaign of misinformation by the
> opposition and refused to print articles in favor of the bill. . . .[22]

In spite of this campaign, the birth-control forces lost the
1942 Massachusetts referendum by a margin of only seven to five.
When the next campaign for revision began in 1947, the Springfield hierarchy fired the opening gun by publicly discharging four
leading Protestant and Jewish gynecologists from the courtesy staff
of the Catholic hospital in Springfield because they favored a revision of the state law. The doctors were penalized as doctors for
their opinions as citizens. There was no charge that they had

abused the hospitality of the Catholic institution in any way. During the height of the 1948 campaign for revision, four more eminent physicians were dropped from the staff of a Catholic hospital near Greenfield for public espousal of birth-control rights. The Church in 1948 repeated many of the same tactics used in 1942 and won the referendum battle by about the same proportion after a campaign in which the birth-control amendment was described throughout Massachusetts as immoral legislation and an "anti-baby law."

In Connecticut, with a Catholic population of 48 per cent, six leading physicians were dropped by Catholic hospitals for favoring a change in the antiquated state law, and the hierarchy has defeated the vigorous drive for revision by holding the state Senate in line after birth-control forces have captured the House. The same story of defeat for liberal birth-control advocates has been repeated semi-annually for 25 years, down to 1957. Said Connecticut's Catholic Commissioner of Labor Danaher, in defying the strong backing for revision of the state's laws by leading professors, doctors, and clergymen: "Thousands of citizens join with me in a rebellion against surrender to decadence. . . . A vote for this bill is a vote to destroy this nation. Forbid it, Almighty God, forbid it!" "Decent birth controllers," said the Catholic *Transcript* of Hartford, "patrol the sewers of filth to find companions in their apostasy from decency. . . ." [23]

The discharge of eminent physicians from the staffs of Catholic hospitals in Massachusetts and Connecticut is quite typical of priestly tactics wherever the hierarchy has sufficient power to carry through a boycott program. The policy of discharge is imposed upon priests officially. Father Francis J. Connell, writing in the *American Ecclesiastical Review* of July, 1948, in answering a question as to whether a doctor attached to a Catholic hospital should be dismissed for attending a meeting which favored planned parenthood, said: "If he promises to sever his connections with the planned parenthood movement, he could be retained at the hospital. But if he refuses to make this promise, he should be asked to resign from the hospital staff. This ruling should be applied to non-Catholic as well as Catholic doctors."

I have mentioned the fact that Cardinal Hayes was responsible for the break-up of a birth-control meeting by New York Catholic police. The meeting was held in Town Hall, and Joseph P. Dineen, secretary to the then Archbishop Hayes, frankly admitted to *The New York Times* on the night of the raid: "Yes, we closed the meeting." [24] Similar acts of repression have been instigated by the hierarchy in many parts of the United States. In September, 1940, the Catholic hierarchy of Holyoke, Massachusetts, prevented an address by Margaret Sanger in the First Congregational Church by threatening a boycott of Congregational businessmen. The hierarchy of El Paso, Texas, tried the same maneuver with less success. An El Paso hotel owner who had granted permission for the use of a hall for a birth-control lecture was visited by representatives of the Catholic hierarchy who threatened a boycott unless the lecture was canceled. He hinted that if the Church announced a boycott, he might feel obliged to discharge every Catholic employee on his payroll. The boycott was never declared.

When the *Woman's Home Companion* published editorials favorable to birth control in 1938, the diocesan weekly, *Our Sunday Visitor,* denounced such opinions as "an insult to Catholic intelligence," and urged a nation-wide boycott of all Crowell publications, including the *Woman's Home Companion* and the *American Magazine.*[25] The boycott was a complete failure. The Catholic hierarchy of San Francisco forced the cancellation of an exhibition of the Birth Control Federation at the Golden Gate Exposition of 1939 after the space had been paid for, although a demonstration of the Catholic rhythm method was on display throughout the exposition on the Gay Way of the fair. The Catholic hierarchy of Binghamton, New York, forced a planned-parenthood booth out of the Broome County Health Fair in 1948 by similar tactics. In 1943 staff physicians at St. Elizabeth's Hospital, Elizabeth, New Jersey, were compelled to sign a statement that they would not advise on birth control in the hospital or *in their own private practice outside of the hospital.* "I agree," said the pledge, which was imposed under instructions from Monsignor Glover, "that I will not disseminate any birth-control information and will not be a member of any group or organization which favors birth control or other eugenic activities at variance with Catholic morality." [26]

Maternal-health centers offering contraceptive advice to patients who request it have been forced out of Community Chests in at least twenty American cities by ultimatums from the Catholic hierarchy that Catholic support would be withdrawn unless such maternal-health centers were removed from the organizations.

In New York City fifty-three Catholic charitable and welfare

groups, acting on directives from Cardinal Spellman's office, resigned from the Welfare and Health Council of New York City
because the motherhood centers of the Planned Parenthood Federation, after a stormy contest, had been admitted to membership
in 1953 by a vote of 317 to 259. Speaking for the Archdiocese
of New York, Monsignor James J. Lynch explained that the Catholic Church opposed "any violation of God's law" and therefore
could not co-operate with any groups that encouraged artificial
birth control.[27] (No Protestants or Jews threatened to withdraw
from association with Catholics in the Council because of the
brutal policy prescribed in some cases of childbirth by the Catholic
doctrine of the equality of mother and fetus.) The Catholic boycott almost destroyed the Council, and in 1956 it was ignomini-
ously "re-organized" into the Greater New York Community
Council with the agencies of the Planned Parenthood Federation
denied voting membership.

A similar surrender was forced upon the Planned Parenthood
Committee of Princeton, New Jersey, in August, 1955, when the
Catholic Church boycotted the Community Chest campaign because of the Committee's membership;[28] and in May, 1957, the
trustees of the United Community Services of Washington, D. C.,
by a vote of 45 to 43, denied admission to the Planned Parenthood
Federation of that city because of a threatened boycott by Catholic priests.[29] In Washington, in October, 1956, the hierarchy even
attempted to block an address inferentially favoring birth control
given over the Voice of America by the noted historian Arnold
Toynbee, who declared that "the problem of limiting the birth-rate
will have to be faced. The alternative is starvation." This, said
Monsignor Howard J. Carroll of the National Catholic Welfare
Conference, was regarded "by millions of Christians and non-
Christians alike as immoral and obnoxious." [30]

5

The hierarchy's claim to control the entire ethical code sur-
rounding propagation and childbirth includes the fields of sterilization, artificial insemination, population control, and the so-called
Rh blood factor. Behind the Catholic formula in regard to all of
these "quality" problems in human beings is the philosophy that
creating Catholics is a good thing in itself, and that, even if they
are diseased, feebleminded, and a menace to normal community

life, no *medical* act should be permitted to prevent their conception, their survival, or their freedom to produce other human
beings. Under such a theory of reproduction, eugenics is on the
defensive. "Medicus," whose priestly textbook I have already
mentioned, opens his section on eugenics for priests with the statement: "In our time there has risen a most dangerous movement
called Eugenics. . . . Human nature is more than an animal.
Therefore it must not be made subject to the laws of stock breed-
ing."

With this outlook upon eugenics, it is natural that the Church
should oppose all types of population control except "self-control"
within marriage. The hierarchy freely admits that self-control has
obvious limits. Hence the production of large families regardless
of quality or poverty is an inevitable and recognized result of
Catholic population policy.

Catholic sociologists refuse to concede that there can be any
such thing as overpopulation. The trouble with the world, they
declare, is not too many people but a poor organization of human
resources. "With supplies increasing in proportion to population,"
says the *Catholic Encyclopedia Supplement,* "there is no such thing
as overpopulation."

Such a statement meets with general ridicule in the world of
non-Catholic social science, and in self-defense many Catholic
economists pretend that advocates of population control have not
given due thought to economic reform. Actually, of course, advocates of planned parenthood and population control are usually
advocates of economic improvement also, and only in the segregated culture of the Catholic universities is there any divorce between movements for economic and for biological betterment.

Virtually all of the great population experts of the world
today believe that some form of population control, with child
spacing, is necessary to preserve minimum standards of social
decency.[31] The plain facts seem to make their position incontrovertible. Although modern scientific methods have enormously
increased the world's food supply, modern medicine is keeping so
many more people alive for so much longer, and the world's survival rate is going up so rapidly, that a population explosion is
bound to occur if the present rate of increase continues.

The *Demographic Yearbook of the United Nations* for 1956
showed a world daily increase of 120,000 persons a day, and an
annual increase of 43,000,000—approximately the population of

France. The United Nations statisticians predicted that the world's population of 2,700,000,000 might double by the end of this century, reaching a new total of 5,400,000,000.[32] The population of the United States is now increasing at a rate greater than that of India.[33] The "phenomenal decline in mortality" during the last decade is an event of unprecedented and revolutionary significance. If it continues indefinitely without a reduction in the birth rate, it will mean unspeakable horrors, especially in Asia, which already has more than half the world's population. It will mean also the kind of overcrowding that leads inevitably to war. William Vogt has emphasized these dangers in his *Road to Survival,* and has indicated that many experts consider the United States already overpopulated. Professor Earnest A. Hooton, head of the Department of Anthropology at Harvard, expressed the conviction of most experts in this field when he said in 1941: "The hypocrisy of certain organized religions and governments in endorsing deliberate killing in warfare, for whatever motives, and at the same time opposing the restricting of that fatal overproduction of low-grade human life which leads to warfare, should not be tolerated by the leaders of human biological science." [34]

American Catholic scholars cannot admit the truth of such statements. Vogt's *Road to Survival,* when it appeared in 1948, was denounced in the Catholic press as part of "a war against the child." Various spokesmen for the Church deny that the Church officially teaches Catholic women to have as many children as possible, but the denial will not bear analysis. At one and the same time the priests teach that a "wife may not without sufficient reason deny herself to her husband," [35] and that all contraception is a grave sin. The fear of extreme poverty is not accepted by the priests as a "sufficient reason" for avoiding surplus children. So the Catholic doctrine leads inevitably either to the overproduction of children or to the violation of a "divine" law.

When Catholic organizations choose "the Catholic Mother of the Year," they usually avoid this dilemma by choosing a mother of the upper classes whose husband earns enough money to support an oversized family. The "Catholic Mother" of 1948 had fourteen children, a husband with a very substantial income as a prominent Philadelphia attorney, and a mother who lived with her for twenty-five years and "took over the housekeeping." [36] The "Catholic Mother" of 1957 (ten children, eight living) was also the wife of an attorney who had been president of the county bar association of his home city, and the daughter of the president of the Union Brass and Metal Manufacturing Company. She was the possessor of a ten-room house with enough income to maintain it.[37]

The tensions and strains imposed upon the Catholic family by priestly rules for sex relations ultimately destroy many families. Bishop G. Bromley Oxnam of the Methodist Church brought this out clearly in an address in 1947 before the Planned Parenthood Association of Chicago:

> Roman Catholic insistence on continence as the virtuous method of spacing children is based upon ignorance of the place of conjugal love in the maintenance of the home and a vicious conception of one of the most sacred of human relationships. If we may assume that the normal family should be composed of from three to six children and we face the fact that the child-bearing years of the woman are about twenty-five, the Roman Catholic Church is recommending continence for approximately twenty of the twenty-five years. Psychologically, the inevitable frustration of such a practice means the destruction of the home, and it is therefore sinful. If continence is not practiced, then it means that a woman may be called upon to bear twenty children, which in present society, if we think in terms of the support and education of the child, as well as the life of the mother, is sinful.[38]

In reply to such realism the hierarchy can offer only the Papal defense that quantity production of Catholic souls outweighs all the personal suffering and frustration involved. Dr. Raoul de Guchteneere in his *Judgment on Birth Control* said bluntly:

> The value of progeny is not to be measured by physical qualities but lies entirely in that supernatural destiny which is common to all. Even the marriage of the feebleminded is forbidden only on the ground of their inability to make a valid contract and not on account of the possible quality of the offspring.[39]

American priests console themselves with the thought that their own celibacy provides a "solution" for the problem of over-population. Father Daniel A. Lord said in the thinly disguised fiction of his *Speaking of Birth Control:*

> But the Catholic Church long ago, perhaps without realizing it, solved whatever problem of overpopulation there might be. It stressed the fact that there is a state of celibacy. It encouraged men and women to marry and bring into the world large families; but out of those

families it asked for a generous supply of priests, monks and nuns who
would vow themselves to continuous chastity. Their example inspired
people of the world with the realization of the possibility of purity.
And at the same time the fact of their professional chastity kept them
from increasing the world's population. So without any preaching
about crimes against nature and by example of pure lives lived by men
and women, the Church removed any possible danger of overpopulation.[40]

6

In view of such determined complacency concerning overpopulation, it is not surprising that the hierarchy opposes all kinds
of eugenic sterilization, even when surrounded with the most careful safeguards against abuse. The theologians do not oppose sterilization as a penalty for crime because such opposition would bring
the priests into direct conflict with the enforcement of criminal law.
The Church even condones and accepts capital punishment. But
eugenic sterilization is another matter. Such sterilization, designed
to protect society against the production of feebleminded citizens,
is branded as "interference" with divine law. It cannot be coun-
tenanced even when applied only to those inmates of mental institutions who could thereby gain release.

This attitude has been imposed upon all American Catholic
doctors and nurses by the same Pius XI who ruled against contraception in 1930, and in the same encyclical. Before 1930 many
competent Catholic authorities argued that the state has the same
right to sterilize the feebleminded that it has to vaccinate children,
for its own protection. Then Pope Pius XI, in his *Casti Connubii,*
not only condemned sterilization of the feebleminded but said that
the government, in sterilizing the insane and feebleminded, is arro-
gating to itself "power over a faculty which it never had and can
never legitimately possess." This defiance of modern governments
was justified by Pius XI, who said that "the family is more sacred
than the State and that men are begotten not for the earth and for
time, but for Heaven and eternity." [41]

I have already quoted Father Francis J. Connell, who gave
the doctrine American application by saying, after he had declared
that no Catholic judge could ever approve euthanasia: "Similarly,
in those states which now prescribe or permit eugenic sterilization
for certain types of defectives and criminals, no circumstances can
justify a judge in giving a decision that the law should be put in

operation." It would be interesting to bring a test case in some American court to determine whether a Catholic judge, sworn to enforce the law of his state without reservation, could obey this ecclesiastical edict and still observe his judicial oath. If, in order to obey the Church, a Catholic judge violates his judicial oath after getting a Papal dispensation for the violation, he is considered blameless by Catholic theologians. He is obeying a "higher law," and the Pope is empowered under Canon 1320 to dispense with *any* oath.[42]

Fortunately, neither the people nor the courts of the United States agree that there is anything necessarily wrong in depriving an insane or feebleminded person of the capacity to reproduce by a simple and relatively painless operation which does not even deprive him of the satisfactions of sex. The Supreme Court of the United States approved sterilization of the unfit in a historic opinion written by Justice Oliver Wendell Holmes in 1927, with only one dissenting vote, that of the Catholic Pierce Butler. Justice Holmes said: "It is better for all the world if, instead of waiting to execute degenerate offspring for crime or to let them starve for their imbecility, society can prevent those who are manifestly unfit from continuing their kind. The principle that sustains compulsory vaccination is broad enough to cover cutting the Fallopian tubes." In commenting on the test case he added: "Three generations of imbeciles are enough." [43]

But the opposition of the hierarchy continues to hamper enforcement of the sterilization laws in the twenty-seven states that now have such laws, and to prevent the passage of adequate sterilization laws in other states.[44] The American Human Betterment Association, which is working for sterilization laws in all states, reports the same kind of threats against legislators in this field that the Planned Parenthood Federation reports in the field of birth control.

Most recent of the anti-eugenic campaigns of the hierarchy is the attack on contraception in Rh blood-factor cases. The meaning of the Rh blood-factor in producing subnormal children has been appreciated by obstetricians for only a few years. The problem in such cases is essentially this: In about one marriage in ten a woman with a factor in her blood known as Rh negative marries a man with a factor known as Rh positive. This mismatching of blood may produce a child with congenital blood disease and it may affect the health of the mother very seriously. The exact cause of the phenomenon is not yet understood in all its aspects, but careful studies show that about one in twenty-five of the children of an Rh-negative woman and an Rh-positive man develop congenital blood disease and severe jaundice. Usually the children can be saved, if they are born alive, by immediate, complete replacement of the blood. But in certain cases, if a mother has given birth to one child of this type, she should not have another child for several years, and in some cases she should not have another child at all. With recent advances in scientific knowledge, the specialists can tell quite accurately whether a particular mother should take the risk of having another defective child and what the chances are that such a child will be healthy.

The natural alternative in such cases, if parents do not wish to face the hazards of a second or third defective child, is contraception. Medical science is almost unanimous in favor of providing such an alternative in selected cases if the parents with mismatched blood desire it. But the Catholic hierarchy is no more willing to accept medical common sense in this field than it was to accept medical findings concerning tubal pregnancy before 1945. Contraception even after the second or third defective child in Rh blood-factor cases is still a grave sin in the official Catholic manuals. Father Alphonso Schwitalla, former Jesuit moderator of the Federation of Catholic Physicians' Guilds and dean of the St. Louis University medical school, described the priestly rule graphically in 1947:

A young married couple has an uneventful but intensely happy experience in the birth of their first child. The second child is born sickly with symptoms that are today but too easily recognized. The health of the child wanes and the child dies. The third child might be stillborn and premature; the fourth might survive the threats of delivery but may present a pitiable appearance with its characteristic facial habitus or, which God may forbid, its continuous convulsive state, and its accompanying mental retardation. . . .

The physician will counsel the application of one of his favorite contraceptive devices. It is here that the moral aspects of the Rh factor come into play . . . contraception is no answer to the reality of the suffering endured by the young married couple under those conditions; rather must the couple be safeguarded and strengthened and protected against the inroads of a false philosophy of life which would see in physical suffering the deepest and greatest of all human misfortunes and which would neglect for such a misfortune the sublime teachings of Christ Who by word and example taught the inexhaustible sublimity

of human suffering, the ennobling character of agony. . . . An ery-
throblastic infant is destined for the eternal bliss of heaven as much as
any other infant. . . .[45]

When one reviews the whole range of priestly dictation in
matters of sex, the conviction is reinforced that the twisted and
bizarre "principles" of the Catholic sexual code cannot be explained in rational terms. Some of these "principles" contradict
the most fundamental facts of human experience. Many Catholic
laymen believe that the whole priestly system of sexual dogma is a
direct result of celibacy, a compensation for thwarted instincts and
suppressed desires. They see in celibacy the explanation for the
restless pugnacity of the priests and the craving for authority, and
they see only one way to normalize and modernize the priesthood.
For centuries individual reformers have suggested a married priesthood.

Some governments and local dictators have tried to compel
priests to marry, but the Holy See has repudiated the attempt.
Likewise the Holy See has, thus far, resisted every petition from its
own priests to do away with celibacy although it may some day be
compelled to yield to pressure in this matter. Immediately after
World War I the new Czechoslovakia seemed about to reach a
healthful solution of the problem by establishing a married Catholic clergy for its national church, after the priests themselves had
voted by an overwhelming majority to abolish celibacy.[46]

The notion of this natural remedy for sexual extremism is not
unthinkable, since celibacy is a disciplinary requirement, not an
infallible dogma; it was ordained definitely as late as 1139 A.D.,
and it does not apply today to the Oriental section of the Roman
priesthood before taking orders. Young Roman Catholic priests of
the Eastern rites habitually rush to marry just before taking orders
because they are not permitted to marry afterwards. There is no
indication that the Church itself suffers from this modified rule,
although the Holy See is now moving to curtail the practice, and it
will not permit priests to marry a second time.

The primary reason why celibacy continues in the United
States may be as much economic as traditional or religious. Unmarried priests are able to live together cheaply on much less than
a family income. If celibacy were abolished for priests, it would
have to be abandoned for nuns also, and, as I have pointed out in
the first chapter on education, the educational structure of the

American Church rests upon unmarried nuns who work for maintenance only. In order to maintain its power structure, the Church is likely to continue the present priestly sexual code for a long time, even though that code runs counter to all that modern science has discovered about the basis of the normal personality, and even though the Church permits part of its priesthood to lead normal lives and to rear families.

The leading Catholic publishing house of Great Britain published a booklet in 1957, *Married Men as Ordained Deacons,* in which the author advocated the use of married deacons to "help ease the priest shortage, and . . . as a possible step toward the re-unification of the Christian Churches of the West." The quoted words are from the description of the book by America's leading Catholic paper, *The Register.*[47] But the *Register*'s editor hastened to explain that this was an item of news and not of editorial opinion. A great body of sentiment against celibacy exists in the Catholic clerical world, but no priest dares to express any negative opinion in public without precautionary, protective phrases.

8

Marriage, Divorce, and Annulment

1

MARRIAGE, SAYS THE Roman Catholic Church, along with some Protestant groups, is a sacrament.[1]

This statement has a good, safe ring, and most non-Catholics do not stop to think what it means. Many people feel a certain sense of relief that there is a large and powerful organization in the world working for the stability of the marriage relationship. So many present-day forces are working in the opposite direction that serious-minded people tend to welcome Catholic conservatism on marriage and divorce even when they do not accept Catholic formulas for their own personal conduct.

The statement that marriage is a sacrament implies a great many things that are not explicit in the words themselves. The doctrine does not mean, as many non-Catholics believe, that all marriages are sacred. It implies that a Catholic marriage, besides being a contract, is also a sacrament, and is thus distinguished from outside marriages, which are inferior. It gives theological sanction to the priestly policy of systematic discrimination against non-Catholic marriage.

In practice in the United States Catholic priests frequently "dissolve" non-priestly marriages of Catholics and non-Catholics summarily with greater speed than the most debonair judge would permit in the most casual Reno divorce court. I put the word "dissolve" in quotation marks because the priests cannot dissolve any marriage completely in the United States without recourse to our courts, and technically they do not dissolve: they annul. With complete aplomb, they go through the motions of declaring that a valid American marriage does not exist, and when non-Catholics are involved with Catholics, they often do this with studied unconcern for the traditions of non-Catholic marriage. When Catholics

185

alone are involved in a marriage, the priests are much more cautious about any move to annul it. Then they require elaborate and detailed "evidence" to prove that the marriage was never consummated, or that it was not a bona-fide affair. If the evidence meets the technical requirements of Catholic ecclesiastical law, the Catholic marriage courts declare a marriage annulled in Catholic law without any reference to American marriage law. For priests the marriage law of the Church is higher than American law.

When the Catholic hierarchy says that marriage is a sacrament, it means that marriage is not merely a contract between two persons regardless of their religion. It means that religious faith must always be taken into account in deciding whether any union of any particular man and woman is a "real" marriage or an immoral agreement for fornication. It means that the sacramental element lifts Catholic marriage to a high level as a channel of divine grace. This divine grace is lacking, naturally, in non-Catholic marriage. Marriage, according to this theory, is an ecclesiastical rite and not a civil ceremony. Its highest form must be sealed and celebrated before someone who has power over sacraments, and, in Catholic doctrine, only the priesthood of the Roman Catholic Church has this complete power. Hence, in general, no Catholic can be "really" married without his priest.

In spite of this rigid rule for Catholics, the Church is charitable enough to recognize the validity of Protestant marriage for baptized Protestants, even admitting that, in theory at least, it qualifies as a sacrament. But in practice priests are likely to treat Protestant marriages as quite second-rate. In fact, for many centuries the Church denied that Protestant clergymen had the right to marry anybody at all. Then, when the number of "bastard" children became embarrassingly large and "unmarried" families rose to positions of power in Europe and America, the Church reluctantly concluded that it must give up its efforts to control all Christian marriage. So the concession was made in the *Ne Temere* decree of 1908 and in Catholic Canon Law that Protestants can legitimately marry without benefit of priests.[2] But the Pope may reassert at any time his supreme authority over all Christian marriage and declare that no marriage of Christians anywhere is genuine without the special blessing of his priests.

Since most Protestants have little concern with the sacramental aspect of marriage, the average American Protestant who wishes to marry is free to ask either a clergyman or a government official to perform the marriage ceremony for him. American law recognizes civil and religious ceremonies as equally valid so long as a license for marriage is secured from a government bureau. In most American Protestant churches a bride's choice between a clergyman and a government official for her marriage ceremony is simply a matter of personal taste. Her church does not penalize her in any way if she chooses the non-ecclesiastical ceremony. It is assumed that marital promises are morally binding whether they are made in a parsonage, a church, or a courthouse. A non-Catholic American who had been married by a justice of the peace would be outraged beyond words if anyone in his own circle of faith and friendship asserted that he was less married than if he had been married in a church.

American Catholic priests cannot permit their people to take this tolerant and co-operative attitude toward all legal forms of marriage. They are compelled by Rome to support the narrow and exclusive Roman marriage system that has been transferred bodily to American shores from countries where the priests rule over the marriage policies of the government. Accordingly, the American Catholic Church maintains on American soil a whole elaborate system of ecclesiastical marriage, separation, and annulment that is outside American law and, supposedly, above American law. In reading the following pages, the nature of this dual system must be constantly borne in mind in order to avoid confusion. The American Catholic people, because they are Americans, must *always* obey American marriage law when they marry, separate, get a divorce, or ask for marriage annulment; and *in addition* they must obey Catholic marriage law if they wish to remain good Catholics. When they marry, separate, or secure an annulment in the American legal system, the priests do not recognize the moral validity of any of these acts unless parallel proceedings are conducted within the Catholic system.

The whole complicated system of the Catholic Church for marriage, annulment, separation, and divorce goes back to two key dogmas, a positive one and a negative one. The positive doctrine is that the Church has the supreme mission to marry, just as it has the supreme mission to teach. John G. Brunini, in his authoritative summary of Catholic faith, *Whereon to Stand,* declares that "the Church regards Matrimony as a sacrament over which she alone has jurisdiction, and jurisdiction which she cannot transfer; she cannot permit any other agency to take over the administration of those laws with which she has surrounded the sacrament." [3]

The negative doctrine is expressed not only by Mr. Brunini but also by the most liberal leader American Catholicism has produced, Monsignor John A. Ryan: "According to the Catholic position, the State has no right to make laws affecting the validity of the marriage of baptized persons. . . . She does not admit that human welfare, or social welfare, is promoted by State recognition of any marriage that she pronounces invalid, nor by State prohibition of any marriage that she declares to be valid." [4] Monsignor Ryan's interpretation is based squarely upon Canon Law, for Canon 1038 declares: "The supreme authority of the Church alone has the right to authentically declare in what cases the Divine law forbids or annuls a marriage." [5]

There you have the Catholic marriage gospel in its full presumption. The Church not only claims the right to govern all marriages of its people but also denies the right of the government to pass laws in conflict with its own rules. The most that the hierarchy will concede to any government is that the people have the right to adopt certain rules concerning the purely "civil effects" of marriage. The government, for example, may compel all brides and grooms to register with a government bureau and secure a license, or it may prohibit marriages below a given age. The priests tell their people that they should obey such regulatory laws because they are not of the essence of marriage. As Brunini puts it, "the State is without power to function in the spiritual realm, nor can it be given it. Hence the Church commands that all her children observe the marital laws which both she and the State have established, *in so far as those of the latter do not conflict with her own.*" [6] (Italics supplied.)

This claim is contrary to the spirit and the letter of American law and American tradition, but in this respect the American Catholic bishops have no choice. They are heirs to the ecclesiastical traditions of medieval Europe, and no Boston Tea Party in the field of Catholic marital law has yet given them freedom from those traditions.

The Roman Catholic Church, it should be remembered, acquired power over marriage in Europe at a time when the conception of the modern, democratic welfare state was unknown, and it continued to hold power over marriage rites in many states largely by default. For perhaps three hundred years after the eleventh century the Church exercised complete authority over both the religious and the civil aspects of marital life, and during that period the Christian courts were the only courts in which married people could seek redress from grievances. The priest determined whether men and women were living in sin or in holy matrimony. Not until the Reformation did the institution of marriage achieve any freedom from ecclesiastical control, and not until the last century did all the European governments establish marriage as an independent civil institution available to all persons on a basis of equality.

The Roman Church has fought the modern trend toward democratic control of marriage with every weapon at its command, particularly in countries like the United States where the people believe that they have the same right to pass marriage laws that they have to pass any other laws. The American priesthood has begged, threatened, and excommunicated in order to hold American Catholics in line with the marriage rules laid down for European Catholic nations. The Church has never abandoned one iota of its sweeping claim that the marriage of a Catholic performed by a government official is not a marriage at all but, as Pius IX described it, "low and abominable concubinage." [7]

2

Because the Catholic marriage system grew up gradually over a period of several centuries, Catholic marriage law is exceedingly complex. In many respects it is obscure, and it has many historical features that are quite meaningless to Americans. In essence there are five grades of marriage in the Catholic system and four types of nullity. (These classifications are wholly my own, and do not correspond to the formal Catholic classifications.)

Grade 1: "True" marriage of Catholics by a priest. This is the highest form of marriage, valid and absolutely indissoluble.

Grade 2: Mixed marriage of a Catholic with a Protestant, Jew, Greek Orthodox, or pagan, performed by a Catholic priest after all the *cautiones* or pledges (which I shall describe later). Such marriage is valid only with a special dispensation by a local bishop or the Pope, and it is so decidedly second-rate that it cannot be performed in a Catholic church without special permission.

Grade 3: Protestant marriage for Protestants. This is less sacred than Catholic marriage but "legitimate."

Grade 4: Pagan, Jewish, and Moslem marriage for non-Christians. This, also, may be "legitimate" but it is distinctly inferior, one level below Protestant and Greek Orthodox marriage because there is nothing sacramental about it.

Grade 5: Civil marriage for non-Catholics. This is tolerated by the Church as an unpleasant necessity.

Below these five grades of legitimate marriage are four types of "attempted" marriage that are either voidable or completely void. They may be listed as general types of invalid marriage.

Type 1: Mixed marriages involving a Catholic and non-Catholic without special dispensation by the Church and solemn pledges by the bride and groom. These are absolutely void under Canons 1061 and 1070.

Type 2: Mixed marriages of a Catholic and a non-Catholic before a non-Catholic clergyman or justice of the peace. These also are absolutely void under the same canons.[8]

Type 3: Marriages of Catholics by government officials or non-Catholic clergymen except when the parties are in danger of death. These are invalid under Canons 1098 and 1099.

Type 4: Catholic marriages never consummated, and several other types of marital union that remain legitimate until they are proved void by credible evidence and the action of an ecclesiastical court.

The non-Catholic who reads these classifications is bound to ask what is the point of such elaborate provisions. He would ask the same question with even more bewilderment if he could run through the enormous volumes of detailed rules for procedure in Catholic marital cases, which are published by American Catholic publishers. He would view with dismay the pretentious, competing system of Catholic law that exists in the United States today, with its marital courts, ecclesiastical lawyers, appellate machinery, lengthy affidavits, and tedious transcripts of evidence. If he could find a priest who would answer questions frankly, he would probably be told that modern American priests are bored with and resentful of the whole paraphernalia of medieval Catholic marriage institutions that have been imposed upon American Catholics by the Roman Curia. He might be told also that, in spite of the imposing "front" of the separate Catholic marital system in this country, most American Catholics live, love, marry, and get divorced in much the same manner that non-Catholics live, etc., because, after all, they are Americans who live under American law, and American law is still supreme over Catholic law even in the field of marriage.

3

For non-Catholics the most offensive part of the Catholic marriage code is the rule on mixed marriages. A non-Catholic who wishes to marry a Catholic must enter the marriage relationship not as an equal but as a lowly subordinate. Catholics must marry Catholics; that is the general rule of the Church. It is not merely an *error* for a Catholic to marry a Protestant or a Jew; it is a *sin*. To marry a Protestant is a minor sin; to marry a Jew is a more serious sin. In any case a Catholic who marries either a Protestant or a Jew without special dispensation and written promises to rear an exclusively Catholic family commits a mortal sin and is subject to immediate excommunication.

This system of family segregation and family subjection to priests has been consecrated by the highest agencies in the Church and expressed in Papal encyclicals and Canon Law. There is nothing in American Protestant or Jewish practice that quite equals its narrowness and severity.[9] Protestants and Jews often frown upon mixed marriage, but they do not deny the validity of the marriage of Protestants and Jews before Catholic priests. "The Church," says the Canon Law, "forbids most severely and in all countries marriage between a Catholic and a heretic or schismatic. If there is danger of perversion for the Catholic party and the offspring, such marriage is also forbidden by the Divine law." [10] In practice "heretic" means Protestant, and "schismatic" means Greek Orthodox. Jews, Moslems, and, in general, non-baptized persons exist on a special tertiary level.

It was this mixed-marriage rule of the Church that kept former King Michael of Rumania from marrying Princess Anne of Bourbon-Parma in a Catholic church, in June, 1948. The bride was a Roman Catholic, and Michael, as a member of the Greek Orthodox Church, refused to promise that all their children would be brought up as Roman Catholics. The Church therefore refused to marry him, and declared that his marriage to Anne with a Greek Orthodox ceremony was "no marriage."

The Church even forbids every Catholic individual involved in a mixed marriage to participate in a Protestant marriage ceremony *after* he has received the blessing of his Church in a valid Catholic ceremony. Theoretically the Protestant ceremony nullifies the previous Catholic one. The famous Olympic weight-throwing champions, Harold Connolly and Olga Fikotova were the victims of this prohibition in 1957 when they were married in Prague in three ceremonies, civil, Catholic, and Protestant.[11] (Harold was an American Catholic and Olga a Czech Protestant.) The Church did not object to the civil ceremony, since it is required by law, but Harold "automatically incurred the penalty of excommunication" when he agreed to an additional Protestant ceremony. The announcement of the penalty caused such a storm of angry protest that the Church later indicated that Harold could stay in the fold after due penance.

The severe Catholic prohibition of marriage with Jews or other non-Christians is contained in Canon 1070, which reads: "A marriage contracted by a non-baptized person with a person who was baptized in the Catholic Church or who has been converted to it from heresy or schism, is null." The impediment to marriage between a Catholic and a Jew is called an "annulling impediment," whereas the impediment to marriage with a Protestant is only a "prohibitory impediment." Even when Catholics receive a special dispensation to marry non-Catholics, they cannot receive a Nuptial Mass (Canon 1102), and they can be married in a church only by another special dispensation.

If the general rule against marriages with Protestants, schismatics, and Jews were strictly enforced, the divisive effects upon American life would be appalling. We would have an American community split cleanly down the middle by religious bigotry. The sorry tale of Pakistan and India might be repeated in this hemisphere.

The actual situation that many families face today as a result of the Catholic rule on mixed marriage is equally serious for them. Thousands of American homes have a Catholic wife and a non-Catholic husband, or a Catholic husband and a non-Catholic wife, living in continuous tension because priests habitually interfere to enforce the pledges exacted at the time of marriage.

Catholics are conditioned from the time of childhood to accept and to endure this priestly interference, and to look down upon marriage that is not controlled by priests. Discrimination against Protestants and Jews in marriage is part of the curriculum of the parochial schools. Little Catholic children are taught that it is wrong to "keep company" with non-Catholic boys and girls. A teacher-training handbook written by two Sisters of Notre Dame and published under the Imprimatur of Cardinal Spellman offers these typical "examples" for class discussion:

> Marian refused to go out with Gilbert, a non-Catholic, because she feared a friendship might form that would lead to mixed marriage.
> Ellen C., who was keeping company with a non-Catholic young man, felt that a strong attachment was forming which might lead to a mixed marriage. After a long struggle with herself, she gave him up.[12]

As Catholic children grow older, they are taught the rule of Canon 1099 that if they should be foolish enough to marry a Protestant or a Jew without the blessing of the priest, they would not be married at all, and the bishop could dissolve their marriage without any trial. So, millions of good Catholic girls in America are conditioned to approach marriage with non-Catholics as a phenomenon of low ethical significance. To be "really" married, they feel, they must be able to persuade their non-Catholic fiancés to accept priestly rules. Also, if they marry at a lower level, they are not obliged to take their marriage as seriously because there can be an ecclesiastical annulment.

When a Catholic girl finally decides to marry a non-Catholic, and the priest is unable to persuade her to abandon the notion, he has the power to grant her a dispensation if she observes certain conditions. If the prospective groom is a Protestant, the local priest or bishop can grant the dispensation. If the prospective groom is a Jew, the process is more difficult and complicated. No local American bishop has power to permit a Catholic to marry a Jew. Permission for such a marriage must be secured from Rome, and the cash "offering" for the dispensation goes to Rome.[13]

The Catholic girl who wants to marry a non-Catholic is told that her marriage will be absolutely void unless she can persuade the non-Catholic man to sign a written pledge agreeing to give his Catholic wife full freedom to practice her faith and to bring up *all* their children in the Catholic religion. Many American priests require in addition that every non-Catholic involved in a mixed marriage attend a six-session proselyting course in which the priest makes every effort to convert the non-Catholic to Catholicism.

Unless the non-Catholic groom becomes a convert before marriage, the bride cannot ordinarily be married in the church proper or receive the Nuptial Mass, even after both parties have signed the pledge requested by the priest. The official pledge required of the non-Catholic reads:

I, the undersigned, not a member of the Catholic Church, wishing to contract marriage with N.N., a member of the Catholic Church, intend to do so with the understanding that the marriage tie cannot be dissolved except by death, and promise her on my word of honor that she shall enjoy free exercise of her Catholic religion, and that all the children of either sex born of this marriage shall be baptized and educated in the faith and according to the teachings of the Roman Catholic Church.[14]

In addition to this pledge, signed in varying forms by both the Catholic and the non-Catholic, another pledge must be signed by the Catholic party "to prudently work for the conversion of the non-Catholic." Canon 1062 makes this second pledge compulsory.

The prenuptial agreements and records used by the Archdiocese of Milwaukee show that a Catholic girl who enters into a mixed marriage before a priest must not only sign all of the pledges I have just described, but also make a written pledge not to practice birth control at any time. She must declare in her signed statement that she will "hereby give to the Most Reverend Archbishop of Milwaukee as the representative of the Roman Catholic Church . . . the right to enforce each and every promise herein contained in the event of the violation of the same by either party or both. . . ."[15] This is a legal sanction for priestly interference in regard to such matters as the care of the children in the event that the Catholic mother should die.

Under these compulsory pledges, imposed upon all Catholic young people by Papal decree, no reciprocity or compromise with a Protestant or Jewish spouse is permitted. The non-Catholic must not attempt to persuade the Catholic to become a Protestant, for example. That is strictly forbidden. The boys born of the marriage cannot be brought up as Protestants and the girls as Catholics. Such a compromise is not permitted.

Although a large proportion of the non-Catholics who sign such humiliating pledges are men, the non-Catholic men do not carry out the promises as faithfully as women. It is part of the traditional chivalry of American men to cater to women in marriage as a proof of affection. The priests take full advantage of this tradition, but when the marriage ceremony has once been performed and the home established, there is a tendency for the mixed family to adopt the religion of the wife or no religion at all. Of course, the pledge to raise all children of mixed marriages as Catholics is not enforceable in an American court.[16] Parents are free to bring up their children in the faith which they currently choose.

For most Americans there is something distinctly unsporting in taking advantage of the high exaltation of young love to impose upon one of the parties in marriage a proselyting agreement. Many non-Catholics evidently sign such a pledge with mental reservations because they consider it coercive. Catholics as well as non-Catholics violate the pledges so frequently that the priests are thoroughly alarmed. The fundamental fair-mindedness of the American people is conquering the narrowness of priestly practice. Young Catholics are rebelling against the use of marriage to obtain "converts" and to establish Catholics as a separate class in a tolerant American community. There are at least 85,000 priestly mixed marriages a year in the United States, and recent studies by priests show not only that such marriages are increasing rapidly in spite of ecclesiastical pressure but also that a very large proportion of mixed families are lost permanently to the Church.

Professor John J. Kane of Notre Dame has predicted that Catholic mixed marriages are likely to increase in the next generation to between 40 and 50 per cent—they are now averaging between 25 and 35 per cent.[17] This prediction, presumably, concerns only the priestly mixed marriages that are recognized by the Church as valid. There may be as many as 50,000 other mixed marriages a year without benefit of a Catholic priest. It is quite possible that even now more than half of all marriages involving Catholics in the United States are mixed marriages.

It is generally admitted by the priests that both the principals and the children of such mixed unions are falling away from the Church in "appalling" numbers. A recent study summarized in the Catholic weekly *Ave Maria* estimated that the pledges to bring up children as Catholics in mixed marriages are kept in only about 30 per cent of the cases.[18]

This intermingling of the Catholic people with people of other faiths is causing the American hierarchy great anxiety. Father

Francis J. Connell speaks of "the terrible inroads on the Catholic faith caused by mixed marriages." One of the Church's leading theologians, Father Stanislaus Woywod, has advocated the complete abolition of all dispensations for mixed marriage in the future. "We must keep our young people," he said, "from unnecessary association with non-Catholics by persuading them, as much as may be, to attend Catholic high schools and colleges." [19]

DON'T MARRY A CATHOLIC, shouts an advertising headline published in many newspapers in 1956 by the Religious Information Bureau of the Knights of Columbus. "From long experience," the ad says, "the Church knows that the permanence and the harmony of family life are often jeopardized by mixed marriages, and, because of the religious division, the children often grow up in an atmosphere of religious indifference." [20] The K. of C. ad might have said also "in an atmosphere of tension, bitterness, and distrust, produced largely by the interference of priests who take upon themselves the responsibility of enforcing the mixed marriage pledges." The divorce statistics bear out this hypothesis. The divorce rate in mixed marriages is more than twice the rate for marriages of unmixed faith.[21]

4

"The valid marriage of Christians, consummated by the conjugal act," says Catholic Canon Law, "cannot be dissolved by any human authority for any reason; death alone can dissolve the bond." [22] We shall see in a moment that other things besides death *can* dissolve the bond if Catholic petitioners are resourceful and lucky enough, but in general it is true that the rule of the Church is: No divorce for Catholics who marry Catholics with a full Catholic ceremony.

The theological basis for this rule is a trifle more substantial than the Biblical basis for the Church's birth-control doctrine. Two of the four statements of Jesus about divorce in the New Testament reflect total opposition to divorce, while two others indicate acceptance of divorce for adultery and the right of remarriage for the innocent party.[23] Christendom is divided in its interpretation of these Biblical passages. The majority of American Christians do not take either the mild or the severe passages as binding directives on believers today. The burden of proof is on those who declare that the founder of Christianity intended to institute a new set of rules about marriage and divorce, since the Jewish law permitted some divorce.

The Catholic hierarchy in this country goes to great extremes to maintain the letter of the Catholic divorce rule. The hundreds of thousands of young Catholics who married hastily and not too wisely during the war period are told that, no matter what the provocation, they may never remarry and start life over again. The prohibition against the marriage of divorced persons is nominally carried so far that a Catholic social worker may not, under threat of excommunication, advise a Catholic woman to marry her lover even when she is openly living in sin with him and both are eligible for marriage under American law. Father Francis J. Connell says:

> For even though her position is at stake, the social worker may not give advice that will indirectly induce her client to violate the law of God. Similarly, when the social worker finds a couple living together unmarried and incapable of entering marriage because of some impediment of divine law (but permitted to marry by civil law) she may not suggest a civil marriage, even as a mere formality to obtain civil effects. Indeed, in the United States, where the Third Council of Baltimore inflicts a censure of excommunication on a Catholic who attempts remarriage after a civil divorce, a social worker might so concur in the commission of this sin by her counsel as to incur herself the same penalty.[24]

This edict is handed down, as we shall see, by a hierarchy that permits nullification of marriages in its own courts on grounds that would be regarded as too flimsy for consideration in the courts of any state of the Union.

"The state," says the *Catholic Almanac* of 1948, "has no right to grant divorces since it has no authority to annul a valid marriage." [25] This flat denunciation of American legal principles places the American hierarchy in a somewhat delicate situation. Catholic moralists in the United States do not quite dare to instruct Catholic judges and lawyers to avoid all divorce cases. (This would disqualify many Catholic judges and deprive many Catholic lawyers of a living.) They resort to an elaborate moral make-believe to maintain the nominal existence of Catholic rules while these rules are ignored in practice. A Catholic judge may marry divorced Catholics if refusal might jeopardize his judicial position, but in that case he must admonish the sinful bride and groom privately of "the enormity of their sin and the invalidity of the marriage." [26] After he has administered a solemn oath to the bride and groom as a government official, he is obligated as a "good" Catholic to tell them that the oath is morally worthless.

Such a Catholic judge is also permitted to pronounce a divorce for Catholics under the casuistic theory, expressed by Father Connell, that "the act of the Catholic judge in pronouncing a divorce is merely an official declaration that the state regards the *civil* effects of marriage as no longer existing." He cannot dissolve the "real" marriage which was made in a church. This can be dissolved only by the Church. The Catholic judge must sign the solemn legal phrases of the American divorce decree with the mental reservation that he is not actually loosing the bonds of matrimony at all.

The Catholic opposition to sensible divorce laws is probably more important for non-Catholics than any other part of the hierarchy's marriage code because it affects every effort to secure honest and comprehensive divorce legislation. Our divorce laws, as everybody knows, have become almost as much of a national scandal as divorce itself. As divorces increase, the abuses of inadequate and contradictory state laws become more obvious. Hypocrisy and perjury are part of the daily routine in American divorce courts. A New York City investigation in 1948 revealed what every informed New Yorker already knew, that thousands of New York divorces are secured every year by fraud and perjury because the state's antiquated laws permit divorce for adultery only. The New York bar association demanded liberalization of the laws, but the Catholic hierarchy said "No." The "No" was still effective in 1957.[27]

Catholic political blocs in all parts of the country fight bitterly against intelligent liberalization of divorce statutes. The priests cannot admit that divorce may be at times an unfortunate but fundamentally moral remedy for a situation that is worse than divorce. Under their Roman instructions they must continue to oppose all rights of divorce for non-Catholics as well as Catholics. They must continue to say that every Catholic marriage is made in heaven, even if one party becomes an insane murderer and destroys the opportunity of normal life for a whole family.

It would be a mistake, however, to conclude that the Church always tries to preserve the home intact. Legal and permanent separation without remarriage is permitted in the Catholic system for many reasons, and among the reasons are some that are strictly denominational and theological. Sometimes, when there is a choice between preserving a home as a non-Catholic home and saving the Catholicism of a husband or wife, the hierarchy chooses the Catholicism at the expense of the home itself.

The Canon Law permits separation not only for adultery and habitual crime but also for simple differences in religious conviction "if one party joins a non-Catholic sect; or educates the offspring as non-Catholics." This rule is so sweeping that it is a ground for separation if a parent who has been married by a priest sends a child to an American public school without the priest's permission. In some cases it is also ground for the complete nullification of a mixed marriage.

When husbands and wives are separated because of some misconduct, Catholic priests are directed to place the children if possible with the innocent party, but not in all cases if the innocent party is a Protestant or Jew. In that case the Canon Law says that "if one of the parties is a non-Catholic, the Catholic party is to have charge over them, that they may be raised as Catholics, unless the bishop decides differently for the sake of the welfare of the children, always safeguarding their Catholic education." Under this rule Catholic education is officially placed ahead of general welfare. This rule explains why in the domestic-relations courts of the United States the representatives of Catholic charitable organizations frequently fight for the placement of children with a guilty parent in a separation proceeding when the guilty parent is a Catholic and the spouse is non-Catholic. The theory of this policy is that a bad Catholic is a better risk as a parent than a good Protestant or Jew because loyalty to the Church is of the essence of goodness.[28]

A similar emphasis and partisanship can be noted in the policy of Catholic charitable organizations in the placement of dependent children for adoption in our large cities. The preservation of their Catholicism is considered more important than the general quality of the home that is chosen for them. Even if the choice lies between a first-class semi-Catholic home and a much inferior practicing Catholic home, the Catholic charitable organizations choose the practicing Catholic home. They insist that the parents must have been married in a church to qualify as Catholic parents.

The Catholic hierarchy in New York has been particularly

possessive and narrow in blocking the appointment of Jewish probation officers in the city's Children's Court. It insists that Catholic children should be handled by Catholic probation officers. As a result, competent Jewish probation officers on the civil service list have been repeatedly refused positions in the Children's Court because of their religion, while vacancies have remained unfilled.[29]

The most striking example of the hierarchy's determination to put denominational interests first in domestic-relations courts came in 1957 in the famous case of Hildy McCoy Ellis, the six-year-old girl who was born of an unwed Catholic mother in Massachusetts in 1951, and finally possessed—in Florida—by Jewish foster parents, Mr. and Mrs. Melvin B. Ellis. Under a 1950 Massachusetts statute, foster parents are required to be of the same faith as the adopted child "when practicable." Most Americans would approve of such a law, if administered with discretion. Hildy's mother, not desiring to keep her child, had given her to the Ellises with full knowledge (they said) that they were Jewish. When the hierarchy heard of the preliminary adoption, the power of the state government and the complementary power of the greatest Catholic machine in American politics were united to take Hildy away from the Ellises and return her, not to her mother, but to a Catholic orphan institution and thence to an unidentified Catholic foster home.

Hildy had been treated with the utmost affection and tenderness by her Jewish foster parents. In desperation, they fled from Massachusetts to avoid a court decree ordering her return, and finally were apprehended in Florida. When the government of Massachusetts, aided by Archbishop Richard Cushing, attempted to bring the Ellises and Hildy back north for trial and separation, Governor Leroy Collins of Florida refused extradition in a historic edict which brought tears and cheers from millions of Americans.

The great and good God of all of us, regardless of faith, grants to every child to be born first the right to be wanted and secondly the right to be loved. Hildy's mother denied both of these rights to her. . . . It was the Ellises in truth and in fact who have been the persons through whom God has assured to Hildy these first two rights as one of His children.[30]

It is interesting to note the version of this case which was given to the Catholic people and the public by Church leaders. Monsignor Francis J. Lally, editor of the (Catholic) Boston *Pilot,* defended Archbishop Cushing's position in the Jesuit magazine *America* in an article which did not even disclose the fact that his Church sought to take Hildy McCoy away from the Ellises and return her not to her mother but to a strange Catholic foster home.[31] "The Church," he said in a letter to a Protestant publication,[32] "has, in fact, nothing whatever to do with this case of the removal of Hildy McCoy from the Ellis home." Archbishop Cushing himself, in addressing 1,100 Catholic followers for one hour on the McCoy-Ellis case, assured them solemnly that the case did not involve a religious issue.[33] Could a more patent falsehood be contrived in words?

It is not surprising that the McCoy-Ellis case, with the possible exception of the Spellman-Roosevelt correspondence of 1949, did more than any other incident in recent years to destroy public faith in the integrity of the hierarchy. The *New York Post,* in denouncing the Massachusetts law for placing "religious labels" above "real children," quoted a courageous Catholic judge from Massachusetts who asked: "Is it a Christian thing to destroy the love and affection which have grown up between the child and the only ones she has ever known as father and mother?" [34]

The clearest proof that Catholic divorce policy is narrowly denominational is the so-called Pauline privilege. This is a special ecclesiastical device for permitting a convert to Catholicism to obtain a "divorce" and marry again if his spouse refuses to cooperate. It is comparatively rare in the United States because there are many other devices in the Catholic marriage system for nullification that offer easier roads to marital freedom. The Pauline privilege is based upon the "interpretation" and development of a brief passage in 1 Corinthians 7 in which St. Paul said: "If any brother have a wife that believeth not, and she be pleased to dwell with him, let him not put her away. And the woman which hath any husband that believeth not, and if he be pleased to dwell with her, let her not leave him. . . . But if the unbelieving depart, let him depart. A brother or a sister is not under bondage in such cases. . . ."

This passage could easily be interpreted as applying to the Corinthians only, or as permitting separation without divorce, or as having no legal force whatever today, since Paul said specifically in stating the doctrine that he spoke for himself and not for his Lord. But the official Catholic interpreters of ancient times saw an opportunity for gaining infidel converts by inflating this passage into a plan for a special kind of "divorce." The plan was finally written into the Canon Law with many added features, and its present form is clearly summarized by Father Connell: "Two unbaptized persons are married. Later one is converted to Christianity and receives Baptism. The other refuses to dwell with the convert, or is a menace to the latter's faith and religious practices. When these conditions are present, the convert is free to leave the unbaptized partner and marry a Christian; and this new marriage dissolves the bond of the previous union. Even though many years have passed since the conversion took place, the Pauline privilege may be used if the requisite conditions exist." [35]

This device is particularly useful in dissolving a Jewish marriage when a Jewish wife wishes to divorce her husband and marry a Catholic. All she needs to do in that case is to join the Church and then go through the motions of asking her Jewish husband to become a Catholic and continue living with her. If he refuses, she may get a civil divorce for its purely "civil effects" without committing sin, and then marry a Catholic under the fiction that the Jewish marriage was wiped out by her new and "holy" marriage.

The technical skill displayed in the development of the Pauline privilege as a proselyting device is eclipsed by the ingenuity of ecclesiastical annulments. There is almost no type of marriage that cannot be annulled somehow under the complex rules of the Catholic marriage courts if a determined spouse is willing and able to go to the expense of prolonged litigation, and uses sufficient patience and ingenuity in constructing a plausible case.

The annulment process is used eagerly and frequently by American Catholics as a kind of Catholic substitute for divorce. Hundreds of annulments of valid civil marriages are granted each year by the Catholic hierarchy in the United States without reaching public attention. The Church's annulment statistics tell only a fragment of the real story. The rest of the story is contained in tables and reports that never reach the public.

If the student of Catholic marriage accepted the hierarchy's official statements about annulments as the whole truth, he would believe that the Church granted very few annulments. The Roman Rota, the highest Church court, to which all marriage cases go on final appeal, announced in its annual report for 1946-47 that in ten years it had granted only 335 marriage annulments, and had rejected 498. This story was given great prominence in the American press, and the casual reader was left to infer that the Roman Church grants only a few score annulments a year in the whole world. Actually the annulment cases which reach the Rota are trifling compared to the thousands of cases in which annulments are granted by local courts and from which no appeal to the Rota is made by either party.

American Catholics rarely go to the Rota for a marriage annulment if they fail to secure one from the local bishop, since they can step outside the Catholic system altogether and get divorce or annulment in American courts, a solution that is not open to the faithful in Catholic countries like Spain, Italy, and Portugal. In any case, American Catholics must go to the American courts to obtain a valid divorce or annulment; for them the decrees of the priests are theological surplusage, having moral validity only within the Catholic community.

When a Catholic American wishes to have his marriage annulled, usually in order to marry another Catholic, and he believes that there may be some technical ground for annulment, he goes to his priest and asks for a decree. If the case is simple, the local bishop acting through a subordinate can grant the annulment himself without any trial. If there is some doubt about the facts in the case, the Catholic goes to the diocesan marriage court of three judges, usually priests, chosen by the local bishop.[36] The local bishop is himself a judge ex officio in this court of first instance, but frequently he appoints a mature priest to act in his place. Each local Church court has a "defender of the bond," a priest who challenges every attempt to dissolve a marriage by raising technical objections.

If the annulment is denied by majority vote in this local court, the litigant can appeal to another three-man Church court of the archbishop of the province, and if the petition is again denied, he can appeal to Rome to the highest court, chosen by the Pope. The process of appeal is prodigiously long and quite expensive, and few Americans ever bother to use it. The Rota, in fact, is used chiefly by marriage litigants in Catholic countries in cases involving a large amount of property where title to the property would be affected by priestly decisions because Catholic marriage law has the force of civil law.

In most American state courts annulments of marriage are not easy to secure. To get a legal annulment of a marriage under

American law it is usually necessary to prove actual coercion, fraud, or some physical disability such as impotence. The Catholic annulment system is much more lax and loose than the American system. This laxness was developed in Europe, where divorce is prohibited in Catholic countries and where the pressure of outraged victims of mismating forced the priests to offer some methods for escaping from unhappy marriages. The Catholic system permits annulments for a whole series of reasons not recognized by American law, some of which seem fantastic or purely theological to non-Catholics, and some of which have no relation to the conduct of the parties involved.

These reasons for annulment are classified as "diriment impediments" to marriage. A diriment impediment is an impediment that is serious enough to nullify a marriage automatically. (A milder impediment is called "prohibitory," and such an impediment "seriously forbids but does not annul" a matrimonal contract.[37]) Some diriment impediments are really serious, such as an existing marriage, coercion, or blood relationship. Others are obviously denominational devices designed to prevent Catholics from falling in love with non-Catholics, and eventually to capture non-Catholic families for the Church by breaking up mixed marriages.

Any Catholic who has married a non-Catholic without getting his spouse to promise that all their children will be reared as Catholics can easily secure an annulment from a local bishop without any judicial formalities by proving that his original marriage was not "correct in form." The Canon Law says that such a marriage is null and void from the beginning, so the priest does not need to submit the case to a tribunal. He delivers a one-sheet Decree of Nullity after making sure that the former marriage was actually performed in the way described. A modest fee—usually $15—is asked for this service.[38]

Usually the Catholic marriage-court official who issues such a Decree of Nullity can gather the evidence very easily by getting an admission from the non-Catholic party that the marriage was not performed in the prescribed Catholic form. Here is an actual letter asking for such an admission (with initials) sent out by the marriage court of the Archdiocese of Washington:

ARCHDIOCESE OF WASHINGTON
The Tribunal
1719 Rhode Island Ave. N. W.
Washington 6, D. C.

Dec. 2, 1952

Dear Mrs. F:

R. F. F. has requested that he be declared free to contract a new marriage in the Church. He bases his plea on the fact that although he is a Catholic, his marriage with you was never contracted in the presence of a priest.

My purpose in writing is to acquaint you with Mr. F.'s request and to invite your comments on it.

With best wishes, I am

Sincerely in our Lord,
(Signed) Reverend E. Robert Arthur
Vice-Officialis

Here is the Decree of Nullity used in such summary proceedings in Minnesota:[39]

Since it has been clearly proven to me from certified, authentic documents that the marriage attempted on September 7, 1929, between ...., a non-Catholic, and ...., who was clearly bound to adhere to the canonical form of celebrating marriage according to Canons 1094 and 1099, was null from the beginning because the proper canonical form was lacking, I, the undersigned delegate of the Bishop of the diocese of Winona, according to the instructions laid down by the Sacred Congregation on sacramental discipline on August 15, 1936, declare that the aforesaid marriage was null and void before God and the Church.

(Signed) ....Official
................................Notary

Any Catholic who has married anybody, Catholic or non-Catholic, before a Protestant minister, Jewish rabbi, or justice of the peace can get an ecclesiastical annulment by this short-form decree simply by proving the facts of his marriage. The Church declares that all such marriages are void for Catholics *even when the fact of the possibility of easy annulment is one of the reasons for choosing this method of marriage.* So the irresponsible party in a marriage is allowed by the Church to use his own irresponsibility to gain release from an obligation, a principle that is flatly at variance with the ethical principles of American law.

The Catholic annulment system requires no proof of misconduct on the part of husband or wife in securing an ecclesiastical annulment. A perfect marriage can be annulled as easily as an imperfect marriage, if the canonical form of the marriage has been incorrect.

Altogether, there are at least half a dozen devices in Catholic Canon Law for dissolving mixed marriages without formality. When a Catholic marries a Jew without special dispensation, the marriage suffers from what is called the diriment impediment of disparity of cult, and can be quickly annulled. When a Catholic marries a Protestant without priestly blessing, the marriage can also be annulled without formality because of the milder prohibitory impediment called mixed religion. Thus, the Jewish marriage is one step lower than the Protestant, but both are classed as non-existent when a Catholic wishes to dispose of a non-Catholic spouse and marry another Catholic. The children of the annulled marriage are illegitimate unless a Catholic priest brings them into the fold by approved formula.

If a Catholic marries a non-Catholic outside of the Church and later repents and persuades the non-Catholic also to repent, the Church may validate this invalid marriage by a special retroactive device called *sanatio in radice,* meaning a "healing at the roots." [40] This legitimizes the once-illegitimate children and erases the sin of adultery.

One of the oddities of the ecclesiastical annulment system is that even a formal Catholic marriage can be easily annulled for what is called "the diriment impediment of crime." If, for example, a married man who is planning divorce commits adultery with a girl whom he promises to marry, and later marries her according to his promise, he can get this marriage annulled even if his first marriage was terminated by death instead of divorce. The priests argue that the man's association with his second wife began in crime, and that this justifies annulment on moral grounds.[41] Thus the ordinary rules of chivalry are completely reversed. The assumption that a man who seduces a woman has a special obligation to offer marriage is discarded in favor of a purely theological concept that allows the guilty person to use guilt as a shield.

The thousands of inexpensive annulments secured directly from priests in one-sheet decrees are not entered in the Church's public statistics and reports. Officially they are not called annulments but "declarations of invalidity." Yet these easy annulments constitute the overwhelming majority of all annulments granted to Catholics in the United States. The Pope has become so disturbed about their numbers that the Congregation of the Sacraments has sent a special warning message about them to the American hierarchy. The figures that caused Papal alarm have never been made public, although marriage reports are sent by each American diocese to Rome every year. If two studies by priests can be taken as typical, probably 10 per cent of Catholic marriages in the United States are *subject* to quick annulment for one cause alone, that of participation in the ceremony by a Protestant clergyman or justice of the peace. At a conservative guess, it is probable that 33,000 marriages of Catholics each year in the United States are void under the Church's discriminatory rule against all Protestant, Jewish, and civil marriages for Catholics.[42] How many of the 33,000 Catholic brides and grooms avail themselves of the opportunity to secure quick annulment of these marriages from their priests will probably never be known. The Church is privileged to keep its annulment statistics secret, since its annulments do not have any recognition in American law.

The Sacred Congregation of the Sacraments sent the following warning about easy annulments to American bishops on September 23, 1938:

> The Sacred Congregation is avowedly disquieted at the overwhelming number of summary cases [of annulment] . . . where there is a patent lack of juridical form of marriage. In no other nation in the world is there such an alarming disproportion between formal and informal cases. Special surveillance must be exercised by all Ordinaries over all such cases because of the gravity of the problem involved and the striking preponderance of informal cases.[43]

The "patent lack of juridical form" to which the Congregation refers is mixed marriage with Protestants or Jews without benefit of priests. The disproportion to which the Congregation refers still exists in the United States without substantial change, but the detailed figures are still secret. It is easy to see why the hierarchy keeps them secret. The facts about summary annulments could scarcely be made public without revealing the fact that perhaps several hundred thousand supposedly respectable married persons of Protestant and Jewish stock are living in adultery in unions with Catholics that have no standing in Catholic moral law, and that can be annulled without giving the non-Catholic parties any hearing. This summary condemnation of the marriage status of non-Catholics might handicap the Church very seriously in winning converts among those whose children have been classified as bastards.

5

When short cuts to annulment are unavailable, the Church provides a number of special, elastic interpretations of marriage vows that can be used to dissolve a marriage. One of these elastic devices is the theory that there must be an "interior consent" to a marriage or it is void from the beginning. There is sound common sense in such a rule in cases of fear and coercion, but the priests have stretched it to include many cases of apparently valid marriage in which a married person changes his attitude toward his spouse long after marriage, and then announces that he never consented to the marriage in the first place. The hierarchy has developed the theory that the failure to consent to a single, doctrinal essential in marriage voids the whole affair.

Any Catholic, for example, can obtain an ecclesiastical annulment if he can prove that in entering marriage he made it a condition that he should not have children, or that the parties agreed that they *could* get a divorce if the marriage proved to be unsuccessful. In such cases the hierarchy holds that the parties to a marriage never actually consented to full marriage. They made a mental reservation about two essentials of marriage, children and indissolubility.

It is easy to see how simple it is for many persons to secure ecclesiastical annulments under such a rule, especially since the priests do not require proof that the mental reservation of one party has been disclosed to the other party in the marriage. The Roman Rota said in a case which was confirmed on July 30, 1924, that "an intention, even on the part of only one of the parties, though not manifested to the other, if it excludes the obligation itself regarding any of the three essential blessings of marriage; that is, children, indissolubility, or fidelity, renders the marriage null." [44] On November 28, 1928, the Rota granted annulment to a Catholic girl who married a Protestant infected with syphilis on the ground that they agreed they should not have children on account of the danger to health involved. The annulment was granted not because of the syphilis or the desire to separate but because of the couple's "intention to exclude the obligation" of having children. On February 11, 1928, the Rota granted an annulment for an "agreement" not to have children even when the man strenuously denied any such agreement. The husband had been heard by several persons to say that he was "utterly averse" to having children.

Similar reasoning makes it easy for a Catholic court to find a pretext for ecclesiastical annulment of a Protestant marriage on the ground that the bride and groom "excluded the obligation" of indissolubility when they took their vows. Virtually all American Protestants are at least aware of the fact when they marry that they can get a divorce if their marriage turns out to be a failure. If they admit this to each other and indicate that they concede the possibility of terminating their marriage by divorce if it turns out to be a disaster, the Catholic Church holds that their marriage is void from the beginning.[45]

The Pope, incidentally, although he has conceded the validity of ordinary Protestant marriages since the new Canon Law was promulgated in 1918, still claims the power to annul any Protestant marriage anywhere by virtue of his supreme power over all Christian marriage. In the Helena case of September 30, 1919, the Pope, on recommendation of the Rota, nullified the marriage of a non-Christian man to an Anglican woman simply as a special religious favor to the man, who wished to become a Catholic and marry a Catholic girl.[46] The marriage annulled had nothing to do with the Catholic Church.

All Protestants who married Jews before 1918 are still living in sin, according to Catholic doctrine, and their children are illegitimate. This is true because the right of a Christian to marry a non-Christian without benefit of a priest was not recognized before the promulgation of the new Canon Law in 1918, and the new dispensation is not retroactive.[47]

Only a few of the most famous cases of Catholic annulment ever reach the attention of the public, and frequently the American press refrains from candid discussions of these annulments. When Admiral Ellery Stone, former head of the Allied Control Commission in Italy, married an Italian countess before a cardinal in St. Peter's on April 7, 1947, the American press included the fact in its news dispatches without elaborating on the facts that Admiral Stone's second wife, who had been married to him in a Protestant ceremony, had just divorced him in Reno a few weeks before. The Admiral could remarry in good conscience because he had been converted to Catholicism and, according to *The New York Times,*[48] his "second marriage was not recognized under Canon Law."

Rudy Vallee's fourth marriage, in September, 1949, in Oakland, California, was described by the Matrimonial Court of the Archdiocese of Los Angeles as his "first valid marriage," and he was permitted to marry a new wife in the church although he had two living divorced wives. This matrimonial legerdemain was made possible by the Church's rule that when a baptized Catholic is married outside the Church the marriage does not count as valid under Canon 1094. Father Daniel Collins, secretary of the Matrimonial Court, explained that "the Church presumes, when they contract a valid marriage, that they are sorry for their past misdeeds." [49]

The general tendency of the hierarchy is to nullify a non-Catholic marriage as swiftly and graciously as possible if a noted person is thereby won over to the Church, or held within the Church. Marconi was allowed to free himself from a marriage with an Anglican bride before an Anglican minister in 1927 after thirteen years of married life, in spite of the fact that he and his bride under oath had taken each other for better or worse forever. The Church said that the marriage had never existed because the parties had agreed "not to resist divorce in case of dissatisfaction with the marriage." [50] The Duke of Marlborough and Consuelo Vanderbilt were given an annulment in 1926, more than thirty years after their marriage, and after they had lived together ten years, on the theory that Miss Vanderbilt had been "coerced" in marriage by her mother.[51] Our American courts, of course, would never listen to such a theory in a case in which the lady continued to live with her husband long after release from the initial coercion. But the Roman Rota evolved the "explanation" in this case that the bride of thirty years' standing did not know that her marriage had already been invalidated by the lack of consent under Catholic law, and that this lack of knowledge excused her from prompt action.

There are signs that American Catholics are beginning to resent the purely ecclesiastical and artificial standards of the Catholic marriage courts. They would like to apply modern standards of social science to marital difficulties instead of the unrealistic traditions imported from Catholic countries of Europe. Some attempts have been made recently to use the marriage courts as tribunals for psychiatric therapy and intelligent marriage counseling. The Roman Curia immediately scented danger.

In 1938 the Congregation of the Sacraments deplored the tendency in the United States "to consider the ecclesiastical tribunal as a kind of clinic for unhappy marriages where the judges are bound to adjust situations at all costs, or at least with exaggerated leniency." American priests were warned that "such an erroneous attitude would wound the sacred bond of Christian marriage." Marriage, the Congregation insisted, is still "indissoluble by divine origin." [52]

9

Censorship and Boycott

1

WHEN A NON-CATHOLIC AMERICAN picks up his newspaper and reads that Cardinal Spellman or some other dignitary of the Roman Catholic Church has directed Catholics to boycott the motion picture *Baby Doll,* he is likely to think of the event as a spontaneous and isolated outburst of moral indignation. Such an interpretation is almost certain to be wrong. Catholic cardinals are not isolated and they are rarely spontaneous. The censorship system of the Roman Catholic Church in the United States is neither a spasmodic nor an intermittent phenomenon. It is a highly organized system of cultural and moral controls that applies not only to books, plays, magazines, television, and motion pictures but to persons and places as well.

The censorship system of the Church is very ancient, deeply imbedded in ecclesiastical tradition, and notoriously unpopular with both Catholic and non-Catholic intellectuals. It was John Milton who expressed the attitude of self-respecting authors of the seventeenth century in his *Areopagitica* when he ridiculed the literary censorship of priests by saying:

> To fill up the measure of encroachment, their last invention was to ordain that no book, pamphlet or paper should be printed (as if St. Peter had bequeathed them the keys of the press also out of Paradise) unless it were approved and licensed under the hands of two or three glutton friars. . . . Sometimes five Imprimaturs are seen together dialogue-wise in the piazza of one title-page, complimenting and ducking each other with their shaven reverences. . . .

The London *Times* echoed this sentiment in 1949 when it said: "There is something intensely repugnant to the liberal mind

212

in a coalition between priests and policemen for the maintenance of religion and virtue." [1]

In a sense the Catholicism that the hierarchy imposes upon its people is itself a great system of censorship, a system of condemnations and taboos of which the boycott of certain works of literature and art is a relatively minor phase. We have seen that the Catholic hierarchy does not hesitate to condemn or boycott certain individuals or whole classes of persons wherever the Church is strong enough to enforce such strictures. A Catholic boycott may apply to the sporting world, the graveyard, or the entire Jewish community.

In Brooklyn, the largest Catholic diocese in America, Leo Durocher could not resume the managership of the Brooklyn Dodgers in 1948 until the Catholic boycott against him had been lifted. He was the victim of Catholic sexual censorship because of a slightly irregular marital relationship.

We examined in the last chapter the special annulling impediment applied by Catholic priests to Jews in mixed marriage. This extreme rule against mixed marriage with Jews is, in a sense, a censorship of all Jews as Jews, a form of discrimination against their ideas as well as their personalities.

The Church's censorship of apostates is even more severe. No true believer may eat, play, or do business with a moral leper who has been excommunicated by name from the Roman Catholic Church. If a renegade from the Church is buried in a Catholic cemetery, he must be dug up as promptly as possible and moved away. Until he is moved away, the whole cemetery or churchyard where he is buried is defiled.[2]

All these practices of censorship, boycott, and taboo are imposed upon the faithful as doctrinal directives by their bishops, or by the Congregation of the Holy Office in Rome. Obedience to such directives is a serious matter for good Catholics. The Holy Office is successor to the body that once recommended the burning of heretics, and that condemned Galileo for heresy. Today it does not burn people, but it continues to proscribe plays, books, films, newspapers, and magazines. It holds the power of economic life and death over many authors, editors, publishers, and producers who must rely upon American Catholics for patronage and support.

Because good Catholics are accustomed to the imposition of general boycotts and taboos by their priests, the censorship of literature and art is accepted as part of the Church routine. Catholics are taught that the Roman Catholic Church is the supreme guardian and purveyor of truth, that the Pope has infallible judgment in moral matters, and that "union of minds requires not only a perfect accord in the one Faith, but complete submission and obedience of will to the Church and to the Roman Pontiff, as to God Himself." The words are those of Leo XIII in his *Chief Duties of Christian Citizens.*

With this theoretical background it is natural that Catholics should regard the censorship system of their Church as primarily a Catholic affair. But is it primarily a Catholic affair? It would be fortunate if the effects of censorship could be limited to Catholics, but in real life Catholics, Protestants, Jews, and unbelievers are exposed to the same plays, books, magazines, and films. The strictures of the Catholic hierarchy upon its own people cannot be isolated from the life of the rest of the community. Likewise, the liberties of the general population are bound to affect Catholics because Catholics constitute so large and organic a part of the general public.

Catholic censorship, therefore, cannot be considered in isolation. It is an important factor in American social policy, and it cannot hide behind the protective screen of a single faith. Since it affects the lives of so many non-Catholics it must be submitted to non-Catholic analysis and judgment. The question, then, that will concern us in this chapter is not whether Catholic censorship is a good thing for Catholics but whether it is a good thing for the American people.

2

The least important part of the Catholic censorship system is the part that is commonly supposed to be most important. I refer to the famous *Index librorum prohibitorum,* or list of books that Catholics are forbidden to read.

Although the *Index* lists very few books in English, it still bans about 5,000 works, including some of the world's greatest literature. The ban applies to all of Anatole France, Maeterlinck, and Zola; much of Voltaire, Descartes, and d'Annunzio; the love stories of Balzac, Hugo's *Les Misérables;* all the novels of Dumas (father and son) except *The Count of Monte Cristo;* Kant's *Critique of Pure Reason,* Bergson's *Creative Evolution,* Gibbon's

Decline and Fall of the Roman Empire, Renan's *Life of Christ,* Taine's *History of English Literature,* Rousseau's *Social Contract,* and Thomas Paine's *The Rights of Man.* The first official *Index* was published only in 1559, but throughout the Middle Ages the Church, by decrees of bishops or of councils or of Popes, proscribed and burned objectionable books. Then book censorship was entrusted to a special Congregation of cardinals in Rome called the Congregation of the Index, and, more recently in 1917, to the Congregation of the Holy Office, the Roman Inquisition, whose procedure and decisions are usually clouded in impenetrable secrecy. The bishops, however, have retained their ancient right to forbid books and other publications within the territorial limits of their dioceses. The *Index* was revamped by Leo XIII, and has been reissued and brought up to date by his successors.[3]

When modern printing presses began to pour out tens of thousands of new books every year, the Roman hierarchy realized that the *Index* could not keep pace with the heretical output, and the function of censoring books was left primarily to local bishops. Every bishop of the Church throughout the world was made a special agent of the censorship. He was directed and empowered to condemn all "anti-Catholic" books, plays, magazines, and films in his own diocese. Since all bishops are appointed by the Pope, the Roman directives on this subject have been obeyed with great alacrity.

Today the Catholic theologians do not bother to place many objectionable modern books on the *Index* because the Church's world-wide system of local condemnation and boycott is far more efficient than any general black list could possibly be. Occasionally the Congregation of the Holy Office makes an exception in the case of a contemporary author whose whole outlook on life seems to be opposed to Catholic teaching—the French existentialist, Jean-Paul Sartre, is an illustration. All of his books were put on the *Index* in October, 1948. In May, 1952, all the works of the French novelist André Gide were placed upon the *Index,* and the works of the Italian novelist Alberto Moravia were banned at almost the same time. In 1956 two best-sellers of Sartre's friend, Simone de Beauvoir, were condemned, *The Mandarins* and *The Second Sex.* The Vatican rarely awards American authors this special distinction, perhaps because the American hierarchy is anxious to present the Church to the non-Catholic public as a champion of freedom.

The directives for the maintenance of the Catholic censorship system are specific and astonishingly detailed. The moral manuals for priests even suggest how many pages a book should ordinarily have to be called a book, and how many pages may ordinarily be read without endangering the soul. (The numbers are 160 and six respectively "if the book is dangerous to faith and morals.")

The general rule is: "All men are forbidden to read books that are contrary to faith in God, good moral conduct and Christian virtue"—a rule so sweeping that it can be interpreted as banning a large proportion of all modern works on science, medicine, and morals. In practice this rule means that no Catholic is allowed to read knowingly and without special permission any book attacking any fundamental doctrine of the Catholic Church. "The Church is not afraid of truth," says Father John C. Heenan in his *Priest and Penitent,* "but She is very much afraid that a clever presentation of falsehood will deceive even the elect." [4] The Church teaches that literature is "immoral" if it is opposed to Catholic standards, and that "no one has a 'right' to publish such literature any more than one has a right to poison wells or sell tainted food." [5]

The general subject of book censorship is included in Canons 1384-1405 of the Codex. For brevity's sake I shall quote here, as above, from the most authoritative Catholic work on doctrine, Father Henry Davis's four-volume *Moral and Pastoral Theology.* Catholic bishops must enforce a boycott against all of the following classes of books, as described in the words of Father Davis:

1. Books by any writers which defend heresy or schism, or attempt in any way to undermine the very foundations of religion;
2. All books . . . which affect to prove that true divorce is permissible in the case of adultery;
3. Books which attack or hold up to ridicule any Catholic dogma, such as the creation of man, original sin, the infallibility of the Pope;
4. Books which professedly treat of, narrate, or teach matters that are lewd or obscene, such as the defense of methods of birth control.[6]

Catholics are directed to be on the watch for such books and to denounce them. As Father Davis puts it: "All the faithful, and those especially who are clerics, or who hold high positions, or who are learned should denounce any book which they consider dangerous." Under Canon 1397, it is the duty of a Catholic bishop to keep secret the name of any person who wishes to denounce a book privately.

When a book has been denounced by official authorities it is a grave sin for a Catholic knowingly to buy, sell, borrow, own, read, or lend it to any other person. The penalties apply to booksellers, publishers, readers, and reviewers unless they secure special permission to handle contraband goods. Father Davis says:

> Excommunication, specially reserved to the Holy See, is incurred *ipso facto*, by the publisher of any book written by apostate, heretic, or schismatic in defense of apostasy, heresy, or schism; it is also incurred by those who defend the said books prohibited by express mention and by name by Letters Apostolic. Furthermore, the same excommunication is incurred by those who knowingly read or keep such books without due permission.

Similar punishments are meted out to Catholics who read newspapers and magazines condemned by the hierarchy. Under Canon 1386 no priest or member of a religious order may publish anything, even on profane subjects, without permission of his bishop; and under Canon 1404 Catholic booksellers must get permission from the Holy See to handle any forbidden book, and then they must not sell such a book to the faithful until they have made certain that the buyer has obtained special permission to read it. Students for the priesthood, while studying in Catholic seminaries, are not permitted to read daily newspapers which meet with the disapproval of the hierarchy. "Catholics," said Pius XI in an Allocution on December 20, 1926, "may not support, favor, or read papers which are edited by men whose writings are in notable opposition to Catholic doctrine in faith and morals. . . ." [7]

Nominally it is a mortal sin under Canon 1399 for any Catholic to read *this* book without special permission, since it comes within the forbidden categories. In the library of the Catholic University of America it is put in a special locked section, not open to the public. During the course of a debate in which I engaged at the Yale Law School with Father Robert T. Hartnett, editor of *America,* the Jesuit leader admitted that even a Yale Catholic student under Church law would not be permitted to own this work without episcopal permission.

Catholic scholars and writers may easily secure special permission to read forbidden books and magazines by paying a small fee, but that permission is instantly withdrawn if it appears that the victim is drifting from faith. The bishops themselves have graciously exempted the bishops themselves—and all archbishops and cardinals—from any restraints on reading. Under Canon 1401 it is presumed that they are beyond temptation, and can read any obscene or heretical book without injury to their consciences.

The hierarchy will not even permit its people to read the Protestant and Jewish books included in a joint interfaith bibliography. The most authoritative American journal for priests, the *American Ecclesiastical Review* of September, 1946, published the following question and answer on this point:

Question. A "religious book list" has recently been published by the National Conference of Christians and Jews. What should be the attitude of Catholics toward such a list, and what would be its practical use as far as Catholics are concerned?

Answer. . . . the impression naturally given . . . is that it is quite commendable for the adherents of each of these three denominational groups to read the books which explain and defend the religious beliefs of the other two. Now, this would be strictly forbidden to Catholics . . . such a list might be an incentive to violate the rules which the Catholic Church, in her capacity of defender of the Christian faith, has wisely laid down for the spiritual protection of her children.

So Catholics in the National Conference of Christians and Jews continue to persuade Protestants and Jews to read Catholic books but forbid Catholic readers to dip into Protestant and Jewish books.

This complete absence of cultural reciprocity might not be considered serious if the boycotted books were merely partisan denominational tracts. Actually the Catholic boycott includes all books which specifically oppose the major social policies of the Church even when those policies have no direct bearing on worship or theology. No book favoring sterilization of the feebleminded, birth control, euthanasia, artificial insemination, therapeutic abortion, cremation, humanism, state operation of all colleges, divorce, or complete separation of church and state can be deliberately and knowingly read by a good Catholic.

If the Catholic hierarchy could extend to all American literature the system of censorship that it has developed in Catholic countries, the rule would be applied to all books and magazines that expressed any criticism of the Church. Father Francis J.

Connell, dean of the School of Sacred Theology at the Catholic University of America, was extraordinarily frank about this when writing in the *American Ecclesiastical Review* for January, 1946, on "Preserving the Faith Inviolate":

> We believe that the rulers of a Catholic country have the right to restrict the activities of those who would lead their people away from their allegiance to the Catholic Church . . . they possess the right to prevent propaganda against the Church. This is merely a logical conclusion from the basic Catholic tenet that the Son of God established one religion and commanded all men to accept it under pain of eternal damnation.

What it means for the hierarchy to "possess the right to prevent propaganda against the Church" in a Catholic-dominated country may be appreciated by looking at the new republic of Eire, in which the Roman Catholic Church has a privileged position in the constitution. I have discussed this situation in detail in *The Irish and Catholic Power*. Technically religious freedom is permitted for non-Catholic sects, but Catholic censorship standards are enforced by a Censorship of Publications Board, which for many years consisted of four Catholic laymen and a priest-chairman. Between 4,000 and 5,000 books are banned, including many of the most famous best-sellers of the American book clubs and works of noted Irish authors who have called themselves Catholic. Nominally the ban is imposed in almost all cases for sexual frankness. The list of authors who have some banned books on the list includes Sherwood Anderson, Hamilton Basso, Taylor Caldwell, Theodore Dreiser, Graham Greene, William Faulkner, Ernest Hemingway, Sinclair Lewis, Arthur Koestler, J. D. Salinger, Quentin Reynolds, John Steinbeck, Thomas Mann, James A. Michener, and Aldous Huxley.

No item of Catholic policy has done more to alienate the intellectuals from the Church than literary censorship. Some Catholic writers are openly defiant concerning it. The Catholic novelist Graham Greene has declared:

> In common with other Catholics, I have little regard for the *Index* in the rare cases when it deals with imaginative writing. The Roman *Index* is not an infallible document and sometimes makes mistakes as absurd and regrettable as British judges, juries and magistrates.[8]

Spain is the only country in Europe where the Vatican has achieved sufficient union of church and state to prevent the publication of every book on the *Index*. Perhaps the Church could impose the complete ban in the Irish Republic if the hierarchy insisted upon such an extreme measure for the thought control of the 95 per cent Catholic population, but Catholic political leaders advise against it on the ground that the Church must be on its good behavior if the Republic is ever to absorb Northern Ireland. In the Pope's home country the literary community is bitterly scornful of Church censorship, and of almost everything else that is ecclesiastical. "In Italy," says the Catholic writer Bernard Wall, "the literary intelligentsia is anti-clerical almost to a man, and priests, peasants and members of the clerical bourgeoisie either do not read at all or do not read 'profane' books." [9]

3

The machinery that the Church uses in the United States to enforce its boycott of unfriendly literature is quite elaborate. There is machinery for handling books by non-Catholics and machinery for sifting out every printed work of Catholics that touches on religion and morals. Non-Catholic publishers who print criticism of Catholic policy are threatened with boycotts and flooded with very unpleasant letters of protest. As a result of this type of pressure scarcely any publishers in the United States will even consider any manuscript that might expose them and their textbooks to a Catholic boycott.

Ordinarily the hierarchy boycotts heresy more ruthlessly than vulgarity. "Heresy," as Bernard Wall points out, "is in practice far less tolerated than crime, being considered a crime in the most important field of all—that of theology." The Church subjected the *Encyclopedia Britannica* to a critical siege for years because its biography of the Virgin Mary suggested that the apostles knew nothing about the Virgin Birth. The *Encyclopedia* changed a few words but stood by the substance of its interpretation.

The hierarchy has two instruments for critical attack upon any book or magazine which is considered offensive to clerical taste: a literary journal called *Books on Trial,* published in Chicago, which sends out a kind of black-and-white list of current publications, ranking these publications according to conventional clerical reactions; and the National Organization for Decent Literature, which is a subsidiary of the Archdiocese of Chicago. *Books on Trial* is a reasonably dignified critical journal. The monthly newsletter of the N.O.D.L. is essentially a propaganda blacklisting device, widely used throughout the country by policemen and Catholic-dominated prosecutors to ban both genuine pornography and serious, realistic literature. (I have discussed this organization in detail in my 1955 book, *The Right to Read*.) It claims to be "in no sense an exclusively Catholic movement," but it is controlled completely by the hierarchy, with Bishop John J. Dearden of Pittsburgh as head and Monsignor Thomas J. Fitzgerald of Chicago as executive secretary. Its lists of "objectionable" publications are prepared by the Chicago Archdiocesan Council of Catholic Women.

Although this organization scored a considerable victory in its fight against horror comics from 1954 to 1956, it has earned a reputation for repressive stupidity by including in its black lists a large number of distinguished modern novels. In May, 1957, the American Civil Liberties Union published an open letter signed by 162 distinguished authors and publicists condemning the N.O.D.L. for conducting punitive boycotts against booksellers and newsstand owners who would not accept its "suggestions" for banning disapproved books. Among the books on N.O.D.L. black lists recently have been *Mr. Roberts* by Thomas Heggen, *Antic Hay* by Aldous Huxley, *The Catcher in the Rye* by J. D. Salinger, *The Young Lions* by Irwin Shaw, *From Here to Eternity* by James Jones, *Native Son* by Richard Wright, *Pride's Castle* by Frank Yerby, and *A Rage to Live* by John O'Hara.

Occasionally a devout Catholic in public office applies the principles of the N.O.D.L. to literature or art without any apparent prodding from the supervisory organization. It was Mayor James M. Curley of Boston who, in October, 1946, banned the exhibition by the Copley Society of eleven modern paintings of the Temptations of St. Anthony on the ground that they were "an insult to the great organized society, the Catholic Church." [10]

The internal, preventive literary censorship of the hierarchy is both negative and positive. Every American diocese has an internal censor who is also a priest. Ordinarily, every book on religion or morals by a Catholic must be examined before publication by the censor of the diocese where it is to be published. Before a book is published, the diocesan censor reads it carefully, stamps his *Nihil Obstat* on the fly-leaf if he finds nothing objectionable, and turns it over to his bishop for the necessary Imprimatur ("let it be printed"). A Catholic publisher who issues a book on religion or morals without this Imprimatur risks immediate excommunication and nation-wide boycott under Canon 2318. Also, says the *Catholic Encyclopedia,* "Catholic laymen must not write for newspapers or periodicals hostile to Catholicism or morality, unless for a just and reasonable cause approved by the local ordinary."

The Imprimatur of a bishop is a kind of negative guarantee that there is nothing very wrong with the book from the point of view of Catholic doctrine. It is not a guarantee that everything in the work meets with the hierarchy's approval. In order to make clear the meaning of a *Nihil Obstat,* placed in a book by the diocesan censor, and an Imprimatur, placed there by the bishop, the Archdiocese of New York has taken to printing the following statement of explanation with the Imprimatur:

The *Nihil Obstat* and *Imprimatur* are official declarations that a book or pamphlet is free of doctrinal or moral error. No implication is contained therein that those who have granted the *Nihil Obstat* or *Imprimatur* agree with the contents, opinions or statements expressed.[11]

Important condemned books frequently receive special detailed hostile reviews in the Catholic press and denunciations from the Catholic pulpits. *Raintree County* was singled out for special denunciation by the New York hierarchy in February, 1948, on three counts: because it was a Book-of-the-Month Club selection, because it was written by an author who came "from public school, where he did not learn anything about God," and because "the Virgin Birth, the Resurrection, the virginity of Mary, the divinity of Jesus Christ Himself are derided in terms of lascivious and unquotable blasphemy." Father Harold Gardner, literary editor of *America,* found that Pearl Buck's *Pavilion of Women* was "a failure as a means of intellectual understanding, and it fails on the precise ground that it distorts the one supreme element necessary for that understanding, the reality and truth of the soul, of marriage, of love, of truth, as they are found in Catholic Christianity." [12]

The Catholic censors are particularly bitter against any Catholic who is either a "renegade" or a critic of Catholicism. Betty Smith, the author of *A Tree Grows in Brooklyn,* married outside the Church, and when her remarkable novel appeared, Monsignor Belford of Brooklyn condemned any reader of the book as an accomplice in a mortal sin.[13] A Roman Catholic congressman attacked Miss Smith in Congress, and his speeches were printed in *The Congressional Record* and circulated in Brooklyn.

When the liberal Catholic novelist Harry Sylvester wrote *Moon Gaffney,* one of the most candid novels that has been written about his Church in many years, the reviewer of the *Catholic World* found that "he dissipated his power in a thousand different directions, ranting, suggesting, shouting, sneering, never really sustaining a point and proving it to the satisfaction of the initiated reader. . . ."

4

Unfortunately, the most effective and devastating Catholic censorship of books takes place in the small towns and villages of America, in schools and libraries whose officials do not dare to make a public issue of the event. Liberal, non-sectarian textbooks are frequently removed from *public* schools because some local school board is unwilling to resist the local hierarchy. In 1947 a popular and scholarly textbook, *Health Problems: How to Solve Them,* by Doctors Brownell, Williams, and Hughes, incurred the wrath of the local Catholic hierarchy in North Tarrytown, New York, because it ridiculed the ideas that knocking on wood, carrying a rabbit's foot, and saying "God bless you" when a friend sneezes have any connection with good health or good fortune. "If they [people who are superstitious] believe that faith healing cures human ills," said the authors, "or that whiskey is a sure cure for snakebite, or that pre-natal desires of expectant mothers are transmitted to the unborn child, then the effects are likely to be quite tragic." The head of the local Catholic parish demanded that the book be eliminated from *public* high schools on the ground that if the children were taught that good health was completely a matter of science, it would destroy faith in the accomplishments of prayer. The Board of Education yielded to the pressure and cut from the book two pages containing the offending passages.

In Catholic schools such censorship of books is automatic, and even includes heretical lecture notes as well as textbooks. The censorship code for Catholic students in non-Catholic institutions was set forth clearly in January, 1948, by Vincent B. Balmat, Chancellor of the Diocese of Cleveland, in a public letter.

Canon 1374 gravely forbids Catholics to attend non-Catholic schools unless the Bishop judges that adequate precautions are taken and satisfactory conditions maintained to avoid danger of weakening or loss of faith. Catholics are forbidden by Canons 1398 and 1399 to read or keep books which deny or make light of any point of Catholic belief or practice. This prohibition includes textbooks and lecture notes, as well as reference material. This law of the Church is dispensed by the Holy See only under rigid and unusual circumstances when it is necessary to read the books to refute them, or for an equally important cause.

Many Catholic literary people seem to be unhappy under the system of censorship. In fact, they writhe in misery when they discuss the state of the Catholic literary world. Very few lay writers of any intellectual stature are willing to accept such tight controls, and even priests are sometimes bitterly critical of the yoke they cannot throw off. There is only one lay Catholic magazine of any consequence in the country, *The Commonweal,* and it is neither fearless nor independent when some basic doctrine of the Church is challenged. Almost all the other widely known magazines are edited and managed by priests. The diocesan weeklies are little more than house organs for the hierarchy, carefully censored and filled with slanted news sent out from the humming Washington headquarters of the National Catholic Welfare Conference.

The state of literary criticism and literary knowledge in this sequestered cultural world has caused many Catholic writers to burst out in wrathful denunciation. Even *America,* which is edited entirely by Jesuit priests, occasionally allows a frank statement. C. J. Maguire, a Catholic teacher, writing in *America* for February 8, 1947, said: "The belief [in the Church] seems to be that wide reading in and of itself is subversive, suspicious and rarely to be sanctioned . . . the Catholic is faced with a program that lays stress, by abstention and implication, upon juvenility and ignorance in the field of literature." Father John W. Simons, writing in the issue of December 28, 1946, described the "chief Catholic error" as "a moralism unsupported by esthetics," and declared, "It is a melancholy fact that the science of literary criticism among Catholics in America is practically non-existent."

Michael de la Bedoyere, editor of Britain's *Catholic Herald,* said bluntly in his *Christian Crisis:*

We have almost reached the stage in Catholic public opinion when nothing is regarded as Catholic unless a religious or pious or apologetic label can be attached to it . . . the name is freely bestowed upon a second-rate professor who writes Catholic Truth Society pamphlets, the story-writer who resolutely shuts his eyes to reality and indulges in edifying talks, the picture maker who devotes himself to "sacred art . . ." [14]

Another Catholic critic, Erik von Keuhnelt-Leddihn, writing in the *Catholic World* of May, 1947, puts much of the blame on Catholic publishers who feel compelled to be prudish for business reasons. One Catholic publisher, he said, considered the word "womb" unprintable, and he added:

We know of a Catholic publisher who had printed a novel but refused to publish it at the last moment because it mentioned (a) a laxative and (b) permitted a young man to kiss a girl in a dark room. This momentous decision was said to have been reached after canvassing the reactions of nuns who read the page proofs. . . . A book called *Married Saints* used for refectory reading in a convent had the most innocent passages deleted such as, "She dearly loved her husband," and "She milked the cows. . . ."

The net result [of this prudery] is a fatal lowering of the Church in the eyes of non-Catholics, who might otherwise be friendly disposed. . . . They are horrified and often fatally repelled when they see manifestations which characterize rather a narrow backwoods sect than a Church of the world of all ages.

Under the Catholic code these criticisms represent the extreme limit of what a Catholic writer can say about Catholic literary censorship and still write for the Catholic press. He cannot discuss freely the fundamental principles of the censorship, the truth of any particular Church doctrine, the right of priests to prevent Catholics from reading critical books, or the mind-deadening effect of repetitive ritual. Occasionally, however, a Catholic writer dares to point out that in a nation that cherishes freedom of speech the Catholic censor's stamp of approval is a kiss of death. Catholic books may sell well among Catholic readers, but most non-Catholic Americans carefully avoid any book that bears the official Imprimatur. Conversely, when the hierarchy, acting through Catholic government officials, succeeds in "suppressing" a book in a Catholic city like Boston, the "award" is often more valuable than a Pulitzer prize.

The embarrassment of Catholic writers under the censorship of their Church is mild compared to the resentment of American non-Catholic scholars and librarians. Public librarians in recent years have been subject to steady pressure from local Catholic organizations in all parts of the United States to remove from their shelves books that are unfavorable to the Church's doctrines. In many cities and towns they have been forced to yield to that pressure. When Catholic critics cannot secure the removal of a disapproved book from the shelves, they frequently ask that a Catholic book be purchased and displayed as a corrective.

The American Library Association became so alarmed by this pressure and similar attempts at censorship that it made plans at its 1948 annual convention to fight back with a black list and boycott of its own. It was proposed that any librarian who yielded to un-American censorship by religious or patriotic groups should be condemned by an organization of his own profession and publicly blacklisted. It was suggested that it is the duty of librarians, if necessary, to become martyrs to the cause of free speech even if defiance means the loss of a job. President Paul North Rice of the Association, addressing 6,000 librarians, warned that intellectual freedom was being destroyed by censorship and asked:

> Should a small religious minority be allowed to keep off the shelves of a library a biography of their founder that does not depict her as they feel she should be depicted? Should copies of *The Nation* ever be removed from library shelves? Should libraries in the South fail to have current books on the race problem or novels on the problem that may be offensive to perhaps even a majority of their constituents? Should witch hunts for subversive books persuade librarians not to stock a book because it is friendly to Russia or a communistic idea? The answer to all these questions is, of course, an emphatic no.[15]

The Boston *Pilot* replied by saying that "just as we are not free to take as food for our bodies matter that will disease, deprave and destroy them, so too for our minds—far more precious—we may not take ideas that similarly vitiate the very functions for which the mind was made." [16] It requires only a little reflection to see that this analogy between the brain and the stomach is somewhat disingenuous.

5

The power that the hierarchy exerts in the American newspaper world is, for the most part, external. Although the Church has more than three hundred newspapers and magazines in the United States, including four foreign-language dailies, the only official Catholic daily newspaper in English died many years ago. (In several cities the Hearst press so nearly approximates the hierarchy's attitude on public questions that the need of a denominational daily is not apparent.) "Independent" newspapers owned by Catholics are sometimes more zealous than official organs. In cities like Boston and Chicago the solicitude shown for the local hierarchy by papers owned by non-Catholics could scarcely be improved upon by diocesan newspapers.

If the quality of the diocesan press can be accepted as evidence of the character of Catholic journalism, the Catholic people are fortunate that they have no daily newspaper owned by the hierarchy. The diocesan papers, understaffed with poorly paid writers, ordinarily make no attempt at fair play in their news columns or independence in their editorial columns. The Brooklyn *Tablet,* which has the third largest circulation of any weekly paper designed for one diocese only, is probably the most deliberately partisan newspaper in the United States, with the possible exception of the *Daily Worker.* The Catholic *Register* of Denver, with a circulation of about 800,000 and thirty-five separate diocesan editions, uses the techniques of yellow journalism, substituting miracles and magic for vice and violence. It is now the most important and representative weekly of the American Church.

American priests habitually use their pulpits to condemn any newspaper that publishes material critical of the Church, and they are particularly vehement in condemning any editor who publishes facts unfavorable to priests and nuns. Whenever a newspaper prints a news-story reflecting upon the character of a priest, local Catholic organizations, directed by priests, write, telephone, and telegraph vigorous protests to the editor, and frequently approach the business office of the newspaper with threats to boycott the paper's advertisers. As a result of this policy of siege and boycott, very few publishers in the United States are courageous enough or wealthy enough to deal frankly with Catholic social policy or stories of priestly crime.

In 1944 *Time* magazine rendered a great public service by printing a detailed description of the way in which the Catholic hierarchy attempts to suppress stories of priestly crimes.[17]   On September 11, 1944, the Scripps-Howard San Francisco *News* printed a brief item saying that a Roman Catholic priest had been arrested for drunken driving with a woman companion, and had pleaded guilty in a Madera, California, courtroom. Other San Francisco papers were afraid to print the item. Monsignor Harold E. Collins, acting for San Francisco's Archbishop Mitty, got wind of the impending publication of the story and asked the *News* to suppress it. A courageous editor not only refused, but published the fact ten days later that the priest had paid a $250 fine.

Then the Catholic hierarchy went to work to punish the *News*. Archbishop Mitty directed his clergy at a semi-annual conference to tell their parishioners about the "antagonistic" and "bigoted" attitude of the *News*. He declared that if this informal procedure were not effective, he would write an official letter to be read in every pulpit in the diocese condemning the *News* for its hostility. Catholic advertising was temporarily withdrawn from the Saturday religious page of the paper.

Frequently the Church succeeds in intimidating the most powerful newspapers by this policy of organized protest and boycott, and, in many cases, the facts suppressed have great social significance. The Philadelphia *Public Ledger,* in the face of a Catholic threat, once apologized abjectly for printing some disparaging remarks by Katherine Mayo about Catholic missions in the Philippines.[18] Philadelphia, with a population which is almost one-third Catholic, is quite typical of Northern cities in this respect. "No newspaper, however it may feel its oats, can go on belittling the Catholic Church," proclaimed the Right Reverend Edward Hawks in the *Catholic Standard and Times* of Philadelphia. "We all remember what happened to the *Public Ledger*." [19] Four or five of the great newspapers of the country, notably the *Washington Post, The New York Times* and the *St. Louis Post-Dispatch,* occasionally print frank items which can be construed as "anti-Catholic" because of their factual content, but they rarely print an analytical editorial on such items, placing the newspaper itself in a position opposed to the hierarchy.

In cities where the Church is powerful, the hierarchy attempts to censor all advertising of the birth-control movement, even when the advertising consists of dignified statements signed by bishops and rabbis. When the Louisville *Courier-Journal* accepted such an advertisement for planned parenthood, Archbishop John A. Floersh directed all the priests in the Lousville diocese to read a letter to their congregations saying: "The action of the paper in printing such an advertisement is unpardonable, if for no other reason, at least for this that it offends the decency of its Christian readers and constitutes a deliberate assault on their cherished religious principle." The *Courier-Journal* refused to apologize, and replied in an editorial: "It is not insulting for a non-Catholic newspaper to disagree with the Catholic Church." [20] When the *Reader's Digest* reprinted a *Survey* article in 1943 that lauded the work of a birth-control nurse, it was subjected to a similar attack from the National Catholic Welfare Conference, but did not apologize.

Every city editor in the United States knows of the unofficial Catholic censorship of American news, but almost all publishers avoid discussion of the phenomenon because of the fear of Catholic reprisals. The hierarchy itself has avoided public discussion of its boycott techniques in recent years, and has resorted more and more to quiet pressure. It has discovered that public mass movements against courageous editors sometimes prove to be boomerangs. It has discovered also that four or five insiders in a Catholic diocese can simulate a mass movement of protest very successfully.

A Jesuit priest, Charles J. Mullaly, has published in the Jesuit magazine *America* one of the most useful social documents of our time, a point-by-point description of Catholic techniques in boycotting an American newspaper, and a censorship program for priests and laymen.[21] Father Mullaly tells with perfect candor how a priest and four or five Catholic laymen, with the help of an impressive letterhead bearing the names of prominent citizens, can terrorize any editor with the specter of a great wave of Catholic indignation.

The boycott which he describes as a model in the techniques of suppression was organized by the priests of Washington, D. C., when a young girl who had been an inmate of a Catholic home conducted by the Sisters of the Good Shepherd died while trying to escape from an upper window of the home at night. There was, naturally, much speculation in Washington concerning the conditions that had caused the young girl to attempt escape. One Washington newspaper allowed local citizens, in discussing the affair in its letter columns, to criticize the policy of Catholic institutions.

Instead of writing an indignant defense of the Sisters of the Good Shepherd [says Father Mullaly] and thus stimulating a controversy that would have been financially profitable to the offending paper, this Catholic society followed a more practical method of action. Its strategy was aimed at the business office and not at the editorial department. . . . Members of the society interviewed merchants who advertised in the paper and suggested they demand an immediate change of editorial policy, if they hoped to keep Catholic trade. No intimation of boycott was given [*sic*], but these businessmen understood perfectly well that the paper was supported by their advertising, and they hastened to show sympathy for their insulted Catholic patrons. In one instance an advertiser, who used a page and a half daily, immediately cut his space, with the warning to the business office that, if any more insults were published against his Catholic customers, he would withdraw all advertising.

Priests in Washington were told to make a statement in their pulpits "somewhat as follows": "There is a newspaper in this city that is attacking the Sisters of the Good Shepherd. I will not mention its name. This paper is opening its columns to bigots who are insulting the purity of our Catholic Sisterhoods. I do not know what kind of Catholic each of you may be, but as for me, I will fight insults to Holy Mother Church. I do not know what you will do; I will fling any offending newspaper from my house and I will never buy it again." Father Mullaly claimed that "the effect was magical," and that the offending newspaper lost 40 per cent of its circulation in two weeks.

It should be noted that this priestly assault on an American newspaper occurred not because of an editorial attack upon the Catholic faith or because of any expression of editorial sentiment, but because American citizens were *permitted* to express their own personal views in a public letter column that had been reserved for such personal views. Father Mullaly, in triumphant mood, told how the Washington Truth Society was able to function successfully as censor of the Washington press in this manner without any large membership meetings. Its actual work was done by "one active priest in charge, two zealous laymen and a Catholic lawyer or two, ready to give legal advice free of charge. The letterhead was formidable with names of prominent men, but this heavy artillery was brought to bear only when urgently needed. In any city of the United States one zealous pastor with two or three active laymen, together with a legal adviser, could form a Truth Society that would batter to pieces bigotry when found in the pages of any local newspaper."

Father Mullaly concluded this revealing document with a platform of action for punishing critical American newspapers:

1. Do not attack a magazine or newspaper through its editorial departments but act through its business office.

2. When a magazine or newspaper is attacking your religion, write to the business manager and inform him that you will not buy the offending periodical again, and mean it. . . .

4. Call the attention of the merchants with whom you deal to the insults and tell them that as long as they advertise in any offending paper, you will not buy their goods, and mean it. . . .

6. Tell your news-dealer that as long as you see the magazine or newspaper on his stand as an open insult to you, you will not buy from him, and mean it.

Father Mullaly's platform is entirely consistent with Papal pretensions. The Vatican does not stand for freedom of the press as the term is commonly used in the United States. The Church *tolerates* freedom of the press only up to a certain point, and with restrictions. In 1946 Pius XII told a group of American editors that freedom of the press "does not allow a man to print what is wrong, what is known to be false, or what is calculated to undermine and destroy the moral and religious fiber of individuals and the peace and harmony of nations." The Church, of course, is the supreme judge of all requisites of worthy public expression. Most Americans will agree with *The Christian Century* that this is "a totalitarian conception of the freedom of the press." [22]

6

Most Americans probably assume that the Roman Catholic instrument of censoring films, the Legion of Decency, is concerned primarily with what H. L. Mencken once called "translucent drawers." The Legion's name implies that it is the guardian of purity and the logical heir to Anthony Comstock in the pursuit of the lewd, lascivious, and obscene. It pleases the Catholic hierarchy to have Americans take this view of the agency because if it were called the Catholic Political and Doctrinal Censorship it would immediately lose its usefulness to the Church.

Nothing in the public pledge of the Legion of Decency, administered once a year to all Catholic congregations in the United States, indicates its underlying denominational and political objectives. The pledge says:

In the name of the Father and the Son and the Holy Ghost. Amen.

I condemn indecent and immoral motion pictures, and those which glorify crime or criminals.

I promise to do all that I can to strengthen public opinion against the production of indecent and immoral films, and to unite with all those who protest against them.

I acknowledge my obligation to form a right conscience about pictures that are dangerous to my moral life. As a member of the Legion of Decency, I pledge myself to remain away from them. I promise, further, to stay away altogether from places of amusement which show them as a matter of policy.

Actually the Legion of Decency, in its private censorship of several hundred films a year, is far more concerned with Catholic dogma and Catholic social philosophy than with decency. Indecency is only the organization's pretext for extending Catholic influence into the studios. The Legion begins where the censors of the government and the industry leave off. It seeks to rate all films according to a kind of super-code that emphasizes distinctly Catholic taboos, and, at the same time, it tries to prevent the issuance of films containing any material critical of the social policies of the Church.

Naturally it exerts pressure upon the industry in favor of films that treat the Church in a flattering manner. Its value to the Church, in this respect, is inestimable. *Going My Way, Boys Town, Song of Bernadette,* and *The Bells of St. Mary* were probably worth more to the hierarchy in creating good will than all the propaganda produced by the Church's official proselyting agencies in a decade.

The Legion's denominational bias is quite transparent, and has been since the organization was founded in 1934. In 1947 it raised such a clamor against the British film *Black Narcissus* as an "affront to religion and religious life" that the producer was forced to withdraw the picture and make substantial changes to avoid a permanent "condemned" rating. *Black Narcissus* was a fair and realistic film about frustrated *Anglican nuns,* but the Legion could not allow convent life, even non-Catholic convent life, to be exposed to criticism.

The Legion did not dare to boycott completely such a charming family picture as *Life with Father* but it refused to give the film top rating as "unobjectionable for general patronage" because "it presents certain concepts on the sacrament of Baptism which are contrary to Catholic teaching and practice." The harmless and delightful *The Bishop's Wife* was likewise rated not suitable for the whole family because one of its characters, according to the film critic of *America,* was "a dictatorial widow who tells him [the bishop], among other things, that it was she who had him made bishop." Part of the duty of the Legion, it appears, is to protect Catholic youth from the suggestion that bishoprics can be bought in *any* church. Occasionally the Legion breaks out in a purely theological condemnation, as in its objection to *Repeat Performance:* "This film presents as a theory the inevitability of destiny despite the free will of man."

Of the seventy films rated "objectionable in part" by the Legion in 1947, only 40 per cent were called suggestive; the objections to the rest were largely denominational, that is to say, the objections would not necessarily be accepted by good Protestants and Jews as reasons for rejecting a film. About one-third of the "objectionable in part" films were given this low rating because of "light treatment of marriage and divorce." In priestly parlance this does not mean what it means to non-Catholics. If a script writer assumes that divorce may be an unfortunate but practical way to terminate an unhappy marriage, that assumption is called "light treatment of marriage and divorce."

In fact, the most common indictment of films marked "objectionable in part" by the Legion in its 1945-46 reviews was the phrase "Reflects the acceptability of divorce." Some of the films so branded undoubtedly treated family life in a frivolous and irresponsible manner, but many others were in accord with the highest non-Catholic moral ideals.

Gentleman's Agreement, the famous film on anti-Semitism, voted by New York film critics as the best film of 1947, was given a Grade III "objectionable in part" rating because the heroine, played by Dorothy Maguire, had once been divorced, and it was improper to imagine that a divorced person could ever be happily remarried. That was also the reason *Miracle on 34th Street,* one of the most suitable family pictures of its year, was similarly rated; Darryl Zanuck had refused to make the divorced lady of the story into a war widow to suit the Legion of Decency.

William H. Mooring, the Catholic convert who writes the syndicated motion-picture reviews for the Catholic diocesan press of the United States, summed up in the Brooklyn *Tablet* of January 31, 1948, his reasons for failing to give *Miracle on 34th Street* his blessing:

> Unfortunately, the people who adhere rigidly to Legion of Decency ratings and firmly refuse to patronize pictures that are classified as "objectionable in part," had to forego the pleasure of seeing it. *Miracle on Thirty-Fourth Street* introduced the subject of divorce.
>
> The reference was entirely gratuitous. The leading feminine character, nicely played by Maureen O'Hara, was a divorcee. She was a sophisticated career woman, so the writers assumed she must also be a divorcee. She had a little daughter who proved a pivotal character, but the little girl could just as easily have been a niece, or a young sister or a child adopted by an unmarried professional woman. Spinsters have been known to make admirable foster mothers, and there's no law against it.

Some defenders of the Legion insist that it is only exercising the American right of free criticism—and no one is disposed to deny that right whether exercised by a church or by any other social institution. This claim, however, is entirely specious. The Legion goes far beyond free criticism and organizes punitive boycotts against theaters for *future* films, when a theater owner defies its rulings. The boycott directives usually go out in the columns of Catholic film critics. When, in 1953, the Legion condemned *The Moon Is Blue,* William H. Mooring not only denounced the film because "its theme is seduction" and because of its "pseudo-naïve badinage about promiscuity" but published instructions for future boycotts as follows:

> Catholic organizations everywhere should immediately implement the terms of our annual Legion of Decency pledge by:
>
> 1) Causing all theater owners to know that as Catholics and members of the Legion of Decency they are under solemn pledge to "stay away *altogether* from theaters which show immoral films as a matter of policy. . . ."

2) By refusing to patronize any of the films released by a company distributing or offering *The Moon Is Blue.* . . .[23]

When the Legion condemned *The French Line* in 1954, Cardinal Stritch in Chicago officially called for a permanent boycott of any theater which refused to cancel the film; and in Buffalo, Bishop Burke, in the words of the *Catholic Almanac,* "urged his people to protest by phone or letter, or in person to any theater scheduling the picture; if the picture were shown anyway, he urged that managers be informed that the offending theaters would be boycotted for six months." [24]

The Legion consistently fights any reference in the films to any person or fact in history that would reflect upon the Church's character. In 1947 it induced Metro-Goldwyn-Mayer to alter Dumas's *The Three Musketeers* in several important particulars. Thomas Brady, writing in *The New York Times* of December 7, 1947, said that the Legion of Decency's Hollywood representative, Father John J. Devlin, suggested the complete elimination of Cardinal Richelieu from the film because Dumas's characterization of the cardinal as a worldly and unscrupulous man was offensive to the Church. Father Devlin was not satisfied to take the clerical garb off the cardinal and omit all religious functions. The studio finally made Richelieu into a mere caricature of a stock villain, without clerical trappings or clerical title. "In fact," said *The New Yorker* in commenting upon the transformation, "if it were not for his doublet and hose, you could hardly tell him from the standard Hollywood version of a Fifth Columnist or crooked used-car dealer." [25]

When Samuel Shellabarger's novel *Captain from Castile* was filmed, Twentieth Century-Fox was warned by the Legion of Decency that its villainous priest of the Inquisition was not true to history. Two scripts of the play, according to *The Nation,*[26] had to be torn up, and a doctored script substituted that mollified the Legion of Decency by depicting the villainous priest as one who was not cruel and did not accept bribes. When Greene's *The Labyrinthine Ways* was made into the film *The Fugitive,* even the fact that the author is a Catholic did not save the story from mutilation. The priest of the novel, who liked brandy and a mistress and had an illegitimate child, was made into the insipid, sinless hero of one of the world's dullest films, dutifully heralded by the Catholic diocesan press as one of Hollywood's greatest productions.

The distortion of famous literary works has become such a commonplace in Hollywood that it excites little attention. Thomas Brady's above-mentioned article in the *Times* described other changes forced in *The Three Musketeers* and in other works of art. "Constance, the married mistress of D'Artagnan in the novel," Mr. Brady said, "will be unmarried on the screen, her unsympathetic husband becoming her cruel father." A new Columbia film on Lucrezia Borgia may be compelled to suppress the fact that she was the illegitimate daughter of Pope Alexander VI. And producer Geiger, in order to avoid Catholic criticism, has felt compelled to doctor the Berthold Brecht-Charles Laughton version of the play *Galileo,* so that the screen adaptation "will present Galileo's opposition as general scholastic authoritarianism rather than specific religious inquisition."

The Legion of Decency itself is not content with "general scholastic authoritarianism." It is ecclesiastical through and through. Its tactics and methods of operation are all directed by the hierarchy. It is an organic part of the Catholic Church, staffed by the clergy, and administered since 1936 by the Archdiocese of New York. The public pledge of the Legion was ordered by Pope Pius XI in his encyclical *On Motion Pictures.* Probably 10,000,-000 persons have taken the oath, at one time or another, and all Catholic organizations are directed to enforce boycotts whenever possible. Boycotts are frequently spearheaded by the Catholic War Veterans, whose members make excellent marchers and aggressive pickets.

Local bishops claim the traditional right to go beyond the censorship of the Legion of Decency and "censor films which are admitted to the general list," but usually they abide by the list printed each week in all diocesan newspapers throughout the country and posted at the doors of the churches. The actual first-judgment reviewing of films is done in New York by a revolving committee of alumnae of Catholic women's colleges, known colloquially as "Mrs. Looram's ladies," since they are headed by a Mrs. James F. Looram. The literature of the Legion has never made public the special qualifications of the censors for their work.[27]

Since 1951 the power of the Legion has sharply declined both in Hollywood and throughout the country. The turning point came when Cardinal Spellman and the Legion denounced an Italian film, *The Miracle,* as a "sacrilegious and blasphemous mockery of Christian religious faith" when it was exhibited in New York. Under Catholic pressure the licensing authorities of both New York City and New York State banned the picture from public exhibition.

The Miracle was not by any stretch of the imagination an obscene film. It told, in sensitive fashion, the story of a demented goat-tender (Anna Magnani) who, while tending her goats, was plied with wine by a bearded stranger, was seduced (off-stage), and later gave birth to a child. In her mental confusion she imagined that she had been impregnated in some miraculous way by St. Joseph, her favorite saint. She found refuge in a village church where she gave birth to her illegitimate child. Cardinal Spellman and the Legion objected to the film because of an implied analogy with the Virgin Birth; it was apparent that their real protest was theological, although, oddly enough, the film had been produced, directed, and acted entirely by Catholics, who saw nothing sacrilegious in it.

The producer of *The Miracle* fought back; he carried his case to the United States Supreme Court and won from that Court a unanimous decision.[28] American films henceforth cannot be subjected to blind, prior restraint by film censorship boards. They are entitled, as any other medium of communication is entitled, to the free speech guaranties of the First and Fourteenth Amendments. Since this historic decision, the pronunciamentos of the Legion have become more and more ineffective. Cardinal Spellman's denunciation of the Elia Kazan film *Baby Doll,* in 1956, did not prevent its exhibition in many theaters or destroy its financial prospects. (Incidentally, the Cardinal did not bother to see *Baby Doll* before condemning it.)

Films condemned by the Legion have more than doubled during the last decade, and theater owners are becoming more and more independent of its censorship power. One reason is that the arbitrary, sectarian basis of the Legion's standards is becoming year by year more apparent. In 1956 it condemned a French movie, *Letters from My Windmill,* for "disrespectful presentation of religion" because it pictured the gluttony of a medieval priest while serving Mass, although this same picture had been approved by the highest-ranking Catholic film authority in France, Canon Jean Dewavrin, director of the Centrale Catholique du Cinema.[29]

When the film *Martin Luther* was introduced, the Legion did not quite dare to give it a C ranking along with imported obscene pictures, but the censors gave it a special "Separate Classification" as a film containing "theological and historical references and interpretations which are unacceptable to Catholics." It was denounced as "a theological fraud and historical farce" by Father Urban Adelman, editor of the *Catholic Home Journal,* and it was banned altogether by Catholic pressure in Quebec, the Philippines, Peru, and Egypt.[30]

7

Catholic techniques in censoring radio and television are so similar to the methods used in dealing with newspapers that they need no detailed description here. The Church does not require any separate Legion of Decency in the radio and television field partly because its own bishops can easily handle the slight deviations from doctrinal conformity on the air. In an encyclical letter of 16,000 words (summarized in *The New York Times* of September 12, 1957) Pius XII imposed upon the bishops responsibility for "supervision" over the air as well as the films, and urged upon them the duty of "positive action and authority" in censoring these media. The central Roman Pontifical Commission for Didactic and Religious Motion Pictures has now been changed to the Pontifical Commission for Motion Pictures, Radio and Television, and it is presided over by an Irish-American bishop. Part of his task is to promote Catholic Action groups in all countries to see that nothing "offensive" to the Church ever reaches the air waves.

In general, all the major religious bodies in the United States have a privileged position on the air, and the Catholic Church shares in the privilege. In general, no radio or television network permits any direct or specific criticism of any religious body, although Catholic radio orators like Fulton J. Sheen are freely permitted to indulge in violent attacks on religious liberalism—the group that embraces Unitarianism, Universalism, liberal Congregationalism, and liberal Judaism. The immunity of Catholicism is perhaps a little more pronounced than that of other denominations because it extends into many matters of social and educational policy. The hierarchy, by bringing its sexual, medical, and educational code within the sacred sphere of its religious dogmas, is able to protect itself against purely political and secular criticism.

Because of the general taboo against any "attack" on a religious faith, no person in the United States is permitted to suggest on the air that the Catholic Church is the chief enemy of modern sex education or of birth control or of scientific methods of dealing with venereal disease, although every specialist in these fields is aware of the fact. Nor is any person permitted to describe on the air the methods and regulations used by the hierarchy in opposing the American public school or in supporting fascism in Spain. (A slight break-through of this blockade came in 1956 and 1957 in New York, with the "Mike Wallace Program" on Channel 5, which specialized in controversy and won a large audience; but it is too early to predict that this program has started a trend.) The restrictions upon American freedom on the air are substantial. "More people are influenced by what they hear than by what they read or see." [31] More than 90 per cent of American families have radio sets, and those sets have more than 130,000,000 potential listeners. The television statistics are almost as colossal.

When Walter Winchell, speaking on a national hook-up in February, 1947, gave a mild endorsement to planned-parenthood activity, he and his radio sponsors were subjected to a concerted attack in all parts of the United States. The country's leading Catholic family journal, *Our Sunday Visitor,* declared that "the Jergens Company [sponsor] owes an apology to those religious organizations in the United States which do try to defend the moral law." [32] When the priest-president of Notre Dame was allowed to attack birth-control teaching on the air and a New York station gave the birth-control forces an opportunity to reply, an Episcopal clergyman who participated in the birth-control broadcast was not even permitted to include in his discussion the phrase "unmarried medieval theologians" to identify the historical origin of the opposition.

When the well-known radio team of Jinx Falkenburg and her husband, Tex McCrary, in a broadcast over New York's WNBC on February 11, 1948, permitted a young Negro couple with three small children to describe the benefits that child spacing, as taught by the Planned Parenthood Federation, had brought to their home, thousands of letters of protest from Catholic sources poured into the National Broadcasting Company, many of them containing the same misspelled words and showing complete ignorance of the nature of the Falkenburg-McCrary program.

Under pressure, the National Broadcasting Company felt

compelled to take an apologetic and conciliatory attitude. Its officials did not dare to attack the intolerance and bigotry that lay behind the directed campaign. Catholics were assured that "it was not the intention of Jinx and Tex or Station WNBC to offend any listener." Mr. McCrary had said at the end of the offending broadcast: "After hearing of your Federation's efforts, I feel sure that we are rapidly progressing to the point where procreation of man will be on as scientific a basis as animals or hybrid corn." The Catholic press swooped down upon this sentence with glee. The beleaguered Jinx and Tex inserted the following "explanation" in a later broadcast:

> . . . and, Jinx, remember the other day we had three guests on the program, telling the story of the Planned Parenthood Association? Some of the objectives of this group have, of course, been the subject of considerable controversy on moral grounds, and it is a matter of sincere regret to us that parts of the program offended the convictions of some of our listeners.
>
> One impression I would like to correct is that we intended to compare in any way the reproduction of man to that of animals and hybrid corn. That was not our purpose. We recognize, with all right-thinking people, that the creation of a human soul out of nothing is a divine act. What we intended to express on our program was our gratification that in terms of money and research, we are beginning to realize that the heredity of man is more important than the heredity of lower forms of life.[33]

Occasionally a powerful broadcasting company has the courage to defy Catholic pressure. On April 29, 1948, after elaborate precautionary consultations with Catholic as well as non-Catholic authorities, the American Broadcasting Company prepared to broadcast a wholesome and scientific script on venereal disease, "VD: a Conspiracy of Silence," written by the United States Public Health Service and the Columbia University Radio Program Bureau. The Archdiocese of New York would not give approval in writing, and, shortly before the broadcast, the Church expressed official opposition privately. In spite of pressure from New York and Washington Church headquarters and from the Catholic War Veterans, the program was broadcast as scheduled with the modification of only a few words. The public response was enthusiastic and almost unanimously favorable. The *Catholic News* protested vainly that the program "was not only distasteful but shocking."

The public thought otherwise, and an implied Catholic boycott died before it was born. In August, 1948, Dwight D. Eisenhower, as president of Columbia University, urged the radio industry to assist in a "critical job of education" by carrying such programs locally.[34]

Catholic censorship of radio programs is effective largely because of its nuisance value. According to the informal practice of the industry, the great broadcasting companies undertake to give equal time to any religious or moral or educational group of any importance that feels that it has been misrepresented or maligned by a critic on the air. Because of this rule, a station permitting any criticism of Roman Catholic policy, or of distinctively Protestant or Jewish policy, is immediately besieged with demands for the right to answer the impeachment. So, program directors live in terror of all critics of any religious group, and they have a special fear of the Catholic counterattack on any critic because the Roman hierarchy is the most dogmatic and aggressive.

The hierarchy takes full advantage of the fear and obsequiousness that it finds in almost every studio. Its leaders freely use the great networks for so-called religious broadcasts that are interlarded with political and partisan propaganda. For years Bishop Fulton J. Sheen used the most important religious period on the American radio, "The Catholic Hour" of the National Broadcasting Company, to broadcast, free of charge, innuendoes and pronouncements against political and religious liberalism, birth control, reasonable divorce laws, the government of Yugoslavia, and any other target that inspired his wrath. He was freely permitted to insult American non-Catholic family life, under the guise of attacking Communism. In a March, 1947, "Catholic Hour" broadcast he declared: "There is no doubt that the philosophy of America today regarding family life is just the same as Russia's between 1917 and 1935, namely belief in divorce, free love and a queer system which in a compound word rejects both birth and control."

Neither Bishop Sheen nor the other Catholic speakers on this program were censored. They reached 103 stations during this period, and 52 stations during "The Hour of Faith" of the American Broadcasting Company, all free of charge.

When Catholic censorship of literature and motion pictures is considered in the larger perspective of American life, there

seems little to recommend it. No one questions the religious freedom of the hierarchy or its right to influence its people in matters
pertaining to the moral aspects of art and literature. Nor does
anyone question the fact that Catholic censorship has eliminated
some unwelcome vulgarity from the lower reaches of pornographic
commerce. But the censorship operations of the hierarchy have
gone far beyond religion and decency. They have extended into
the world of politics, medicine, and historical truth. They have
impaired the integrity of the media of information serving non-
Catholics as well as Catholics. Most important of all, the hierarchy
has stifled self-criticism among its own people by refusing them
permission to read both sides of vital controversies on matters of
social policy. Such repression is directly contrary to the American
conception of freedom of thought. Because most Catholics are
good citizens and good Americans, it seems inevitable that sooner
or later they will recognize the censorship system of their priests
for what it is, a survival of medieval authoritarianism that has no
rightful place in the democratic American environment.

Perhaps this thought was in the mind of the Catholic historian Mason Wade when he said to a 1948 meeting of Catholic
authors in Boston:

> In recent years there have been certain signs that we Catholics,
> who once hailed the American traditions of tolerance and freedom
> because they enabled us to exist as a tiny minority in an overwhelming
> Protestant U.S.A., are becoming somewhat bumptious, now that our
> unified strength outweighs the disordered ranks of a dying Protestant-
> ism. We seem to be adopting the Puritan attitude of "I will not. Thou
> shalt not." A strong majority, like the original settlers of Massachusetts
> Bay, may thus coerce a wavering minority along the road of rectitude,
> but no tactics on the part of a strong minority are more apt to unite
> the majority against it.
>
> Americans have always peculiarly loved liberty, and we Catholics
> may be launching a boomerang against ourselves when we attempt to
> impose our discipline upon our fellow Americans who are not Catho-
> lics.[35]

One of the most noted American Jesuits, Father John Courtney Murray, in a much publicized article in 1956 on "Literature
and Censorship" gave some hope to Catholic liberals by suggesting
that an ordinary father and mother are not "qualified to act as
censor within society at large, or to decide what literature and

movies may be displayed before the public." He called for "professional competence" in literary critics, and deplored "methods of action which verge upon the coercive." "Censorship is no job for an amateur," he said.[36]

His inferences were hailed as hostile to the stupid pressure tactics of the N.O.D.L. and kindred Catholic censorial groups, but his language, as befitted a Jesuit who was questioning established clerical institutions, was general and ambiguous. He did not question the fitness of bishops to establish and direct a censorship system. He did not dare to attack the central fortress of Catholic intellectual suppression, Canon 1399 of the Code, which imposes an internal censorship on the mental activities of all Catholics. "This canonical discipline," he explained, "is outside our present subject . . ." At the end of his article appeared the tell-tale legend, "Published with ecclesiastical approval."

10

Science, Scholarship, and Superstition

1

IN ITS RELATIONS WITH science the Roman Catholic Church operates on three levels, the upper scholarly level, the priestly level, and the level of popular superstition. The priest acts as a mediator between the upper and lower levels, striving to reconcile the extremes and keep them both in the one true Church. His task is exceedingly difficult. He is not a free agent and he does not operate under American controls. He must stand with one foot in the twentieth century and the other in the thirteenth. The resultant straddle is extremely painful and embarrassing for many a priest.

In the United States the straddle between science and superstition is even more painful for educated Catholic laymen than for priests. They tend to believe in the American gospel of science because they have been reared in the American atmosphere, and, at the same time, they wish to be loyal to their priests. Those priests, however, are directed from Rome, and Rome has given many hostages to medieval superstition. No American priest can be faithful to his trust unless he continually promotes and exploits practices that the educated Catholic must scorn as primitive deception.

The Catholic novelist Harry Sylvester, in his *Moon Gaffney*, tells how a sensitive and cultured young Catholic, afflicted with paralysis, is shipped away to Lourdes by his devout parents on the assumption that he can be cured by some magic power in the waters that flow from the spot where the Virgin Mary spoke with Bernadette Soubirous in 1858. The young man is secretly so infuriated by the superstitions of his father that he prays fervently that no chance circumstance will cure him. He would rather not be cured at all than have his cure associated with such superstitions.

Not many Catholics would go that far; but there are enough educated believers to put the priests on the defensive in their practices of traditional magic. The hierarchy is exceptionally sensitive about the charge that the Church exploits the superstitions of the ignorant, perhaps for the reason that so many people believe the charge. Millions of Americans oppose the Church primarily because they believe that it has not adjusted its teachings to modern knowledge.

How much *has* the Church adjusted itself? How much has it changed its attitudes and techniques since the seventeenth century, when it condemned Galileo for asserting that the earth moves around the sun?

Verbally, the Church has changed a great deal. In encyclical after encyclical recent Popes have proclaimed their steadfast devotion to science. If a student of the problem failed to note the qualifying phrases and conditions in Papal pronouncements, he might easily believe that the Church has always been the arch foe of superstition and the fearless champion of science.

The Jesuits have even evolved an "explanation" for the condemnation of Galileo, which reconciles the Church's blunder with the doctrine of the infallibility of the Pope. Galileo, it seems, was condemned by a "commission," not by the Pope himself. The Pope, when he ratified the sentence that condemned the scientist, was not acting in his official capacity as pastor of the human race. In any case, Galileo was not condemned for teaching the truth but for being too *abrupt* about it. He persisted in teaching as a *fact* something that should have been taught only as a *theory*. Ergo, "it will be found that the Galileo case furnishes splendid evidence of the Church's truly scientific attitude and procedure." [1]

Pope Pius XII, in his address before the Pontifical Academy of Science in 1939, declared that the Church "throughout the centuries has proved to be the mother of science and progress." Pius XI in his encyclical on *Christian Education of Youth* declared that "science, scientific methods and scientific research . . . have nothing to fear from the full and perfect mandate which the Church holds in the field of education." In the Jesuit pamphlet quoted above, Father Scott says:

It is historically certain that from the beginning of Christianity to the present day the Catholic Church has been the greatest friend and supporter of science. . . . Whenever you hear that the Church is opposed to science, you may be sure that either the Church is misrepresented or that the science in question is pseudo-science.

It would be comforting to accept this optimistic view. There is no doubt that today the Church accepts many of the *findings* of science which it once rejected, including the teachings of Galileo —although Galileo's books were not removed from the Catholic *Index* finally until 1822. Today science is lauded and "recognized" on all top levels of Catholic life in the United States. The American Catholic universities have created many learned societies that are indistinguishable in their use of technical language from all the other learned societies. Probably it would be safe to say that the Catholic laboratory technician is free to agree with his non-Catholic colleagues in respect to 90 per cent of their scientific conclusions.

But the Catholic hierarchy still does not accept either the method or the conclusions of science when the results of scientific inquiry conflict with priestly belief and practice, and every Papal endorsement of science is made with this spoken or unspoken reservation. In fact, the mechanism of priestly control over science and the fundamental theory on which the mechanism works are essentially the same today as they were in the Middle Ages. The technique for disciplining a rebellious scientist has changed; the principle has not.

The theory behind the Church's control of science is that all truth is divided into two grades, divine and human. Divine truth comes from God via the Roman Catholic Church; human truth comes from finite reason, experience, and observation. Divine truth is per se infallible; human truth is always subject to correction by divine truth. If the two conflict, that conflict *ipso facto* proves that the supposed human truth is not truth at all but falsehood.

Pius XI described the Church's guardianship over truth in his encyclical on *Christian Education of Youth:*

Nor does she, the Church, prevent sciences, each in its own sphere, from making use of principles and methods of their own. Only while acknowledging the freedom due to them, she takes every precaution to prevent them from falling into error by opposition to divine doctrine, or from overstepping their proper limits, and thus invading and disturbing the domain of faith.[2]

That is the *theory* for priestly control of science. The mechanism is arbitrary and authoritarian. In the Catholic system every judgment by a scientist or a philosopher concerning the nature of the universe, the relation of man to that universe, the institution of the family, or the moral principles of human conduct is subject to review and condemnation by a supreme court composed of priests and presided over by the Pope. This is the Congregation of the Holy Office, the same commission that establishes the clerical code for doctors and nurses; it is composed of nine cardinals and acts wholly in secret. It pledges its victims in advance never to reveal the facts or processes of their inquisition. It is appointed entirely from above, and contains no American and no lay scientist. It is even more independent of democratic influences today than it was in the Middle Ages, for then the Church occasionally held a General Council of the higher clergy. As we have seen, the modern Catholic Church has held no General Council of its clergy since the Pope was declared infallible in 1870, and it *never* holds a plenary conference of Catholic people.

Joseph Bernhart, in describing the vast powers of the Holy Office over the modern scholar in *The Vatican as a World Power,* wrote:

The ancient palace of the Holy Office, which stands alone to the side of the colonnade of St. Peter's, still evokes the sombre mood which has always been created by the name and the work of the Inquisition. . . . How many fall a victim to its spiritual inquiry no one can so much as guess, because even the Catholic who is summoned before it for some such purpose as to renounce an error is bound to maintain silence throughout life. Not only does the theologian engaged in teaching and writing stand under the supervision of the Holy Office and owe it an explanation for every departure from the prescribed teaching, but even the specialist in a profane science is under its jurisdiction. It may investigate the conclusion arrived at by an historian, or the system of a philosopher, a sociologist, or a political scientist, in so far as these touch upon questions of Church law and social ethics. It opposes the biologist and geologist when they reach conclusions at variance with orthodoxy; it disciplined Galileo and threatened Columbus. The spirit of resistance to innovations that seem dangerous abides today, though the measures employed are different. . . . It is evident that the General Inquisitors of the Holy Office—they are still so-called —have a broad field in which to carry on their activities.[3]

Although all Catholic scientists are subject to this Congregation of the Holy Office without recourse or appeal, they are, in practice, allowed great liberty as long as they do not encroach upon priestly preserves. Then the Holy Office may become firm and even vindictive. The penalty of excommunication and expulsion faces any scholar in a Catholic institution who dares to disagree openly. Usually Catholic scholars do not disagree openly. Either they submit quietly or slip out of the Church quietly, since the penalties of public defiance are painful in the extreme.

The general effect of this supervision of all science by priests is to create a special kind of ecclesiastical anti-science in the Church which the educated Catholic does not dare to evaluate candidly and openly. The special effects of this anti-science may be summarized briefly under six heads: (1) the system permits the continued exploitation of the poorer and more ignorant Catholic people by practices which have been discarded as medieval superstitions by nearly all other religious groups in the West; (2) it limits the physical scientist not so much by thwarting his research as by preventing him from drawing logical deductions from his data; (3) it imposes dogmatic restrictions upon Catholic social science, especially in the analysis of family and population problems; (4) it shades history in order to exalt Catholic accomplishments and conceal the devastating effects of clerical control in the past; (5) it makes the Catholic philosopher an underling of the theologian; (6) it reduces the Catholic universities to the lowest scientific level in American education.

2

The most important and lucrative form of anti-science in the Church is the exploitation of miracles and relics. Many non-Catholics imagine that relics are used by Catholicism merely as symbols of faith and devotion. Nothing could be farther from the truth. The Church, even the American Church of the present day, still operates a full-blown system of fetishism and sorcery in which physical objects are supposed to accomplish physical miracles. Sometimes it is claimed that these physical objects also accomplish spiritual miracles and change the physical or spiritual destiny of any fortunate Catholic who relies on them.

I have before me as I write[4] a four-page circular called *The Scapular Militia* issued by the Carmelite National Shrine of Our Lady of the Scapular, of 338 East 29th Street, New York. It bears the official Imprimatur of Archbishop (now Cardinal) Spellman, and it was issued at the height of the war in 1943. The slogan emblazoned on its cover is "A Scapular for Every Catholic Service Man," and it carries, underneath a picture of Mary, Joseph, and St. Simon Stock, the specific guaranty in heavy capitals: WHO-SOEVER DIES CLOTHED IN THIS SCAPULAR SHALL NOT SUFFER ETERNAL FIRE.

Originally the circular contained, in a pocket on the back page, a small cloth scapular to be tied about the neck of a member of the armed forces. The circular not only makes the flat promise, quoted and requoted from the Virgin Mary, that the wearer cannot go to hell, but it cites the miraculous effects of the charm in protecting Franco's soldiers from death in the Spanish civil war:

> In a book currently appearing in this country we read: "The Carmelite Fathers of Spain tell us that letters constantly poured in from the front during the Spanish war (1936-39) describing Scapular miracles. Whole regiments wore the Scapular openly on their breasts. . . . A Carmelite Father showed the present writer a letter from a classmate who was directly fired upon by *four machine guns,* from a distance of 700 or 800 metres for a period of fifteen minutes, and who wrote in a token of gratitude to Our Lady of the Scapular, saying simply: 'And here I am.' " (Haffert, 1940)
>
> Today about *one hundred plenary indulgences* can be gained annually through the practice of the Scapular Devotion, not to speak of *almost countless days* of partial indulgences, all applicable to the souls in Purgatory.
>
> Besides this a Scapular wearer can assure his liberation from Purgatory *on the first Saturday after death.*

The scapular itself is free, but, at the bottom of the circular, over the Imprimatur of Cardinal Spellman, is the suggestion: "Donations to support the Scapular Militia will be gratefully accepted." An inside page contains the precautionary statement:

> A Scapular is not a talisman. It is not a rabbit's foot. It is the sign of devotedness to the Blessed Virgin, just as the carrying of your mother's picture in a fold of your wallet would be a sign of your devotedness to her.

Probably this final precautionary statement was added by a diocesan censor. At any rate, it illustrates quite admirably the technique of the hierarchy in handling matters of fetishism. The

Carmelite Fathers are permitted to collect money by exploiting a scapular in the most explicit language as a divinely guaranteed rabbit's foot. Then, in a few relatively inconspicuous lines in the text accompanying the scapular, the hierarchy disowns the idea. If a critic had attacked Cardinal Spellman for exploiting Catholic soldiers during the war by permitting such an appeal to superstition the Cardinal would undoubtedly have replied by saying that he was "misrepresented" by "bigots," and he would have quoted the above precautionary insertion as proof of his innocence. But, in fact, the offending circular did not promise salvation to those devoted to the Virgin; it promised salvation to those physically "clothed in this scapular."

The scapular racket has been promoted with renewed zeal in the American armed forces in the decade since World War II. All Catholic chaplains in the forces have received scapular "faculties" as well as Carmelite scapular literature telling how the Virgin Mary told St. Simon Stock that "anyone who is clothed in this [scapular] shall not suffer eternal fire," and will escape from purgatory on the Saturday after death. Five and one-half million scapulars have been distributed to armed service members in this way, and the Scapular Militia in 1957 set 1,000,000 scapulars a year as the promotion goal for the future.[5]

Actually, scapulars are not so important in the Catholic system of sorcery as relics. The number of working relics in the world has increased since the Middle Ages, and the Church continues to expand the supply every time a new saint is created. It is part of the official doctrine of the Church that true relics of Jesus and the saints are entitled to veneration if properly approved (Canon 1283), and no limit is set upon their miraculous power. Officially they cannot be sold, but they can be systematically exploited by the faithful, for their own profit and the benefit of the clergy. To avoid the charge of exploitation, the Church solemnly declares that it "does not guarantee the genuineness of a single relic," but it continues to give "episcopal authentication" to thousands of them.

Miraculous relics apparently had no place in the teachings of Jesus. Christian martyrs were the objects of veneration very early in the history of the Church, but it was some time before the custom of honoring their relics began. Once established, the custom spread rapidly. Graves were rifled and bones of the martyrs sold for large sums. New supplies of relics began to appear miraculously. The discovery of the alleged cross produced a whole crop of "miracles" and, as the *Hastings Encyclopedia of Religion* says sardonically, "a few years later the holy wood of the cross had almost filled the whole world."

Paulinus developed the intriguing theory that the part of the cross kept at Jerusalem gave off fragments of itself without diminishing. Thousands of holy garments and portions of the bodies of the saints began to appear throughout Europe. The coat of Jesus was exhibited at Trèves, the holy shroud at Turin, and the swaddling clothes at Aachen. By the time of the Reformation there were embarrassing duplications. Calvin discovered that he had been kissing a stag's bone when he had thought he was kissing the arm of St. Anthony, in Geneva; and that the supposed brain of St. Peter, kept at St. Peter's altar, was actually a pumice stone. He said:

It is almost incredible how the world has been cheated. I can mention three foreskins of our Saviour's circumcision, fourteen nails exhibited for the three driven into the cross, three robes for Christ's seamless garment over which the soldiers cast lots, three spears by which our Saviour's side was pierced, five sets of linen cloths in which his body in the tomb was wrapped.[6]

The relics industry in the United States has been more carefully regulated than in Europe, but it has not been entirely suppressed. In fact, it has been stimulated by two official practices of the Church, the creation of new saints and the use of relics in the building of new church altars. "It is necessary for the valid consecration of an altar," says the *Catholic Encyclopedic Dictionary,* "whether fixed or portable, that it contain, sealed into the sepulchre, relics of at least one martyr." If 14,000 Catholic churches in the United States have an average of four altars each, this requirement calls for 56,000 relics of martyrs in this country alone. New churches, of course, require new relics or portions of old ones.

Although relics, under Canon 1289, cannot be sold, there is a brisk trade in articles associated with certain relics. In the New York *Catholic News* of September 20, 1947, appeared a large advertisement, with reproduction of a "photograph" of Jesus taken from the Holy Shroud in Turin, with this written guaranty:

The negative from which this photograph was made lies in the Holy Shroud and was developed in the Tomb during the hours Our

Lord lay there before the Resurrection. The urea vapors emanating from the body acted on the aloes within the Shroud, creating the indissoluble pigment, aloetin, which was absorbed by the Shroud linen, thus forming the True Image of Christ. . . . The official Vatican Newspaper says: "Twenty centuries ago the Apostles saw and kissed this same living Face."—Monsig. Aureli, Director, *Osservatore Romano*.

In return for my $2 check, International Religious Art of 287 Commonwealth Avenue, Boston, sent me "the True Face of Christ from the Holy Shroud of Turin." An accompanying letter dated October 7, 1947, said:

As copyright owners in the Western Hemisphere we pay a royalty to the Official Photographer of the Holy See, Cav. G. Bruner, and to the Prince Archbishop of Trento, Italy, and these funds are for the rebuilding of the College of Priests and the Cathedral in Trento which were severely damaged during the war. . . . We can ship these to you for $18 per dozen.

This racket was discontinued and repudiated by the Boston hierarchy after my published exposure. It was somewhat more crude, but not much more unethical, than many standard forms of exploitation practiced by the Church.

The leaders of the American Church are still officially recognizing the multiple relics of Europe and the multiple miracles accomplished by those relics. The *Catholic Almanac* of 1948, page 250, says:

There are various relics of the true cross to be found principally in European cities: Brussels, Ghent, Rome, Venice, Ragusa, Paris, Limbourg and Mt. Athos. The inscription placed above the cross is preserved in the Basilica of the Holy Cross of Jerusalem at Rome. The crown of thorns is kept at Paris. One of the nails was supposedly thrown into the Adriatic to calm a storm; another was made into the famous iron crown at Lombardy; another is in the Church of Notre Dame, Paris. The sponge is in Rome at the Basilica of St. John Lateran. The point of the lance is in Paris, the rest is in Rome. The robe is in the Church of Treves. The tunic is in the Church of Argenteuil near Paris. A part of the winding sheet is in Turin. The linen with which Veronica wiped Christ's face is in Rome. Part of the pillar of the Scourging is in Rome, part in Jerusalem.

3

For many years the Western Hemisphere had a shortage of relics, but this deficiency is being rapidly eliminated by the creation of new saints. Pope Pius XII created eight new saints in the first seven months of 1947; Pius XI had at least 531 beatified and at least 31 canonized, including 136 English Catholic martyrs of Protestant persecution. Through a curious oversight, the Popes did not canonize a single United States citizen until 1946; and the one then chosen, Mother Cabrini, had been born in Italy and did not become a United States citizen until she had lived in this country for twenty years. In view of America's new financial and moral importance in the Church, the needs of American Catholicism cannot be overlooked. The National Catholic Welfare Conference has already submitted a petition to canonize 116 American missionary martyrs in one bloc.[7] The granting of this petition would give the United States no more than its fair share in the relics industry, since there are now 283 formally canonized saints of whom only one is American (by adoption), and the new American plan would give this nation only 29 per cent of the saintly total.

The relics of a new saint may be just as effective as those of an old one. In fact, the effectiveness of relics is usually considered a preliminary condition of sainthood, almost as important as the character and lifetime accomplishments of the saint himself. The present machinery for creating saints by beatification and canonization is based upon a definite mathematical plan for miracles. Usually those miracles are associated in some way with the saint's relics. As Joseph Bernhart points out in describing the Church's machinery for creating saints, beatification comes only after a petition has been submitted to the proper authorities showing saintliness and "at least two miracles *after death*" [8] (italics supplied). After an "investigation" made by Catholic devotees, and after beatification, which confers only limited and local sainthood, the saint may be canonized. He then becomes the object of universal veneration in the Church. This final honor is attained only if the saint's relics or spirit have performed *new* miracles after beatification.

"Clear proof of at least four miracles is required as a condition of canonization," says the introduction to *The Book of Saints*.

"It must be shown in each case that the fact alleged as miraculous has really taken place, that it cannot be explained away or attributed to any natural cause, and that the miracle directly followed upon an appeal to Almighty God through His servant departed this life." [9]

Why does the Church insist that a physical miracle performed *after death* is necessary to qualify a dead man for sainthood? Because the miracle is proof of the fact that he has already passed through purgatory and reached heaven, and thus his sainthood is verified. As *The Book of Saints* puts it: "Canonization is the official recognition by the Church of the fact that one of her children has won his place in Heaven; and since Almighty God alone can make known this fact to mankind, every canonization essentially depends on proof that miracles have been wrought in witness thereto."

What kinds of miracles are accepted by the hierarchy as evidence of sainthood? In this respect the hierarchy is very lenient. In practice the miracles are nearly always subjective miracles performed for those who are already devout, and they are "investigated" by persons equally devout. The miracles are usually described in very general terms, often with no specific data as to location or time. They may have occurred many years before the "investigation," since under Canon 2101 the discussion of the virtues of a proposed saint does not ordinarily begin until at least fifty years after his death.[10]

Here, for example, as reported in the Catholic press, are the "two further miracles" which occurred after beatification, and which were accepted as genuine by the Vatican, when a nineteenth-century nun of the Sisters of Charity, Catherine Laboure, was canonized in August, 1947. She had died many years before and her remains had been carefully preserved.

The first, occurring the same year as her beatification, concerns Josephine Goudret, who was suffering from a serious heart ailment and had received the last sacraments. After imploring the intercession of Blessed Catherine, she was cured—a cure that was confirmed by two doctors who attended her and by four experts sent by the Congregation of the Rites.

The second miracle wrought through her intercession occurred in 1937. A sister Irene Pascal of the Daughters of Charity had undergone four operations for adhesions, but doctors declared her condition incurable. Yet on the sixth day of a novena to Catherine the nun was completely cured.[11]

The first miracle wrought by Mother Cabrini which was accepted for her canonization occurred in a Chicago Catholic hospital in 1921, four years after her death. A nurse accidentally bathed the eyes of a newborn baby—or *thought* she bathed the eyes of a newborn baby—with a 50 per cent solution of silver nitrate instead of a 1 per cent solution. The baby appeared to be blind and developed pneumonia. The doctors gave up hope for him, but a Catholic superior of the nurse pinned a relic of Mother Cabrini on the baby's gown, and the Sisters prayed for the child all night. He improved rapidly and became a normal child.[12] Silver nitrate in 50 per cent solution is a powerful caustic, but the eyelids of a wriggling infant readily go into spasm when an attempt is made to separate them, and the solution from an eyedropper may easily fail to reach the eyeball. The Massachusetts Eye and Ear Infirmary has a 1933 case on record in which a baby's sight survived a supposed treatment of 100 per cent—not a 50 per cent—composition of silver nitrate.

The canonization of a saint is prodigiously expensive, and it is surrounded with much formality and fuss. Many Catholic writers deplore the costly production methods, but they do not venture to describe the process as a scheme for exploiting the superstitions of the ignorant.

Joseph Bernhart writes:

> The process of beatification, and still more noticeably that of canonization, consumes huge sums of money which the petitioner—an Order, a family, a diocese—must raise. All members of the Congregation of Rites swear a solemn oath to spurn every bribe but it may well be that deference to national wishes proves under given circumstances not without influence upon the readiness of the Curia to act.

Religious orders, particularly hospital orders, frequently go about the business of saint-making with much gusto, since a saint and shrine are very effective devices for money-raising. An order of nurses will spend a great deal of time and money, if necessary, in searching for miracles that can be used to establish a patron saint for a hospital. Recently, for example, the Institute of Gray Nuns of Montreal initiated a movement to canonize the foundress of the Sisters of Charity of the General Hospital of Montreal. They went back forty-seven years to discover a miracle which consisted of a cure "in a case of pulmonary tuberculosis" achieved by the candidate-saint after she was dead. Eight nuns, priests, and Catholic doctors came to Montreal and appeared as witnesses with counsel before a tribunal headed by an archbishop in the effort to "prove" this miracle. The tribunal held twelve sessions and prepared a two-hundred-page dossier "which the Vice-Postulator will take to Rome, where the Congregation of Rites will examine the evidence and decide whether the reported miracle will be admitted." [13] If that miracle is accepted, there will probably be another long and expensive promotion process before the foundress-nurse is finally eligible for sainthood and a shrine.

But when the saint finally "arrives," she may be extremely profitable. In New York, the tomb of Mother Cabrini, according to *Ave Maria,* draws almost ten thousand visitors a day. The visitors file past a lifelike image of the famous saint in repose, many believing that they are viewing her miraculously preserved body— whereas the image is plastic and the shrine possesses only the bones.

In Chicago, the nuns who belong to the order which Mother Cabrini founded have recently announced a $4,500,000 addition to their Columbus Hospital, "containing a national shrine to Mother Cabrini." A Mr. and Mrs. Thomas Warner of Chicago have presented St. Peter's with a 20-foot, 25-ton statue of the saint, which was unveiled in the presence of the American Ambassador to Italy. When Mother Cabrini was canonized in Rome, fifty thousand tickets for the ceremony were given out; but this was not enough to meet the demand, and eager Americans offered as much as $200 for a ticket.

When a shrine becomes famous for its relics, the Catholic Travel League organizes pilgrimages to it. Six "developed" shrines in New York State drew 750,000 visitors in 1955.[14] St. Anne de Beaupré, twenty-one miles from Quebec, drew its largest annual attendance in history, 1,815,000 visitors, in 1955, bringing the total visitors since the shrine's establishment in 1658 to 30,620,-000—with 614 organized pilgrimages and more than half a million Masses.[15]

The shrine of St. Anne de Beaupré first began its climb to fame when St. Anne, the mother of the Virgin Mary, "cured" a man of "rheumatism of the loins," about 1676, after he had placed three stones on the foundation of the church. Although two French towns claimed all of St. Anne's bones in the Middle Ages, one turned up in Quebec in 1870. A cardinal presented "the wrist bone of St. Anne" to the shrine, and a monsignor brought it across the ocean with much ceremony.

Of course, nobody knows who the mother of the Virgin Mary was. Nobody knows where or when she was born, lived, or died. Nobody knows where she was buried. She is not even mentioned. in the Bible. *The Biographical Dictionary of the Saints,* by the Right Reverend F. G. Holweck, Imprimatur of the Archbishop of St. Louis, admits, page 79, that "not even the identity of her name is firmly established."

4

The exploitation of scapulars, ancient knucklebones, rusty nails from "the true cross," and pictures engraved on grave-clothes by urea goes on continuously, while the hierarchy professes enthusiastic admiration for science on the upper cultural level. The Church is wise enough not to impose compulsory belief in relics upon the wealthy and the educated. In the upper Catholic world, in fact, relics are regarded with a kind of amused tolerance. "No Catholic is formally bound to the positive veneration of relics," says the *Catholic Encyclopedic Dictionary,* "but is forbidden by the Council of Trent to say that such veneration ought not to be given."

This means in practice that the "honest" Catholic scientist disregards the whole relics industry, and keeps his mouth shut. He concentrates, if possible, on those subjects farthest removed from priestly exploitation. Catholic scientists are famous for their investigations of the weather and earthquakes. Occasionally a leader of the Church turns in disgust on the commercial exploitation of shrines and relics and describes the practices in blunt language. The late Monsignor John L. Belford, one of Brooklyn's most noted Catholic leaders, once published an article in the *Homiletic and Pastoral Review* on "Shrines: Their Use and Abuse"; in this article he deplored the fact that some shrines "have appealed to the greed which is one of the foul characteristics of human nature," and condemned the "commercialism which surrounds shrines." He said:

It is not easy to draw the line between devotion and superstition, but there are places at home and abroad where devotions are practised and promoted as a means to gather money. . . . Catholics are ashamed and non-Catholics are horrified. It is a crime to gather money —even to build a church—at such a cost to real religion. . . . The use of relics is, of course, approved by the Church. In that use we profess unqualified faith, but we do loathe, despise and condemn the contemptible practise of applying the relic with one hand and collecting money with the other.[16]

The exploitation of some shrines became so scandalous before World War II that the Sacred Congregation of the Council issued a special decree on June 7, 1932, deploring wild and unjustified tales of miracles and the association of pleas for money with tales of miraculous accomplishment.[17]

In recent years the hierarchy has added political purposes to other features of its shrine promotion. Of the two greatest shrines in the world today, the French Lourdes and the Portuguese Fatima, made sacred by visits of the Virgin Mary to the earth, the more famous one, Fatima, is now used by the Church chiefly as an emotional symbol in the war against communism. The most famous shrine in the Western Hemisphere, Guadaloupe, is being used as a weapon against Mexican public schools.

I am not concerned here with the religious significance of apparitions, but with the use that the hierarchy makes of apparitions in the fields of science and politics. There need be no doubt in the mind of anybody that actual cures have been wrought at certain Catholic shrines. We have learned a great deal about psychosomatic disabilities and the therapeutic effects of hopeful enthusiasm since Bernadette Soubirous spoke with the Virgin Mary at Lourdes in 1858. The piles of discarded crutches at Catholic shrines are real enough; the only controversy is as to their meaning. Many sincere, educated Catholics argue that there is ample evidence of supernatural intervention of some sort; and the Church includes many genuine mystics who believe in direct communication with the supernatural.

The Church admits that "only a very small percentage of the sick are cured" at Lourdes. It claimed "300 to 400 cures which medical science cannot explain" up to 1931, and 33 definitely miraculous cures.[18] Perhaps one person in a thousand is helped physically. Whatever may be the truth behind the statistics, it is not wholly irreverent to suggest that unmitigated adoration has its therapeutic value entirely apart from the validity of the object adored.

Whether the priests recognize this elementary truth or not, they certainly promote Mariology as one of the most important parts of Christian faith. The various shrines visited by the Virgin Mary have become enormously profitable financially and spiritually. Mary Immaculate has been made the official Catholic patroness of the United States. Catholic annals, however, do not report any visitation by the Virgin Mary to the United States.

For a few days in 1945 it seemed that this condition might be remedied. A small Bronx boy named Joseph Vitolo, Jr., who had seen the motion picture *Song of Bernadette,* saw an apparition of the Virgin Mary seventeen times. New York's *PM* described the phenomenon on November 5 of that year:

Twenty-five thousand persons, according to a police estimate, swarmed yesterday to the vacant lot in the Bronx where a nine-year-old boy and his friends have built a crude shrine on the spot where he says he saw an apparition of the Virgin Mary last Monday.

The boy, Joseph Vitolo, Jr., 3194 Villa Ave., saw the apparition, according to his friends, after three small Negro girls had fled from a dancing white cloud in the lot, which lies on the Grand Concourse, 150 feet south of Van Cortlandt Ave.

Joseph was quoted in Sunday's *Bronx Home News* as saying: "I saw the Virgin Mary with long blond hair and a sort of light around her. She wore a blue dress that turned to pink and stood behind a golden table and four chairs.

"There was a candle on the table, and I took it and tried to hand it to another boy, but it disappeared."

Joseph . . . says his vision was "completely different" from that seen by Bernadette in the movie.

Two women claim that their children have benefited miraculously from Joseph's apparition.

New York priests co-operated in this performance cautiously, but the hierarchy was noncommittal. The Virgin Mary had promised Joseph that a well would appear in the vacant Bronx lot after her last appearance—at Lourdes it had been a spring. When the well failed to appear under the skeptical scrutiny of the world's shrewdest newspapermen, the New York hierarchy let the matter drop.

In the promotion of antiscientific legends and incredible dogma Pius XII has, in the last decade, carried the Papacy back toward the Middle Ages by several of his encyclicals and other pronouncements. Indirectly he has widened the gap between the Church and all those branches of modern Christendom which profess some allegiance to scholarship and science. In his 1950 encyclical, *Humani Generis,* he denounced attempts to adjust Catholic teaching to modern "relativist" knowledge, and declared that when the Popes have reached a solution of a matter, all the world must understand "that it can no longer be considered an open question among theologians." [19] He proclaimed as infallibly proved and true, in November, 1950, the dogma that the body of the Virgin Mary was taken up literally into heaven after her death. Unhappily, a scholarly writer in the *American Ecclesiastical Review* of August, 1950, had not been warned of the new Papal "discovery" in advance. He showed that Catholic research indicated that "we do not have a genuine historical tradition on the Assumption" of the Virgin Mary, and that "in the patristic tradition of the first six centuries we find a void regarding this problem." [20]

Nevertheless American priests, apparently with full Papal approval, are going ahead with the promotion of Mariology to the point where the unofficial worship of the Virgin is changing the whole theological base of Catholicism—and making co-operation with Protestantism more than ever impossible. In 1954, the Very Reverend John A. Flynn, president of Catholic St. John's University in Brooklyn, announced at a Marian Year Convocation that it is "not unlikely" that Mary will be proclaimed within a century as "Co-Redemptrix of the human race," participating "with her Son in the power of ruling the World." [21]

In recent years priestly promotion in the field of Mariology has centered on Fatima, the Portuguese hamlet where the Virgin Mary made six appearances to three peasant children in 1917 just before the Bolshevik revolution. The messages she delivered to these children were most timely; in fact, they showed a considerable comprehension of the delicate position of the Vatican in European politics. Her political forebodings were conveyed to three shepherd children of ten, nine, and seven who had never gone to school.

The gist of the Fatima message was that a "horrible, horrible" war was coming, and that the one way to avoid it was "consecration of the World to my Immaculate Heart." "If my requests are granted Russia will be converted; there will be peace. Otherwise Russia will spread its error throughout the world giving rise to wars and persecutions against the Church." [22]   One part of the Virgin Mary's message was kept secret by the Church and can be used by the Vatican at its discretion. It is to be released in 1960.

The Catholic hierarchy did not appreciate at first the unique importance of the miracle of Fatima. Five years after the event the *Catholic Encyclopedia Supplement* did not even mention it. Neither Benedict XV nor Pius XI showed any signs of interest. Then the struggle between the Church and Communism became more intense, and it was noted that the Portuguese peasant children had received a supernatural message on the subject of Russia. Some genius in the Church recognized the possibilities of the situation, and an international promotion campaign for Fatima began under Pius XII, who had become Pope in 1939. The trickle of Fatima literature became a flood. Dozens of books and pamphlets were written by Catholic authors on the subject, and recently a whole section of a Catholic press exhibit was reserved for Fatima literature exclusively. In 1937, twenty years after the event, the only surviving member of the childish trio of Fatima, Lucia Aborbo, who had become a cloistered nun, communicated to priests for the first time many important additional parts of the Fatima story that she had never mentioned before.[23]

The spot where the six apparitions of the Virgin appeared in Fatima has now become a shrine more popular even than Lourdes. Sometimes more than 700,000 people visit the shrine in a single month. American publishers and newspapers co-operate in developing the cult, and American newspapers that refuse, as a matter of policy, to accept advertising for any article or book that attacks the Catholic Church are quite ready to accept advertising that describes the Fatima occurrence as a proved fact. Respectable book reviewers attest Fatima's value. *The New York Times,* which is scrupulously fair in its general news coverage, published on September 7, 1947, a Macmillan advertisement for *Our Lady of Fatima* by William T. Walsh; the advertisement described the story of Fatima as "historic fact established by overwhelming testimony." In the same issue the *Times* carried a commendatory review by a Catholic priest, Father John S. Kennedy, implying complete acceptance of Catholic claims. The Macmillan advertisement said:

 . . . it [the story] is vitally important to every person in the world. For the Lady foretold the Bolshevik Revolution, the horrors of

World War II, and the menace that Marxism offers to the entire world at this moment. She warned that unless her wishes were carried out, every country in the world would be overcome by communism in some form.

"Fatima statues" have been circulated in Europe and America with enormous public fanfare and detailed reports in the Catholic press. Each statue during its journey has had many "miracles reported along its path." Some "Fatima statues" are duplicates of an original done, under the direction of the nun Lucia, by a sculptor-priest, who also talked with the sole survivor of the three peasant children of Fatima and wrote a book about the apparitions.[24] The American duplicate was flown from Lisbon to the Azores, brought to Canada for a tour of its five leading cities, and welcomed to American soil in Buffalo on December 8, 1947, by 200,000 persons. More than three million people viewed the statue during the first year of its American pilgrimage. Several leading New York newspapers gave the statue enormous display. Duplicate, 25-inch models of the statue, with gold-leaf decorations and crystal eyes, were sold for $60.[25]

Virtually all publicity about the statue has coupled the miracle of Fatima with the Church's drive against Communism. At the June, 1948, commencement of Fordham University, the then president of that institution of higher learning, Father Robert I. Gannon, suggested that "the women of Italy saved Western Europe at the polls" in April, 1948, largely because "Our Lady of Fatima was at the side of her divine Son." [26]

Many Catholic intellectuals are shamefaced about this exploitation of apparitions. They are willing to admit that the "messages" given to the world by this means do not seem to be any more coherent or plausible than those of the average spiritualist medium—and the Church rejects spiritualism flatly.[27] Nominally the Catholic intellectuals are not bound by the rules of their Church to take the apparition stories seriously as long as they do not repudiate the inspiring legends publicly. Even Bishop Sheen, when he described the miracle of Fatima on a nation-wide hook-up in 1947, and coupled it with an attack on Communism, ended his breathlessly reverent description by disowning any attempt to establish the miracle as fact. He declared: "We are not concerned about proving the authenticity of these phenomena at Fatima, for those who believe in the realm of the spirit and the Mother of God need no proof, and those who reject the Spirit would not accept it anyway."

5

While many parish priests are operating on the lower level of popular superstition, the Church is attempting to hold the allegiance of educated Catholics in the upper world of science. The task is made easier by the fact that the Catholic educational system is largely segregated from the rest of American culture. Students who stay within the closed Catholic system are indoctrinated with the dogma that the Church is the mother of all learning. Sometimes they complete their education within this system without ever hearing a criticism of the Church's scientific limitations. The segregated learned societies of the Catholic colleges are carefully quarantined against heresy.

In this upper world of Catholic learning the language of the hierarchy in dealing with scientific matters is well modulated. Official and public encouragement is given to scientific research. The theory of evolution receives somewhat frosty treatment but it is not excluded from Catholic halls of learning altogether. Catholic theologians have not actually accepted the theory of evolution *in toto,* but they have given Catholic scientists permission to believe it if they wish, as long as they teach it merely as a hypothesis and not as a fact, and as long as they do not attempt to draw any philosophical inferences from it.

Dr. William Agar in his *Catholicism and the Progress of Science,* one of the volumes of the "Christendom Series" edited by Carlton Hayes and others under the Imprimatur of Cardinal Spellman, states the extreme limit beyond which a Catholic scientist cannot go in compromising with secular science. He points out that "the Catholic view of man . . . precludes the acceptance of evolution of man *as a whole* from animal life," but it is perfectly permissible for a Catholic to believe "the scientific theory . . . that life has developed from life with change and specialization from simple beginnings up to the manifold types now existing." [28] It is permissible provided the modern believer also believes in the *special* creation of the soul at some point in the evolutionary process and accepts the doctrine that all members of the human race are descended from two parents, Adam and Eve.

Although Pius X directed all Catholics as late as 1909 to regard the creation narrative and the story of Adam's fall as historical, the hierarchy is now very charitable about the dates of Adam's appearance in history. "The Catholic Church," says Dr. Agar, "has never been wedded to any particular chronology in spite of the current notion that the date of Adam's creation had been definitely fixed." It is interesting to note that Dr. Agar in this standard defense of Catholic science does not mention relics, saints, scapulars, or apparitions. The whole territory of priestly anti-science is carefully avoided as outside the scope of the progress of Catholic science.

While educated Catholics make concessions to modern science on paper, the parish priests in many parts of the United States still bitterly assail the theory of evolution. They do not agree that an uninterrupted development of life from formless beginnings to the twentieth-century man can be as divine as "special" creation. They frequently ridicule the idea of evolution without rebuke from their superiors. The *Catholic Almanac* declares that "no system even of mitigated evolution has been scientifically proved."

The leading Catholic newspaper in the United States, *The Register,* headed its 1953 review of Julian Huxley's *Evolution in Action* with the phrase "Darwinian Claptrap" and branded as "wholly without foundation" the belief that "Darwin's theory of natural selection explains the origin of species." [29] In August of that year, the newspaper's associate editor, Father Paul Hallett, bitterly assailed *Life* magazine for circulating "misinformation" in favor of evolution through its notable scientific series, "The World We Live In." [30]

The National Catholic Educational Association has had a hard time keeping "atheistic" evolution out of Catholic textbooks. Father Paul Carroll, a Jesuit biologist who made a survey of Catholic college biology textbooks for the Association in 1940, declared that "the great majority of the books give either false or inaccurate accounts" of the Catholic fundamentals. He stressed the fact that good Catholic teaching must include "a single pair of progenitors of the human race" and the conception that "a human body is formed in a special way," and he concluded his analysis by quoting with approval the statement: "Loose-thinking Catholics often tell you that the Church has not condemned evolution. The truth is that you are a heretic in a dozen ways if you admit what the

world is calling evolution. . . . The evolutionists have an answer
. . . an irritating, erroneous, unproved and unprovable one—and
one condemned by the Church." [31]

In areas where the Catholic Church is strong, priests frequently attack the teaching of evolution in the public schools.

6

On the whole, the Church is less charitable to heresy in the
social sciences than in the physical sciences. No matter how
overwhelming the evidence may be, no Catholic social scientist is
permitted to declare publicly that birth control, socialism, civil
marriage, remarriage after divorce, or sterilization of the feebleminded is a scientific solution for a social problem. All these solu-
tions, of course, have been specifically denounced by the Popes.

The limitations imposed upon the social scientist by Catholic
discipline are usually stated with considerable moderation in order
to avoid ridicule. The Right Reverend Francis J. Haas, dean of
the School of Social Science at the Catholic University of America,
describes these limitations suavely (italics supplied):

> In the Catholic institutions of higher learning, *due regard being
> given to the requirements of the natural and divine law,* there are no
> restrictions on the biologist, chemist or physicist in *assembling* data or
> in *proposing* new formulas, regardless of how novel his discoveries may
> be. The social scientist enjoys the same freedom in *gathering* data on
> all subjects, no matter how unpalatable such data may be to those who
> would not want them brought to light in assembled form. . . . More
> than this, he is entirely free, *within the framework of the Church's
> social teaching*—which rests on the common good and which in turn
> is based on human needs—to *propose* any formula or remedy which
> he can demonstrate will advance human well-being.[32]

More specific is a sociology professor from the same university, Father Paul H. Furfey, in a chapter on "Supernatural Sociology" in his *Fire on the Earth:*

> The Catholic sociologist, then, enjoys complete freedom of investi-
> gation in the social field, but he is not allowed to rely upon merely
> human science as the sole means of procuring individual and social
> well-being. . . . It is dangerous, then, for a Catholic sociologist to
> deal with social problems by the methods of purely natural science if,
> in doing so, he conveys the impression that this purely natural treat-

ment of social questions represents the complete mind of the Church.
. . . We ought constantly to emphasize the fact that no important
problem can be solved without taking the supernatural into account.[33]

The effects of priestly limitations upon scientific thinking are
evident in nearly all Catholic textbooks on sociology and in the
voluminous pamphlet literature of Catholic organizations. Perhaps
the most serious limitation is evident in the analysis of population
problems. I have already quoted the declaration of the *Catholic
Encyclopedia* on this point: "With supplies increasing in proportion to population, there is no such thing as overpopulation." This
must be the standard answer of all Catholic sociologists to worries
about population. "A high birth rate is still the best and most
practical way of bettering human generations," says Father Edgar
Schmiedeler, director of the Family Life Bureau of the National
Catholic Welfare Conference, in a widely circulated 1942 tract
called *A Holy War*. This same tract quotes Father Thomas V.
Moore, "eminent psychologist of the Catholic University of America," as follows:

There can be little doubt that the heredity of intelligence is governed by the law of the regression of the mean, with the exception of
rare types of mental defect. If that is the case, moronity has a biological trend to eliminate itself. We need not fear, therefore, that in helping the poor to have children and in caring for them that we are going
to spread moronity. If these poor people are of low grade intelligence,
the children they bring into the world will be distinctly higher than
themselves.[34]

In the fields of philosophy and history, the Catholic restrictions upon scientists are almost equally onerous. The mind of the
Catholic philosopher is not free to roam over the field of speculation and select for himself the system that satisfies his reason most
completely. His conclusions are predetermined. He must always
come out at one place, the classical philosophy of St. Thomas
Aquinas. According to Canon 1366, philosophy must be taught
by the professors according to the manner of the Angelic Doctor,
without deviating from his doctrine and principles.

The narrow outlook of Catholic philosophy has been imposed
upon the academic world by the Popes themselves. Pius IX decreed that "it is the duty of every philosopher who wishes to be a
son of the Church—as indeed it is the duty of philosophy itself—

never to say anything contrary to what the Church teaches, also to withdraw opinions about which the Church may have admonished him." [35] Leo XIII issued a special encyclical ordering the entire cultural system of the world Church to recognize St. Thomas Aquinas as supreme thinker. "We most strenuously exhort you, Venerable Brethren," he said, "that . . . you reinstate and as widely as possible propagate the inestimable wisdom of St. Thomas." [36] Is it surprising that *The Basic Writings of St. Thomas Aquinas* has become a standard textbook in Catholic college philosophy, and that many Catholic students never hear of the great modern philosophers whose works have superseded St. Thomas in the non-Catholic world?

The famous ex-priest, Joseph McCabe, in describing his experiences inside the Church where he was a teacher of philosophy for four years, said that he "remained ignorant of the very names of the chief English, German and American thinkers of the time; and I did not read or have any opportunity to read a single line of Mill or Spencer, Lotze or Herbart, Nietzsche or Hartmann, Green or Bradley, Seth or Royce, until I had quitted the Church."

Unhappily, this insulation from non-Catholic culture is admitted by some Catholic observers to be quite typical of many Catholic universities in the United States. The head of the Department of Psychology at the Catholic University of America, when called upon to testify in a 1943 hearing on censorship by the Post Office Department, admitted under cross-examination that he had never heard of Sholem Asch, Theodore Dreiser, Ernest Hemingway, D. H. Lawrence, John Steinbeck, Thomas Wolfe, Maurice Maeterlinck, or John Dos Passos. He had heard of Thomas Mann but did not know who he was.[37]

The present condition of Catholic philosophy in the United States may be judged from the fact that Bishop Fulton J. Sheen was a professor of philosophy at America's leading Catholic institution of learning, the Catholic University of America, for many years. The following sample of his "philosophy," taken from his *Communism and the Conscience of the West,* indicates his reliance on necromancy or astrology:

As Americans we cannot be unmindful of the relation of this country to the Woman to whom God gave the power of crushing the head of the serpent. The Council of Baltimore on December 8, 1846, consecrated the United States to the Immaculate Conception of Our Blessed Mother. It was only eight years later that the Church defined her Immaculate Conception. It was on December 8, 1941, the feast of the Immaculate Conception, that the United States went to war with Japan. It was on May 13, 1945, Mother's Day, the day on which the entire Church celebrated Sodality Day of Our Lady, that the United States Government proclaimed a National Thanksgiving for V-E Day. It was on August 15, 1945, the Feast of the Assumption of Our Blessed Mother, that victory came to us in the war with Japan. It was the nineteenth of August, 1945, that the United States Government declared official V-J Day and this happened to be the anniversary of one of the appearances of Our Lady of Fatima. On September 1, 1945, the first Saturday of the month which our Lady of Fatima asked should be consecrated to Her, General MacArthur accepted the surrender of Japan aboard the *Missouri*. It was on September 8, 1945, the Birthday of Our Lady, that the first American flag flew over Tokyo, and as it was unfurled General MacArthur said: "Let it wave in its full glory as a symbol of victory for the right." [38]

It is easy to see why the hierarchy has chosen St. Thomas Aquinas as a model in philosophy. He was completely devout and completely authoritarian. He declared that "philosophy is powerless with regard to anything that depends on faith." He constructed a neatly segmented world in which the philosopher was in perpetual subordination to the priest, and he saw nothing inconsistent in this because he was both a philosopher and a theologian. In the Thomistic system there is a body of received, supernatural truth transmitted by God to a grateful humanity through the Roman Catholic Church. The Church has the right to persecute the apostate and the heretic, even to kill them if they persist in their heresy. In the last analysis the Church has authority over the state and must be its master.

It is natural that the struggle between this kind of theology, dressed up as philosophy, and free speculative inquiry should reach the American philosophical organizations. To avoid taint and trauma the Catholic philosophers usually stay away from gatherings where their authoritarian views may be challenged, and in their own Catholic Philosophical Association the faith is carefully preserved. In recent years an attempt to get Catholics to co-operate with non-Catholic philosophers in "The Conference on Science, Philosophy and Religion in their Relation to the Democratic Way of Life" has been successful only because the sessions of this conference avoid any forthright discussion of the Papal control of Catholic philosophy.[39]

7

Catholic history-writing differs from non-Catholic history-writing chiefly in its emphasis. In Catholic histories the centuries of Catholic domination in Europe are described with nostalgia, almost as if this period had been a golden age of culture and humanitarianism. The French Revolution and the Reformation are both described as essentially godless attacks upon a superior culture, and some Catholic writers are not above suggesting that the worst evils of Nazism, fascism, and Communism have come from anticlericalism and Protestantism. Catholic school histories emphasize the persecution of Catholics in England by Protestant monarchs, and pass over lightly the horrors of the Inquisition in Europe and Mexico.

Even the most eminent Catholic scholars indulge in astonishing "interpretations" of European history. Jacques Maritain, Catholic philosopher, who was appointed to a chair at Princeton in 1948, says, in discussing the excesses of the Church and clergy in the Middle Ages: "The Church, as such, was not involved in these excesses but they were produced within the Church." [40]

The Catholic Action Manual by Monsignor Luigi Civardi states a typical Catholic historian's view of the past:

> Before the French Revolution, society, with but rare exceptions, was organized on a Christian basis. Political and social ordinances, public and private justice, and institutions, were all inspired by Christian principles. . . . Liberalism, child of that bloody mother the French Revolution, and grandchild of rationalist Protestantism, broke up the framework of the Christian civitas, that glory of bygone days, by proclaiming religion to be but a private affair and relieving the governments of any duty in its regard.[41]

In American history as taught in Catholic schools, there is much emphasis upon the role of Catholics in winning the West and aiding the American Revolution, although there were hardly any Catholics in the thirteen colonies at the time of the Revolution. The Declaration of Independence is solemnly described as a document largely derived from Catholic inspiration. This view is defended in detail by the 1948 *Catholic Almanac:*

A study of its [the Declaration's] philosophical principles reveals them to be derived from the traditional streams of Catholic philosophy. These principles when found in the works of non-Catholic writers are but a borrowing of Catholic doctrine.

Two outstanding Catholic churchmen whose philosophy and thought contribute to the excellence of the Declaration of Independence are St. Thomas Aquinas and St. Robert Bellarmine [an Italian cardinal]. . . . A comparison of sections of the Declaration of Independence with selections from the works of these two renowned Catholic theologians, reveals a striking similarity of thought and identity of political principle.[42]

In this version Thomas Jefferson is not mentioned, but Catholic historians are willing to give him some credit for the Declaration of Independence if it is understood that his ideas came partly from Cardinal Bellarmine. John Locke is another matter. It is generally admitted that Locke was Jefferson's chief inspiration, but Locke's books are still on the Catholic *Index,* and the *Catholic Almanac* does not mention him.

The Catholic *Register* went so far, in a 1956 editorial in honor of Bellarmine's birth, as to say that he "might be described as the 'ghost writer' of the Declaration of Independence." [43] The editorial ascribed to Bellarmine a strong faith in "the people" as against "the totalitarian state," whereas the actual Bellarmine was primarily a champion of the Papacy against hostile European princes. "Freedom of belief," he once said, "is pernicious; it is nothing but the freedom to be wrong."

The only evidence, incidentally, that the Jefferson-Bellarmine legend has anything behind it except wishful thinking is the fact that Madison once included Bellarmine in a list of authors he recommended to Jefferson—but Bellarmine was one of 122 authors so listed! Jefferson read many books, and if he ever read Bellarmine or was influenced by Catholic thought, the literary remains we now possess do not prove it. Catholic scholars admit that "none of the Founding Fathers seems to have given the slightest hint that they were in any way acquainted with the works of the greater among the schoolmen." [44]

Some Catholic writers have "discovered" that George Washington became a Catholic. A picture of the Blessed Virgin was found in his household after his death. What did this mean? David Goldstein, columnist and convert, writing in the Boston

Pilot of February 21, 1948, celebrated Washington's Birthday by saying:

There was a still more basic reason for the friendliness of Washington towards Catholics. He was a Catholic in spirit, so much so, that there is warrant for believing that he became a son of the Catholic Church before he died. Some of the reasons for so believing are the statements of Old Juba, Washington's trusted slave, who said that he used to row a priest across the Potomac to visit him; and that "Marse George made the sign of the Cross befo' he eat"; also the "tale of the skeleton in the family closet," the conversion of George to "Papistry"; and the statement of Bishop Carroll that Washington died as did Emperor Valentinian, who was received into the Church before his death. Bishop Carroll's statement was so interpreted by Father Laurence J. Kenny, S. J., who made a special investigation of the Washington conversion tradition for the Denver *Register*.

Distortions of history in Catholic textbooks that vindicate fascism and cultural tyranny are less humorous. Father John Laux's *Church History,* used in American Catholic high schools, may be taken as an illustration (Benziger; Imprimatur Cardinal Hayes). Its emphasis throughout is in favor of imposed authority rather than democracy. It introduces a hostile discussion of the French Revolution by saying: "Absolutism, free thought, infidelity, licentiousness, the sneers of Voltaire and the seductive democratic theories of Rousseau had done their work. France was ripe for the Great Revolution."

Father Laux declares that the Masonic order "has always, especially in the Latin countries of Europe and America, openly and secretly attacked Christianity." He describes Pius IX's 1864 *Syllabus* as a condemnation of "pantheism, naturalism, socialism, communism, freemasonry and other forms of religious liberalism" but neglects to point out that the encyclical also specifically repudiated the separation of church and state, and branded religious freedom as one of the "principal errors of our time." Father Laux frequently attacks the "atheistic communism" of Russia, but does not even mention fascism or suggest the connection between Mussolini, Hitler, and Franco.

Here, for example, is what the Catholic high-school students are told about Franco by Father Laux—and this is *all* that they are told about him.

In the elections to the Constitutional Cortes held in July [1931] the Socialists and Freemasons won the largest number of seats. The new Republican Constitution was adopted on December 9. Complete separation of Church and State is decreed, but the religious paragraphs prove conclusively that by separation the anti-Catholic politicians of Spain mean complete domination of the Church by the State. The most radical anti-religious provisions are the following: the dissolution of marriage by mutual consent; State monopoly of education; abolition of the Concordat with the Holy See; suppression of all State subsidies to Catholic worship; dissolution of the Society of Jesus and confiscation of all its property; subjection of all Religious Orders to an arbitrary regime.

Following the advice of the Holy Father, the Bishops of Spain accepted the Republic, reserving their right to work for the revision of the unjust provisions of the new Constitution.

In 1936 the Leftists abetted by the Communists formed a new Government called "The Popular United Front." A reign of terror ensued during which bishops, priests, nuns and laity became the victims of extreme persecution. All Church property was confiscated. On July 17, 1936, the murder of a deputy who had denounced the government for these atrocities precipitated a crisis. The army, led by General Franco, and supported by the conservative political parties who had meanwhile united and later became known as the "Nationalists," moved against the Popular Front Government. A civil war had begun. It lasted almost three years, ending on March 28, 1939, with the victorious entry into Madrid by General Franco's Army. The conduct of the war by the Popular Front Government was marked by an excess of anti-religious fury. Countless churches and Religious institutions had been profaned and destroyed. Nine bishops and thousands of priests and nuns were slain. Great massacres of the faithful laity took place. On the day of victory Pope Pius XII sent this message to General Franco: "Raising our hearts to God, we thank Him and your excellency for the desired victory of Catholic Spain and pray that this beloved country, having found peace, may renew with vigor her ancient Christian traditions which made her so great. With these sentiments we send your excellency and the whole Spanish people our Apostolic blessing. . . ."

General Franco completed his work of reorganization by announcing himself as "the Supreme Chieftain responsible only before God and History." In October, 1939, General Franco condemned atheism connected with the invasion of Poland, and for this was commended by the Holy Father. Somewhat later the Spanish Government decreed restoration of clergy salaries by the State and also took measures to repair the damage done by the "Reds" to the Church property. It also returned to the Jesuit Order the properties which had been confiscated by the Republic. Another measure taken was that of suppression of Masonry. Early in 1940 General Franco stated in regard to the European war that "Spain has united her voice to that of the Catholic Church" and to those states who desire to bring about peace.[45]

8

The total effect of cultural schizophrenia upon Catholic scholarship has been enormous. The scientific output of American Catholicism is insignificant, and the fact has been admitted again and again with much breast-beating by eminent Catholics. Priestly control has so stifled and misdirected the scientific spirit in Catholic institutions that first-class scientific research is rare. Three decades ago a study by Professors H. C. Lehman and Paul A. Witty of starred names in *American Men of Science* showed that less than one per cent of these eminent men of science were Catholic, the lowest proportion of any religious group in the United States. The Catholic Church also has the lowest proportion of scholars on the faculties of state universities of any religious group in the United States. In subsequent decades there have been no indications of significant change in these proportions.

A 1953 study by Robert H. Knapp and Joseph Greenbaum of academic distinctions and awards found the Catholic institutions of learning lowest in science, social science, and the humanities— "consistently the lowest of all seven partial indices." [46]

A study begun by Professor J. A. Reyniers of Notre Dame, and summarized in *America,* showed that, just before the war:

> On the basis of productive scholarship we have no prominent universities. Among the schools which have reached the university status, we are at the bottom of the list of published research, just as our medical schools are at the bottom of medical rating lists. The over-all picture is still blacker. . . . There is only one-fourth as much productive scholarship coming from Catholics as our numbers warrant. . . . Neither in its quantity nor its quality is there the slightest room for complacency about Catholic scholarship.[47]

Such humility is refreshing, and it can be useful if Catholic scholars will begin to admit the causes of their lowly place in the world of science. Lehman and Witty at the end of their 1927 study of men of science said: "The conspicuous dearth of scientists among the Catholics suggests that the tenets of that church are not consonant with scientific endeavor."

11

Fascism, Communism, and Labor

1

In 1944 the Catholic Information Society of New York issued
under the Imprimatur of Cardinal Spellman a pamphlet called
Is the Pope Fascist? Among other things it said: "It is beyond
dispute that the Pope was the only [*sic*] world leader before 1939
to speak out fearlessly and dogmatically against the twin evils of
fascism and nazism."

Presumably this pamphlet marshals the best evidence available to support this astounding claim and to demonstrate that the
Vatican is not fascist. Yet it does not mention Franco, Argentina,
Tiso, the Ethiopian war, or the corporate state; and the quotations
from the Popes themselves not only ignore these subjects but fail
to mention democracy, the principle of dictatorship, or Mussolini's
and Hitler's methods in destroying democratic political opposition.
Both the pamphlet and the two Popes quoted, Pius XI and Pius
XII, ignore the one great force in Europe that opposed fascism
and its concepts most consistently, the socialist movement. Although the Popes are represented as speaking fearlessly and dogmatically against fascism, there is not a quotation in the pamphlet
that is specific, fearless, or dogmatic in condemning the two primary doctrines of fascism, political dictatorship and the corporate
state. With one exception, the quoted "criticisms" of fascism are
simply counterattacks upon Mussolini and Hitler for their encroachments upon the educational and political preserves of the
Catholic Church.

In one respect, of course, this Catholic pamphlet is correct.
The Pope is not *specifically* fascist. No Pope has ever stood up
and said publicly, "I am a fascist." Nor, for that matter, has any
Pope ever said, "I am a democrat." Popes do not commit themselves in that fashion when they have faithful subjects on both sides

274

of a war or political conflict, and we have already seen that the Church is officially neutral concerning all forms of government. It is a necessary part of Papal political technique to be general and vague concerning the forms of state control when the institution of the Catholic Church needs the support of dictators as well as presidents.

Moreover, no one can say correctly that the majority of American Catholics have ever been fascist, or that the American hierarchy is fascist *at the present time*. (There may have been legitimate doubt about the hierarchy in the thirties.) The Father Coughlins and the Christian Front are not representative of American Catholicism today. American Catholics who fought in World War II were just as heartily antifascist as their comrades, and no one can question their loyalty or heroism.

Unfortunately it must be pointed out, at the risk of seeming to be unappreciative, that there were more Catholics who fought against the United States in World War II than for it, and that the Church dignitaries blessed them all with equal unction. The Pope, as the Primate of Italy, naturally blessed his own people with considerable warmth when they fought against American troops, and he also blessed German soldiers at the Vatican several times during the war. The benediction was duly noted by the semiofficial Vatican newspaper, *Osservatore Romano*. He did not protest when Italian bishops enthusiastically wired Mussolini their pious hope that he would "crown the unfailing victory of our arms by planting the Italian flag over the Holy Sepulchre." [1] These unpleasant recollections are called to mind only to show that the whole question of the Vatican's relations to fascism cannot be dismissed by emotional utterances about slaughtered Catholic heroes. Such utterances raise the embarrassing query: *Which* heroes?

In the postwar alarm about Communist expansion, the American people were not in a mood to listen to any discussion of fascism and its relationships with the Vatican. In the public discussions of the critical election in Italy in April, 1948, scarcely any American commentators stopped to ask what kind of government the Vatican would have built in Italy if it had been completely victorious. (The Vatican and its allies won the election easily; but the victory was far from complete, because it was accomplished by a coalition that was by no means united on all major issues.) Nor did any American newspapers discuss the question how the Vatican could dominate a whole string of Catholic political parties in Europe while its American votaries professed to believe in the separation of church and state.

No one doubted after the Italian election of 1948 that the Vatican was attempting to establish in Italy, as in other European nations, a conservative and proclerical regime. It did not attempt to conceal its partisan participation in the election campaign. The Pope declared that failure to vote would be a mortal sin, and the parish priests told the people how to vote and how not to vote. There was an open and reckless disregard for the provision in the Lateran Treaty that prohibited priests from participating in partisan politics. Cardinal Schuster of Milan excommunicated a priest for participating in left-wing meetings, and instructed the clergy of his diocese to refuse absolution to members of "movements contrary to the Catholic religion." [2] Later on, in July, 1949, Pius XII issued a famous decree under which every Catholic sympathizer with Communism anywhere in the world might have been excommunicated. But he never had the courage (or stupidity) to apply the excommunication threat to the opposition parties in Italy, partly because the Communists had won over millions of Italian Catholics to their cause and had developed the largest Communist Party in the world outside of the Soviet Union.

On March 3, 1948, eighteen archbishops and fifty-five bishops of southern Italy issued a pastoral letter to their flocks saying that "nobody can, at the same time, be a good Catholic and a Socialist." In the province of Turin, Catholics were even forbidden to belong to socialist co-operative societies. "Already," said the Brooklyn *Tablet* in a dispatch from Rome shortly before the election, "the 4,500,000 members of Italian Catholic Action are being mobilized to ensure victory for the Christian Democratic Party and the defeat of the People's Democratic Front, a coalition of Communists and left-wing Socialists." "The thousands of parish priests," remarked *The New York Times,* "are concentrating their efforts on the women voters, who are regarded as generally more strongly attached to religion than are the men."

In the United States also the hierarchy abandoned all pretense that it was independent of politics, and threw all of its resources into the fight for the Christian Democratic (Catholic) Party of Italy. Millions of dollars in aid for good Catholics in Italy went from good Catholics in the United States. Hundreds of thousands of letters addressed to Italians went out from the United States urging them to stand with the Vatican. In one Brooklyn church, choirboys distributed through the congregation assembled for Mass copies of a political form letter for transmission to Italy, of which 250,000 copies had been made by American Catholics.[3]

Probably Pope Pius XII, who is a shrewd political strategist, knew exactly what he was doing in backing the conservatives so openly. He reasoned that, in view of Western commitments, he could not lose so long as he was presented as opposing Communism. He had his ear tuned to American public opinion, and the American public had completely forgotten fascism in the panic caused by Communist aggression. Postwar America, in fact, seems to be suffering so acutely from emotional fatigue that it cannot muster the energy to pursue the twin villains of fascism and Communism at once.

The Russian Communists themselves, of course, are largely to blame for this strange denouement. They not only have frightened the Western world by their aggressiveness but also have muddled the antifascist forces of the West by their semantic inanities. By using the word "fascist" as a rogues'-gallery label for all their enemies, they have whitened the word and created a new disposition in the West to be charitable to the underlying pro-clerical concepts. "After all," many honest antifascists are saying, "Communism is the present danger. The Roman Catholic Church may be superstitious and reactionary but it *is* an enemy of Communism. Why not forget fascism for the moment, take one danger at a time, and go along with the conservative policy of the Church until we see daylight?"

The Catholic hierarchy in the United States is taking full advantage of this new and unexpected benevolence. It nominates itself as archenemy of America's archenemy, Communism; and simultaneously it is building the legend that it has always been opposed to fascism. It is adding to the current babel by using the word "fascist" almost as carelessly as the Communists use it. In American Catholic parlance today, "fascist" is a general-utility cuss word, applied loosely to any non-Communist who is critical of the Roman Catholic Church and also wants more state control of social and educational institutions. The word is rarely applied by Catholics to Franco or Salazar, but "the anti-Catholic Government of Northern Ireland" is called "this noisome remnant of fascism." [4]

In view of the confusion and the importance of the issues involved, it is worth while asking certain fundamental questions concerning the Roman Catholic Church and its record in dealing with fascism. Is the Church fascist? Has it actually opposed European fascism? Has it collaborated? Has it changed its attitude since the war? Can we afford to ignore its relations with fascism even temporarily in order to resist Communist aggression more effectively? Can we trust the Vatican to use *any* victory in Europe to extend democracy?

Both the American Catholic people and the American Catholic hierarchy are very sensitive about these questions, because they have an acute sense of guilt about fascism. The hierarchy, in order to protect its record, is making many wild and unfounded statements about its own antifascism. Many individual Catholics are indignantly insisting upon the right to repudiate any purely *political* policy of the Vatican. They are demonstrating their right by criticizing fascist-American co-operation before and during the war. I am sure that millions of American Catholics would adopt as their own the 1937 statement of the Catholic writer William Teeling: "The political policy of Rome seems to become more and more identified with organizations on totalitarian lines. That Rome should feel it wise to work with dictators is not regarded happily by those democratic countries who are striving against dictatorship at every turn." [5]

2

The Catholic hierarchy did not seriously oppose the seizure of power by Mussolini in Italy in 1922, or urge its people to come to the defense of democratic institutions, or specifically declare its opposition to dictatorship. Pius XI, who had become Pope shortly before Mussolini's march on Rome after serving as Archbishop of Milan, was noted for his distrust of democracy and was so definitely antisocialist that he declared in his encyclical on *Reconstructing the Social Order* that socialism "conceives human society in a way utterly alien to Christian truth. . . . No one can be at the same time a sincere Catholic and a true Socialist." [6]

How different the future of Europe might have been if he had made a similar utterance concerning fascism! Instead, as Cardinal of Milan, he gave Mussolini's blackshirts a place of honor in the unveiling ceremonies for the Unknown Warrior in Milan Cathedral, and studiously refrained from attacking the political principles of the blackshirts. (I lived in Milan during the first summer of fascist rule.)

The noted Catholic scholar, Professor D. A. Binchy of University College, Dublin, in his *Church and State in Fascist Italy,* says of Pius XI: "He believed that democracy was too feeble and incoherent to serve as a dam against the Communist tide, and a strange irony made him turn to the new form of authoritarian government as offering the only hope of successful resistance." [7] In a nation that was nominally 99 per cent Catholic, the Church probably had the power to destroy fascism at the source, but chose instead acquiescence and, in the end, co-operation.

While Pius XI did not endorse fascism specifically in the twenties, he came so close to it that the distinction was scarcely noticeable. On December 20, 1926, he declared that Mussolini was "the man sent by Providence," and his successor as Cardinal Archbishop of Milan called Mussolini "the new Constantine." In the United States, as Professors Gaetano Salvemini and George La Piana of Harvard have pointed out in their *What to Do with Italy,* the highest American cardinals echoed the praises for Mussolini.[8] The Bishop of Cleveland called him the "Man of Destiny," and Cardinal O'Connell of Boston, who had received a high fascist decoration, exalted him as "a genius in the field of government, given to Italy by God." Cardinal Hayes received four fascist decorations, and also responded with gratitude.

Throughout the world in this period, Catholic writers echoed the fascist disparagement of democracy without rebuke from their superiors. In 1931, England's most noted Catholic propagandist, Hilaire Belloc, said in describing Italy: "The anti-Catholic and Masonic organizations have been effectually got rid of by the happy suppression of Parliaments and all their sham authority, which is but a mask for a few rich men controlling a corrupt machine." [9] Thirteen years after Mussolini came to power, another noted British Catholic, Christopher Dawson, who has been named as one of the "forty contemporary immortals" among the Gallery of Living Catholic Authors, said:

. . . There seems to be no doubt that the Catholic social ideas set forth in the encyclicals of Leo XIII and Pius XI have far more affinity with those of fascism than with those of either liberalism or socialism. In the same way, it is clear that Catholicism is by no means hostile to the authoritarian ideal of the state. Against the liberal doctrines of the divine rights of majorities and the unrestricted freedom of opinion, the Church has always maintained the principles of authority and hierarchy and high conception of the prerogatives of the state. The ruler is not simply the representative of the people, he has an independent authority and a direct responsibility to God. His primary duty is not to fulfill the wishes of the people but to govern justly and well, and so long as he fulfills this duty any resistance on the part of the people is a grave sin.[10]

In Italy, the "grave sin" of resistance to Mussolini by individual Catholics soon came to an end when the Pope jettisoned the unofficial Catholic Popular Party, which had been led by the priest Don Sturzo, and finally signed the Concordat and Lateran Treaty with Mussolini's government on February 11, 1929.

In perspective, the Lateran Treaty seems to be one of the most important and one of the most tragic events in modern history. It gave Mussolini the confidence and respectability that he needed to begin his campaign of international aggression. In return for official peace, Mussolini gave the Vatican some very handsome concessions. The Lateran Treaty provided for: (1) the establishment of the Vatican State with extraterritorial rights and about $90,000,000 in reparation for the old Papal States; (2) the adoption of a rule that "apostate or suspended priests may not be employed or continued in employment as teachers or in any office or post which brings them into direct contact with the public"; (3) separate prisons for priests convicted of crime; (4) the reestablishment of "the Catholic Apostolic and Roman religion as the sole religion of the state"; (5) Catholic teaching of religion in the public schools with the right of Catholic bishops to remove any teacher of religion at will; (6) partial support of priests by the public treasury.[11]

The treaty, of course, was dishonored by Mussolini almost as soon as its ink was dry, and the Pope then scolded the dictator with a few sorrowful and indignant phrases in his encyclical *Non Abbiamo Bisogno*. It is this encyclical that is used in American Catholic propaganda to prove that the Pope was antifascist. Actually, the Pope never bothered to condemn the dictator for murdering Italian labor leaders or suppressing the democratic rights of Italy's masses or destroying the freedom of the press and of teaching.

His only genuine antifascist—as distinguished from antiliberal—utterance was his attack on Mussolini's anti-Semitic laws of 1938. By that time, his experience with Hitler had taught him that he could not afford to condone racial fanaticism officially. But Pius XI and his successor have continued to profit by those sections of the Lateran Treaty that discriminate against both Jews and Protestants. Even today there is no way in which a Protestant or Jew can get a divorce in Italy, while Catholics can get a marriage annulled if they can convince an ecclesiastical court of the justice of their case. The Union of Italian Jewish Communities has been just as unsuccessful in demanding equal treatment for Jews as the Council of Protestant Churches of Italy has been in demanding equal treatment for Protestants. "In all manifestations of social and political life," said the Vatican's *Osservatore Romano* on September 18, 1946, "the equalitarianism of religions and cults is an absurdity." [12]

3

The signing of the Lateran Treaty cleared the way for Vatican approval of Mussolini's war on Ethiopia. "On the plains of Ethiopia," said Cardinal Schuster of Milan on October 28, 1935, as reported in *Popolo d'Italia,* "the Italian Standard carries forward in triumph the Cross of Christ, smashes the chains of slavery, and opens the way for the missionaries of the gospel." The Catholic press in the United States was not so enthusiastic, but it promptly began sniping at the League of Nations and the "barbaric" notion of sanctions against Italy, and it was supported in this attitude by the Jesuit organ in Rome, *Civiltà Cattolica.*[13] The Vatican brought pressure to bear on South American states to oppose League sanctions, but the campaign was scarcely necessary. The League was dying on its feet from moral anemia. It required no special gift of prophecy for me to write from Milan to *The Nation:* "If Italy cannot be persuaded or compelled to use the machinery of the League of Nations, that outcast institution will have no place to lay its head."

It has remained for a Catholic writer, Count Michael de la Bedoyere, editor of Britain's *Catholic Herald,* to write the most sweeping indictment of the Vatican and the Ethiopian war:

Italy, reputedly a Catholic nation—wherein a Catholic revival was proceeding—attacked with the might of modern armaments a small and weak native people for purposes of naked imperialistic conquest. She did this, moreover, in defiance of the Covenant of the League of Nations and the Kellogg Pact, after having actually sponsored Abyssinia's membership in the League. . . . It would be difficult to find a clearer case on paper of deliberate and unjust (and cowardly) aggression in the face of international machinery, accepted by Italy and expressly designed to prevent the recourse to force as the instrument of policy. . . . Yet so far from protesting against such action, the Church seemed to condone and to defend it. The Catholics of Italy enthusiastically supported the Duce; the clergy, even the higher clergy, apparently allowed nationalism completely to overshadow their moral sense and the traditional teaching of the Church about just and unjust wars; even condoning the affair.[14]

Meanwhile, the Vatican had been drawing nearer and nearer to fascism in its economic and social program. Pius XI's ambiguous encyclical of 1931 on *Reconstructing the Social Order* seemed to advocate an authoritarian, corporate state as a solution for the world's economic ills. It avoided direct opposition to fascist organizations and advanced a program that was strikingly similar to the economic program of fascism. It denounced socialism explicitly, and called for a dual labor movement under Catholic influence to combat the movements of the left. Pointing out how Mussolini's corporative organizations prohibited all strikes and lockouts, the Pope said: "Little reflection is required to perceive the advantage of the institution thus summarily described; peaceful collaboration of the classes, repression [*sic*] of Socialist organizations and efforts, the moderating influence of a special ministry." [15] The only criticism of fascism that the Pope ventured in this encyclical was that the corporative organizations were "excessively bureaucratic and political." There was no suggestion that they also murdered the champions of democracy.

In the United States, the Catholic bishops echoed the Pope's principles of "co-operation," in a vague plan for "social reorganization" that suggested a voluntary industrial parliament of employers, workers, and the government, with the government serving as an innocuous adviser. In this plan, as in its victorious campaign against the child-labor amendment to the Constitution, the American hierarchy sought to use liberal slogans to oppose the expanding power of a democratic welfare state.

4

After these years of collaboration with fascism, it was not an accident that, when the republican-socialist revolution began in Spain in 1931, the Church was universally recognized as a partisan in the struggle. At the beginning, the war in Spain was not a clean-cut struggle for and against fascism, but it soon became that.

The political war which preceded the formal Spanish civil war was largely a struggle for the schools. The Spanish Church had controlled education for centuries and had left almost half the Spanish people illiterate. I wrote to *The Nation* from Madrid in 1933:

> In the background of the capital-labor struggle that is going on in Spain is the struggle between the socialistic state and the Catholic Church for control of national culture. The issue involved is not freedom of worship—the churches are open and well attended, and the clergy is outspoken in opposition to the government. Other important issues are involved. Who shall control the schools? Shall the government continue to support the ordinary priesthood?

The Republican government realized that it had to begin from the bottom and teach Spanish children the alphabet of democracy. It ordered the schools taken away from the Jesuits, but it never acquired the power and the money to carry out its program. As a result, the population was profoundly divided when the official civil war finally began in 1936. Many good Catholics fought with the Republicans, but the hierarchy, the Falange, and the landholders stood together. A pastoral letter signed by nearly all the bishops of Spain urged support for the Franco rebellion as "the Crusade of Spanish Liberation." [16]

In the end, it was the international power of the Vatican that determined the issue. The Roman Catholic Church in the United States played a decisive role in preventing the lifting of the embargo on arms to Spain—arms that would have saved the government from Franco's rebels. Secretary of the Interior Harold Ickes in his diary in May, 1938, in a comment on President Roosevelt, remarked: "He said frankly that to raise the embargo would mean the loss of every Catholic vote next fall and that the Democratic members of Congress were jittery about it and didn't want it done." [17]   While Mussolini and Hitler rushed support to Franco, the American Catholic press described the battle as a holy war for the preservation of Christianity and denied that Franco was getting help from Hitler. Communist support from Russia gave the Church its opportunity to paint the battle as a Christian-Communist death struggle. In American Catholicism only a few faint voices were raised in dissent and those voices were almost drowned in bitter denunciation. The Catholic *Commonweal,* which, with the Chicago *New World,* had stood almost alone in favor of neutrality toward Franco, admitted in 1947 that it lost one-fourth of its circulation in a single year as the price for this policy.

The attitude of the American hierarchy was summed up by *America* on August 20, 1938:

> Warning is again cried that Secretary Hull and the Administration are contemplating the lifting of the embargo of shipments of airplanes and war materials to Spain. Immediate action, by way of individual and public protests, by way of letters and telegrams, must be taken against this dangerous procedure. . . . Lift the Spanish embargo and the United States is on the sure road to war. Let us keep out of Spain! Let us refuse to make bloody dollars through munitions profits. Furthermore, let the United States continue to refuse to come to the aid of Moscow's satellite, the Red regime of Barcelona. Lift the embargo and this country becomes an ally of Communism abroad and a tool of Communism here at home.

Franco and the American Catholic lobby won, and the prewar story is now ancient history. But the postwar story is part of the same serial, with all the same actors except Hitler and Mussolini. Franco no longer greets American diplomats with pictures of Hitler and Mussolini displayed on the wall behind his chair, but he has established in Spain a clerical-fascist state that goes far beyond Mussolini's fascism in recognizing the Church as a partner in the totalitarian government.

In the fake "election" of July 6, 1947, when Franco had a law of succession passed by a "referendum," making Franco head of the Spanish government for life, the Catholic Primate of Spain, Enrique Cardinal Pla y Deniel, openly rallied the vote for him by a political pastoral letter addressed to all churches. The ballots contained no alternative to a pro-Franco vote, but the cardinal saw nothing inconsistent in this limitation, or in the regulation that made opposition to the Franco regime a crime. "Women voters," said *The New York Times* in describing the election, "turned out in greater numbers than men, partly, it is said, because of pressure from the clergy to vote for Generalissimo Franco."

The law of succession describes Spain as a "Catholic kingdom," and, in this kingdom, Franco has restored control of education to the Church, made Catholicism the official state religion, declared in article 6 of his bill of rights that public "ceremonies and manifestations other than those of the Catholic religion will not be permitted," and made it impossible for anyone who has ever been baptized as a Catholic to be married except by a priest. The Spanish law of primary education of 1945 makes it obligatory for all teachers in state schools to take a course in Catholic doctrine before they can teach; and article 5, chapter II, section I, says that "primary education, inspired with a Catholic sense and consistent with Spanish educational traditions, will conform to the principles of the Catholic dogma and faith and to the prescriptions of Canon Law."

These specifications are listed in Emmet J. Hughes's *Report from Spain,* in which he summarizes with the bitter honesty of a devout Catholic what he believes to be the "dominant characteristics of the contemporary Spanish Church . . . an overriding dedication to institutional self-interest; a tough, prideful imperviousness to criticism; a profound suspicion of any intellectual inquisitiveness; a contempt for any kind of education which is not synonymous with indoctrination; a sharp distrust and hostility toward any political or social movement that could be called radical, leftist, or liberal; and a respect that approaches reverence for power in any form." [18]

In this new Spain, the little children in all schools are told that "Spain is a totalitarian country and its Chief is His Excellency the Caudillo, Generalissimo of the Armies on land, sea and in the air, and Chief of the Government which is made up of twelve ministries." In the manual for religious instruction, *Nuevo Ripalda,* as cited by Mr. Hughes, Spanish children in all religious classes in the nation are given the following interpretation of freedom:

Q. What are the freedoms which liberalism defends? A. Freedom of conscience, freedom of worship, and freedom of the press.
Q. What does freedom of the press mean? A. The right to print and publish without previous censorship all kinds of opinion, however absurd and corrupting they may be.

Q. Must the government suppress this freedom by means of censorship? A. Obviously, yes.

Q. Why? A. Because it must prevent the deception, calumny and corruption of its subjects, which harm the general good.

Q. Are there other pernicious freedoms? A. Yes, freedom of propaganda, and freedom of assembly.

Q. Why are these freedoms pernicious? A. Because they serve to teach error, propagate vice, and plot against the Church.

5

The Roman Catholic record vis-à-vis Hitler is not as black as its record in Spain, but many Catholic sources can be cited to show that Vatican policy in Germany when Hitler was rising to power was designed to save the Church, not democracy. The Church permitted German Catholics to be National Socialists but not socialists. The Catholic Center Party, before it finally dissolved itself, undoubtedly stood for democracy, but it served chiefly to weaken the anti-Hitler labor forces. The Christian trade unions actually became a subordinate part of Ley's Labor Front before they were abolished.

Those German priests who wished to follow parishioners into the Nazi party were saved from this blunder by Hitler's unequivocal stand in favor of state control of education and his scathing denunciations of Christianity. When the Rome-Hitler-von Papen Concordat of 1933, negotiated for the Vatican by Cardinal Pacelli (later Pius XII), proved to be a scrap of paper in spite of the fact that Hitler had announced himself a member of the Roman Catholic Church just before its signing, the Church's subsequent attacks upon Hitler gave it new standing in England and America. These attacks, as De la Bedoyere points out, "were as popular with the world as the Abyssinian affair had been unpopular." But the popularity was scarcely deserved. The attacks were directed primarily against Hitler's incursions into "Catholic territory." The Church never excommunicated Hitler or—but let a Catholic editor summarize my doubts. De la Bedoyere says (italics supplied):

Pius XI issued in 1937 the encyclical, *Mit Brennender Sorge,* in which, with considerable skill, the extravagances of German Nazi doctrines are picked out for condemnation *in a way that would not involve the condemnation of political and social totalitarianism.* . . . They powerfully served to restore the international, moral, and spiritual prestige of the Church, which had been so shaken by the Abyssinian war. Nonetheless, the Concordat was not denounced, diplomatic relations between the Holy See and Berlin were not broken, the civil allegiance of Catholics to the Nazi Reich was not made impossible; still less, of course, was German foreign policy, involving the destruction of Catholic Austria and largely Catholic Czechoslovakia, in any way reprobated.

On the eve, then, of the new European war we find the Church endeavoring still to maintain, even at high cost, contact and friendship with all the conflicting interests, save only Bolshevism. . . . No breach sufficient to undermine the national loyalty of the Catholics in Germany either to Hitler's internal or external policy had been made.[19]

When the war began, the Catholic hierarchy in Germany continued to be concerned chiefly with Catholic rights and privileges. The pastoral letter of German bishops on Nazi persecution of June 26, 1941, was wholly ecclesiastical, bemoaning the lost privileges of the Church and the lost control of schools, but not revealing any animosity to dictatorship as such, or any opposition to Hitler's war.

Meanwhile, when Engelbert Dollfuss established in Austria for a few brief months what Teeling calls "the first Catholic model government in Europe," he received, on the day he ascended to power, a special telegraphed blessing from Cardinal Pacelli as Papal Secretary of State.[20] To this day Dollfuss is considered the model statesman of Catholicism. He called his state the "German Corporative Christian State," and he called the day of its inauguration "Catholic Day." He smashed the independent unions, massacred the Social Democrats, and destroyed freedom of the press. His ideals may have been noble, but the state that he actually established was a fascist state. The judgment is not mine but that of many Catholic and independent critics. "In reality," said Don Sturzo, Italian Catholic leader, "it is a dictatorial state with a Catholic and fascist predominance." "It was," said Teeling, in his *Crisis for Christianity,* a "totalitarian state working with the Church." [21]

Professor Charles Gulick in his monumental study, *Austria from Hapsburg to Hitler,* calls the state that Dollfuss established "The Clerical-Fascist-Police State," and quotes the chief author of the constitution as saying that the Economic Council of the regime had been planned "in perfect accordance with the encyclical *Quadragesimo Anno."* This 1934 constitution definitely discriminated against non-Catholic teachers in public schools, and under its partisan provisions, as Professor Gulick points out, "the Clerical Fascists methodically abolished all kinds of Socialist organizations and crippled, prostituted or destroyed institutions and arrangements that embodied the political, economic and social gains which had been secured only after decades of effort." [22] After Dollfuss had been assassinated, it did not take long for the Nazis to move in.

While Hitler was rising to power in Germany a clerical-fascist state emerged in Portugal under a Catholic dictator, Oliveira Salazar. Free speech was promptly suppressed and opposition parties were destroyed. The Portuguese constitution of 1933 was partially based upon the *Quadragesimo Anno* of Pius XI, and partially upon Italy's fascist constitution. The Concordat of 1940 between Portugal and the Holy See,[23] which is considered a model of Catholic diplomacy, did not technically "establish" the Church itself, but it legalized subsidies to Catholic schools, outlawed divorce for all Catholics, and provided that even in schools maintained entirely by the government the Catholic religion should be taught, and that "in no case shall religious instruction be given by persons not approved by the ecclesiastical authorities." Portuguese missions in the colonial empire became the monopoly of the Catholic Church, subsidized by the state as agencies of Portuguese imperialism.

One indication of the amount of democracy in Portugal is that for twenty years no president was opposed in an "election." The Portuguese system of dictatorship has been quite satisfactory to the Church, and probably no nation in the world today is praised by the hierarchy more consistently as a successful exhibit of Catholicism in action.

6

The Second World War imposed new strains on Vatican diplomacy but did not alter its fundamental policy. In the period before Pearl Harbor, when American aid against Hitler was desperately needed, the overwhelming majority of the Vatican's representatives in this country railed at the possibility of American intervention, in language that was strikingly similar to Soviet propaganda in the period of the notorious Hitler-Stalin pact. "Let those who have started this war finish it," said Cardinal O'Connell to a Boston Congress of Catholic Women eight months before

Pearl Harbor. "It is not our affair." [24] "The present conflict," said Bishop Francis Beckman, of Dubuque, in a radio speech over the Columbia network in July, 1941, "is not a 'holy war,' least of all a just war; but a war of one imperialism against the other in which godlessness is incidental to all belligerents." [25]

When Hitler conquered France, and a collaborationist regime was set up in Vichy, the Vatican rushed to the support of the aged Catholic leader, Pétain, and hailed the "spiritual rebirth of France." When Pétain gave back to the Church many of the special ecclesiastical privileges that had been lost under the Republic, the Church responded, even in the remote French islands of the Caribbean, by praising Pétain at the expense of the resistance movement. In Spain, as Emmet Hughes points out, the Bishop of Madrid in 1944 issued an order that excluded all Frenchmen not loyal to Pétain from the Catholic chapel connected with the French embassy. At home, most French Catholic leaders welcomed Pétain with open relish.

The psychology of that welcome has been described by Father Georges Didier, French Jesuit, writing in *America:*

The defeat of 1940 appeared to all Frenchmen as a terrible, incredible catastrophe. But . . . the Catholic conservatives experienced a feeling of bitter triumph. For seventy years they had not ceased to warn France that the Republic was leading it to disaster. For seventy years they had cried out that the pacifist illusions of the Left were weakening the army, that divorce, birth control, atheistic schools were sapping the physical and moral resources of the nation. Thus it was that at the moment of sorrowful disillusionment many conservatives felt a strange exhilaration.[26]

The "feeling of bitter triumph" and the "strange exhilaration" among French Catholics were revealed so openly that Father Didier acknowledges "the anguish that gripped us when certain Catholic leaders seemed to make submission to an oppressive and unpopular regime a matter of conscience." He admits the effectiveness of the Communist slogan: "The Church supports Vichy! The Church favors fascism!"

The Church's support of Pétain will not soon be forgotten by the Jewish people of the world, because it involved acquiescence in oppressive anti-Semitic legislation. Vichy's laws were designed to remove Jews from the civil service, from the professions, and from all control of newspapers and radio broadcasting. Jews were limited to 3 per cent of the enrollment in universities. Pius XI had officially condemned anti-Semitism; but when Pétain's ambassador to the Vatican, Leon Bérard, consulted the Vatican about Vichy's discriminatory laws, he reported that "there is no intention to take us to task, in any form or fashion, over our Jewish legislation." The Vatican asked only that the discriminatory laws be applied with charity and that "no provision should be made in our Jewish legislation on the subject of marriage which would provoke difficulties of a religious order." M. Bérard's report describing the Vatican's attitude was discovered in the archives of Vichy's Commissariat of Jewish Affairs after the war.[27]

The postwar Church rallied quickly in France, and the Vatican appointed a nuncio who had not been too friendly with the collaborationsts. The French hierarchy threw its support to a new political party, the M.R.P., which, as Father Didier says, "remained faithful to the spirit of Catholic Action, of which it was born." With De Gaulle's rise toward power and the decline of the M.R.P., the French hierarchy promptly adjusted its viewpoint and found many virtues in the doughty general's R.P.F. One "virtue" was that De Gaulle promised to restore state subsidies to Catholic schools. The restoration came shortly afterward.

The Vatican in all these postwar political maneuvers has been astute enough to choose its martyrs carefully and to drop an unsatisfactory martyr gently. When the Very Reverend Joseph Tiso, priest-president of Hitler's puppet state of Slovakia, tried to build a Roman Catholic fascist state, he had the warm support of the Vatican at first; the Vatican radio said that "his intention to reconstruct Slovakia on a Christian plan is greatly welcomed by the Holy See. The reorganization of the state is to be based on the corporate system, on Christian lines, and modeled on the system which has proved so successful in Portugal." But when Tiso declared war on the United States, called for the deportation of all Jews, and co-operated enthusiastically in the murder of his democratic opponents, the Vatican grew cautious. It never excommunicated him, but it made no great effort to win clemency before he walked to the gallows on April 18, 1947, clutching a rosary.

On the whole, the postwar political policy of the Vatican has been little different from its prewar policy. The Church has been astutely conservative, always adjusting its policies to local conditions. In Belgium the Catholic party is a monarchist party; in the

United States the bishops are learning to use the phrases of democracy as if they had been invented in Rome. Some American bishops have been somewhat more cautious in praise of Franco than they were in the thirties, and *America* in 1948 actually questioned whether a political party based on Christian principles could approve "the monolithic form of Franco's political organizations." *The Commonweal* also has valiantly fought against Catholic favoritism to Franco. But most American Church leaders have continued to favor Franco after the war almost as enthusiastically as they did during the Spanish civil war, and the American diocesan press has continued to carry long eulogies. On December 12, 1948, Pius XII gave Franco his public and "affectionate blessing." A writer in the *Catholic World* said confidently: "It can be factually demonstrated that Spain under the leadership of Don Francisco Franco . . . is a powerful force for good internationally, and that it is actively applying sound social, ethical and cultural principles within the nation itself." [28]   On December 21, 1953, Pius XII conferred on Franco the Supreme Order of Christ, the highest secular decoration granted by the Holy See. Only three other living men possessed this honor.[29]

In Washington, D. C., Catholic legislators have formed a kind of pro-Franco bloc. Many of them supported the disastrous proposal to include Spain in the European Recovery Program. It was a nice sense of irony that led *The New York Times* correspondent in Washington to report on March 31, 1948, that the House of Representatives voted to include Franco's government in the Marshall Plan "less than an hour after the session had been opened with prayer by Monsignor Fulton J. Sheen of the Catholic University of America."

Must we take seriously the threat of a clerical-fascist International? The answer is implicit in the record that I have reviewed. In the years since Mussolini came to power, the *deeds,* as distinguished from the *words,* of the Vatican have strengthened the conviction that it will gladly support a fascist International *so long as it is a clerical-fascist International.* In several great crises in Europe the Vatican has, through passive and active collaboration with fascism, thrown the balance of power against democracy. It has never spoken out against fascist dictatorship with one-tenth of the ferocity of its attack on Communist dictatorship. Committing itself against even democratic socialism, it has aligned itself with the most reactionary forces in Europe and Latin America.

Surely it is not an accident that the two most fascist nations in the world today—Spain and Portugal—are Catholic nations whose dictators have been blessed by the Pope and are conspicuously loyal to him!

The Vatican's affinity with fascism is neither accidental nor incidental. Catholicism conditions its people to accept censorship, thought control, and, ultimately, dictatorship. Says Count Coudenhove-Kalergi, who was reared as a Catholic:

> Catholicism is the fascist form of Christianity of which Calvinism represents its democratic wing. The Catholic hierarchy rests fully and securely on the leadership principle with the infallible Pope in supreme command for a lifetime. . . . Like the Fascist party, its priesthood becomes a medium for an undemocratic minority rule by a hierarchy. . . . Catholic nations follow fascist doctrines more willingly than Protestant nations, which are the main strongholds of democracy. . . . Democracy lays its stress on personal conscience; fascism on authority and obedience.[30]

7

Most Americans agree with the Church's opposition to Russian Communism but have some misgivings about the hierarchy's anti-Communist campaign. Is that campaign really based on lofty moral sentiment, or on self-defense, or is it a form of temporary opportunism developed for trading purposes? There is an element of truth in all of these interpretations, but non-Catholics are not sure what are the proportions of moral idealism, self-interest, and political strategy. Certainly the world Communist movement is sufficiently anti-Christian to evoke genuine Christian opposition, and there is no doubt that Moscow threatens the very life of the Catholic Church in many parts of the world. A counterattack by all the clergy, Catholic and non-Catholic, against such a movement is inevitable.

The theory that anti-Communism may be a temporary Vatican policy designed for more effective trading with the enemy should not be overlooked. Following the principle that the Church is indifferent to all forms of government, the Vatican is ready to make shrewd and surprising deals in balance-of-power politics. The whole history of the Church indicates that it will compromise with almost any form of dictatorship if there is a sufficient *quid pro quo*. At the international conference in Genoa in 1922, marking the entrance of the Bolsheviks into international gatherings, the Vatican was ready to begin negotiations with the Bolshevik government; and an agreement could have been reached if Moscow had been willing to grant a degree of freedom to the Roman Catholic Church in Russia. At the present time the Church cannot compromise with Communist Russia because the Soviet Union offers nothing in return.

But cannot the Church which made a concordat with Hitler, and kept it until he destroyed it himself, compromise also with Moscow—at a price? That speculation seems idle now, but it should not be banished altogether from serious discussions of Vatican policy. There is so much basic kinship between the doctrinal absolutism of the Vatican and that of the Kremlin that the possibility of ultimate collaboration on a basis of mutual self-interest cannot be dismissed as unthinkable. Both organizations believe in censorship and reject democracy as a form of government for themselves. Both are seeking to extend their authority by developing groups of loyal followers within other jurisdictions. The distorted Communism of the Kremlin is a fanatical religion, with commissars instead of priests. Communists and Catholics, as Reinhold Niebuhr has said, are "rival absolutists." It is not too difficult for men to pass from one absolutism to another. "If we are to judge by the writings of the outspoken apologists of Catholicism in Europe and America," says Professor Sidney Hook, "they are just as ready, if necessity arises, to baptize Marx as they once baptized Aristotle." [31]

The kinship between Catholic and Communist political policy has been noted by Europe's leading Protestant theologian, Karl Barth, in an acid comment that he made to a Jesuit journalist in 1948:

> To be honest, I see some connection between them [Roman Catholicism and Communism]. Both are totalitarian; both claim man as a whole. Communism uses about the same methods of organization (learned from the Jesuits). Both lay great stress on all that is visible. But Roman Catholicism is the more dangerous of the two for Protestantism. Communism will pass; Roman Catholicism is lasting.[32]

(I have discussed this analogy at great length in my 1951 book, *Communism, Democracy and Catholic Power*.)

Meanwhile, the Roman Catholic Church has become the world's loudest opponent of Moscow's brand of Communism, and there is no doubt about its anti-Communist zeal. Pius XI's 1937 encyclical on *Atheistic Communism* is the law and the prophets of Church political policy, and the American hierarchy has made anti-Communism the central theme of its ministry since the end of World War II. "Communism," said Leo XIII, is "the fatal plague which insinuates itself into the very marrow of human society only to bring about its ruin." "Communism," said Pius XI, "is intrinsically wrong, and no one who would save Christian civilization may collaborate with it in any undertaking whatsoever." [33]

In American Catholic propaganda, Russian Communism is literally and figuratively a devil. For the priests it is a happy eventuality that their fears coincide with American national fears. In the national anti-Communist symphony, the double brass of the Catholic section blares loudly, and the Catholic priests obviously enjoy their pro-American role in the noisy performance. The diocesan Catholic press of the United States has been essentially a pro-war press since 1945, featuring murdered nuns in Communist China and murdered priests in Yugoslavia, along with the Communist coup in Czechoslovakia, the Communist struggle for power in Italy, and the imprisonment of Cardinal Mindszenty in Hungary.

It is scarcely necessary to say that many of the hierarchy's fears about Communism's present leaders are justified, and that Russian aggression threatens world peace. That, at least, is my opinion, and I will not permit skepticism concerning the role of anti-Communism in Catholic politics to mitigate the judgment. It is natural that any believer in democracy should feel some sympathy for the Church's apprehension about Communism, even when he questions the hierarchy's consistency and motives.

But many questions naturally occur to the independent student concerning Catholic anti-Communism. How much of it is genuine and justified alarm and how much is cultivated, clerical hysteria? How much of economic and political reaction is included in the composite product, "anti-Communism," which the hierarchy is offering to the American public as a single, patriotic package?

There are many evidences that Catholic anti-Communism in the United States is unbalanced and emotional, and that it is using the legitimate apprehensions of the American people to protect what *The Christian Century* once called "shady and reactionary allies, whose opposition to communism represents nothing more than a desire to preserve old privileges." The examples of this policy in action are too numerous to mention.

The American hierarchy has repeatedly represented the Mexican government's desire for control of elementary education as Communistic. Archbishop Stepinac's martyrdom in a Yugoslav prison was dramatized by the hierarchy as undiluted religious persecution, although Stepinac had collaborated openly with rebel forces led by the notorious Croatian Fuehrer, Ante Pavelitch.

In the United States after World War II, the Catholic organizations and the Catholic press enthusiastically backed the undiscriminating policies and theatrical behavior of the House Committee on un-American Activities, headed by J. Parnell Thomas. Priests in various parts of the country attacked well-known anti-Communist independent liberals as "communist sympathizers" if they dared to question Catholic policy. Usually the priests made use of some Catholic lay organization as a "front" for this political activity, but their propaganda was circulated in the churches at regular religious gatherings.

The priests of Pittsfield, Massachusetts, defeated proportional representation in that city in 1947 by persuading their parishioners that it was a dangerously revolutionary measure. On the Sunday before a popular referendum on the question, a surprise unsigned statement attacking the reform was read in all Catholic churches, and one leading priest characterized the reform as "the most vicious thing that ever was presented to the people of this city." [34]

Catholic war veterans have frequently appeared in the press in recent years as the self-confessed leaders of raids on leftist headquarters. Their fury has been whipped up by officially approved Catholic publications. The Catechetical Guild of St. Paul—listed by the *Catholic Almanac* as one of the "Catholic pamphlet publishers in the United States" and headed by a priest, Father Louis A. Gales—distributed in 1947 a comic-strip pamphlet called *Is This Tomorrow?* in which Communist mobs were depicted as attacking St. Patrick's Cathedral with torches and nailing the cardinal to the church door in imitation of the crucifixion. When the Detroit police department banned this comic pamphlet in that city, on the ground that it would provoke racial violence, and threatened to arrest anybody who sold it, the editor of the *Catholic Digest,* which had carried the pamphlet as a supplement, informed the police chief: "Then you'll be arresting twenty or thirty pastors who will be selling it next week." [35]   The Detroit police backed down. Incidentally, a single New York priest sold more than seven thousand copies of this pamphlet inside his church.

The phenomenon called McCarthyism, which did so much to discredit American culture throughout the world for almost a decade, was largely a product of the fanatical support of the Catholic diocesan press for the late senator from Wisconsin, Joseph R. McCarthy. McCarthy used the Catholic War Veterans and other Catholic organizations as shock troops in his campaigns, and he had the enthusiastic support of the Catholic clergy and all but three or four of the American Catholic publications. His unbalanced anti-Communism, which did not discriminate between liberalism and subversion, was heartily hailed by thousands of priests. He was repeatedly described by Catholic clerical leaders as a great American, a great Catholic, and "a deeply religious man," while his exaggerations and misrepresentations were condoned. Only one Catholic bishop dared to challenge him vigorously during the days of his ascendancy, the liberal Bishop Bernard J. Sheil of Chicago, and he was promptly demoted by Cardinal Stritch.[36]

It was not an accident that when McCarthy died in May, 1957, four bishops, twenty monsignors, and seventy-five priests assisted at his funeral Mass. "The Senator," said the Baltimore *Catholic Review* in its elegy, "was a Catholic, honestly and without display, a man who believed what we believe about God and about men, about right and about wrong, about justice, charity, prudence, temperance." [37]

Although the Catholic Church in Europe has been traditionally antisocialist, the American Church is not antilabor, and even its antisocialism is due more to historical accident and jealousy of the modern welfare state than to any reasoned allegiance to capitalism. Some members of the American hierarchy are quite gentle in their opposition to socialism, and quite anticapitalist in many of their utterances. Father J. Edward Coffey expressed a typical current view of this liberal wing of American Catholicism in *America* in 1946 when he said: "The awful things the encyclicals and textbooks used to say about it [socialism] . . . are all valid still as anathemas for communism. . . . But not for the 'socialism' of Norman Thomas, Ignazio Silone, Leon Blum, Ernest Bevin or the Scandinavian co-operative states." [38]

In fact, if the first European socialists had not been anticlerical, the history of Catholicism in Europe might have been quite different. As it was, the economic liberalism of Leo XIII and Pius XI in their two famous economic encyclicals, *Rerum Novarum* and *Quadragesimo Anno*, was largely derivative, a reaction to the pioneer liberalism of European socialists which echoed many of socialism's aspirations while opposing the socialist state. Today, the Catholic churches of Europe frequently collaborate with local social-democratic parties, and even the Catholic parties themselves endorse the lesser socialist objectives. The Church, however, always clashes with the socialist movement on two fundamental issues: the supreme power of the democratic state over all aspects of secular life, and the superior claim of public schools in the education of the people.

Today the Church's official opposition to democratic socialism appears to be more a matter of political strategy than of principle. Catholics do not necessarily oppose public ownership of many leading industries. The Church's seven Catholic political parties in Europe frequently make deals with socialist parties for joint programs which have many socialistic features—and the Vatican withholds its veto. Catholics have been permitted to belong to Britain's Labor Party since 1931, although it is officially socialist. Capitalism is frequently denounced and disparaged in official Church publications. Catholic leaders explain this adjustment by claiming that the Church merely opposes the materialism in the socialist movement, not the gospel of economic betterment. They would like to reconcile Catholicism and social democracy in spite of the repeated declarations of the Popes that no good Catholic can be a socialist.

When, before Adenauer's victory in the 1957 elections in West Germany, German Catholics were told by the Bishop of Muenster that as a matter of "conscience" they were forbidden to vote Socialist,[39] the real reason for the prohibition was not the socialism of the Socialists but the fear that a Socialist victory would take money and power away from the Church. Socialists in Europe have been the foremost opponents of grants of public money to Catholic schools.

In practice the American Church has no settled philosophy of labor except the general humane concept of personal kindness and fair play. Its vague pronouncements on labor policy are more sentimental than fascist. The Church believes in private property if responsibly administered, and in "good" labor unions. It favors an "industry council plan" for settling industrial problems "based on democratically selected councils of employers' associations and labor unions." It refuses to face the problems of ownership and class power squarely.

When clerical privileges and Roman dogma are not involved, the American hierarchy is frequently quite liberal in its policies on race relations and civil rights. Its recent pronouncements on fair play for Negroes in employment and in the educational world have greatly strengthened the movement for racial justice in this country.

When the Supreme Court announced its famous decision of May, 1954, outlawing racial segregation in the public schools as unconstitutional, the Catholic hierarchy and the American Catholic press, even in the South, hailed the decision as a "great triumph of democracy," [40] in keeping with Christian principles. Catholics were ordered, in several dioceses, to put the decision into practice by desegregation of parochial schools. This opposition to segregation is not a new Catholic policy, although it came as a new policy to many Southern parishes where segregated Catholic schools had been operating for many years. Actually, the Church has taught for some time that even the state's laws against interracial marriage have no binding moral validity. [41]

In the Northern and border states desegregation has been almost universally accomplished in Catholic institutions, but in the old South, where segregation is traditional, the Church has not been able to enforce its rulings. Archbishop Joseph F. Rummell of New Orleans not only ordered desegregation in the Catholic schools of his diocese in 1956, but threatened excommunication for any Louisiana legislator who voted for a state law imposing segregation on Catholic schools—not because this violated the American Constitution but because it violated Canon 2334. Although he was hailed in the North for his courage, his own people did not immediately accept his edict, and he was forced to suspend its enforcement.

It is interesting to note that in this struggle no member of the Catholic hierarchy suggested that the Catholic people of each diocese or of the United States should be allowed to decide questions of racial policy for themselves. There was no formal consultation with the Catholic people even in the grave crisis in the South. The directive on race came from Rome, with no apology for its arbitrary character. When New Orleans laymen appealed to the Vatican, they were promptly rebuffed.[42]

While the leaders of the Church were persuasive and intelligent in describing the wrong done to American children by segregating them according to race in separate schools, no member of the hierarchy ventured to draw the obvious parallel that segregation of children in separate schools by religion might also injure them and the community. In each case the policy adopted—desegregation in one case and segregation in the other—was declared to be "of faith," which means in practice that it was imposed without recourse by directives coming from Rome.

Meanwhile the hierarchy, although it is opposed to racial segregation in the South, may emerge from the struggle unwittingly as the chief beneficiary. If public schools are superseded in several Southern states—and at the moment this seems to be a genuine possibility—any private schools which replace them may divide along denominational lines. Catholic private schools would emerge with new status, and possibly with new grants of public (local) funds, if they added some non-Catholics to their boards of control and nominally accepted some non-Catholic students. It is not surprising that the racial struggle in the South has caused a number of Northern Catholic editors to express anticipatory pleasure over the impending decline of the prestige of the "public school monopoly."

In general, American priests tend to be sincerely pro-labor, because of their own humble beginnings, and because the Catholic concentration in large industrial centers gives Catholics more than their share of American union personnel. Bishop John F. Noll claimed in 1946 that Catholics constituted 40 to 50 per cent of American trade-union membership.

American labor leaders welcome Catholic support with reservations. They know that, while local priests may be sincerely prolabor, they are subject to the orders of a foreign government that may suddenly impose an anti-labor policy on them when the interests of the Vatican seem to demand it. They are aware of the reactionary political role played by the Church in many European countries and are naturally suspicious of any attempt by American Catholicism to build up a separate national organization for Catholic labor. A.C.T.U., the American Association of Catholic Trade Unionists, which has been organized to develop

Catholic power in the labor movement, is a small and relatively unimportant organization that has never attained the menacing proportions of the dual Catholic labor organizations in Quebec and in Europe. It works inside the unions as a Catholic pressure group. On its tenth anniversary, in 1947, it had perhaps 2,000 members in the whole country.[43] It has never gained more than 5,000 members in a labor movement numbering above 16,000,-000. One reason for this lack of success is the complete subordination of the organization to priestly advisers. Like all other Catholic lay organizations, it has no mind of its own. The constitution of its Detroit branch, which I quoted in my *Communism, Democracy and Catholic Power,* reads:

> In the event of insoluble dispute over any question of policy, tactics, principle or leadership, the counsel of the Most Rev. Archbishop shall be the final determinant.

A.C.T.U. has been frequently criticized even by Catholic labor leaders, because they doubt the wisdom of establishing a labor body on denominational lines within a larger democratic movement. Daniel Tobin, Catholic former head of the International Brotherhood of Teamsters, expressed the view of most American labor leaders when he said in his union journal: "I have repeatedly advised our membership that under no circumstances should we allow religious cliques of any kind within the organization of labor." At present A.C.T.U. work is largely confined to fighting Communist influence, and its successes have been scored chiefly because the overwhelming majority of labor-union members in the United States are also anti-Communist.

The most questionable feature of Catholic labor policy in the United States is the hierarchy's doctrinaire opposition to the expansion of government social services. Cardinal O'Connell in Massachusetts and Cardinal Hayes in New York were largely responsible for the defeat of the 1924 child labor amendment to the federal Constitution. They misbranded the measure "The Youth Control Amendment" in their propaganda, and argued that it would interfere with the parental control of children in the home. They did not speak for the whole Church, however, and perhaps the Church's attitude might be different in facing the same issue today.

The American Church has many advanced economic liberals whose views on economic policy are as far removed from fascism as from laissez-faire capitalism. The voting record of Catholic senators and representatives in Washington in recent years has placed the Catholic legislative bloc distinctly left of center. The great Catholic population blocs in our cities are largely labor blocs whose members tend to march forward with New Deal Democrats. Many of the priests march along in the same procession, trying hard to make themselves believe that the most modern ideals of economic reconstruction come directly from the vague and amorphous pronouncements of Leo XIII and Pius XI.

12

The Catholic Plan for America

1

BACK IN THE DAYS of the most virulent anti-Catholic bigotry, when "The Menace" was a national institution and candidates for public office openly reviled the Pope, one dramatic question was frequently asked at anti-Catholic mass meetings: "What will become of American democracy if the United States is captured by the Papists?" That last word was usually hissed or whispered in a way to make shivers run up and down the spine.

The question was more reasonable than its source. In fact, the bigoted character of the source has tended to divert attention from a valid and important question. Many American liberals have been deterred from an honest analysis of the implications of Catholic rule by fear of being associated with anti-Catholic fanatics. They have allowed the Catholic hierarchy, unchallenged, to use American freedom as a cloak for the systematic cultivation of separatism and intolerance among the American Catholic people.

Recent developments in Europe and Latin America suggest that the future role of the Roman Catholic Church in American politics should be re-examined with some care. What would happen to American democracy if our alleged thirty-five million Catholics grew to be a majority in the population and followed the direction of their priests? Suppose that, on some magic carpet of time, we could pass over the next two centuries and find ourselves in a predominantly Catholic America. What would American democracy look like?

The democratic *form* of our leading institutions might not be altered very much. Probably the most striking effect of Catholic control would be apparent in the *spirit* of those institutions and the *use* to which they would be put. The Catholic hierarchy is perfectly willing to compromise with democratic forms of government so long as its own special areas of power are respected. In a Catholic America the principal institutions of American democracy might be permitted to continue if they were operated for Catholic objectives.

The most striking and immediate result of Catholic ascendancy in our democracy would be the transfer of control of education, religion, and family relationships to the Catholic hierarchy. After Catholics had attained a majority in three-fourths of our states, this transfer could be accomplished by three comprehensive amendments to the United States Constitution. Let us draft them in outline, with our pontifical tongue in cheek.

The first Catholic amendment to the Constitution might be called, for educational purposes, the "Christian Commonwealth Amendment." Let us assume that it might include all of the following statements:

1. The United States is a Catholic Republic, and the Catholic Apostolic and Roman religion is the sole religion of the nation.
2. The authority of the Roman Catholic Church is the most exalted of all authorities; nor can it be looked upon as inferior to the power of the United States government, or in any manner dependent upon it, since the Catholic Church as such is a sovereign power.
3. Priests and members of religious orders of the Roman Catholic Church who violate the law are to be tried by an ecclesiastical court of the Roman Catholic Church, and may, only with the consent of the competent Catholic authority, be tried by the courts of the United States or the states.
4. Apostate priests or those incurring the censure of the Roman Catholic Church cannot be employed in any teaching post or any office or employment in which they have immediate contact with the public.
5. Non-Catholic faiths are tolerated, but public ceremonies and manifestations other than those of the Roman Catholic religion will not be permitted.
6. The First Amendment to the Constitution of the United States is hereby repealed.

The second Catholic amendment to the Constitution of the United States might well be described for propaganda purposes as the "Christian Education Amendment." It could be expected with confidence to be phrased in forms like these:

1. American religious education belongs pre-eminently to the Roman Catholic Church, by reason of a double title in the supernatural order, conferred exclusively upon her by God Himself.
2. The Roman Catholic Church has the inalienable right to supervise the entire education of her children in all educational institutions in the United States, public or private, not merely in regard to the religious instruction given in such institutions, but in regard to every other branch of learning and every regulation in so far as religion and morality is concerned.
3. Compulsory education in public schools exclusively shall be unlawful in any state in the Union.
4. It shall be unlawful for any neutral or non-Catholic school to enroll any Catholic child without permission of the Church.
5. Since neutral schools are contrary to the fundamental principles of education, public schools in the United States are lawful only when both religious instruction and every other subject taught are permeated with Catholic piety.
6. The governments of the United States and of the states are permitted to operate their own schools for military and civic training without supervision by the Roman Catholic Church, provided they do not injure the rights of the said Church, and provided that only the Roman Catholic Church shall have power to impart any religious instruction in such schools.
7. With due regard to special circumstances, co-education shall be unlawful in any educational institution in the United States whose students have attained the age of adolescence.
8. The governments of the United States and the states shall encourage and assist the Roman Catholic Church by appropriate measures in the exercise of the Church's supreme mission as educator.

The third Catholic amendment to the Constitution of the United States might be called the "Christian Family Amendment," although, in the campaign for its adoption, the sanctity of womanhood and the defeat of Communism would, doubtless, play a major part. The amendment conceivably could read:

1. The government of the United States, desirous of restoring to the institution of matrimony, which is the basis of the family, that dignity conformable to the traditions of its people, assigns as civil effects of the sacrament of matrimony all that is attributed to it in the Canon Law of the Roman Catholic Church.
2. No matrimonial contract in the United States that involves a Catholic can be valid unless it is in accordance with the Canon Law of the Roman Catholic Church.

3. Marriages of non-Catholics are subject to the civil authority of the state, but all civil laws that contradict the Canon Law of the Roman Catholic Church on marriage are hereby declared null and void.
4. All marriages are indissoluble, and the divorce of all persons is prohibited throughout the territory of the United States: provided that nothing herein shall affect the right of annulment and remarriage in accordance with the Canon Law of the Roman Catholic Church.
5. Attempted mixed marriages or unions between members of the Roman Catholic Church and non-Catholics are null and void, and the children of such unions are illegitimate, unless a special dispensation is obtained from the ecclesiastical authority of the Catholic Church.
6. Birth control, or any act that deliberately frustrates the natural power to generate life, is a crime.
7. Direct abortion is murder of the innocent even when performed through motives of misguided pity when the life of a mother is gravely imperiled.
8. Sterilization of any human being is forbidden except as an infliction of grave punishment under the authority of the government for a crime committed.

I remember a verse from Job which is appropriate at this moment: "If I justify myself, mine own mouth shall condemn me." That is meant for Catholic liberals whose temperature has been rising while they have been reading these three amendments. As most of my readers have doubtless guessed, there is not an original thought and scarcely an original word in my entire three Catholic amendments. They are mosaics of official Catholic doctrine. *Every concept, almost every word and phrase, has been plagiarized line by line from Catholic documents.* The most important phrases are derived from the highest documents of Catholicism, the encyclicals of the Popes. The provisions on education come from Pius XI's *Christian Education of Youth,* and those on family life from his *Casti Connubii,* both of them accepted universally in the Catholic Church as the Bibles of present-day educational and family policy. A few provisions are taken directly from Canon Law, the recent laws of Catholic countries like Spain, and the 1929 Concordat between Mussolini and the Vatican, all of which have been publicly approved by Catholic authorities. Only place-names and enabling clauses have been added to give the Papal principles local application. The sources are listed in the Notes.[1]

2

There is no Catholic plan for America distinct from the Catholic plan for the world. The hierarchy's techniques of promotion vary from country to country, but the master plan is only one plan and the world-wide strategy is directed from Rome. In a Catholic world *every* national government would establish the Roman Catholic Church in a unique position of privilege, and support its teachers and priests out of public revenues. That is what the Holy See has *always* demanded in every country where it has had the power to support the demand with reasonable strength.

In any Catholic state, schools receiving public funds would be either entirely Catholic or operated under Catholic moral supervision. Vituperative attacks on the clergy would be suppressed, and all books directly attacking the hierarchy or its doctrines would be forbidden. Non-Catholic sects would probably be permitted if they were relatively quiet and confined their ceremonies to their own property. The Church would have sole authority over the marriage and separation of Catholics, and complete veto power in censoring all books, magazines, newspapers, and films. The Vatican would be the chief organ of international peacemaking, and the Pope would be the world's highest arbiter. In each nation the Church would play the leading role in mediating between the propertied classes and organized labor.

There is nothing fanciful about this picture except that it has not yet been realized in the United States. The essentials of the Catholic plan for America, and for all nations, are self-evident in Papal encyclicals and the Canon Law. The record is neither secret nor mysterious, although its full implications are not always clear to Americans because the most aggressive and offensive features of the plan are not stressed in non-Catholic countries.

The Catholic hierarchy proposes to realize the Catholic plan for America by maintaining and increasing the present Catholic population, by expanding the Catholic schools with the aid of public money, and by infiltrating and penetrating non-Catholic organizations with faithful Catholic laymen who will act as consecrated missionaries for the Church. This latter activity is the special task of the over-all co-ordinating organization of Catholic laymen, Catholic Action.

Although its techniques are sometimes conspiratorial rather than democratic, there is nothing particularly wicked or sinister about Catholic Action, unless the goal that it seeks is considered sinister. Catholic Action is a "lay apostolate" working for a totally Catholic civilization—political, medical, cultural, economic, and religious—a civilization in which the Catholic Church will be "the mistress and guide of all other societies." [2] It is completely subordinate to the hierarchy, being described by Pius XI as "the participation of the laity in the apostolate of the Church's hierarchy." In the United States, in a sense, Catholic Action is simply the total network of Catholic lay organizations, inspired by a set of militant shibboleths. It has a separate department in the over-all organization of American Catholicism, the National Catholic Welfare Conference, but it works largely through other organizations.

"Catholic Action itself," says *The Catholic Action Manual*, "is an army involved in a holy war for religion." The military symbolism is not accidental; the whole emphasis of the organization is upon a crusading faith, inspired with militant confidence that the Catholic Church can conquer the earth if its followers obey their priests with military precision. Its members are urged not to marry the enemy, for fear that mixed marriage will pervert their Catholic zeal. Father James J. O'Toole puts this warning graphically in his official pamphlet for members, *What is Catholic Action?*:

A few days ago a young woman said to a priest, "Father, I'm going to join one of those Catholic Action groups."

Father was a bit surprised. He glanced at the girl, then turned his eyes to the window. Finally he spoke and his words were unexpected. "Just what for?" he asked.

It was the young woman's turn to be surprised. She got off a preliminary "We-ll" and waited for words to come. None came. "I just thought I'd like to," she floundered helplessly.

"My dear girl," said the priest, "on yonder table I see the picture of a rather handsome young man. If I'm not mistaken you're keeping company with him at the present moment. Now I happen to know that he's not a Catholic . . ."

"What's the matter with that?" interjected the young woman quickly.

Father looked out of the window again. It was a long time before he answered. When he did it sounded as if he were talking to himself. "People who go in for Catholic Action," he said slowly, "are people who have definitely determined to follow the mind of the

Church in their daily life so that they may use their influence sincerely to conquer other souls for Christ." [3]

Catholic Action was relatively unknown to the non-Catholic people of the United States until 1948, when its notable success in helping to swing the Italian election of that year to the Christian Democratic (Catholic) Party advertised its techniques and its growth. In most of its activities in the United States, it is open and aboveboard, attempting to inspire such standard organizations as the Knights of Columbus and the Catholic War Veterans to zealous service for their priests and the Church. Its techniques of penetration into non-Catholic organizations are not always so candid. The priests choose Catholic laymen from Catholic Action to infiltrate non-Catholic organizations in much the same manner that Communists are chosen to infiltrate labor unions and political parties for the Kremlin. Says *The Catholic Action Manual:*

> The layman is not surrounded by that net of prejudice and distrust that secularism has woven around the sacred person of the priest; he is not suspect of pleading his own cause, or fulfilling a professional job; and so he can penetrate into areas where the priest can never set his foot; and can gather great sheaves where the priest would find nothing but dry and prickly stubble.[4]

The cell technique employed by Communism to infiltrate other bodies is frankly used by two affiliated Catholic organizations, the American Association of Catholic Trade Unionists and the Young Christian Workers or Jocists.[5]

The chief role of Catholic Action is in politics, where it serves as a general denominational pressure group "not only outside all parties but above them." How far above all parties it functions is a matter of dispute. Its nonpartisanship is nearly always fictional because, in practice, it throws its support to Catholic parties when some issue arises that is vital to the priests. In the United States, Catholic Action has not yet become very important because the hierarchy is not yet ready to participate openly and officially in partisan politics, as it participates in Europe. The American hierarchy is shrewd enough to know that American voters would reject a political party controlled from Rome almost as decisively as they now reject, and properly, a political party controlled from Moscow. Accordingly, Catholic Action in the United States is still largely in the talking stage. It is a manufacturer of wordy propaganda which seems to the outsider so abstractly theological that it is bound to repel all except the devout.

3

How fanciful is the picture of an American nation under Catholic cultural and moral control? What evidence is there, aside from wishful thinking, that a Catholic hierarchy can control a nation that has democratic institutions? One answer comes from Ireland; and I have discussed the operations of the Irish clerical state in *The Irish and Catholic Power.* Another answer comes from the Catholic nations of our own hemisphere where, to the north and to the south of us, the Catholic hierarchy is now giving a working demonstration of the Catholic plan in action.

Quebec is essentially a Catholic clerical state existing within a troubled and divided Canadian democracy. Mexico would be a clerical state today if the Mexican revolution had not been led by anticlericals, and it might revert to that condition again if the present government should succumb to continuing clerical pressure.

There are many worth-while exhibits of the Catholic plan for America in our own hemisphere. Let us look at a few of them.

Quebec is the most solidly Catholic section of our continent and, as one Catholic writer has said, "one of the few remaining almost completely Catholic communities in the world." It has no divorce,[6] no birth control, and no public schools. Its capital city of Quebec has no public library. It is a cultural desert in a progressive, democratic Dominion, and its Catholic separatism is one of the chief factors in its cultural isolation.

The Catholic teachers of Quebec receive about one-half the rate of wages paid to non-Catholic teachers.[7] Nearly all the Catholic children stop school at an early age and go to work, after a few underprivileged years in parochial classrooms. Until 1943 the province had no compulsory-education laws, and even today the law requiring attendance up to the age of fourteen is not enforced in most rural districts. The province spends about one-third as much per capita on schools as does Ontario.

Although Quebec's citizens are not compelled as taxpayers to support their priests directly, the government renders indirect support in many ways to the Church; Catholicism is, in effect, the state religion. There is a crucifix in every courtroom and a Catholic officeholder in virtually every political office. The Church controls almost all the social services of the province. The Catholic historian Mason Wade says that Papal flags and portraits are more prevalent in Quebec than in Rome.[8] The Catholic hierarchy dominates the whole cultural life of the area with the exception of a few islands of English-speaking culture in the cities. It is a French hierarchy but not a *contemporary* French hierarchy, since its point of view is hostile to emancipated modern France. It is anti-American, anti-British, anti-Parisian, antiscientific and, until recently, notably sympathetic with fascism.

These are sober facts that liberal Catholic writers have recorded again and again with embarrassment and regret. The fault, of course, is not entirely with the French-Canadian hierarchy; Canada is the victim of a national and linguistic division that has foredoomed the Dominion to social conflict. Quebec is French, and the rest of Canada is, or was, predominantly British. Today, more than half the biological stock of the Dominion is non-British, and the French-Canadian Catholic bloc in the population is increasing at a rate half again as great as that for the rest of Canada.[9] Differences of language and nationality have served to accentuate religious rivalries.

In the light of subsequent events, it now seems clear that Britain made a gigantic political blunder in failing to ordain the separation of church and state when it wrested Quebec from the French. Today the Canadian people are still paying a heavy price for that blunder, and the policy which has brought them to their present predicament was not of their own choosing. England had failed to separate church from state in the home country before the British conquest, and its policy of public support for religious schools, a policy still in force, became a part of the basic constitution of Canada.

From the beginning, the Catholic hierarchy of Quebec has fostered and developed French-Canadian separatism against the Canadian national spirit and the influence of modern culture. It was the priests, in the early days of settlement, who watched the incoming ships for heretics and would not permit a Huguenot to land. It was the priests who stimulated the policy of importing shiploads of Catholic orphan girls who were married when they were still children and told to replenish the earth with good Catholics. With priestly encouragement the girls were married at fourteen and fifteen, and the boys at eighteen and nineteen. Bachelors were taxed and prizes given to large families.

The oversized family was feasible in the early days because every extra child became a useful worker on the patriarchal farm. "The rule in all respectable Canadian homes," according to Canon Lionel Groulx, "was, at one time, to reach a dozen children and even go beyond the second dozen." "The family," says Sister Marie Agnes of Rome Gaudreau, Ph.D., "gathered at the long dinner table, with twenty-five or twenty-six of the household participating in the noonday mirth, was once a fine substitute for outside distractions." [10]

When the struggle between the Gallican and Papal parties split French Catholicism at home, and the French Church declined in power, the Quebec hierarchy remained faithful to the Pope. It developed its own anti-Parisian and anti-urban provincialism. It censored French books and boycotted French liberal ideas. When France itself disestablished the Church and dethroned the priests in the public schools, Quebec still clung to a culture that was neither French nor Canadian but primarily Roman. When, in the 1860's, it became clear that the Italian kingdom would sooner or later seize Rome from the Pope, it was the Bishop of Quebec who recruited the first Canadian overseas contingent to fight as Papal Zouaves for the Vatican.

Aggrieved nationalism played a major role in keeping the Church supreme among the French-Canadian people. Clerical power was rapidly declining when the British conquest revived it and gave it new significance. "The defeat of the French on the Plains of Abraham," says Riddell,[11] "was a victory for Roman Catholicism in Quebec. . . . [It] made the Roman Catholic clergy . . . the leaders of the people against the policies of their conquerors. In this way the clergy became the logical and actual, though not the legal, successors of the French civil authorities who had returned to France."

The hierarchy fought the English language and won. It fought the idea of neutral schools and won. In both cases its victories were closely tied up with French patriotism and hostility to British rule. For forty years the British attempted to maintain neutral schools and then, defeated by the priests, finally accepted two private-school systems for Quebec, a Catholic system and a Protestant system, both supported by public appropriations and both controlled by private committees. Since Quebec is almost entirely Catholic, the adoption of this scheme meant the virtual surrender of public education to the Church.

Today, nearly all the Catholic young people of Quebec are segregated in the Catholic educational system from the kindergarten through the thirty-one "classical colleges" which have been set up by the hierarchy for the higher education of the faithful. Only a few ever reach the colleges. The program of training in these classical colleges is wholly clerical, and the curriculum is saturated with Catholic doctrine. The discipline is rigid, and every subject is compulsory. The philosophy of St. Thomas Aquinas is the crowning glory of the cultural mélange, and there is less science and mathematics in the curriculum than in the average non-Catholic Canadian high school.

Most of Quebec's children stay for a while in the educational strait jacket of the parochial-school system, completely insulated from non-Catholic culture, and then drop out. The failure of the teaching nuns to hold their interest is not surprising. A leader of Quebec's rural teachers' union protested in 1947 against the system that permitted children to learn history from nuns "who never read a newspaper nor listen to the radio." [12] A survey of the Quebec schools in the thirties revealed the fact that the average teacher of French-Catholic rural schools received less than $200 a year and held only an elementary-school diploma.[13]

The French-Catholic educational system has spread outward from Quebec to several other provinces because of the compromise between the hierarchy and the Dominion government on the separation of church and state. The Church claims public funds for its schools directly or indirectly in many non-Catholic provinces. Ontario, Saskatchewan, and Alberta have two school systems, a regular system and a separate system, both supported by taxpayers' contributions.[14] The Catholic taxpayers who support the separate system are excused from paying taxes for the regular system. In Ontario, Catholic families may start a separate school in a district and secure tax funds for it before a public school has been established. This bizarre arrangement, essentially a system of denominational rebates, was developed partly because the English Protestants of Quebec asked for support of their separate schools, and their demands were used as an argument for Catholic special privilege in non-Catholic territory.

The dual school system is being used aggressively by the Catholic hierarchy to build up segregated Catholic "colonies" in many parts of the Dominion, notably in northern Ontario. Says the Catholic William Teeling:

The French Canadians are determined if they possibly can to spread their own influence and the influence of their church throughout the whole Dominion. They do this in a systematic manner. By a federal law new seats in Parliament can only be created in the newly populated provinces when a certain number of people have settled there. The French Canadians, true to their traditions, commonly breed families of 8 and 10. They no longer try to keep the younger children in Quebec. They send them out as colonists to Manitoba, Saskatchewan and Alberta. They make a point, however, that these French Canadians shall go to a new district where there is not yet a member of Parliament. They continue sending people to this district until there are a majority of French Canadians there and enough to elect a new member. This done, they open up a fresh district. . . . Their population is increasing so much faster than that of the Anglo-Saxon races in the Dominion that they will soon be able to outnumber them.[15]

The Catholic success in outbreeding Protestant Canada is openly encouraged by the priests; and the recent decline of the Catholic birth rate in industrial centers like Montreal is, likewise, deplored by the priests. The oversized family is still exalted as the true Catholic family. There was official rejoicing in 1946 when the vital statistics of the parish of Notre Dame D'Herbertville in Quebec showed that Catholic families in that parish maintained an average of more than twelve children per family, and that one hundred mothers had produced 1,262 Catholic children.

In economic and political affairs the Quebec hierarchy has won the distinction of being the most reactionary clerical group north of the Rio Grande. It fought against woman suffrage so effectively that women could not vote in Quebec until 1944. The hierarchy backed Catholic Premier Maurice Duplessis in imposing upon the province an extra, local censorship of films, which even extends to 16-millimeter films shown by educational organizations after approval by the Canadian National Film Board.[16] It organized a Catholic labor movement, the Federation of Catholic Workers, which opposed international unions that had their headquarters in the United States. This Catholic labor organization frequently serves as a "company union," and stands for "the necessity for the maintenance of the inequality among social classes." [17] In 1940 Cardinal Villeneuve forbade all Canadian priests to give their names or votes to Premier Aberhart's Social Credit Party in Alberta, and today the whole force of the hierarchy is being quietly mobilized against the national organization, the Co-operative Commonwealth Federation, whose program resembles that of the British Labor Party.

Although the Quebec hierarchy does not officially favor separation from Canada, there is no doubt that its total influence tends to be opposed to the Dominion government. The hierarchy has never regarded the Canadian articles of confederation of 1867 as an actual or potential constitution for a new democracy. In practice, those articles have been treated as a declaration of an armistice between a Catholic and a non-Catholic nation, and the hierarchy has considered itself the special guardian of French-Catholic rights under the armistice terms.

But it should not be imagined that the reactionary and separatist policy of the hierarchy represents all of Quebec's Catholic people. Quebec Catholics cannot control their priests any more than British and American Catholics can, but they can criticize privately. A strong anticlerical movement has begun in Quebec, and it may possibly change the future of the whole Dominion. In 1947 the Catholic journalist Richard Pattee, after deploring the loss of more than 100,000 French-Canadian Catholics in recent years, declared that "the mind, the spirit and the economy of Quebec are in a state of crisis." Mason Wade, Catholic historian, described the new anticlericalism among Catholics in *The French Canadian Outlook:*

In the past, because of the great services of the clergy to national survival and because of the fact that it is democratically recruited from the people, anti-clericalism was confined to isolated individuals among the elite. . . . Today there is a growing feeling among all classes that the national debt of the French Canadians to their clergy has been paid with interest; there is a bitter resentment of the abuse of clerical privilege and of the alliance of the clergy with the haves rather than the have-nots. . . . Public opposition to the clergy still involves virtual exclusion from the French Canadian nationality . . . but private opposition is widespread. . . . It is important to recognize that this is very largely a Catholic anti-clericalism. It is not anti-Catholic, and its adherents include anti-clerical clerics.[18]

So it is evident that the Catholic question in Canada is exceedingly complex, and that not all opponents of the hierarchy are outside the Church. The cultural cleavage in the Dominion is due partly to the failure of non-Catholics to make a reasonable effort to accommodate themselves to the French language. Even in Quebec, very few of the English-speaking people bother to learn French, while more than one-third of the French Canadians speak English.

The major lesson for the United States in the Canadian experience is quite clear. A nation that compromises with the Catholic hierarchy on the control and support of common schools is doomed to be either a clerical state or a house divided. In Canada the Roman Church has built a state within a state because the British government permitted public revenue to be used for a school system that conditioned Catholic children to be Catholics first and Canadians second. Many Canadians believe that it is too late now to rescue the province of Quebec from medieval forces and that, like Eire, it should become a separate nation.

4

At first glance there would seem to be little resemblance between the French-Canadian Catholicism of Quebec and the Spanish and Portuguese Catholicism of Mexico and South America, but the hierarchy's underlying philosophy is the same at both ends of the hemisphere, even if its tactics vary. One phenomenon common to both ends of the hemisphere is a growing anticlericalism among intellectuals.

As an exhibit of Catholic culture, Latin America is not regarded with great pride by the hierarchy. During the period of more than four hundred years since Catholic warriors took possession of the area in the name of Catholic sovereigns, the Roman Church has failed so notably in its efforts to capture the loyalty of the masses of the people that the region is still largely a missionary territory. Much of its money comes from Catholic contributors in the United States, and an astonishing proportion of its priests are foreigners from Spain and Italy. Nominally the area claims—if Mexico, Central America, and the West Indies are included—a Catholic population of 160,000,000, almost five times the Catholic population of the United States. Brazil is rated by some as the No. 1 Catholic nation of the world. But the Church has such a small following among the educated classes that it cannot recruit even enough local priests to man its ecclesiastical establishment in

316   AMERICAN FREEDOM AND CATHOLIC POWER

Brazil. For centuries it has had to import its most important Church leaders from Europe, and today more than half of its Religious are Spaniards and Italians.

Most Latin-American intellectuals scorn the Church as an institution for women and peasants, and recognize the priest only for marriages and funerals. "The Latin-American mind," says E. Stanley Jones, "has had no resting place between infallibility and infidelity." Latin-American males of the educated classes have, in general, chosen infidelity or complete indifference, and today the Church is in critical condition because of their desertion. The *Catholic Almanac* of 1957 published a survey saying that the "great body of people of Latin America live outside the Church. . . . Only about 10 per cent actually practice the faith." Earnest appeals are being made almost weekly in the cathedrals of New York, Boston, Chicago, and other American cities for priestly recruits for these Latin-American "Catholic" countries, and there are more than six hundred Catholic missionaries from the United States serving in the region.

For American students of Catholicism, the area south of the Rio Grande is significant chiefly as an exhibit of Catholic policy on church and state in nations that are predominantly Catholic. When an American Catholic bishop says fervently that he accepts the doctrine of the separation of church and state, the skeptical inquirer may turn his eyes southward and see what the bishop means by this profession of an American doctrine.

The Latin-American spectacle is not reassuring. In every nation in Latin America today the hierarchy is trying to get special privileges and financial support from the governments for its churches and schools. In nine of the twenty republics south of the Rio Grande, Roman Catholicism is the official state religion and receives some kind of financial aid from the governments. In the other eleven republics the hierarchy never ceases to demand this church-state alliance as a basic right. In some of the nine special-privilege countries, Church-dominated governments discriminate against non-Catholics as openly as does the regime of Franco in Spain, and religious liberty for Protestants is only nominal.[19] Pius IX won a permanent position of special privilege for the Church in several Central American countries by concluding a series of concordats with these nations. The concordat with Honduras, which may be taken as typical, says in Article I: "The Catholic Apostolic Roman religion is the religion of the Republic of Honduras, and it will be kept fully without modifications, and always with all its rights and prerogatives to which it is entitled by the law of God and the prescriptions of the Holy Canons." [20]

Argentina, Bolivia, Colombia, Costa Rica, the Dominican Republic, Panama, Paraguay, Peru, and Venezuela have given the Catholic Church both a privileged position in the law and some financial support. In countries like Peru and Argentina the hierarchy controls and censors public-school education and harasses Protestant clergymen. In Colombia scores of Protestant clergymen and laymen have been killed, largely by mobs incited by local priests. In all of these Latin-American countries, Franco and Salazar have been held up as Christian models by Spanish and Portuguese priests, who served through World War II as cultural agents for the clerical fascism of their home countries. Franco's picture was displayed almost universally in Latin-American monasteries during the Spanish civil war, and Catholic, pro-Franco demonstrations were held inside and outside Latin-American churches.

Thomas J. Hamilton of *The New York Times,* writing during World War II, predicted that "should fascism ever gain a real foothold in Latin America, it will show the clear inspiration of the propaganda which Franco has hurled against us continuously ever since the end of the civil war." Harold Callendar of the *Times,* reviewing fascist influence in ten Latin-American republics shortly before our entrance into World War II, found "among many Catholics, lay and clerical, marked suspicion of the influence of the United States, and in some cases a leaning toward the totalitarian side." [21] John Dewey's books were burned in Brazil, and Peru followed the example of Franco in forbidding Protestants to hold services outside their established churches. The editors of the *Commonweal* published an article in 1947 that deplored "the identification between Catholicism and reaction which obtains in nearly all South America." [22]

5

In this hemisphere, Mexico continues to be a striking exhibit of a Catholic plan for an American country—an exhibit of priestly ignorance and priestly ambition that finally provoked an extreme and violent reaction. Today the Church in Mexico is denied many of the basic liberties that it possesses in non-Catholic countries, largely because its priests have become identified in the minds of the people with exploitation, superstition, and tyranny.

Catholicism came to Mexico with the Spanish conquest, and priest and conquistador worked hand in hand to convert, to subdue, and to exploit the Indian masses for a church-state empire that used religion for political purposes in all its imperial adventures. The Church grew rich and powerful as an arm of the state, and the priest as politician, moneylender, landowner, and magician ruled the most backward section of the mestizo and Indian population with a strange mixture of medieval and primitive superstition. "For nearly three hundred years," says Henry Bamford Parkes, "Mexico remained feudal and Catholic—a country where landed aristocrats dominated a population of peasants and where the right to think was narrowly restricted by the clergy." [23] By the time the new nation had achieved independence, perhaps half the land and capital wealth of the country was in the hands of the clergy.

Even the lesser priests rebelled, and the first great hero of the first Mexican revolution, Hidalgo, was an excommunicated parish priest whose followers carried a picture of the Virgin of Guadaloupe as the banner of the revolution. Since that day, in 1810, the Catholic hierarchy in Mexico has been in open alliance with one or another reactionary military leader against every effort to extend the scope of democratic power. When Benito Juarez tried to enforce the constitution of 1857, he recognized the clergy as his chief opponents, and ordered the confiscation of all Church property except the actual church buildings. When the Church survived the revolution and continued to ally itself with reactionary forces, the constitution of 1917 provided for confiscation even of the church buildings, and priests were forbidden to control primary schools, perform religious ceremonies outside of their churches, wear clerical costumes on the street, or organize political parties. Foreign priests were forbidden to serve in the churches, and the state legislatures were given power to limit the number of priests in their various jurisdictions.

When President Calles began to enforce this constitution for the first time in 1926, the Roman hierarchy declared a three-year strike, and, throughout the world, Vatican influence became strongly anti-Mexican. Pope Pius XI virtually sanctioned civil war in three encyclicals, calling upon the people to put God's law (Catholic law) above Mexican law. Representatives of the Vatican used every known type of moral and political pressure to induce the United States to intervene against the Mexican government. There broke out a religious civil war in which all thought of religious liberty and impartiality was abandoned. The Church was attacked as an enemy of the state, and replied in kind.

In recent years the hostility of the government toward the Church has declined, and many observers see a future of peace and co-operation. But nominally all the provisions of the constitution of 1917 can be enforced by executive decree at any time, and some of them are actually enforced. The Church is fighting the "socialistic" public schools and operating Catholic schools under other names, with thousands of pupils in the district of Mexico City alone. It is maneuvering constantly to build up new political movements for a reactionary rebellion. The Catholic archbishops have specifically forbidden their people even to study the facts of socialism, and have urged children to resist their parents if those parents insist on sending them to public schools.[24]

In 1937, and later, the Mexican clergy backed the new counterpart of the Spanish Falange, the Sinarquista movement, which, as Catholic journals admitted, opposed democracy and advocated a new aristocracy of reaction under the guise of "the restoration of a Christian social order . . . through peaceful and disciplined idealism," and which condemned the class struggle and attempted to "revive the spirit of Christian tradition and morality." [25] This Sinarquista movement is frankly described by the *Catholic Almanac* of 1948 as a "Catholic party." It was outlawed by the Mexican government early in 1949.

Many times, while living in the heart of Mexico's most Catholic section in Michoacan, I have seen the long lines of peasants and fishermen creeping on bare knees to the shrines of Tzintzuntzan. I have talked with their priests, teachers, and public officials, and observed the Catholic Church in action in this typical Mexican Catholic village. In 1948 the Smithsonian Institution published a thorough and impartial survey of this little village of Tzintzuntzan, written by George M. Foster, which described candidly, among other things, what the Catholic Church has accomplished after four hundred years of domination.[26]

Today Tzintzuntzan has a public school, but not through the co-operation or encouragement of the priests. When it was established, it met the "active opposition of all the fanatically Catholic population." A priest sponsored a private Sinarquista school in the local convent and almost destroyed the public school by declaring it out of bounds for all Catholics. He excommunicated parents who sent their children to the public school, even though his Sinarquista school taught only elementary reading and writing, whereas the public school, with nine trained teachers—all practicing Catholics—gave the students a modern curriculum without charge.

The priest, in this one little village of poverty-stricken peasants and fishermen, by 1945 took an estimated 30,000 to 40,000 pesos a year for the Church, while the entire municipal budget was 2,675 pesos. (The peso was then worth about 20 cents.) "It is probable," says Mr. Foster, "that the total amount spent on civic improvements and government, apart from the school, is from a tenth to a twentieth of the income of the Church itself, not counting other religious expenses of the population." The "other religious expenses" of the people are substantial, and the priest profits from them. In the 1930's the parish priest derived an estimated income of 2,000 pesos from the Church's annual festival alone, and 300 pesos from each of three other special days. Peasants too poor to bring money are encouraged to bring corn, beans, and wheat, which the priest sells for himself.

It is this basic exploitation of the common people by the priests that has created an almost fanatical anticlericalism in Mexico, an anticlericalism that has little connection with anti-Catholicism. Some of its disciples, in fact, are priests—Tzintzuntzan itself now has a priest who co-operates with the public school and tells his people that they may send their children to it. Most of Mexico's people and many of its leaders are still devout Catholics, but the most progressive and intelligent are determined that the Church shall never again re-establish cultural and political control of the nation in the name of religion.

Former President Lazaro Cardenas once expressed the thought behind Mexico's Catholic anticlericalism when he told a group of Mexicans who had criticized the government's public-school policy:

> You claim that liberty of conscience is recognized by all nations living under a regime of social and democratic morality, but the Catholic Church has always undermined any liberty of conscience. . . . Under such conditions, Catholic authorities cannot be included within the sphere of culture to which you now appeal. . . . In Mexico, the Roman clergy has been the instigator and sustainer of most of our

bloody internal warfare and is still guilty of treachery to the fatherland.[27]

The Mexican government's attitude toward the Church is more charitable today largely because the people are winning their long fight for the separation of church and state.

6

What are the actual prospects for Catholic control of the United States? Bertrand Russell said twenty years ago that he thought the Roman Catholic Church would dominate the United States "in another fifty or one hundred years" and "by sheer force of numbers." Many Catholic leaders have echoed that prophecy. Father James M. Gillis, editor of the *Catholic World,* predicted in 1929 that "America will be predominantly Catholic before the present younger generation dies." [28]

Such prophecies deserve serious consideration even if they seem to be extreme. In our individualistic nation a closely knit political organization does not need a majority of the people to control the government. As a pressure group it may operate on the balance-of-power principle, which has been so useful in giving Catholic political parties in Europe a dominating position. Already Catholicism has enough power in the Northern cities of the United States to capture more than its *pro rata* share of political spoils, and it has enough power in national politics to destroy the political career of any national leader who challenges its program openly and specifically. In the presidential campaign of 1948 neither leading candidate or party dared to mention the Catholic Church's drive for federal funds for its schools, although this drive had been one of the most vital issues before the preceding sessions of Congress. In the presidential campaign of 1952 all candidates dodged all questions of church and state wherever possible, largely because of the fear of Catholic reprisals. It is evident that the Catholic hierarchy already has almost complete veto power over the free discussion of some issues by both of our major political parties.

Aside from the development of this negative veto power, there are two positive roads to domination that the Catholic Church may take: the increase of the Catholic minority to a majority in the population, and the capture of our public-school system. We have already seen that the Catholic Church has not in recent years gained proportionately on non-Catholic elements in the population by conversions or accretion. Probably its losses far exceed its annual total of converts. The Church's gains from immigration have almost ceased, although new strength from abroad may come with Catholic displaced persons. The hierarchy's most substantial hope for transforming a Catholic minority into a majority lies in a differential birth rate.

Are American Catholics outbreeding the non-Catholic elements in our population? Probably they are. Some Catholic publicists answer the question with a confident assertion that already one baby in every three born in the United States is a Catholic.[29] No scientific answer is possible because there are no national statistics on birth rates by denominations. The priests themselves believe and boast that Catholic families are rapidly gaining on the "degenerate" non-Catholic people who practice birth control. They deplore the fact that the birth rate of their people is declining as Catholic families move into the cities and become corrupted with modern ideas, but in their own journals they continue to exult in the fact that the *comparative* birth rate is apparently favorable to Catholics. They are encouraging their people in the race for numerical supremacy with all the fervor at their command, ignoring the fact that it is the poorest and the most ignorant of the Catholic people who obey priestly commands most readily and who breed the largest families.

The Right Reverend John J. Bonner, diocesan superintendent of schools of Philadelphia, boasted in 1941 that the increase in the Catholic births in Philadelphia in the preceding decade had been more than 50 per cent higher than the increase in the total population, and that Philadelphia "will be fifty per cent Catholic in a comparatively short time." [30] Father Joseph M. Egan, a Catholic seminary professor of Rochester, published in 1948 a study of Catholic and non-Catholic birth rates in New York State; it indicated that, in the four years from 1943 to 1946 inclusive, the annual rate of natural increase of Catholics was more than four times that of non-Catholics. His conclusions were partially based upon unverified assumptions, but his case was persuasive.[31] If the disparity in birth rates which he claimed should continue indefinitely, it would not be long before the United States became a "Catholic" country by default.

But no matter what may be the outcome of priestly plans for numerical supremacy, the struggle for power in America will not be settled merely by numbers. A nation is not necessarily a clerical state because the majority of its people are nominal Catholics; France is a "Catholic" country, but it is not a *Catholic* country.

My own conviction is that the outcome of the struggle between American democracy and the Catholic hierarchy depends upon the survival and expansion of the public school. Even if the differential Catholic birth rate should soar in the United States, as it has soared in Quebec under the goading of the priests, the Catholic hierarchy could never make the United States into a clerical state unless it captured the public-school system or regimented a majority of American children into its own parochial-school system. There is no doubt that the hierarchy would like to capture our public-school system, as it has captured the systems in Catholic countries and in some of our own Eastern cities. Failing in that ambition, it would like to fragmentize our "godless" culture, under the guise of "Christianizing" it, by establishing strong competing schools of its own in every American community.

The danger is real, but the possibility seems remote that the battle between public and parochial education will be won by the hierarchy. Non-Catholics are aroused as never before to the perils that threaten the public school. Many of the American Catholic people are no longer responding as they once did to the priestly appeals for separation and segregation. They have become Americanized in the true sense of that much-abused word. As I have already pointed out, only half the Catholic children of the United States are in Catholic schools, and some very able Catholic experts predict that the drift of the future will be toward public schools.

More important than this fact is the fact that the economic structure of Catholic schools is threatened with collapse by the growth of modern liberalism among young Catholic women. The Catholic school system is essentially an enterprise of nuns who work without salaries. If the supply of nuns should be cut off, the system would rapidly disintegrate. "By no stretch of the imagination," said Father William J. Ferree in the August, 1944, *Bulletin of the National Catholic Educational Association,* "could they [Catholic educational and charitable works] ever be supported if their staffs were salaried."

Catholic young women, reared in the free and hearty atmosphere of modern America, are beginning to regard the whole segregated system of nuns, wimples, and convents as medieval posturing and useless mortification. Thousands of them are volunteering eagerly for social-service work but refusing to become nuns. In the *Catholic Mind* of April, 1956, Sister Mary Emil of Margrove College said some very frank things about the decline of the number of nuns in the United States:

> There is a vocation crisis. It would seem that there is not a Motherhouse in the country where the authorities are not wringing their hands over the Sister shortage as the number one problem. Everywhere the story is the same—classrooms with two, three and four times as many children as there should be, sick old Sisters teaching. . . . Postulants continue to enter our novitiates, but there are not enough. Every Mother General will tell you that she could use tomorrow twice as many Sisters as she has now.

If the present attitude of emancipated Catholic young women continues, the hierarchy may ultimately be forced by economic pressure to turn over a large part of its private-school system to democratic public control. For it should be remembered that a Catholic school which is compelled to hire a lay teacher must pay about four and one half times the wages of a nun.[32]

Meanwhile, as the cost of maintaining segregated schools increases, and as the public-school system is improved from the kindergarten through the state university, the Catholic system finds itself more than ever on the defensive. The invitation to join the American community without reservation becomes more and more appealing. In the long run I think that the invitation will be accepted, and I think that the fundamentally democratic and cooperative outlook of the average American Catholic layman will triumph over a medieval ecclesiastical machine—*provided* we cherish and develop our public schools.

13

Tolerance, Appeasement, and Freedom

1

IT IS APPARENT from the analysis in the preceding chapters that the American Catholic problem is this: What is to be done with a hierarchy that operates in twentieth-century America under medieval European controls? We have reviewed the major facts which seem to demonstrate that many of the hierarchy's social and political policies are incompatible with Western democracy and American culture. Many liberal Catholics are in essential agreement with this analysis of the problem and feel that their Church must be rescued from an authoritarian-minded hierarchy.

What policy should non-Catholics adopt in facing this situation? Is it possible to find a basis for unity or a working plan for co-operation with the Catholic hierarchy? Is compromise desirable in order to avoid the bitterness and social waste of religious conflict?

There is no doubt that most non-Catholic Americans want co-operation among all religious groups and dread the effects of sectarian bickering. They feel that any division of the nation into hostile factions is an injury to all citizens. In spite of the Catholic hierarchy's official intolerance and separatism, many liberals would make almost any compromise with the hierarchy which would lead to the give-and-take of mutual adjustment.

Unfortunately, the whole history of the Roman organization in the United States indicates that co-operation is not feasible in the major areas of Catholic authority. The Church co-operates gladly with civic and military power, but it refuses to yield a single inch in compromising its claims to absolute supremacy in religious, educational, and moral life. Its rigidity of doctrine and discipline is as unmistakable today as it was when the Reformation split the Christian world in the sixteenth century. The hierarchy has rejected all co-operation based on equality and mutual self-respect.

The story of non-Catholic attempts to co-operate with Rome is long and tragic.[1] Eager Christian idealists, visualizing the glories of a united Christendom, have again and again put their pride in their pockets and made humble advances to Rome in order to find a basis for compromise between the Roman and non-Roman branches of the faith.

When the Society for the Union of Christendom was formed in London in 1857, the Holy See boycotted the whole work of the organization. There was a faint ray of hope momentarily at the World's Parliament of Religions in Chicago in 1893, when Cardinal Gibbons agreed to open the proceedings by reciting the Lord's Prayer before the representatives of all the world's leading faiths. But this Parliament of Religions treated people of all religious faiths upon a basis of equality, and Leo XIII could not tolerate such tolerance. Two years later he sent a public letter to the United States opposing Catholic participation in such "promiscuous religious meetings."

The World Conference of Christian Churches, sponsored by the Episcopal Church of the United States, tried, before World War I, to get co-operation for unity discussions, but received nothing except polite refusals. Even Lord Halifax and Cardinal Mercier could make no headway against Roman exclusiveness in the Malines conversations which began in 1921; by the time the Lausanne conference on Christian unity opened in 1927, all Catholics were forbidden to participate in any way. The final seal of Papal infallibility was placed upon the Church's policy of non-co-operation when Pius XI in 1928 in his encyclical on *The Promotion of True Christian Unity* said: "The Unity of Christians cannot be otherwise obtained than by securing the return of the separated to the one true Church of Christ from which they once unhappily withdrew."

As if to add insult to injury, the hierarchy, after it had refused to discuss church unity any further, sought to conceal its own intransigence by establishing a system of "Church Unity Octaves" of prayer. The project was begun in New York in 1928 at about the time that the Holy See had finally rejected all co-operative movements for Christian unity. It was designed to "promote" through prayer "a reunion of Christendom under the authority of the Vicar of Christ," the Pope. Catholics who pray for the absorption of all non-Catholic bodies into the one true Church are assured even today of "the many indulgences with which the Church Unity Octave has been enriched." [2]

The Vatican reiterated and underscored its opposition to joint meetings with other faiths when it warned all Catholics not to participate in the special assembly of the World Council of Churches in August, 1948, at Amsterdam. Pius XII had become slightly alarmed by a new tendency of Catholics "in various places" to join in religious meetings with other Christians. Said the Congregation of the Holy Office on June 5, 1948: "Since indeed in both of the aforesaid meetings and outside of them acts of mixed worship have not infrequently been held, all are again warned that any communication in religious worship with non-Catholics whatsoever is entirely forbidden according to the norms of Canons 1248 and 731, paragraph 2." [3] "The Catholic Church," said Pius XII in a radio broadcast to German Catholics on September 5, 1948, "is inflexible before all that might even have the appearance of a compromise or adjustment of Catholic life with other denominations." He was just as intransigent in a Holy Office pronouncement in December, 1949, on the Ecumenical Movement when he stressed the "truth" that "union may be attained only in the truth." He clearly meant *Catholic* truth.

The Church took a similar position when it was invited to send representatives to the Second Assembly of the World Council of Churches at Evanston, Illinois, in August, 1954. In a pastoral letter, Samuel Cardinal Stritch, as Archbishop of Chicago, declared: "We wish it to be clearly understood that the faithful of the Church are not permitted to attend the assemblies or conventions of non-Catholic organizations or councils . . . she [the Catholic Church] is now as she always has been the only Spouse of Christ. . . ." [4]

Even President Truman's good-hearted and rather naïve appeal for "religious unity" in 1951, when he declared in a Washington speech that he had been trying to "bring a number of the great religious leaders of the world together" to affirm "those religious and moral principles on which we all agree," was rather haughtily dismissed by the Jesuit magazine *America*. In the issue of October 13, 1951, the editors said: "The Holy Father could scarcely give the impression that other 'religious leaders of the world' were on a par with the Vicar of Christ. The President's proposal, on this score, was much too ambitious."

The Papal doctrine of non-co-operation with other religious

groups on a basis of mutual respect also applies to the lower levels of American community activity. In districts where the Church is weak, local bishops will participate occasionally in co-operative ventures on the civic level, but they always refuse co-operation if any suggestion is involved that any other church has a parallel claim to the possession of divine truth. While Protestants are permitted to attend Catholic services if they wish without incurring any penalties, a Catholic who attends and participates in a religious service under Protestant auspices is guilty of grave sin. The Holy Office on May 31, 1922, declared that Catholic missionaries may not even recite funeral prayers at the burial of non-Catholic heretics.[5] When an inquirer asked in the columns of the Brooklyn *Tablet,* "Is it right for a young Catholic man to sing in a Protestant church on Sundays in order to make some extra money?" the official priestly answer declared that it was not, and that, if singing meant an "active part in a Protestant religious service," it was forbidden by divine law.[6]

The hierarchy is particularly hostile to such co-operative religious and moral organizations as the Y.M.C.A., because it fears that young Catholic men will learn in such organizations a respect for "heretical" Christianity. The Congregation of the Holy Office issued a special attack in 1920, in the form of a letter to all bishops, urging them to "guard young people carefully from the contagion" of this and similar organizations, and charging that the Y.M.C.A. was "doing great harm especially to Catholic youth by drawing them away from the faith under the pretext of affording them opportunities for physical culture and education." [7]

Catholics are absolutely forbidden to join secret societies like the Masons, Odd Fellows, and Knights of Pythias. "Freemasonry is forbidden under pain of excommunication," says the *Catholic Almanac* of 1948; "membership in the following is forbidden under pain of grievous sin: Odd Fellows, Knights of Pythias, Sons of Temperance, and the Independent Order of Good Templars. The same applies to secret societies of women." One reason for these sweeping prohibitions is that these societies have developed certain moral and social ceremonies that have some general religious connotation, and the hierarchy will not approve Catholics' receiving religious inspiration from any other source except the Roman system. To join the Masons is worse than to join the Odd Fellows or Knights of Pythias because Masonic orders in Europe have been pioneers in opposing priestly control. Priests are also forbidden to join Rotary Clubs, apparently because these clubs emphasize mutual respect for all faiths on a basis of equality.

When the admirable project for education in interracial and interfaith co-operation known as the Springfield Plan had operated successfully for several years in Springfield, Massachusetts, the Catholic hierarchy began a counterattack upon the plan, because it was inculcating too much broad-mindedness among the children in the public schools. It was, and is, a scheme for breaking down racial and religious barriers by making the children actually acquainted with the various races and religions in their own community. The plan of operation was acceptable to the Catholic hierarchy until it was discovered that charts and books used by the children were, by inference, placing all faiths on the same plane.

Then the *American Ecclesiastical Review,* through Father E. D. Benard of the Catholic University of America, jumped to the attack. Under the Springfield Plan, it was charged, a "glittering miniature tree," standing beside the teacher's desk in a junior high school, had three prisms on its top branch, one for Protestants, one for Roman Catholics, and one for Greek Catholics. All the prisms were the same size. This was dangerous heresy, and was, according to Father Benard, "directly contrary to Catholic teaching. The Catholic Church believes and insists that there is only *one* true religion, not many. . . . We might with perfect consistency, if this is to be our standard, have another prism on the tree, of the same size and brightness, to signify atheism. Why not?" [8]

The hierarchy also protested when a Jewish teacher engaged in the Springfield Plan took the children to a Jewish synagogue to let them see for themselves what the Jewish faith represented. This, said the hierarchy, was contrary to Canon 1258 of Catholic Canon Law, and must not be repeated. But they said:

Of course, if a non-Catholic or number of non-Catholics, adults or children, wish to attend Mass in a Catholic Church and then have the service explained to them by a priest, there would be no objection from the Catholic standpoint. Non-Catholics might consider this an illogical position. . . . In reality, it is eminently logical. The Church welcomes those who wish to know more about her teachings and practices, because the Catholic Church is the true Church, the one to which all men are obliged to belong.

Thus, Protestants, Jews, and liberal Catholics who try to co-operate on a basis of equality and self-respect almost always encounter the impregnable fortress of priestly intolerance. Expressed in the authoritative language of Father Francis J. Connell, this intolerance means that "no one has a genuine right, as far as God's law is concerned, to profess any religion except the Catholic religion . . . it must be remembered that a Catholic cannot advocate such a plan [complete religious toleration] on the basis that all religions have a genuine, God-given right to exist. Such a right belongs only to the one [Catholic] religion founded by Jesus Christ for all men." [9]

Probably the majority of American Catholics would reject such an arrogant philosophy with as much disgust as non-Catholics, but they have no opportunity to vote on the narrow doctrine. It is even possible that the majority of American priests would reject such narrowness if they could vote secretly and without penalties. Many of them are self-consciously defensive about the expression of priestly bigotry in a country like the United States, and their superiors are compelled to exert constant discipline to prevent the development of broad-mindedness. "If some of our fellow-citizens of other denominations," says Father Connell, "fail to see the reasonableness of the position taken by those of us who are Catholics, and consequently denounce us as bigots or fanatics, we are not allowed to compromise on a single point in order to appease their indignation."

2

The hierarchy's narrow conception of tolerance and intolerance goes back to a medieval conception of limited freedom, which the Jesuits defend with such confusing casuistry that a Catholic treatise on freedom frequently resembles a Communist treatise on democracy. In such a treatise the standard meanings of words are often reversed or modified to fit a prefabricated conclusion that "true" freedom comes to men only through the Roman Catholic hierarchy.

Under the doctrine of the divine right of kings, freedom was a *privilege* conferred upon the people by the divinely chosen monarch. The Catholic doctrine of freedom is as bald and antiquated as that. It has not yet been revised to square with modern political science. Freedom of thought in the official Catholic system means freedom to accept Catholic truth, not to reject it. The *Catholic Almanac* defines freedom of thought as follows: "Liberty to think the truth. In our day the expression has come to mean liberty to think as one pleases; this is an error. Our rational nature demands that we think only the truth, whatever the impact of outside forces or our own appetites." [10] And, of course, supreme religious and moral truth comes to men only through the Church. Such truth is an ecclesiastical entity, unchanging and unchallengeable, over which the Church has a permanent monopoly. As Ignatius Loyola put it: "Therefore, if anything shall appear white to our eyes which the Church has defined as black, we likewise must declare it to be black."

In his famous letter to Cardinal Gasparri of May 30, 1929, Pius XI declared that "in a Catholic State liberty of conscience and liberty of discussion are to be understood and practiced in accordance with Catholic doctrines and Catholic laws." Catholic pronouncements make it perfectly plain that in the ultimate Catholic society all religious and cultural freedom will be subject to Catholic restrictions.

Freedom for non-Catholic believers or for unbelievers is a temporary device of expediency, not a God-given right. When the American Catholic Philosophical Association published a special study on St. Thomas Aquinas and American freedom in 1947, it flatly condemned the theory that "freedom of religion means the freedom to worship or not to worship. That is not the real meaning of the freedom of religion." And it went on to say that freedom of religion was the right "to enjoy a right given by the Author of nature and nations. . . . Because religion is a matter of basic justice, freedom of religion does not mean the liberty to be religious or non-religious." Nor does it mean freedom to be an individual mystic, divorced from religious ceremonies. "Religion must be expressed by external actions performed in a church at an orderly and proper time. . . . Human beings are not free in such matters. . . . Free speech is not free to injure faith, hope, charity, prudence, justice, temperance, truth or any other virtue protecting the welfare of the individual or society." [11]

The official world organ of the Jesuits, *Civiltà Cattolica* of Rome, published in April, 1948, a striking statement concerning the Catholic philosophy of tolerance and freedom for non-Catholics:

The Roman Catholic Church, convinced, through its divine prerogatives, of being the only true church, must demand the right of
freedom for herself alone, because such a right can only be possessed
by truth, never by error. As to other religions, the Church will certainly never draw the sword, but she will require that by legitimate
means they shall not be allowed to propagate false doctrine. Consequently, in a state where the majority of the people are Catholic, the
Church will require that legal existence be denied to error, and that if
religious minorities actually exist, they shall have only a *de facto*
existence without opportunity to spread their beliefs. . . . In some
countries, Catholics will be obliged to ask full religious freedom for
all, resigned at being forced to cohabitate where they alone should
rightfully be allowed to live. But in doing this the Church does not
renounce her thesis, which remains the most imperative of her laws,
but merely adapts herself to *de facto* conditions, which must be taken
into account in practical affairs. . . . The Church cannot blush for
her own want of tolerance, as she asserts it in principle and applies it
in practice.[12]

Such frank speaking about the most fundamental rights in the
American Constitution, coming from the highest cultural sources
in Catholicism, would produce a wave of anti-Catholic sentiment
in the country if the dicta were translated into colloquial English
and distributed widely. American Catholics who believe in American principles of freedom are embarrassed and mortified by such
obviously un-American doctrine.

An attempt is being made to counteract the effect of reactionary dogmas upon the American non-Catholic public. The Knights
of Columbus have conducted for several years a campaign of advertising to "interpret" Catholic belief to the American people in
such a way as to destroy certain "misconceptions" about it. Unfortunately the campaign has used all the familiar devices of secular misrepresentation. An advertisement published in *Liberty* in
June, 1948, under the heading "You Hear Strange Things about
Catholics," may be taken as an illustration of casuist techniques.
It adopts the transparent device of misstating slightly the major
criticisms of non-Catholics about the hierarchy's reactionary dogmas; then it denies these misstatements lustily, attempting to give
the casual reader the impression that the underlying criticisms on
which the misstatements are based are also untrue. This device is
called by logicians "the fallacy of irrelevant conclusion." Described algebraically, it runs like this: Critics of Catholicism say
that X is true about the Catholic Church. We, the Knights of

Columbus, say emphatically that X' is *not* true about the Catholic Church. If we say it often enough and loudly enough, most people will accept the denial without noticing that we are denying X' instead of X.

To see how the hierarchy is using the Knights of Columbus to twist its own teachings, let us examine the advertisement I have mentioned. I shall put on one page the actual quotations from the K. of C. advertisement, and on the opposite page the exact statement of Catholic doctrine that the hierarchy did not state in frank terms. The evidence for the wording of the actual doctrines of the Church is all contained in Catholic sources, and the reader may find references to them in the Notes.[13] It will be seen that the exact statements of Catholic doctrine are almost as objectionable as the straw men which the Knights of Columbus demolish.

The "Erroneous Ideas" as Advertised
by the Knights of Columbus

1. You hear it said that Catholics believe all non-Catholics are headed for Hell.

2. That they believe non-Catholic marriages are invalid.

3. Some think Catholics believe the Pope is God.

4. That he can do no wrong.

5. That they owe him civil allegiance.

6. And that he should have the political power to rule America.

7. It is said that Catholics want religious freedom only for themselves.

8. That they oppose public schools [as an evil which should be destroyed].

9. And separation of church and state as an evil which should be destroyed.

10. The claim is made that Catholics pay the priest for the forgiveness of their sins.

11. That they must buy their departed relatives and friends out of Purgatory.

12. That they adore statues.

13. Are forbidden to read the Bible.

14. Use medals, candles, and holy water as sure-fire protection against the loss of a job, lightning, or being run down by an automobile.

What the Hierarchy Actually Teaches

1. Non-Catholics who deliberately reject Catholicism are headed for Hell.

2. Non-Catholic marriages involving a Catholic are invalid.

3. Catholics owe "complete submission and obedience of will to the Church and to the Roman Pontiff, as to God Himself."

4. The Pope can do no wrong when he speaks as head of the Church in matters of faith and morals.

5. They owe him civil allegiance in matters of morals, education, and priestly rights.

6. He should rule America in moral, educational, and religious matters.

7. They advocate complete religious freedom for non-Catholics only as a temporary concession in non-Catholic countries, and in Catholic countries they restrict other cults.

8. They oppose public schools for Catholic children as an evil which should be destroyed.

9. They condemn financial separation of church and state and advocate support of both Catholic schools and churches by public taxation.

10. They pay the priests for Masses and those Masses are recognized as factors in securing forgiveness of sins, granted by priests.

11. They pay established fees for priestly Masses for the dead, and the Church guarantees that these Masses will help departed souls in Purgatory.

12. They *venerate* statues.

13. They are forbidden to read any non-Catholic version of the Bible.

14. They use scapulars, relics, and similar articles with the written assurance of their priests that these articles will help to protect the faithful against disaster.

Does this type of advertising pay? Probably it does. The Knights of Columbus received almost 150,000 inquiries from their first series of ads, and appropriated $350,000 for their second (1949) series.

The American people have been conditioned by the commercial techniques of press, screen, and radio to accept off-center truth in advertising with a complacent lack of discrimination. The mildness of a cigarette, the tastiness of a pudding, and the truth of a religion often seem to be less important in scoring an American success than the endless assertion of mildness, tastiness, and truth. It requires an act of faith to agree with Darwin: "Great is the power of steady misrepresentation, but the history of science shows that fortunately this power does not long endure." [14]

The attempt of the hierarchy and the Knights of Columbus to soften the impact upon American public opinion of Rome's arrogant teachings is significant chiefly because it shows how embarrassed some American Catholics are by the medieval doctrines of Rome. They are attempting to disguise the worst features of their own faith by adroit double-talk. Their attitude raises a question and a hope. Is there any possibility that Catholic social policy may be modernized and modified by appeasement and friendly co-operation?

3

Many sincere non-Catholics feel that they should co-operate earnestly with the Catholic hierarchy in every good cause even under the most humiliating conditions of non-reciprocity. They reason that, in spite of the narrow-mindedness of the priests, personal friendship between non-Catholics and Catholics and mutual activity will, in the long run, break down extreme dogmatism more effectively than counterattack. They would, therefore, ignore the antidemocratic social policies of Rome and attempt to keep relationships between American Catholics and American non-Catholics entirely upon the affirmative level.

The argument for this policy is especially persuasive in this country because priestly bigotry is on the defensive in the American environment. Time and intermarriage are on the side of mutual compromise; many liberals reason that drift and delay may

be wiser than frank speaking about Catholic reaction at this junc-
ture in our history.

Among the advocates of this policy of appeasement and limited co-operation are many idealists of unquestioned integrity.
Among these advocates are also many cowards and politicians. It
is difficult to isolate the idealism from the cowardice in passing
judgment upon this group. The refusal to face unpleasant facts in
the field of religious controversy frequently passes for "tolerance"
and "broad-mindedness."

This last comment applies especially to social psychologists
who evade the problem of Catholic power by assuming that the
primary difficulty lies in personal adjustment between Catholics
and non-Catholics. Frequently the problem is described in terms
of "tensions" between groups which do not "understand" each
other, or it is represented as arising from "prejudice." There is no
doubt that adjustment, prejudice, and group tensions all play their
part in the Catholic problem, but the basic difficulty is a set of
intolerant clerical policies imposed upon the Catholic people of the
United States from abroad in such a way that they cannot be
shaken off by co-operative effort and compromise at the lay level.

Professor Gordon Allport of Harvard has written a book
called *The Nature of Prejudice* which may be taken as a model for
all those who wish to escape genuine responsibility for meeting
the challenge of Catholic hierarchical power. It omits almost all
reference to those separatist and intolerant policies of the hierarchy
in the areas of creedally segregated schools, mixed marriage, divorce, birth control, and censorship—the policies that actually
cause most of the tensions between Catholics and non-Catholics
in the United States. To class the opposition to these policies with
"prejudice" is irresponsible. Prejudice is by definition an opinion
based on pre-judgment, arrived at without sufficient preparatory
examination of facts. The liberal opposition to Catholic hierarchical policy in the United States today is based on post-judgments,
derived from actual, careful examination of documented examples
of ecclesiastical intolerance and separatism.

It should not be forgotten that in a democratic society adjustment to reactionary clerical policies can mean the surrender of
basic liberties. There are times when the highest duty of a citizen
is to increase the tensions between social groups temporarily until
the threat of the triumph of reactionary policies is past. It is possi-

ble that we have arrived at such a moment in the history of the United States in dealing with Catholic hierarchical policy.

Unhappily, many of those who preach what is called "understanding" between religious groups actually advocate silence concerning all controversial issues. They have chosen this evasive way because it is the easiest way, and because it gives them a reputation for tolerance without the unpleasant necessity of fighting intolerance. This observation applies especially to the most noted "tolerance" group in the United States, the National Conference of Christians and Jews. It attempts to meet the problem of Catholic-non-Catholic conflict in America by avoidance of the main areas of conflict, and by counterattack upon those who oppose bigotry within ecclesiastical institutions.

It is a tripartite body of Protestants, Catholics, and Jews, with a large national membership, many branch offices in important cities, and a very impressive program of financial expenditures, much of which is spent on publicity. It is supported generously by Ford money. It has grown rapidly in recent years and has received much favorable publicity in the American press. It attempts to operate entirely on the level of the *status quo,* never questioning the fundamental doctrines of its three constituent religious groups.

The Catholic Church has given relatively little active support to this movement, although the hierarchy in seventy-five dioceses has announced its willingness to permit Catholics as individuals to take part in its activities. In twenty-five dioceses the bishops are openly opposed to the Conference, and in twenty-five other dioceses they are officially "neutral." The Vatican itself is apparently not friendly to such organizations; in 1954 it ordered all Catholics in Great Britain to resign from the British counterpart, the Council of Christians and Jews.[15] The *American Ecclesiastical Review,* in September, 1948, warned Catholics against the organization because it held school meetings in which ministers, priests, and rabbis appeared on the same platform and spoke of "the common positive elements of all the faiths." Catholics were reminded that they must oppose such indifferentism and "defend the basic truth that there can be only one true religion, and that is Catholicism."

The Conference blandly ignores these attacks and acts as if devout Roman Catholics could be full-fledged, bona-fide members of the triple alliance. The few Catholic leaders who actively cooperate with the Conference are given unusual publicity, and the public impression created by the publicity is that the Catholic

Church believes in the same kind of interdenominational co-opera-tion that is endorsed by liberal Protestants and Jews. The Con-ference, of course, never criticizes the Roman Catholic Church for intolerant and separatist policies. The official who had charge of the organization's activities in the fields of the press, radio, motion pictures, and advertising for a long time was a Catholic who had been secretary of the National Council of Catholic Men.

The organization's most conspicuous activity has been the promotion of "American Brotherhood Week," a concentrated cam-paign period during which subscriptions are solicited for interfaith work with the commitment: "I pledge allegiance to this basic ideal of my country—fair play for all. I pledge unto my fellow Ameri-cans all of the rights and dignities I desire for myself."

No one can doubt the high motives of the Conference's lead-ers. The question that honest critics are bound to ask about such a movement is whether it has a moral right to ignore the discrimi-natory practices of Catholicism while conferring upon the hier-archy the protective coloration of "fair-play" slogans. The Confer-ence is extremely vigorous in criticizing anti-Semitism in Europe as well as in the United States, but it never includes in its literature or speeches any criticism of the basic anti-Semitism of priestly doctrine. It never asks why the Catholic Church rates marriage with a Jew in a special low category—beneath marriage to a Protestant—by the device which is called an "annulling impedi-ment." It never demands reciprocity in tolerance for Protestants in those areas in which the Catholic hierarchy practices humiliating discrimination against them. (The president of the organization, a Protestant clergyman, commended Cardinal Stritch in great headlines in the Catholic press when he refused to permit Catholics to attend the Evanston session of the World Council of Churches.)[16]

The pledge of the National Conference of Christians and Jews offers "unto my fellow Americans all of the rights and dignities I desire for myself," but the Conference makes no attempt to induce its Catholic members to keep that pledge in intermarriage. A Protestant bride, marrying a Catholic groom, is not given the same "rights and dignities" to bring up her children in her own faith. Likewise, as I have pointed out in the chapter on censorship, the Conference itself is defeated in its attempts to develop mutual understanding between faiths by the exchange of representative literature of each faith. The distinctively Jewish and Protestant books advertised by the Conference in its "Religious Book List" may not be read by Catholics, but the public is not told of this censorship; nor has the Conference ever challenged the narrow dictum of the hierarchy on this point. Instead, the Conference has quietly surrendered the enforcement of its fair-play pledge in this area, and has broken down its lists of religious books into four groups, Protestant, Jewish, Catholic, and "Goodwill Books for All." The goodwill books, approved by an interfaith committee, are subject to Catholic veto, and any Catholic may read them without endangering his soul. Protestant and Jewish readers are encouraged to read the books on all four lists; Catholics are forbidden to read any but the books on their own and the goodwill list.

Thus the whole underlying concept of the free exchange of ideas between the three faiths is vitiated, while the Conference officials remain silent. The casual reader of the organization's literature is not told that Catholics are forbidden to read the Jewish and Protestant lists, and he would naturally infer from the publication of the tripartite list of titles in a single cover that Catholic authorities give complete freedom for cultural reciprocity in this matter.

Most serious of the omissions in the Conference program is the failure to speak out on the separatist Catholic policy concerning public schools. A major part of the energy of the Conference is spent in bringing children of different faiths together for training in intergroup co-operation. The Conference leaders are frank and fearless in opposing racial segregation in schools. They deplore everything that keeps American children apart except the one factor that does most to separate them, the Catholic parochial school.

There is no doubt that the parochial school, whatever may be its virtues, is the most important divisive instrument in the life of American children. It keeps Catholic children separated from the main body of American childhood during the most impressionable years of life and develops in them a denominational narrow-mindedness. The system also gives to both Catholic and non-Catholic children an exaggerated sense of religious distinctions. The Conference does not dare to point out this elementary fact, and by joining in an alliance with the Catholic Church the liberal leaders in the Conference have surrendered their right to campaign against the divisive philosophy of Catholic education.

The Conference's own activities scarcely touch the one section of American school life that most needs assimilation, the population of the Catholic parochial school. At the same time, the

Conference helps to circulate descriptions of the Catholic theory of education that represent the policy of segregation in its most favorable light. Here, for example, is an apologia for Catholic segregation, written obviously by a Catholic, for distribution in the organization's pamphlet *Building Bridges:*

> Catholics believe that religion should be an integral part of education if we are to have a religious-minded people. Therefore it [the Catholic Church] has established in America at great sacrifice and expense parochial schools and colleges. These are supported by Catholic citizens who are taxed for public schools as well. Protestants for the most part believe in a state supported school system, controlled by no religious group and in which religion is not taught. While our public education thus reaches all children it provides only secular knowledge, and there is serious question whether the exclusion of religion has not led to loss of religious faith and loyalty among our people.

There is no mention here of the basic facts that the public schools are democratically controlled by all the people, while the Catholic schools are not democratically controlled; that Catholic parents are not free to decide for themselves whether they will send their children to public schools; and that Catholic families could save themselves double expense and acquire superior education by using the public schools.

In passing judgment on the National Conference of Christians and Jews, no phrase seems more neatly descriptive than a phrase used by Arthur Schlesinger, Jr. in another connection when he protested the "growing homogenization of American society." The enemy of the true liberal, he pointed out, is "a conspiracy of blandness seeking to bury all tension and conflict in American life under a mass of platitude and piety."

4

Although there are millions of individual Catholics in the United States who disagree with the policies of their Church, there is no substantial, organized movement to reform the Church's central structure of power from within. In this respect the situation has not improved in recent years. American Catholicism is still a colonial dependency within a complete system of ecclesiastical imperialism, and there are few signs of American rebellion.

In 1953, in *The Irish and Catholic Power,* I expressed an optimism about certain slight rebellious trends within the American Church which has not been justified by the events. These slight rebellious trends have been manifested chiefly in the small New York weekly, *The Commonweal,* and in the Jesuit magazine *America.* They are worth examining briefly.

The Commonweal, which probably exerts more influence outside Catholic circles than inside the Church, has a circulation of only 21,000. Its Catholic lay editors are genuine liberals in the areas of social and economic reform, and their discussions of political events often parallel the editorial pages of the *New Republic.* They attack McCarthyism and Franco, and they frequently deplore the more stupid manifestations of Catholic censorship. But they never squarely challenge those features of Catholic authoritarian rule that non-Catholics consider basic—and objectionable. While they may ridicule a specific blunder committed by the censors of the Legion of Decency, they do not challenge the rule behind that censorship, Canon 1399, which gives the bishops the right to ban all reading matter and films critical of ecclesiastical policy. They obediently endorse the clerical suppression of birth control, and publish persuasive defenses of the theory that public money should be used to finance Catholic schools. They never demand plenary participation by laymen in the making of church policy.

In spite of such public submission to clerical rule, *The Commonweal* editors are treated with extreme coolness by the Catholic press and clergy. They are permitted to function on the periphery of American Catholicism without official hierarchical approval, as an exhibit of clerical tolerance in a non-Catholic country. Apparently that permission is given with some reluctance, since Cardinal Spellman's Chancery Office has announced in writing: "It is unfortunate that *The Commonweal* is described as a 'Catholic' magazine, for actually such is not the case." [17] More direct attacks upon the magazine have been made in standard Catholic journals. "Frankly," said Bishop Joseph McShea, president of the American Catholic Historical Society, in 1955, "I think they [the *Commonweal* editors] might do well to omit the word 'Catholic' from their advertising." [18]

In spite of this absence of approval by the hierarchy, *The Commonweal* continues to profess simultaneously its undying loyalty to Catholicism and to American democracy. The editors are embarrassed but not overcome by the seeming contradiction in logic inherent in such ambivalence. They embrace the contradiction quite unflinchingly, since it is their whole purpose in existence to demonstrate that an American can be a liberal democrat and a devout Catholic at the same time. The executive editor of *The Commonweal* said in an article in June, 1953:

> We cannot lose sight of the fact . . . that as Catholics we frankly subscribe to an ecclesiasticism which is non-democratic. For many that is reason enough to doubt the sincerity of our belief in political democracy. Especially for those who regard democracy not merely as a technique of government and a political philosophy but as a substitute for religion, our acceptance of an *authoritarian* Church (which is not at all the same as *totalitarian* Church—a meaningless phrase) is anomalous.
>
> In the Catholic scheme spiritual authority is all-important and the popular will has little or no effect on the government of the Church. If it were proved beyond doubt, for instance, that most American Catholics thought birth-prevention was a good idea, the Church would still hold fast to its teaching that contraception is against the law of God. The Church is democratic only in the sense that the son of a chimney-sweep may sit on the papal throne or a bricklayer's boy may wear the scarlet robes of a Cardinal.
>
> To the Catholic, the Church's authoritarian spirit and hierarchical structure are logical and even desirable.[19]

Most American liberals, while failing to admire the inconsistency of *The Commonweal* in supporting political democracy and ecclesiastical autocracy at the same time, wish the editors prosperity because they see no hope of reforming Catholic reactionary policy except through laymen. And, aside from *The Commonweal,* there is no lay force in American Catholicism which manifests any sign of critical independence. The Knights of Columbus and the Holy Name societies are, in respect to all matters of Church policy, mere creatures of the Catholic bishops. The priests themselves are so carefully fenced in by episcopal regulations that there is no hope of rebellion from that quarter. If, somehow, the American Church is to be liberalized from within, the movement for reform must start with some group akin to the Catholic supporters of *The Commonweal.*

Most non-Catholics will not feel so charitable toward the other slightly rebellious force in American Catholicism, the Jesuits. Some American Jesuits have challenged traditional Catholic doc-

trine on church and state quite boldly in recent years. Most notable of these challengers is Father John Courtney Murray, Jesuit
editor of *Theological Studies,* who has set out to prove through a
series of complicated historical analyses that the religious freedom
and church-state separation of America might possibly win the
approval of Leo XIII if he were alive today. Perhaps, he contends
—but he does not say so—the ultimately desirable society might
look more like the United States than Spain. The present Papal
rules for church-state relationship were made for continental
Europe a long time ago when the Church feared royal absolutism.
The state church does not necessarily represent the "permanent
and unalterable" Catholic aim. In practice the Church has been
accorded better treatment and greater security under the United
States Constitution than in any European country over the same
span of years. Perhaps the American style of church-state relationship may represent the curve of the future. At any rate "the
Catholic ideal" does not *necessarily* imply the reinstatement of
"medieval juridical and political conceptions."

I do not have space here to analyze Father Murray's rather
devious and ambiguous theses. (References to source material are
listed in the Notes.)[20] Suffice it to say that he has stirred up a
theological hornet's nest by opposing even obliquely the ancient
Papal rule that "the state or the civil society is objectively obligated to worship God according to the rite of the Catholic religion." The Vatican, through Cardinal Ottaviani, and the American bishops, through their instrument, the Catholic University of
America, have given him a resounding doctrinal spanking; and the
American diocesan press has lined up against him for daring to
apply to the "unchanging" teachings of the Popes the "pendulum"
theory of interpreting Church law, under which a narrow Papal
mandate may mean one thing to the Catholics of one age and
another thing to the present-day Catholics of the West. For the
time being the Spanish bishops' wing of the Church is triumphant,
and Catholic liberals are covered with confusion, asserting that it
would be "tragically unwise" to apply to all countries the reactionary and discriminatory theories of church-state relationship approved by the Spanish Church and the Vatican.

The New York Times deserves credit for proving that the
"new look" which Father Murray is attempting to impose upon
his Church's theory of freedom is unauthorized. In July, 1953, it
sent a query to the Vatican asking for an authoritative clarification

of the question whether the Catholic Church actually approves the suppression of freedom in Spain, or the more liberal concepts of freedom for non-Catholic minorities being promoted by American Jesuits. In the issue of July 23, 1953, it printed the Vatican's answer under the heading: VATICAN JUSTIFIES VIEWS OF PREL-ATES ON CURBING PROTESTANT MINORITIES.

The Vatican, according to the *Times,* described as "unexceptionable" the March 1953 address of Cardinal Ottaviani, supporting the Spanish bishops' position favoring restriction of Protestant minorities in Roman Catholic countries." Father Murray insisted that Cardinal Ottaviani, in advocating the suppression of freedom for non-Catholics, was "speaking only in his purely personal capacity." But the *Times* showed that the cardinal, who is pro-secretary of the highest Papal Congregation, the Holy Office, was speaking for the Vatican. It said:

> In discussing the purely doctrinal aspect of the church-state issue, Cardinal Ottaviani echoed the views of the Spanish episcopate, not—as he indicated—because they were a specifically Spanish interpretation of Catholic doctrine, but because they were the orthodox interpretation given to it by the Vatican itself through solemn Papal pronouncements in the past. Consequently, he deplored the views of what he called "liberal Catholicism," as expressed by some United States circles inasmuch as, in his opinion, they represented a departure from the true Catholic theological path.

It is clear from this exchange between the Vatican and *The New York Times* that the Church still regards religious freedom for non-Catholics as a matter of time and circumstance—a privilege which may be withdrawn if American Catholics attain a majority in the population.

Regardless of the correctness of Father Murray's rather pleasing attempt to "re-interpret" out of existence some of the more flagrant anti-freedom doctrines of the Papacy—and I think his analysis represents nothing more substantial than scholarly wishful thinking—few students of Catholicism will trust the Jesuits to reform their Church. Traditionally they have been the chief promoters of Papal absolutism, the leading apostles of centralized autocracy. Their propaganda methods, exemplified in their national organ *America,* are not unlike those of Madison Avenue, verbally felicitous and suave, and carefully designed to manipulate the human mind by the techniques of the hidden persuader. With equal urbanity they co-operate with Franco in Spain and his critics in this country. They produce in their highest world journal, *Civiltà Cattolica,* the frank assault on religious freedom that I have quoted earlier in this chapter, while they pose in their American journals as ardent advocates of American democracy and freedom. It is not an accident that the word "Jesuitical" has been incorporated into the English language as a synonym for craftiness.

Father Murray himself, while attempting to rewrite the Catholic church-state policy in a hypothetical future in respect to freedom from restraint, in order to assure non-Catholics that they *might* be given freedom in a Catholic America, is a leading and caustic critic of the *present* American policy of church-state separation in respect to public money. If his dream of Catholic America is realized, the American people will be compelled to support the Church's schools with their tax contributions. He even sees in the Southern battle against the Supreme Court's decision on racial segregation "an important stimulus to the rethinking of the question of state aid to the religious school." [21] In *America,* March 6, 1948, he contended that the whole question of federal financial aid for parochial schools was a question of "legislative expediency, not constitutional law." He could find nothing in the Constitution or the Supreme Court's intepretations of it to justify rejection of Catholic demands for school funds. "The State," he remarked, "is not properly an 'educator.'"

5

Those who have followed my analysis of the Catholic problem thus far will agree that it is already too late to solve the problem by passive measures. The Catholic hierarchy is not passive. It is well organized and well regimented, and it uses astutely the power that it possesses over a nominal American Catholic population of thirty-five million. It seeks to impose its own social, political, and cultural program upon the American community in the name of religion, although a large part of the program has no necessary connection with religion.

It seems clear to me that there is no alternative for champions of traditional American democracy except to build a resistance movement designed to prevent the hierarchy from imposing its social policies upon our schools, hospitals, government, and family organization. It is scarcely necessary to say that a resistance movement can have no place for bigots or for the enemies of the Catholic *people*. Nor can it have any place for those who would curtail the rights of the Catholic Church as a *religious* institution. Its sole purpose should be to resist the antidemocratic social policies of the hierarchy and to fight against every intolerant or separatist or un-American feature of those policies.

Where should such a resistance movement begin? I would not presume to answer that question if the answers were not more or less self-evident. I think it should not begin with any one class of people, with clergymen or the "unchurched" or businessmen. It should begin in the minds of all democratic-minded Americans, Catholic and non-Catholic, who appreciate the danger to our institutions inherent in the hierarchy's policies, and who are resolved to resist without compromise or evasion. The will to defend American freedom from a danger that can no longer be ignored is more important than the method of resistance that may be adopted.

Such a resistance movement should base its activities upon certain broad general principles that will enlist the service of high-minded men of every church and of no church. Its platform of principles and policies might well include certain major objectives in the fields of medicine and general welfare, culture and information, politics and law.

In the field of medicine and welfare, a resistance-movement platform should include the right of every American family to secure information about birth control either from a family physician or from a properly staffed clinic. It should oppose all discrimination against non-Catholic clergymen and doctors in Catholic hospitals. It should resist any solicitation of funds from non-Catholics for Catholic hospitals, unless written assurances are given to contributors that both the surgical and the religious practices of non-Catholic professional persons will be permitted on the same basis as approved Catholic practice. The platform should oppose every attempt by the hierarchy to suppress scientific education concerning sexual problems and venereal disease.

In the field of culture and information, the platform should stand for the American public school, from kindergarten through college, as the foundation of American democracy. It should oppose the use of public funds for salaries, textbooks, bus transportation, or other routine services for all nonpublic schools. It should favor state laws requiring equivalent training for Catholic parochial-school teachers and public-school teachers. It should favor continuous and scientific inspection of all parochial schools to see that the standard requirements of the state are maintained, that classes are taught in the English language, and that textbooks do not distort history, science, and sociology in an opinionated manner for the benefit of the hierarchy. It should favor the exclusion from public classrooms of all teachers who wear distinctively religious costumes. It should oppose all organized denominational censorship of press, screen, radio, and television, and champion actively those newspapers and magazines that have the good old American courage to treat Catholic policies, personalities, and derelictions with impartial candor.

In the field of politics and law, the platform should favor "a wall of separation between church and state," and make it real with no compromise. It should oppose the sending of a formal or informal ambassador to the Vatican, or the holding of any official political conferences with the Papacy. It should favor the registration of all Roman Catholic higher officials operating in the United States under the provisions of the Foreign Agents Registration Law until such time as these higher officials are chosen by the Catholic people of the United States. It should resist the appointment or election of Catholic judges in all states where sterilization laws, applied to the unfit, are on the statute books, unless those Catholic judges publicly repudiate their Roman directives to defy such laws. It should favor the careful review of all tax-exempt real-estate holdings of Catholic bishops in the United States in order to make certain that only property used directly for religious, educational, and charitable purposes is exempt from taxation.

Although I wrote the above planks in the platform of an imaginary resistance movement nearly ten years ago, without great hope that the movement would be a reality in my lifetime, it is a pleasure to report that the movement has developed more rapidly than I had dared to dream. The independent national organization, Protestants and Other Americans United for Separation of Church and State, has successfully promoted the ideal of church-state separation both in Washington and in almost every state of the Union.[22] The American Civil Liberties Union and several powerful Jewish organizations have fought every attempt to use public money for sectarian promotion; and, in general, they have been successful.

Yes, the resistance movement is here, and it is growing with remarkable momentum. On the whole, it is a liberal and constructive movement dedicated to preserving that precious heritage, the separation of church and state. Its ultimate goal is an open and free society.

It should be noted in passing that I have not included in my suggestions for a resistance movement any anti-Catholic political party or any general boycott of Catholic candidates for public office. I regard both of these suggestions as disastrous. The anti-Catholic political movements of the nineteenth century—the Know Nothings, the American Protective Association, and the Ku Klux Klan—degenerated into disgraceful bigotry and fanaticism.

Likewise, any general, blanket boycott of Catholic candidates for public office seems unwise and unfair. Surely an American should not be penalized automatically in political life because he has been born into a certain church, and because, like most human beings, he has continued to be true to the faith of his fathers. At a tense moment in the 1928 presidential campaign, when Al Smith's rather crude and uninformed Catholicism had become a national issue, a Unitarian organization issued a statement of policy on religious tests in politics which, I believe, can be taken as a model for American voters: "No candidate for public office within the gift of the American people should ever be regarded as disqualified for such by reason of his particular form of religious belief."

Having accepted this principle, however, we cannot avoid the further conclusion that a Catholic candidate's attitude toward certain *policies* of his Church is clearly relevant to his fitness to hold public office. This is particularly true when the office which he seeks has great social significance, as, for example, the presidency of the United States. His Catholicism cannot give him immunity from a searching inquiry as to his own personal attitudes toward education, medicine, birth control, and censorship—the areas over which his Church claims a special kind of sovereignty. He has no right to use his religion as a shield to conceal his views on these subjects, or to prevent reasonable questioning.

It seems to me that the reasonable questioning of any Catholic candidate for the presidency might well include these three queries:

1. The Canon Law of your Church (Canon 1374) directs all American Catholic parents to boycott our public schools unless they receive special permission from their bishops. Do you personally approve or disapprove of this boycott rule?

2. The bishops of your Church, in an official statement, in November, 1948, have denounced the Supreme Court's interpretation of the religion clause of the First Amendment and have argued that the Constitution actually permits the distribution of public money on an equitable basis to sectarian schools. At present the Catholic press is promoting a plan for securing grants of federal funds to parents to cover the costs of parochial schools. What is your personal conviction concerning: (a) your bishops' attack on the Supreme Court; (b) the payment of government funds to parents for major parochial school costs; and (c) the payment of tax money for such "fringe" benefits as bus transportation?

3. Your Church denies the right of both non-Catholics and Catholics to receive birth-control information, and in such states as Massachusetts and Connecticut its power has been sufficient to make prohibition of birth control legally binding. Do you personally approve or disapprove of your church's policy on this subject?

It would not have been possible to press home such questions in the Al Smith campaign, because the American people did not know enough about the policies of the Catholic hierarchy at that time to recognize the validity of the questions. Today public knowledge of the whole area is increasing rapidly. One very hopeful sign is that books on Catholic policy are now actually being published and read in considerable quantities by the general public. The surprising success of my own three works in this field needs no comment here. The success of Emmett McLoughlin's *People's Padre* has been notable, partly because it was almost ignored by all the book reviewers in the United States, on the theory that any work by an ex-priest is *verboten*. Plain speaking about Catholic policy is beginning to creep into American fiction, and many publishers are willing to risk publication of such criticism in fiction form when they would not dare to print straight factual analyses. James Gould Cozzens' magnificent novel of 1957, *By Love Possessed,* was more universally praised by literary critics than any other major work of fiction in the United States in recent years, in spite of the fact that it contained the most devastating revelations concerning Catholic policy ever included in an American novel.

The most encouraging phenomenon is that books about Catholicism charged with laughter have scored striking successes in the last three years. When the people begin to laugh at the medieval strictures imposed upon the faithful by their celibate priests, the rule of those priests is doomed. In this class belong three works of fiction, the first of which became a national best-seller: Honor Tracy's *The Straight and Narrow Path,* Ring Lardner, Jr.'s, *The Ecstasy of Owen Muir,* and Roger Peyrefitte's *The Keys of St. Peter.*

Can a resistance movement with such a platform avoid narrow partisanship? Can it challenge the antidemocratic policies of the Catholic hierarchy without attacking the Catholic people? Can it discriminate between an enemy of American freedom and the victims of the enemy?

Frankly, I do not know. Inherent in every vital social movement are the forces that may pervert and destroy it. Even the most idealistic association of free people is subject to exploitation. Extremists often begin by opposing a man's ideas and end by hating the man himself. There is no doubt that any resistance movement against the policies of the Catholic hierarchy in this country would include some extremists of the type who have made anti-Catholicism a national disgrace in the past.

The danger of such corruption and perversion of any resistance movement must be faced squarely by democratic-minded Americans. In cities where ethnic and national distinctions coincide with religious divisions, it is almost inevitable that any defense against priestly policy will be treated by Catholics as an "attack" upon the Catholic community itself. The identification of honest criticism with religious bigotry is exactly what the Catholic hierarchy wants. It can maintain its hold upon democratic-minded Catholics just so long as it can persuade them that it speaks for *them* against their enemies.

At least once in our history the American people have thrown off an alien system of control without losing their moral perspective or their sense of respect for their opponents. In the days of the American Revolution there were some patriots who lost their emotional balance and began hating Englishmen as Englishmen. Most Americans knew that they were fighting not Englishmen as such but an undemocratic system of alien control. When the crisis had passed, the American and British people soon realized that their common purposes far outweighed their incidental disagreements. As the years passed, two great peoples grew closer together because they shared a common heritage. The analogy is not exact, but it contains a suggestion and a hope for the solution of the Catholic problem in the United States.

Calendar of Significant Events, 1947-1957

A list of important events in the growth and containment of Catholic power which occurred between the preparation of the first edition and the publication of the second edition of *American Freedom and Catholic Power*. In assessing events I have relied largely upon the American Catholic press and that invaluable annual guide to Catholic information, the *National Catholic Almanac*.

1947

January, 1947. Illinois Supreme Court, in the McCollum case, affirms legality of religious classes in public schools.

February, 1947. United States Supreme Court in 5 to 4 decision, in the case of *Everson vs. Board of Education,* declares that the First Amendment of the United States Constitution is not violated when a New Jersey school district pays transportation costs of students attending parochial schools.

March, 1947. Methodist Bishop G. Bromley Oxnam, former president of the Federal Council of Churches, attacks "Roman Catholic insistence upon public support of parochial education" as a threat to public education and American democracy.

April, 1947. Six non-Catholic doctors are dismissed from the staffs of three Connecticut Catholic hospitals for publicly supporting a bill in the state legislature that would have permitted birth control.

May, 1947. National Council of Methodist Bishops, and Southern Baptist Convention ask recall of Myron C. Taylor as President's personal representative at the Vatican.

June, 1947. Four leading Protestant and Jewish gynecologists removed from courtesy staff of Mercy (Catholic) Hospital in Springfield, Mass., because they supported a state permissive birth-control law.

July, 1947. National Education Association rejects move to favor the use of public funds for parochial school buses. (Action repeated at later conventions.)

October, 1947. Iowa and Washington state courts rule that use of public funds for parochial school buses is illegal under state laws.

November, 1947. Pius XII, in encyclical *Mediator Dei,* warns against those who "are too much bent on seeking after novelties" and calls on Catholics to "heed with docility" the voice of the Pope.

1948

January, 1948.   *The Nation,* already banned from the public-high-school libraries of New York City, is also banned by Newark high schools by direction of a Catholic superintendent, John S. Herron.

January, 1948.   New national organization, Protestants and Other Americans United for Separation of Church and State, issues first Manifesto, calling for strong movement to support the American concept of the separation of church and state.

March, 1948.   United States Supreme Court in 8 to 1 decision in McCollum case rules unconstitutional religious instruction in public-school classrooms and the use of public money for sectarian promotion.

April, 1948.   Christian Democratic (Catholic) Party, with American Catholic aid, wins Italian national election, but with only 48 per cent of national vote.

June, 1948.   North Dakota, in referendum, bans wearing of distinctively religious garb by public-school teachers.

June, 1948.   Holy Office issues warning that, under Canon 1325, both Catholic laity and clergy are forbidden to participate with non-Catholics in mixed meetings in which matters of faith are discussed.

July, 1948.   Planned Parenthood Association of St. Louis is barred from use of rent-free quarters in suburban health center as a result of Catholic protest.

August, 1948.   Catholic leaders, in Washington hearing, protest right of an atheist to appear on radio programs to explain his case.

October, 1948.   Bishop Carroll of Wichita, before Kansas referendum on state prohibition laws, announces that both "as a Catholic priest and an American citizen" he is opposed to retaining such laws.

November, 1948.   Catholic bishops of United States in official pronouncement, "The Christian in Action," denounce Supreme Court's interpretation of the separation of church and state as expressed in the McCollum decision and favor interpretation permitting public funds for sectarian schools.

November, 1948.   American Federation of Labor endorses federal aid to education, including "health and safety" appropriations to parochial schools.

December, 1948.   Cardinal Mindszenty imprisoned in Hungary. (Sentenced to life imprisonment for treason in February, 1949.)

1949

January, 1949.   With much Catholic support, McMahon-Johnson bill is introduced in U.S. Senate, proposing $25,000,000 expenditure of federal funds for auxiliary services in private as well as public schools. Defeated.

March, 1949.   In New Mexico case of *Zellers vs. Huff,* district court bans religious practices in Dixon "semi-public" schools. Higher court later bans religious garb, and bars 143 priests, nuns, and brothers from teaching in public schools.

April, 1949.   Monsignor William Hart, speaking for Rochester hierarchy, denounces sex education film, *Human Reproduction,* scientific treatment of subject successfully used in Rochester public schools.

April, 1949.   *American Freedom and Catholic Power,* published by Beacon Press, declared unreadable under Canon Law by Catholic spokesmen, and reviewed by only 7 of 150 daily newspapers which received copies for review; national best-seller from June, 1949, to January, 1950.

May, 1949.   Cardinal Spellman denounces Barden bill as "menace to American democracy" because it proposes $300,000,000 federal aid to public schools only. Bill defeated.

June, 1949.   Washington State Supreme Court voids statute providing parochial bus transportation at public expense.

June, 1949.   Cardinal Stritch and Washington Catholic leaders denounce Truman health insurance plan as "fictitious public welfare." Defeated.

July, 1949.   Cardinal Spellman attacks Mrs. Roosevelt.

1950

January, 1950.   Celebration of Holy Year opens in Rome.

January, 1950.   Myron C. Taylor resigns as personal representative of President Truman at the Vatican.

February, 1950.   In Japan, American Occupation authorities, under Catholic pressure, strike out from a book on population problems written by an Occupation adviser all references advocating birth control.

March, 1950.   *Osservatore Romano,* Vatican newspaper, announces that rules prescribing excommunication for any Catholic who joins Masonic bodies are still in force.

April, 1950.   Pius XII in encyclical *Humani Generis* denounces modernist and progressive trends in Catholic theology.

November, 1950.   Pius XII proclaims as infallible truth the dogma of the Assumption of the Body of the Virgin Mary into heaven.

1951

January, 1951.   Motion picture *The Miracle* banned in New York after it is denounced by Catholic archdiocese as an "open insult" to Catholics.

January, 1951.   Holy Office forbids priests to be members of Rotary Clubs or to attend Rotary meetings.

April, 1951.   Two Catholic schools in Maillardville, British Columbia, close doors and send pupils to public schools when local school board refuses to pay bus transportation costs.

July, 1951.   Catholic Archbishop of Verapoly denounces Nehru for recommending birth control for people of India.

October, 1951.   President Truman nominates General Mark Clark to be United States Ambassador to the Vatican, but name is withdrawn after overwhelming public protest.

1952

January, 1952.   Seven physicians of St. Francis Hospital, Poughkeepsie, are asked to resign for supporting Planned Parenthood Association.

March, 1952.   Fourteen Wisconsin "public" schools taught by nuns taken off public payroll for violating separation of church and state.

April, 1952.   James B. Conant, former president of Harvard, challenges dual school system serving different creeds as "divisive" and attacks use of public funds for private schools. Attacked in reprisal by Archbishop Cushing, but later confirmed as High Commissioner to Germany.

April, 1952.   Missouri Circuit Court in case of *Berghorn vs. Reorganized School District* rules out Catholic nuns as public-school teachers because their vows are inconsistent with purposes of public education.

April, 1952.   United States Supreme Court in Zorach case, by vote of 6 to 3, declares released-time religious instruction does not violate First Amendment if given under certain conditions away from public-school buildings.

May, 1952.   United Nations Assembly drops birth-control proposal from agenda after threat by Catholic countries to boycott World Health Organization.

May, 1952.   Holy Office places all the works of André Gide and Alberto Moravia on the *Index*.

May, 1952.   United States Supreme Court unanimously overrules as unconstitutional New York ban on the motion picture *The Miracle*.

September, 1952.   Several American branches of Church of Christ (Protestant) in Italy closed by Italian government; later reopened after protests.

September, 1952.   Efforts to liberalize antiquated Canadian divorce law defeated by Catholic opposition, headed by Quebec.

November, 1952.   California voters in referendum vote 2,323,000 to 2,253,000 to exempt private schools from state taxation.

November, 1952.   Pius XII names twenty-four new cardinals, bringing total to seventy, including one new American, Cardinal McIntyre of Los Angeles.

December, 1952.   National Council of Churches (Protestant) announces general opposition to government aid to parochial schools.

1953

February, 1953.   American Protestant missionaries barred from mission territory in Colombia after Colombian government signs agreement with Holy See providing annual tax grant to Catholic home missions of $420,000.

February, 1953.   Charges filed with State Department that Archbishop O'Hara of Savannah, an American citizen, violates federal double-loyalty law by serving as Vatican Ambassador to the Irish Republic. Dismissed on technicality that position does not require oath of loyalty to Vatican.

February, 1953.   Holy Office announces excommunication of Father Leonard Feeney of Cambridge, Mass.

April, 1953.   Catholic welfare organizations of Pennsylvania boycott Pennsylvania Welfare Conference because of planned parenthood exhibit.

May, 1953.   Fifty-three Catholic agencies resign membership in New York City Welfare and Health Council after it votes to admit Planned Parenthood Committee.

June, 1953.   Missouri Supreme Court rules unconstitutional under state constitution statute providing public money for parochial-school buses.

June, 1953.   Central Conference of American Rabbis opposes both use of public funds for sectarian schools and "released time" classes.

August, 1953.   Holy See signs new concordat with Franco Spain providing for joint appointment of bishops and pledging Spanish government not to legislate in "mixed matters."

1954

January, 1954.   Quebec legislature by vote of 81 to 0 prohibits public distribution of all "books and other publications insulting a religious faith."

January, 1954.   National Council of Catholic Women urges peaceful end of racial segregation in United States public schools.

February, 1954.   Quebec board of censors bars *Martin Luther* film from public exhibition.

April, 1954.   Pius XII, in Easter message, appeals for a ban on nuclear war.

May, 1954.   Supreme Court decision outlawing racial segregation in public schools is generally accepted as "morally binding" by Catholic Church.

May, 1954.   Pius XII condemns independent lay theologians and insists that all theological authorization must come from mandate of bishops.

June, 1954.   Vatican signs concordat with General Trujillo giving Catholic Church special status in Dominican Republic.

July, 1954.   Cardinal Strich, at time of Evanston meeting of World Council of Churches, issues pastoral letter warning against attendance at interfaith religious conferences.

September, 1954.   Bishop Bernard J. Sheil resigns as director of Chicago Archdiocesan Catholic Youth Organization after criticism in Catholic press of his opposition to Senator McCarthy.

October, 1954.   Distribution of King James Version of Bible in public schools by Gideons outlawed by United States Supreme Court.

November, 1954.   Archbishop Alter of Cincinnati, chairman of the Executive Department of the National Catholic Welfare Conference, attacks the "unhistorical interpretation" of the United States Constitution by the United States Supreme Court in forbidding the use of public money for sectarian purposes.

November, 1954.   Organized Catholic opposition defeats $25,000,000 bond issue for New Jersey state medical school; and Catholic medical school is later opened in Jersey City when public medical center is transferred to Catholic control after defeat of a taxpayers' suit charging illegality. December, 1954. Pius XII, gravely ill, recovers.

1955

February, 1955.   Cardinal McIntyre assails National Education Association for being "Hitlerian and un-American" and for attempting to "force all American children into public schools," because it opposes use of public money for parochial schools.

April, 1955.   *Catholic World* in open letter to Eisenhower demands federal funds for Catholic school buildings as a "welfare" grant.

May, 1955.   Missouri legislature defeats bill providing bus transportation at public expense for parochial schools.

July, 1955.   Cardinal Mindszenty released from Hungarian prison, but held in isolation.

October, 1955.   Senate subcommittee on constitutional rights cancels public hearings on violations of religious clause of First Amendment, after promising complete airing.

October, 1955.   Archbishop Joseph F. Rummel suspends Roman Catholic services in Jesuit Bend, Louisiana, because some parishioners decline to accept Negro priest; he is supported by the Vatican.

November, 1955.   Conference of Protestant leaders under auspices of National Council favors religious education for children in public schools but opposes "sectarianism."

December, 1955.   Majority of delegates at White House Conference on Education oppose use of public funds for non-public schools.

1956

January, 1956.   Pius XII approves new "psychological" method of painless childbirth.

February, 1956.   Kentucky court rules that Catholic nuns may teach in costume in state's public schools. (Other issues not involved.)

February, 1956.   New York Welfare and Health Council reorganizes to eliminate Planned Parenthood groups from voting membership.

March, 1956.   Pius XII celebrates eightieth birthday.

March, 1956.   Archbishop Joseph F. Rummel of New Orleans suspends indefinitely plans for racial integration in parochial schools because of opposition of white Catholic parents.

April, 1956.   It is revealed at Washington tax hearing that Catholic orders claim tax exemption from tax on unrelated business income even when they manufacture brandy and operate radio stations for profit.

June, 1956.   Highest Kentucky court condemns gerrymandering of "public" high schools in Marion County by Catholic religious orders and directs end of religious incursions into public schools.

June, 1956.   Congress awards $964,199 to Vatican for war damages by American air raids, although State Department denies any legal obligation.

August, 1956.   Senator John F. Kennedy defeated for Democratic vice-presidential nomination by Estes Kefauver, 755½ to 589.

October, 1956.   Revolt in Hungary; Cardinal Mindszenty finds refuge in American Embassy in Budapest.

October, 1956.   Eisenhower names William J. Brennan of New Jersey to United States Supreme Court, the first Catholic since the death of Frank Murphy in 1949.

October, 1956.   Vermont Supreme Court rules illegal the payment of state funds for tuition to Catholic high schools.

November, 1956.   Facts disclosed at Washington tax hearing show Catholic nuns teaching in public schools are unlawfully exempted from paying federal income taxes on salaries.

December, 1956.   Cardinal McIntyre, in address at Dallas University, reveals new plan to secure federal money for Catholic pupils by legislation resembling G.I. Bill of Rights.

December, 1956.   *Chicago Tribune* television station WGN, under Catholic pressure, bans film *Martin Luther.*

1957

March, 1957.   In Augusta, Maine, Catholic parents threaten, and then retract, move to "dump" 900 parochial-school children on public schools unless their demands for bus money are granted. State courts declare token payment for such purpose invalid.

May, 1957.   After issuance of pastoral letter by Catholic hierarchy, Connecticut legislature, by margin of one vote, authorizes local communities to pay for parochial-school buses.

May, 1957.   In case of Hildy McCoy Ellis, child of unwed Catholic mother, Governor Leroy Collins of Florida refuses extradition of Jewish foster parents, Mr. and Mrs. Melvin Ellis, to Massachusetts, and Florida court later confirms Ellis guardianship.

June, 1957.   Congress without debate and by special statute authorizes Congressmen McCormack and Rooney to accept Vatican political decoration, the Order of St. Gregory.

July, 1957.   Grant of New Orleans television channel to Jesuits by Federal Communications Commission challenged in United States Court of Appeals in suit charging that Jesuit order represents aliens.

August, 1957.   State Department drops proposed treaty with Haiti which fails to guarantee religious freedom and equality.

September, 1957.   Pius XII in encyclical, *Miranda Porsus,* directs establishment of world-wide censorship organization to supervise all motion pictures, radio and television.

Bibliography

Acton, Lord. *Essays on Freedom and Power.* Beacon, 1948.
Agar, William. *Catholicism and the Progress of Science.* Macmillan, 1940.
Ayrinhac, Henry A. *Penal Legislation in the New Code of Canon Law.* Benziger, 1936.

Barclay, Wade Crawford. *Greater Good Neighbor Policy.* Willett, Clark, 1945.
Baron, Salo W. *Modern Nationalism and Religion.* Harper, 1947.
Bates, M. Searle. *Religious Liberty.* International Missionary Council, 1945.
Beck, Sister Mary Berenice. *The Nurse: Handmaid of the Divine Physician.* Lippincott.
Belloc, Hilaire. *The Contrast.* McBride, 1924.
Bernhart, Joseph. *The Vatican as a World Power.* Translated by George N. Shuster. Longmans, Green, 1939.
Betten, Francis. *The Roman Index of Forbidden Books.* Herder, 1912.
Billington, R. A. *The Protestant Crusade.* Macmillian, 1938.
Binchy, D. A. *Church and State in Facist Italy.* Oxford University Press, 1941.
Bouscaren, T. Lincoln. *Canon Law Digest: Officially Published Documents Affecting the Code of Canon Law.* Volume I: 1917-1933. Volume II: 1933-1942. Bruce, 1934, 1943.
Bouscaren, T. Lincoln, and Ellis, Adam C. *Canon Law: Text and Commentary.* Bruce, 1946.
Bovey, Wilfred. *The French Canadian Today.* Dent (Toronto), 1938.
Bowdern, William S. *The Catholic Nurse and the Dying* (pamphlet). Queen's Work (St. Louis), 1945.
Brunini, John G. *Whereon to Stand.* Harper, 1946.
Burns, James A., Kohlbrenner, B. J., and Peterson, J. B. *A History of Catholic Education in the United States.* Benziger, 1937.
Bury, J. B. *History of the Papacy in the Nineteenth Century.* Macmillan (London), 1930.
Butts, R. Freeman. *The American Tradition in Religion and Education.* Beacon, 1950.

Cadoux, C. J. *Roman Catholicism and Freedom.* Independent Press (London), 1937.
Campbell, Paul C. *Parish School Problems.* Wagner, 1941.
Catholic Action Manual, The. By Luigi Civardi. Sheed and Ward, 1943.
Catholic Almanac, 1957 (St. Anthony's Guild, Paterson), 1957.
Catholic Directory, 1957. P. J. Kenedy and Sons.
Catholic Encyclopedia. Encyclopedia Press, 1913.

Chamberlin, William Henry. *Canada, Today and Tomorrow.* Little, Brown, 1942.
Cianfarra, Camille. *The Vatican and the War.* Dutton, 1944.
Connell, Francis J. *Morals in Politics and Professions.* Newman, 1946.
Cook, Robert C. *Human Fertility: The Modern Dilemma.* Sloane, 1951.
Creusen, Joseph. *Religious Men and Women in the Code.* Bruce, 1940.

Davis, Henry. *Moral and Pastoral Theology.* Four volumes. Sheed and Ward, 1935.
Davis, John D. *The Moral Obligations of Catholic Civil Judges.* Catholic University Press, 1953.
Dawson, Joseph M. *Separate Church and State Now.* Smith, 1948.
Deferrari, Roy J., editor. *Essays on Catholic Education in the United States.* Catholic University of America, 1942.
————, editor. *Vital Problems of Catholic Education in the United States.* Catholic University of America, 1939.
De Guchteneere, Raoul. *Judgment on Birth Control.* Macmillan, 1931.
Doheny, William J. *Canonical Procedure in Matrimonial Cases.* Two volumes. Bruce, 1943.
De la Bedoyere, Michael. *Christian Crisis.* Macmillan, 1940.

Elderkin, George W. *The Roman Catholic Problem.* Vantage, 1954.
Ellis, John Tracy. *American Catholicism.* University of Chicago Press, 1955.
Emerson, Thomas I., and Haber, David. *Political and Civil Rights in the United States.* Dennis (Buffalo), 1952.

Fanfani, Louis. *Catechism on the Religious State.* Herder, 1956.
Fey, Harold E. *Can Catholicism Win America?* Christian Century, 1946.
Finney, Patrick A. *Moral Problems in Hospital Practice.* Herder, 1947.
Five Great Encyclicals. (Leo XIII and Pius XI.) Paulist Press, 1947.

Gabel, Richard J. *Public Funds for Church and Private Schools.* Catholic University of America, 1937.
Garrison, W. E. *Catholicism and the American Mind.* Willett, Clark, 1928.
Gasparri, Cardinal. *The Catholic Catechism.* P. J. Kenedy and Sons, 1932.
Gibbons, James Cardinal. *The Faith of Our Fathers.* (63rd ed.) Murphy, 1906.
Grindel, Carl W., editor. *Concept of Freedom.* Regnery, 1955.

Hamilton, Thomas J. *Appeasement's Child: The Franco Regime in Spain.* Knopf, 1943.
Healy, Edwin F. *Medical Ethics.* Loyola University Press, 1956.
Heenan, John C. *Priest and Penitent.* Sheed and Ward, 1938.
Herbst, Winfrid. *The Sisters Are Asking.* Newman, 1956.
Hines, Norman E. *Medical History of Contraception.* Williams and Wilkins, 1936.
Howard, George F. *Religious Liberty in Latin America?* Westminster, 1944.
Hughes, Emmet J. *Report from Spain.* Holt, 1947.

Hughes, Philip. *The Pope's New Order*. Macmillan, 1944.
Husslein, Joseph. *Social Wellsprings*. Two volumes. (Encyclicals and Notes.) Bruce, 1942.
Hutchinson, Paul. *The New Leviathan*. Wilett, Clark, 1946.

Johnson, Alvin W., and Yost, Frank H. *Separation of Church and State in the United States*. University of Minnesota Press, 1948.
Joyce, George H. *Christian Marriage*. Sheed and Ward, 1933.

Landis, Benson Y. *Yearbook of American Churches, 1958*. National Council of Churches, 1957.
Laux, John. *Church History*. Benziger, 1930.
Lea, H. C. *History of Sacerdotal Celibacy in the Christian Church*. Ballantyne (London), 1907.
Lehmann, Leo H. *Mixed Marriage* (and many other valuable pamphlets). Agora Publishing Company (New York).

McFadden, Charles J. *Medical Ethics for Nurses*. Foreword by Fulton J. Sheen. Davis, 1946.
MacGregor, Geddes. *The Vatican Revolution*. Beacon, 1957.
McGucken, William J. *The Catholic Way in Education*. Bruce, 1934.
McKnight, John P. *The Papacy*. Rinehart, 1952.
McLaughlin, Emmett. *People's Padre*. Beacon, 1954.
Manhattan, Avro. *The Catholic Church against the Twentieth Century*. Watts (London), 1947.
Maritain, Jacques. *The Angelic Doctor*. Dial, 1931.
Marshall, Charles C. *The Roman Catholic Church in the Modern State*. Dodd, Mead, 1931.
Marx, Adolph. *The Declaration of Nullity of Marriages Contracted Outside The Church*. Catholic University of America, 1943.
Maynard, Theodore. *The Story of American Catholicism*. Macmillan, 1941.
Mecham, J. Lloyd. *Church and State in Latin America*. University of North Carolina, 1934.
Medicus. *Medical Essays*. (2nd ed.) 1928. Censura Theologica Praecessit.
Meyer, Agnes E. *Out of These Roots*. Little, Brown, 1953.
Moehlman, Conrad H. *The Church as Educator*. Hinds, Hayden and Eldredge, 1947.
————. *School and Church: The American Way*. Harper, 1944.
Moody, Joseph, editor. *Church and Society*. Arts, Inc. (New York), 1953.
Moore, John H. *Will America Become Catholic?* Harper, 1931.
Moore, Thomas Ewing. *Peter's City*. Macmillan, 1930.
Myers, Gustavus. *History of Bigotry in the United States*. Random House, 1943.

Nichols, James H. *Democracy and the Churches*. Westminster, 1951.

O'Brien, John A., editor. *Catholics and Scholarship*. Our Sunday Visitor, 1938,

————. *The Faith of Millions*. Our Sunday Visitor, 1938.

O'Gorman, Thomas. *A History of the Roman Catholic Church in the United States*. (Volume IX of "American Church History.") Scribner's, 1916.

O'Malley, Austin. *The Ethics of Medical Homicide and Mutilation*. Devin-Adair, 1919.

O'Malley, Austin, and Walsh, James J. *Essays in Pastoral Medicine*. Longmans, Green, 1906.

Parkes, Henry Bamford. *History of Mexico*. Houghton Mifflin, 1938.

Pfeffer, Leo. *Church, State and Freedom*. Beacon, 1953.

Redden, John, and Ryan, Francis A. *Freedom Through Education*. Bruce, 1944.

Riddell, W. A. *Rise of Ecclesiastical Control in Quebec*. Columbia University Press, 1916.

Ridley, F. A. *The Jesuits*. Secker and Warburg (London), 1938.

Roemer, Theodore. *The Catholic Church in the United States*. Herder, 1950.

Rommen, Heinrich A. *The State in Catholic Thought*, Herder, 1950.

Ryan, John A., and Millar, M. F. X. *The State and the Church*. Macmillan, 1924.

Salmon, George. *The Infallibility of the Church*. Dutton, 1914.

Salvemini, Gaetano, and LaPiana, George. *What to Do with Italy?* Duell, Sloan and Pierce, 1943.

Sax, Karl. *Standing Room Only*. Beacon, 1955.

Schaff, David S. *Our Father's Faith and Ours*. Putnam's, 1928.

Seldes, George. *The Catholic Crisis*. Messner, 1939.

————. *The Vatican: Yesterday, Today, Tomorrow*. Harper, 1934.

Shaughnessy, Gerald. *Has the Immigrant Kept the Faith?* Macmillan, 1925.

Sheen, Fulton J. *Communism and the Conscience of the West*. Bobbs-Merrill, 1948.

Shuster, George N. *The Catholic Spirit in America*. Dial, 1928.

Smith, Canon George, editor. *The Teaching of the Catholic Church*. (Symposium.) Two volumes. Macmillan, 1949.

Stock, Leo F. *Consular Relations Between the United States and the Papal States*. Catholic University Press, 1933.

Stokes, Anson P. *Church and State in the United States*. Three volumes. Harper, 1950.

Sugrue, Thomas. *A Catholic Speaks His Mind*. Harper, 1952.

Teeling, William. *Crisis of Christianity*. Gifford (London), 1939.

————. *Pope Pius XI and World Affairs*. Stokes, 1937.

Thayer, V. T. *American Education Under Fire*. Harper, 1944.

————. *Religion in Public Education*. Viking, 1947.

————. *The Attack Upon the American Secular School*. Beacon, 1951.

Thomas, John L., S.J. *The American Catholic Family*. Prentice-Hall, 1956.

Vogt, William. *The Road to Survival*. Sloan Associates, 1948.

Wade, Mason. *The French Canadian Outlook*. Viking, 1946.
Wall, Bernard. *The Vatican Story*. Harper, 1956.
Walsh, William T. *Our Lady of Fatima*. Macmillan, 1947.
Ward, Leo R. *The American Apostolate*. Newman, 1952.
Williams, Glanville. *The Sanctity of Life and the Criminal Law*. Knopf, 1957.
Williams, Michael. *The Catholic Church in Action*. Macmillan, 1934.
Woodlock, Thomas F. *The Catholic Pattern*. Simon and Schuster, 1942.
Woywod, Stanislaus. *The New Canon Law: A Commentary*. Wagner, 1918.

Notes

Books listed in the Bibliography are referred to by the author's surname.

It will be seen that in the selection of sources I have relied chiefly on approved American Catholic publications. For the student who wishes to have a small and inexpensive reference library of books and journals, all officially Catholic, I recommend, in order of importance: (1) The *National Catholic Almanac* (annual); (2) The (Denver) *Register* (weekly); (3) *Canon Law* by Bouscaren and Ellis; (4) the Brooklyn *Tablet;* and (5) *America* (weekly). The *Tablet,* a McCarthyite organ, is not representative of the best in Catholicism, but it is recommended because of the fact that it is the largest in terms of bulk of the Catholic diocesan weeklies and carries many details which are omitted in other Catholic journals. The *National Catholic Almanac* can be purchased for $2.50 from St. Anthony's Guild, Paterson, N.J. The *Register,* with 35 diocesan editions, is by all odds the most representative national newspaper of American Catholicism.

Preface

1. This pamphlet, obtainable from the Beacon Press for 50 cents, contains a reply to James M. O'Neill, a reply to a book review by Father Francis J. Connell, and an open letter to the *New York Times.*
2. In the *New York Herald-Tribune,* May 20, 1949.

Chapter 1

Personal Prologue: The Duty to Speak

1. Republished by *America* in the pamphlet by Father George H. Dunne, *Religion and American Democracy.*
2. Beginning in the issue of November 1, 1947, and continuing in 1948. For the long story of *The Nation* ban in New York and elsewhere, see the *New York Times Index* for 1947, 1948, and 1949; *The Nation, passim;* and *The Yale Law Journal,* April, 1950. In Massachusetts, in July, 1948, *The Nation* was banned from all teachers' colleges by an official who admitted that he had not read my articles, but the ban was lifted two months later by the Massachusetts State Board of Education.
3. Mrs. Roosevelt's column on parochial schools and public money appeared in the *New York World-Telegram,* June 23, 1949; Cardinal Spellman's attack in the *New York Times,* July 23; Mrs. Roosevelt's reply in the *New York Times,* July 28.
4. Letter of Arthur Hays Sulzberger, May 10, 1949. In a letter to the *Christian Herald,* published in the issue of September, 1950, Mr. Sulzberger assumed full responsibility for the ban, saying: "My decision

was based on the fact that part of Mr. Blanshard's book was an attack upon faith—not upon church." One wonders where he would classify H. L. Mencken, whose books are advertised. For contemporary accounts of the censorship of this book see the widely circulated article "The Book They Couldn't Ban," by Clarence W. Hall in *The Christian Herald,* July, 1950; and "The Silent Treatment," by Jerry Tallmer, in *The Nation,* July 16, 1949.

5. *The Commonweal* attack, published in the issue of March 12, 1948, by Father George H. Dunne, was a six-page affair which attempted to connect the author by innuendo with bigots who charge that "Catholics store guns in the basements of their churches." The author's reply, which *The Commonweal* refused to publish, was printed in *The Humanist,* August, 1948.

6. The following books and pamphlets, written by Catholic priests and laymen, have been devoted in whole or in part to an explanation of my shortcomings: James M. O'Neill, *Catholicism and American Freedom,* Harper and Brothers; Virgil A. Kelly, *The Truth About Catholics,* Dial Press; Aelred Graham, *Catholicism and the World Today,* D. McKay Co. (New York), 1952. Father George H. Dunne, *Religion and American Democracy,* America Press; *Answers to American Freedom and Catholic Power* (Symposium), Ave Maria Press; Dale Francis, *American Freedom and Paul Blanshard* and *Answering Paul Blanshard,* Ave Maria Press. In addition to these books and pamphlets, *The Commonweal,* early in 1953, carried six editorials and articles largely devoted to a reply to my analysis of Irish Catholicism and my opposition to the service of an American citizen as Papal Nuncio to Dublin. This magazine carried one letter from me in the nature of a rejoinder but refused to publish others exposing the editors' misrepresentations.

7. Various criticisms of O'Neill's interpretations of Catholic doctrine, and his inaccuracies, were published in *The American Ecclesiastical Review,* June, 1952, and February, 1955; in *America,* April 23, 1949; the Brooklyn *Tablet,* September 1, 1956; *Columbia Law Review,* January, 1950 (Pfeffer); *The Christian Register,* March, 1955; in addition to the analysis in *My Catholic Critics.*

Chapter 2
How the Hierarchy Works

1. Since there is no federal religious census, all estimates of religious population groups can be nothing more than estimates. *The Official Catholic Directory,* 1957, estimated the Catholic population of the United States (including Alaska, Hawaii, and the foreign military locations) at 34,386,351 for the year 1956. I have used the round figure of 35,000,000 in this book. The Bureau of the Census estimated that the population of the United States on May 1, 1957, was 170,737,000. Using the round figures of 35,000,000 in a population of 170,000,000, we reach the very tentative conclusion that Catholics

NOTES   369

comprise about 20.6 per cent of the American population. There is much guesswork, and probable padding, in these figures, since the membership statistics sent in by the priests are not scientifically collected or checked. See McLaughlin for comments on the exaggerated Catholic membership claims. The 1958 *Yearbook of American Churches,* published by the National Council of Churches, whose statistics were summarized in the *New York Times,* September 3, 1957, is the best source for Protestant figures. Although the Methodist Church is the second largest single church in the United States, the Baptists lead all other major Protestant groupings in membership, with about 20,000,000, and the Methodists come next with about 12,000,000. World figures for Catholicism are given in the *National Catholic Almanac,* 1957 (hereinafter called *Catholic Almanac*).

Since the Vatican never publishes its financial reports, the statement that the American Church supplies more than half of its contributed revenues can never be scientifically proved, but many Catholic authors have supported this view, e.g., Cianfarra, p. 30; Teeling, p. 158; and Wall, p. 127. The latter says: "It is safe to say that American Catholics pay at least half of the total income of the Vatican."

2. Ellis, p. 21. Shaugnessy has written the classic work in the field of early Catholic statistics; Garrison, pp. 165 ff., has a good discussion of Maryland.

3. See Billington; and Myers, pp. 228 ff. By 1893 the American Protective Association had seventy weekly publications and organizations in perhaps twenty-four states. One of its ex-priest orators accused the Catholic Church of plotting the assassination of Lincoln, a charge that is still being circulated by some anti-Catholic fanatics. The A.P.A. dwindled rapidly after 1900.

4. *The Rights of Man in America,* 1911 edition, pp. 354-358.

5. See *Census of Religious Bodies, 1936,* Bureau of the Census. In a letter in the *New York Times,* May 25, 1956, Henry P. Van Dusen, president of Union Theological Seminary, contended, in discussing world religious statistics, that: "Since, on the average, there is at least one child for each adult, if comparable figures are to be given, the number of Protestant church members must be doubled or the number of Catholic or Orthodox adherents halved." A few Protestant churches in the United States, however, do count children as members.

6. Doheny, II, 544.

7. *Yearbook of American Churches,* 1958.

8. See map of the National Council of Churches, *Time,* October 15, 1956; but Negro church membership was not included, and the overwhelming majority of Negro church members are Protestants.

9. Summarized in the *New York Times,* November 6, 1956.

10. Father Michael N. Kramer in his *Church Support in the United States* said: "According to the general opinion; only about one-half of the faithful support the Church."

11. September 7, 1950.

12. From manuscript of 1956 Washington address.

13. *Register,* May 15, 1955. Possibly the Catholic proportion in Massachusetts is actually just under 50 per cent.

14. *Christian Century,* July 20, 1949.
15. *Census of Religious Bodies,* 1936, p. 8.
16. Bouscaren, *Digest,* II, 444.
17. *Just One Minute,* pamphlet of the Catholic Information Society, 214 West 31st St., N. Y. According to a summary of a spot check across the nation, published in the *Register,* January 2, 1955: "About $25 *per wage earner* is the apparent average annual contribution of Catholic Americans to the Church through regular parish channels." The 1958 *Yearbook of American Churches* indicated average church gifts for all churches of $54 per capita. (*New York Times,* September 3, 1957.)
18. *Life,* July 14, 1947.
19. *Time,* February 15, 1947.
20. *Our Sunday Visitor,* August 29, 1954; but *America,* April 7, 1956, claimed that "nearly one-third of the pre-school children in the nation are baptized Catholics." Thomas, pp. 141 ff., discusses the Catholic birth rate, citing several scientific studies to indicate that, class for class, Catholics are more fertile than Protestants. In the *Register,* October 10, 1954, the editor, Monsignor Matthew Smith, quoted hopefully the estimate of a "business statistics expert" that Catholic births would be "beyond the 50 per cent mark" by 1970, largely because birth control "is not nearly so bad with us as with non-Catholics."
21. Deferrari, *Vital,* p. 144. (Permission for quotations granted by the Catholic University of America Press.) *The Official Catholic Directory,* 1957, claimed 141,525 converts for 1956.
22. *Catholic Almanac,* 1957, p. 350. The world statistics for 1955 are in the *Catholic Almanac,* 1956, p. 339.
23. *The Casuist; a Collection of Cases in Moral and Pastoral Theology,* II, 248. See also Maurice Connor, *The Administrative Removal of Pastors,* Catholic University, 1937.
24. Bernhart, p. 417.
25. *Catholic Almanac,* 1957, pp. 203 ff., has a good workable, elementary description of the Roman Congregations; Bernhart and Wall are useful; Bouscaren and Ellis, pp. 153 ff., give citations of Canon Law for major divisions of the Church; and Seldes discusses the machinery of power very ably. See also the *New York Times,* December 5, 1954, for article by Arnaldo Cortesi.
26. See *Catholic Encyclopedia Supplement,* "Conclave."
27. Statistics from *The Official Catholic Directory,* 1957. In strict usage the word "Sister" is applied to nuns who do not take solemn vows, and who, are, therefore, free to mingle to a limited extent with other human beings, while the word "nun" is reserved for those who take solemn vows and are cloistered. In this book I do not think it necessary to distinguish between the various grades and types of institutes and other organizations of Catholic Religious, and I adopt the common usage of American Catholics in applying the word "nun" to all Religious women who take vows of poverty, chastity, and obedience, and the word "order" to all institutes of Religious. See *Catholic Encyclopedia Supplement,* "Nuns."
28. Herbst, p. 23; also pp. 59-60.
29. Ridley, p. 211, from Part VI, Chapter 1.

30. Brunini, pp. 265 ff., has a good description of a bishop's power and his relations to the Pope; Bouscaren, *Digest,* I, 194 ff., summarizes legal procedure in selecting bishops.
31. Bernhart, p. 403. (Permission for quotations granted by Longmans, Green and Company.) See also the excellent article "Papacy" in the *Encyclopedia Britannica.*
32. Pp. 187 ff.
33. See *A Dictionary of Popes,* by Donald Atwater, Imprimatur Vicar General of Westminster. The reign of Pope John XII (955-964) was a "tale of impiety, debauchery, simony, cruelty . . . crude self-indulgence, and vice." He was charged with "turning the Lateran into a brothel" and "drinking a toast to the Devil." *Life,* June 14, 1948, had a graphic summary of the Reformation and the evils it was designed to destroy.
34. Woodlock, p. 43.
35. David Goldstein, *What Say You?* p. 240.
36. Moody, p. 233.
37. In addition to MacGregor, the reader is referred for accounts of the struggle over infallibility to Salmon; Bury, pp. 47 ff.; Acton, pp. 299 ff.; *Encyclopedia Britannica,* "Vatican Council"; Garrison, pp. 50 ff.; C. J. Cadoux, *Catholicism and Christianity;* J. J. I. Dollinger, *The Pope and Council,* written under the pseudonym of "Janus." A brief statement of the Catholic position, *No Pope Can Be Wrong in Teaching Doctrine,* by Martin Scott, S.J., can be secured in pamphlet form from America Press, 70 East 45th St., New York. A more extensive Catholic account of the Vatican Council is contained in *The Church and the Nineteenth Century,* by Raymond Corrigan, S.J.
38. Marshall, p. 68, from Lord Action, *Correspondence,* I, 103.
39. From *Pastor Aeternus* of Pius XI. See Smith, II, 716 ff.
40. *American Ecclesiastical Review,* February, 1951.
41. Bouscaren and Ellis, p. 866.
42. Ayrinhac, p. 191.
43. O'Brien, *Faith, p.* 126, says: "His [the Pope's] office in the interpretation of Holy Scripture is fundamentally the same as that of the Supreme Court of the United States in the interpretation of the Constitution." *Our Sunday Visitor,* June 20, 1954, produced large headlines (with story to match): "STRUCTURES OF CHURCH, U. S. GOVERNMENT SIMILAR, Our States Like Church's Dioceses; Democracy's Origin is Truly Catholic."
44. Text in *Catholic Encyclopedia,* "Testem Benevolentiae."
45. *The Commonweal, September* 23, 1955, article by William Osborne.
46. *Ave Maria,* October 12, 1946.
47. *Catholic Almanac,* 1948, pp. 414-429, has a good contemporary summary of N.C.W.C. activities, and recent *Almanacs* keep the story up to date. Deferrari, *Vital,* Roemer, and the *Catholic Encyclopedia Supplement* contain historical material.
48. Teeling, *Pius XI,* p. 162.
49. *Catholic Almanac,* 1955, p. 749.
50. *Ibid.,* 1957, p. 609.
51. *Life,* May 27, 1957.

52. *Mystical Body of Christ,* p. 2.
53. P. 117.
54. The official letter, dated August 8, 1949, was not published in Boston until September 4, 1952. It was printed, with the italics I have indicated, in the Irish clerical magazine, *The Furrow,* December, 1952. Cushing's point of view was reflected in *America,* April 30, 1949; the Feeney side of the controversy was given a whole book, *The Loyolas and the Cabots,* by Catherine G. Clark.
55. *The National Catholic Educational Association Bulletin,* May, 1946.
56. A comprehensive discussion of this rule is *Discussion With Non-Catholics,* by Father Stephen J. Kelleher, Catholic University Press, 1943.
57. Davis, I, 282 ff. (Permission for quotations granted by the author.) See also, for detailed samples of intolerance, a series of articles in the *American Ecclesiastical Review* by Father Francis J. Connell, February to April, 1956, on "Cooperation in Non-Catholic Activities."
58. Canon John Vaughan, *Is There Salvation Outside the Church?* p. 14.
59. Religious News Service, as cited in the *Christian Century,* June 9, 1948.
60. *The Outlook for Homo Sapiens,* p. 97.
61. *The Contrast,* p. 160. (Permission for quotations granted by Robert M. McBride and Company.)
62. *Time, January* 29, 1940. LaGuardia's fight against Catholic bingo in New York was described in New York papers of December, 1942.
63. *Boston Pilot,* January 9, 1942.
64. Campbell, p. 195.
65. *Catholic News,* February 14, 1948.

Chapter 3
Church, State, and Democracy

1. The full text of the Lateran Treaty of 1929 is in T. E. Moore, p. 209; the most important sections are printed in the Appendix of my *Communism, Democracy and Catholic Power.* Bouscaren and Ellis, pp. 153-187, includes the most important Canons on Papal and episcopal power.
2. *New York Times,* March 13, 1940. Technically foreign governments have 31 embassies and 15 legations at the Vatican. Only one non-Catholic country, the Netherlands, has a full ambassador.
3. The extraterritorial rights of the Vatican in Italy include thirteen buildings in Rome and the Pope's summer palace, Castel Gandolfo, outside of Rome.
4. Binchy, p. 263.
5. See Pfeffer, pp. 257 ff.; also, for other treatments of the Vatican diplomatic issue, Stock; Stokes; McKnight, pp. 336 ff.; *America,* November 3, 1951; and the *Journal of the Presbyterian Historical Association,* December, 1946, for an article by Dr. Hubertis Cummings on "American Relations with the Papacy," which describes the *New York Times'* mistake.

6. *New York Times,* March 29, 1952.
7. *Atlantic Monthly,* January, 1952.
8. *America,* February 15, 1947.
9. Thomas Sugrue, "Profile of Cardinal Hayes," *The New Yorker,* April 17, 1934. Also Cianfarra, p. 30.
10. Teeling, *Pius XI,* p. 98.
11. *Current History,* August, 1929.
12. Husslein, I, 71. Philip Hughes has a valuable summary of nearly all the important encyclicals from Leo XIII to Pius XII, but not the full, official texts.
13. *The Things That Are Not Caesar's,* p. 34.
14. John R. Bourque, *The Judicial Power of the Church,* Canon Law Studies, No. 337, p. 16.
15. P. 94. (Permission for quotations granted by St. Anthony's Guild.)
16. P. 188. (Permission for quotations granted by Sheed and Ward.)
17. Leo himself did not always observe the "fixed limits," since he declared in his "Chief Duties of Christian Citizens" that "the faithful should accept religiously as their rule of conduct the political wisdom of ecclesiastical authority." (Husslein, I, 159.)
18. Shuster, p. 147.
19. Louis Veuillot, *The Liberal Illusion,* translated by Monsignor George B. O'Toole, National Catholic Welfare Conference, p. 10. (Permission for quotations granted by the N.C.W.C.) See Rommen for complete discussion of the theory.
20. *New York Times,* January 26, 1948.
21. Published by the Paulist Press, 401 West 59th St., New York 19, N. Y.
22. *Register,* August 22, 1948.
23. P. 717.
24. Philip Hughes, p. 126 (Permission for quotations granted by the Macmillan Company.)
25. Connell, p. 33.
26. *Five Encyclicals,* p. 49.
27. *The Contrast,* p. 166.
28. P. 35. (Permission for quotations granted by Macmillan Company.)
29. *Homiletic and Pastoral Review,* November, 1935.
30. Bouscaren, *Digest,* I, 855.
31. *The Contrast,* p. 160.
32. Binchy, p. 494.
33. The oath, prescribed by Canon 332, is in Latin, with various English translations, including one published in this country in 1932 by the Cathedral Library Association of New York. The translation published by the Catholic Truth Society in Ireland, 1948, *The Ceremony of Consecration of a Bishop Elect,* has the following English phrases: "I . . . Bishop-Elect of . . . will now and at all times be loyal and obedient to St. Peter, to the Holy Roman Catholic Apostolic Church and to our Lord Pope . . . I will assist them to hold and defend against every opponent, with due consideration for my own hierarchical position, the Roman Pontificate and the sovereign rights of St. Peter. . . . Such orders as are given by the Apostolic See I will receive humbly and carry out diligently."

34. *Congressional Record,* June 5, 1956, p. 8622.
35. *Catholic Almanac,* 1957, p. 642.
36. H.R. 8383, 85th Congress, First Session.
37. *Church and State Review,* March, 1957.

Chapter 4
Education and the Catholic Mind

1. For detailed educational statistics in this chapter I have relied chiefly upon the *Official Catholic Directory,* 1957, which gives figures for 1956. *America,* April 27, 1957, prophesied an enrollment of about 4,820,000 in Catholic elementary and high schools in 1958; the National Catholic Welfare News Service made the figure 4,640,000 (*Register,* September 1, 1957). This latter estimate is 10.7 per cent of the estimated total number of students in all such schools, public and private, 43,135,000, according to figures given out by the United States Commissioner of Education.
2. Gabel, p. 775.
3. O'Gorman, pp. 317 ff. See Bouscaren, *Digest,* I, 443, for Vatican instructions on church ownership in the United States.
4. *Catholic Almanac,* 1957, p. 473.
5. Deferrari, *Vital,* p. 70.
6. *Ibid.,* p. 138.
7. Deferrari, *Essays,* p. 68.
8. Moehlman discusses the historical background in his *The Church as Educator,* and in his *School and Church: The American Way.* The latter has an excellent Bibliography. See also Pfeffer; Thayer's three works; and, for the standard Catholic interpretations, Burns, Gabel, and Campbell.
9. Canon 1374, Bouscaren and Ellis, p. 704; *Catholic Almanac,* 1957, p. 473.
10. From an unpublished thesis of the Catholic University of America, 1938, by Father Edward C. Bauer, "Educational Costs in Some Midwestern Parochial Elementary Schools." *Time,* in a news story September 20, 1941, estimated that only eleven dioceses enforced the "no absolution" rule strictly.
11. Leo XIII, as quoted by Pius XI, *Five Encyclicals,* p. 60.
12. *Five Encyclicals,* pp. 40, 41, and 48.
13. *New York Times,* January 13, 1930.
14. *Ibid.,* March 3, 1947.
15. *Register,* July 7, 1947.
16. Creusen summarizes all Canon Law on the subject. Bouscaren and Ellis, p. 274, interpret Canon 580? as meaning that "whatever the religious acquires by his industry or personal activity" belongs to the institute, even Christmas presents given to a teacher by her pupils. Fanfani is short and excellent.
17. Deferrari, *Essays,* p. 26.
18. Campbell, p. 66.

19. *Boston Pilot,* June 19, 1948.
20. Canon 555. Boys are officially recruited later for the male religious orders, but the favorite age for recruitment for a seminary is fourteen, according to Father Herman Doerr, a vocation director for the Franciscans. (*Register,* July 31, 1955.)
21. Herbst, p. 60. See also the *Catholic Encyclopedia,* "Flagellants." St. Cesarius prescribed flagellation in his "Rules for Virgins"; and some rules for flagellation were approved by early Church councils.
22. Pp. 2, 27, and 43; published by Newman Bookshop, Westminster, Maryland, 1943.
23. *America,* April 27, 1957, article by Father Neil McCluskey. For earlier discussion on "Fewer Girls Become Nuns," see *America,* April 4, 1941. In September, 1956, the Catholic diocesan superintendent of Sacramento announced that five new school buildings would stand idle for lack of teaching Sisters.
24. *St. Joseph's Magazine,* November, 1956; *Catholic Encyclopedia Supplement,* "Nuns"; *Register,* February 20, 1955, and August 12, 1956.
25. The parochial-school statistics are taken from Bauer, *op. cit.,* note 10, and they cover five elementary schools in Indianapolis in 1937.
26. *Register,* January 24, 1954.
27. *America,* April 27, 1957 (McCluskey); and an unpublished M.A. thesis, Catholic University of America, 1951, "Revenue Procurement in Catholic Schools," by Father Joseph I. Bernardin.
28. Archbishop John F. O'Hara of Philadelphia estimated in 1957 that the Catholic "free gift to public schools" was $1,400,525,036. To reach this figure he multiplied the cost per pupil in public schools for the 1953-54 school year by the estimated Catholic elementary and high-school enrollment. (*Register,* September 1, 1957.) In Ward, p. 184, Bernard Kohlbrenner, professor of the history of education at Notre Dame, estimated that the American Catholic Church actually spends about $200,000,000 annually on its schools. These estimates support the thesis that the Church does not spend even one-third as much on education per pupil as the public schools.
29. See *National Education Association Research Bulletin,* February, 1946. One reason the word "equivalent" is interpreted loosely is that handicapped children must often receive training at home.
30. Gabel, p. 754.
31. Deferrari, *Essays,* p. 241.
32. Campbell, p. 69.
33. Deferrari, *supra.*
34. *The National Catholic Educational Association Bulletin,* XXXIV, p. 396.
35. Published by Bruce Publishing Company, Milwaukee, 1944. Permission to quote denied by publisher in letter of September 3, 1948.
36. *The National Catholic Educational Association Bulletin,* 1942, p. 193.
37. The approved Catholic sources of the eleven statements are as follows, many of them referred to elsewhere in this volume and explained in detail: (1) Enunciated by Pius IX, July 18, 1870, summarized in *Encyclopedia Britannica* article on "Infallibility," and expounded in *No Pope Can Be Wrong in Teaching Doctrine,* by Martin J. Scott, S.J.

(2) Sheen, chap. 10. (3) *National Catholic Almanac*, 1948, p. 253. (4) Louis Veuillot, *The Liberal Illusion*, p. 10. (5) Leo XIII, *Scholastic Philosophy*, text in Maritain, p. 224. (6) Agar, p. viii. (7) Canon 1118, Bouscaren and Ellis, p. 547; see also Joyce. (8) *The Catholic Action Manual*, p. 106; *What is Catholic Action?* by Father James J. O'Toole, Paulist Press, pp. 14-15. (9) Canon 1399, Bouscaren and Ellis, p. 726; Betten, p. 58. (10) Leo XIII, *Christian Constitution of States*, Husslein, Vol. I; and Cardinal Spellman, in the *New York Times*, March 13, 1940. (11) *Five Encyclicals*, pp. 40, 41, and 48, Pius XI on *Christian Education of Youth*.

38. *Social Doctrine in Action*, p. 175.
39. Deferrari, *Essays*, p. 89.
40. *Catholic Educational Review*, May, 1954.
41. P. 381.
42. *Providence Evening Bulletin*, October 31, 1947. Not to be confused with President George N. Shuster of Hunter College.

Chapter 5

Public Schools and Public Money

1. Permission for quotation granted by America Press. This 1937 pamphlet is now out of print.
2. P. 98.
3. *Catholic Education*, June, 1947.
4. This has been established by many studies of crime and juvenile delinquency, but it would be wrong to say that Catholicism is primarily responsible. Poverty and bad housing affect the lives of Catholic workers as well as others in our large cities. Professor Edwin H. Sutherland in his *Principles of Criminology*, p. 194, says: "In America the Baptists and the Catholics have the highest rate of commitment to the prisons which report religious affiliation. This is apparently explained by the fact that most of the Negroes are Baptists and most of the recent immigrants are Catholics." Catholic pre-eminence in the field of crime and juvenile delinquency is notable in our Northern cities, especially in New York. A study, *Crime and Religion*, by Father Leo Kalmer, Franciscan Herald Press, Chicago, 1936, showed that the rate of Catholic criminals committed to prisons in twenty-eight states was about twice that of the Catholic proportion in the population. See Leo H. Lehmann, *The Catholic Church and Public Schools*, Agora Publishing Co. Bishop Gallagher of Detroit declared in 1936, according to the *New York Times* of December 8, 1936: "It is a matter of serious reproach to the Church that more Catholic boys, in proportion to the total number, get into trouble than those of any other denomination. One-fifth of the people of Michigan are Catholics, but 50 per cent of the boys in the Industrial School for Boys at Lansing are Catholics." Father Harold E. Keller, writing in *The National Catholic Educational Association Bulletin*, XXXV, 447, while deploring the fact that the Catholic prison population is out of all proportion to the general

Catholic population, argued that within the Catholic group itself boys who had attended the parochial school had a better chance to stay out of prison than Catholic boys who had attended public school. Actually, I believe that the Catholic hierarchy is responsible for the appalling Catholic crime record in only one respect: the priests encourage over-sized families by their unrealistic policy on birth control, and unwanted and underprivileged children of such families naturally drift from neglect to delinquency.

5. *No Wall Between God and the Child,* National Catholic Welfare Conference, 1947, p. 5.

6. *Federal Aid for American Education* (pamphlet), National Catholic Educational Association.

7. *Senate Hearings on Federal Aid to Education,* p. 245 (April 25, 1947).

8. *42nd Annual Report,* National Catholic Educational Association, August, 1945.

9. October 3, 1925.

10. Pius XI, *Five Encyclicals,* p. 43, said: "Again it is the inalienable right as well as the indispensable duty of the Church, to watch over the entire education of her children, in all institutions, public or private, not merely in regard to the religious instruction there given, but in regard to every other branch of learning and every regulation in so far as religion and morality are concerned. Nor should the exercise of this right be considered undue interference, but rather maternal care on the part of the Church in protecting her children from the grave danger of all kinds of doctrinal and moral evil."

11. All quotations are from Chapter XII, "The Public School Teacher."

12. *Newark Evening News,* April 12, 1943.

13. *Time,* October 22, 1945; see also Dr. Stoddard's *Krebiozen; The Great Cancer Mystery,* Beacon Press, 1955.

14. April 3, 1948.

15. Maine and North Carolina are nominally the exceptions, but even these states have laws which can be construed as limiting certain types of tax expenditure to public schools only. Some states have statutes which prohibit state funds from being used for sectarian purposes, but not local funds.

16. *N.E.A. Research Bulletin,* "The State and Sectarian Education," p. 36. *The United States News and World Report,* December 2, 1955, in a long summary, listed six states as granting free nonreligious textbooks to parochial schools, and twenty-one as granting some tax support for parochial-school buses, but among the twenty-one were several states which sharply limit the transportation appropriations, e.g., to pupils who live along public bus routes.

17. *Everson vs. Bd. of Education of Township of Ewing,* 330 U. S. 1.

18. *Congressional Record,* Senate, October 12, 1943, p. 96.

19. *Senate Hearings* (see note 7), pp. 31 ff.

20. Father McManus told a Senate committee (*ibid.,* p. 240) that "it is a fact for the record that the educational bills which have passed Congress are those which provided funds for the direct or indirect aid of both public and private educational institutions, and the bills which died, Congress after Congress, are those which were discriminatory and

unjust in their failure to count the children in non-public schools among the beneficiaries of the Federal Government's assistance."

21. Father MaManus was quoted in *America*, April 26, 1947, as saying that "Catholic educators will never permit the Federal Government to treat parochial school children as stepchildren, as second-class citizens."
22. *Senate Hearings, op. cit.*
23. *Illinois ex rel. McCollum vs. Board of Education*, 333 U. S. 203.
24. *New York Times*, November 21, 1948.
25. *Christianity and Crisis*, July 5, 1948.
26. *Zorach vs. Clauson*, 343 U. S. 306.
27. See my *Communism, Democracy and Catholic Power.*
28. *Kansas City Star*, April 9, 1957.
29. Brooklyn *Tablet*, November 3, 1951.
30. Bouscaren and Ellis, p. 574.
31. This statement is carried annually in the *Catholic Almanac*, e.g., for 1957, p. 476.
32. By Father John D. Davis.
33. Brooklyn *Tablet*, December 15, 1956; and for Father Blum's addition, *United States News and World Report*, October 25, 1957.
34. *New York Times*, July 12, 1948.
35. Deferrari, *Essays*, p. 30.
36. *Harfst vs. Hogan*, 349 Mo. 808.
37. Personal letter.
38. The report of the N.E.A.'s commission which investigated the North College Hill case was summarized in the *New York Times* of July 11, 1947, together with a statement by Father William McManus of the National Catholic Welfare Conference. See also *Time*, June 30, 1947; the *Christian Century*, May 28, 1947; and Brooklyn *Tablet*, January 24, 1948.
39. *Christian Herald*, February, 1948. A Catholic teacher's defense was published in *America*, November 27, 1948. Pfeffer, pp. 455 ff., has the best legal and factual summary. The case was *Zellers vs. Huff*, 55 N. M. 501; 236 Pac. 2d 949 (1951). The renewal of the battle is described in the *New York Times*, April 17, 1955.
40. See the *Christian Century*, November 3, 1954, "A Kentucky Village Casts a Long Shadow," by Harold E. Fey; and *Church and State Review* (various) from 1953 to date. In the Kentucky case of *Wooley vs. Spalding* the Catholic officials lost, and the courts ordered a new central high school for Marion County, not under Catholic control, but in the contemporaneous case of *Rawlings vs. Butler* the Kentucky court held that nuns could teach in public schools in garb, if qualified. See *Louisville Courier-Journal*, June 23, 1956.
41. The Maine story was in almost all American dailies March 5 and 6, 1957; and in the *Church and State Review*, April and May, 1957. The first legal case, won by plaintiffs, was that of *Squires vs. City of Augusta.*
42. Brooklyn *Tablet*, June 1, 1957.
43. Ward, p. 183.
44. O'Brien, *Catholics and Scholarship*, p. 158.
45. *Ibid.*, p. 182.

46. *America,* January 31, 1948.
47. P. 44.
48. *Catholic School Journal,* June, 1956.
49. Deferrari, *Vital,* p. 109. The Harvard comparison was made by Father John Tracy Ellis, *Register,* September 1, 1957.
50. *America,* April 3, 1948, p. iv, supplement.
51. March 6, 1948.

Chapter 6

The Church and Medicine

1. For his review of the original form of this and the succeeding chapter, I am grateful to one of America's greatest pioneers in medicine and maternal health, the late Robert Latou Dickinson, former president of the American Gynecological Society.
2. Connell, p. 116.
3. See O'Malley, pp. 32 and 39; and *Abortion* by Frederick J. Taussig, M.D., 1936, p. 400.
4. Bowdern, p. 8. (Permission for quotations granted by the Queen's Work, St. Louis.)
5. *Catholic Register,* October 3, 1948. But this extreme care about human souls does not apply in any way to animals. F. A. Westermarck pointed out in his *Christianity and Morals,* p. 389, that "Pope Pius IX refused a request for permission to form in Rome a Society for Prevention of Cruelty to Animals on the professed ground that it was a theological error to suppose that man owes any duty to an animal."
6. Connell, p. 120.
7. *Five Encyclicals,* p. 95.
8. Davis, II, 138.
9. Finney, p. 60. (Permission for quotations granted by B. Herder Book Company.)
10. *Time,* May 31, 1948; and *Catholic News,* May 29, 1948.
11. O'Malley, pp. 250 ff.
12. Medicus, pp. 571 and 536.
13. *State vs. Rudman,* 126 Me. 177; 136 A. 817 and 819.
14. *Reference Manual for Medical Ethics,* p. 34.
15. Davis, II, 165.
16. McFadden, p. 151. (Permission for quotations granted by F. A. Davis Company.)
17. Brooklyn *Tablet,* January 17, 1948.
18. *American Journal of Obstetrics and Gynecology,* XLVIII, 892.
19. McFadden, p. 203. This principle was also embodied in a "Motu proprio" published in *Acta Apostolicae Sedis,* August 15, 1948, p. 305, to come into force June 1, 1949.
20. Bowdern, p. 8.
21. See Davis, IV, 129.
22. Beck, pp. 44 and 45.
23. McFadden, pp. 204 and 205.

24. *Ibid.,* p. 208.
25. Beck, p. 47.
26. McFadden, p. 260.
27. Healy, p. 400. This 1956 work, with the Imprimatur of Cardinal Stritch, has the entire Catholic Hospital Code, and also that of the American Medical Association.
28. *New York Times,* September 2, 1944, and February 8, 1945.
29. De Guchteneere, p. 99.
30. *Catholic Mind,* January 22, 1939.
31. Brooklyn *Tablet,* March 2, 1957.
32. The rule against cremation, contained in Canon 1203, goes so far that relatives are instructed to disregard any request for it in a will, and those who have ordered their bodies cremated are deprived of ecclesiastical burial. See Bouscaren and Ellis, pp. 607 and 625.
33. II, 146. For a contrary view, see article by F. W. Rice, M. D., *Homiletic and Pastoral Review,* August, 1935.
34. P. 221.
35. See Alfred S. Beck, *Obstetrical Practice,* Baltimore, 1942, p. 511; and E. Schumann, *Extrauterine Pregnancy,* Philadelphia, 1921, p. 18. If this ratio is applied to the Catholic baptisms in the United States, and one in fifty mothers die, the total of such deaths is nintey-two annually.
36. *Church and State Review,* September, 1956.
37. *Bradfield vs. Roberts,* 175 U. S. 291. See Pfeffer, p. 176.

Chapter 7

Sex, Birth Control, and Eugenics

1. Davis I, 182. For the following quotations, pp. 178 and 182. An Anglican journal has commented that the "fear of sex . . . has always been an element in Roman Catholicism."
2. See "The Church and Castration" in *New Problems in Medical Ethics,* edited by Dom Peter Flood. The eleventh edition of the *Encyclopedia Britannica,* "Eunuch," said that castrated boys "remained the musical glory and moral shame of the papal choir till the accession of Pope Leo XIII, one of whose first acts was to get rid of them."
3. *Encyclopedia Britannica,* 14th edition, "Celibacy." See also Lea's monumental work on the subject.
4. Gibbons, referring to Matt. 19:27; also contains references to virgin angels. Brunini (Imprimatur Spellman), p. 199, says "virginity is instinctive in the hearts of men."
5. P. 79.
6. McFadden, pp. 136-137.
7. Decree of the Holy Office, August 2, 1929
8. *New York Times,* November 19, 1950.
9. Brooklyn *Tablet,* August 29, 1953.
10. *Five Encyclicals,* p. 56.

11. See Himes, p. 167; and article by John A. Ryan on St. Thomas Aquinas in *Encyclopedia of the Social Sciences.*
12. February, 1938.
13. *Five Encyclicals,* p. 93.
14. *Jewish Encyclopedia,* V, 336.
15. The survey of doctors' opinions was made by Dr. Alan A. Gutmacher of Johns Hopkins. The American Medical Association in 1937 adopted unanimously a report of its Committee to Study Contraceptives, favoring the teaching of contraception in medical schools. See the publications of the Planned Parenthood Federation of America, 501 Madison Ave., New York.
16. I, 46. More conservatively, Dr. Halbert L. Dunn, chief of statisticians for vital statistics, of the Bureau of Census, estimated roughly 350,000 abortions in 1940, or 13.7 abortions per 100 live births, of which one-third to one-half were spontaneous. Special Report, Vol. 15, No. 39, p. 431.
17. P. 34. Queen's Work, St. Louis.
18. P. 13. Paulist Press. Equally illuminating is *Suicide Bent: Sangerizing Mankind* by David Goldstein (a Jewish convert), Radio Replies Press, St. Paul, 1945, Imprimatur Archbishop Cushing.
19. Leo J. Latz, M.D., *The Rhythm of Sterility and Fertility in Women,* 1944, Chicago, 6th ed., 300th thousand, "Published with Ecclesiastical Approval."
20. However, a study, "The Contraceptive Safe Period," by Fleck, Snedeker, and Rock, *New England Journal of Medicine,* CCIII (1940), 1005, concludes that "the safe-period method constitutes a workable form of contraception for a selected group of women." Dr. Dickinson's *Techniques of Conception Control,* obtainable by physicians from the Planned Parenthood Federation of America, discusses all methods of contraception. Priestly ignorance on this subject is indicated by the fact that as late as 1928 medical textbooks used in Catholic seminaries, and written by priests, were giving the young priests information for use in the confessional that was flatly contrary to medical knowledge. Medicus, p. 627, says: "Moreover the woman usually has intense sexual feelings immediately before, during, and immediately after the menstrual period. Conception is most liable during these days. . . ."
21. Latz, *supra.*
22. See *The Churchman,* December 1, 1948, for Professor Sax's description of the 1948 Massachusetts campaign. The Springfield story was mentioned in the *Catholic Almanac,* 1948, p. 771.
23. August 25, 1938.
24. Margaret Sanger, *Autobiography,* pp. 301 ff.
25. *Our Sunday Visitor,* October 2, 1938.
26. See article by Cornelius P. Trowbridge, *New Republic,* January 22, 1945.
27. *New York Times,* January 15, 1953. Other portions of the story were in the *Times,* May 8, 1953, and February 7, 1956.
28. *Ibid.,* August 31, 1955.
29. *Washington Post,* May 1 and 2, 1957.
30. Brooklyn *Tablet.* October 20, 1956.

31. Typical is the statement of Frederick Osborn in his *Preface to Eugenics,* p. 157: "Voluntary control of size of family is essential to any broad program of eugenics in a democracy. And voluntary control is possible only in proportion as birth control is widely available." "If man is determined to control his death rate," says Warren S. Thompson in his *Population Problems,* "there is only one enduring solution of the problem of differential national pressures of population. It is birth control."

32. *New York Times,* May 27 and 28, 1957. Professor Kingsley Davis of the University of California estimated in the *Times* of September 22, 1957, that the world's population will be nearly 13 billion by 2050 if the present rate of increase continues.

33. See Sax; *The Next Hundred Years* by Harrison Brown, James Bonner, and John Weir, Viking, 1957; and the excellent publication *Population Bulletin* of the Population Reference Bureau, 1507 M St., N. W., Washington 5, D. C.

34. Worcester (Massachusetts) *Telegram,* April 25, 1941.

35. Brunini, p. 213.

36. Brooklyn *Tablet,* May 20, 1948.

37. *Congressional Record,* May 13, 1957, p. A 3618.

38. *The Churchman,* November 1, 1947.

39. De Guchteneere, p. 99.

40. P. 31. Queen's Work, St. Louis, 22nd printing, 1946. (Permission for quotations granted by the publisher.)

41. *Five Encyclicals,* p. 96.

42. Bouscaren and Ellis, p. 679.

43. *Buck vs. Bell,* 274 U. S. 200. Justice Holmes is alleged to have said, after his famous sentence, "Three generations of imbeciles are enough," "Pierce Butler dissenting"—under his breath.

44. See the brilliant discussion of this whole field in Glanville Williams; and for counter opinions, Reverend Ignatius Cox, S.J., *The Folly of Human Sterilization,* Paulist Press.

45. Donald C. Kaump, M.D., and Alphonse M. Schwitalla, S.J., "Some Medical and Moral Aspects of the Rh Factor," *The Linacre Quarterly,* January, 1947—official journal of the Federation of Catholic Physicians' Guilds. (Permission for quotations granted by the publisher.) Dr. Philip Levine told the American Medical Association (*New York Herald-Tribune,* January 8, 1948) that about 13 per cent of all marriages are of the mismatched blood type. *The American Journal of Public Health,* February, 1946, p. 105, places the number of stillbirths or child deaths as a result of this factor at approximately 1 in 380.

46. Baron, p. 101. One state in Mexico, Tabasco, decreed for several years that no priest could enter the state unless he was married. Benedict XV, sensing the criticism of celibacy within the Church, went out of his way on three occasions to reaffirm it. "We solemnly testify," he said in an allocution on December 16, 1920, "that the Holy See will never in any way mitigate, much less abolish, this most sacred and most salutary law." Bouscaren, *Digest,* I, 120.

47. *Register,* May 19, 1957.

Chapter 8
Marriage, Divorce, and Annulment

1. The standard Papal discussion of Catholic marriage is Pius XI's *Christian Marriage, Five Encyclicals,* p. 77. Bouscaren and Ellis, chaps. XII to XV inclusive, summarize Catholic law on the subject; and Doheny, Vols. I and II, summarizes the procedure. Bouscaren, *Digest,* is indispensable for cases, and Joyce and Smith give standard Catholic opinions.
2. Joyce, p. 136; and Canon 1099, Bouscaren and Ellis, p. 527.
3. P. 209. Smith, II, 1069, says: "A vital consequence follows from the fact that the marriage of Christians is a sacrament—namely, that everything pertaining to it must be regulated by the Church."
4. Ryan and Millar, p. 50.
5. Woywod, p. 21; Bouscaren and Ellis, p. 431.
6. P. 209.
7. In 1852 in *Acerbissimum.* He also expressed the sentiment in less violent language in his *Syllabus* in 1864. See Schaff, pp. 573 ff.
8. Catholic law treats marriage before a Protestant minister as a more serious sin than marriage before a justice of the peace. Both forms of marriage are invalid for Catholics; but there is no ecclesiastical penalty for civil marriage, whereas the Catholic who marries before a non-Catholic minister incurs excommunication under Canon 2319; Bouscaren and Ellis, p. 463.
9. Orthodox Jewish rabbis are sometimes unwilling to marry Jews to non-Jews, but the Jew who marries outside the synagogue is not penalized or ostracized, and there is no rule on the subject binding all rabbis; nor is there any rule excluding the nonconformist Jew from burial on synagogue grounds.
10. Canon 1060. Woywod, p. 214. See Bouscaren and Ellis, pp. 476 ff., for discussion of Canons 1070 and 1071, barring marriages with Jews because of "disparity of cult." Some authorities (e.g., Smith, II, 1082) use the phrase "difference of worship" to describe the impediment barring marriage to a Jew, and the phrase "mixed religion" for the impediment barring marriage to a Protestant.
11. *New York Times,* March 28, 1957; *Washington Post,* April 27, 1957.
12. *Aids to Will Training in Christian Education,* Frederick Pustet Company, New York, 1943, p. 200.
13. Father Daniel Lord, S.J., in his *Questions I'm Asked About Marriage,* Queen's Work, St. Louis, p. 42, says: "Before a Catholic can marry a Jew permission must be obtained, not from the bishop, but from Rome." See also Bouscaren, *Digest,* I, 181, and II, 31. The rule requires the couple to make an offering, if possible, "proportionate to their means," to be sent to the Congregation of the Holy Office. In practice the Apostolic Delegate may grant the special permission "from Rome."
14. O'Brien, *Faith,* p. 290.
15. *Mixed Marriage,* p. 16, Agora Publishing Co., New York.
16. Probably the best legal summary of this principle is "Religion in the

Upbringing of Children," by Leo Pfeffer, *Boston University Law Review,* June, 1955. In a recent Iowa case, *Lynch vs. Uhlenhopp,* the Iowa Supreme Court refused to enforce a stipulation in a divorce decree which provided that "the said child shall be raised in the Roman Catholic religion."

17. Professor Kane's article was in *The Voice of St. Jude,* June, 1957, and reported in the *Register,* June 16, 1957. The most complete treatment of mixed-marriage problems from the Catholic point of view is Thomas, since he summarizes many studies made by other persons. Annual statistics of *priestly* mixed marriages by dioceses are published annually in the *Official Catholic Directory,* but not summarized. The 1956 *Directory* showed that almost one-fourth of all priestly marriages of Catholics were with non-Catholics—84,720 out of 324,907. However, official figures rarely include the marriages of Catholics with non-Catholics by non-Catholic clergymen and government officials, since these are rated as "no marriages" by the priests. These "invalid" marriages are, to use the words of Father Thomas, "surprisingly high"; in one study they constituted almost 40 per cent of mixed marriages in 132 parishes. *Ave Maria,* November 24, 1956, admits that the number of these "invalid" mixed marriages may be almost as large as the priestly mixed marriages. See also Father Peter Bernardino, "Catholic Loss Through Mixed Marriage," *Homiletic and Pastoral Review,* XXXIV, 1267.

18. *Register,* November 25, 1956.

19. *Homiletic and Pastoral Review,* October, 1934.

20. *American Weekly,* November 11, 1956.

21. One study (*Register,* November 25, 1956) indicates a divorce rate three times higher for mixed marriages. See Thomas, p. 159; *Ave Maria,* November 24, 1956; and also, for a treatment of the whole problem of interfaith marriages, *One Marriage, Two Faiths,* by James H. S. Bossard and Eleanor S. Boll.

22. Canon 1118.

23. The "hard" passages are Mark 10:2-12 and Luke 16:18; the more liberal passages are Matt. 5:31-32 and 19:3-12.

24. Connell, p. 169.

25. P. 231.

26. Connell, p. 30.

27. See *New York Times,* December 5, 1948, and January 29, 1956.

28. Bouscaren and Ellis, p. 462, argue that the antenuptial promises demanded in mixed marriages concerning the rearing of the children as Catholics are enforceable in the Domestic Relations Courts, and they cite *Ramon vs. Ramon,* 34 N.Y. Supp. 2nd series, p. 100. See Father Robert J. White, *Canonical Ante-Nuptial Promises and the Civil Law,* Catholic University of America, 1934.

29. See letter of Dean Kenneth D. Johnson of the New York School for Social Work, *New York Times,* October 29, 1955.

30. *New York Times,* May 24, 1957.

31. *America,* June 8, 1957.

32. *Christianity and Crisis,* June 24, 1957.

33. *Boston Herald,* April 29, 1957.

34. July 8, 1957.

35. *Marriage, Human or Divine*, 1940, Paulist Press, Imprimatur Spellman, p. 39. The appropriate canons are 1120-1124. See also Francis J. Burton, *A Commentary on Canon 1125*, Catholic University of America.
36. Canons 1990-1992, Woywod, p. 329; *Catholic Encyclopedia Supplement*, Courts. See Doheny, II, 581, for appropriate portions of the Instruction of the Sacred Congregation of the Sacraments of August 15, 1936, which is now the basis for procedure.
37. Davis, IV, 98. Bouscaren and Ellis, p. 426, list thirteen diriment impediments which are sufficient to nullify a marriage.
38. Reverend Adolph Marx, *The Declaration of Nullity of Marriages Contracted Outside the Church*, Catholic University of America, 1943.
39. Text in *ibid.;* translation in *The Converted Catholic Magazine*, January, 1947.
40. Canon 1138.
41. Canon 1075 says: "The following persons cannot validly contract marriage: 1. Persons who, during the existence of the same lawful marriage, have consummated adultery together and have mutually promised each other to marry, or have attempted marriage by a mere civil act . . ." Bouscaren and Ellis, p. 484.
42. This "conservative guess" is based on the estimate that there are one-tenth as many voidable marriages among Catholics as full priestly marriages, and that there are 333,138 priestly marriages a year. See discussion above.
43. Doheny, II, 676.
44. The cases described in this paragraph are summarized in Bouscaren, *Digest*, II, 311, 312, and 308 respectively.
45. See *ibid.*, I, 536 for case.
46. Holy Office, November 5, 1924; Bouscaren, *Digest*, I, 553.
47. For a discussion of the effects of the Tametsi of the Council of Trent and the Ne Temere decree of 1908, see Davis, IV, 193-194; and L. H. Lehmann, *Mixed Marriage*.
48. April 8, 1947.
49. *Register*, September 18, 1949.
50. Bouscaren, *Digest*, I, 536.
51. *Ibid.*, p. 523.
52. Doheny, II, 677.

Chapter 9

Censorship and Boycott

1. *London Times Literary Supplement*, October 28, 1949.
2. *Catholic Encyclopedia*, V, 681; and Canons 1173-1175.
3. Betten, pp. 61 ff.; Michael Williams, pp. 107 ff.
4. P. 94.
5. Bouscaren and Ellis, pp. 711 ff.
6. Davis II, 418 ff. More detailed rules are published annually in the *Catholic Almanac*.

7. Bouscaren, *Digest,* I, 610; see also p. 476 for the rule concerning young Religious.
8. *New York Times,* July 11, 1954.
9. Wall, p. 105.
10. *New York Times,* October 3, 1946.
11. *America,* October 1, 1949.
12. *Ibid.,* December 28, 1946.
13. *The Churchman,* March 1, 1945.
14. De la Bedoyere, p. 163. (Permission for quotations granted by The Macmillan Company.)
15. *New York Times,* June 15, 1948.
16. June 19, 1948.
17. October 23, 1944.
18. *Time,* February 15, 1937.
19. Brooklyn *Tablet,* June 19, 1954.
20. *Boston American,* April 24, 1941.
21. *America,* February 11, 1928.
22. *The Christian Century,* July 24, 1946.
23. Brooklyn *Tablet,* June 20, 1953.
24. *Catholic Almanac,* 1955, p. 718.
25. *The New Yorker,* October 30, 1948.
26. *The Nation,* January 11, 1947.
27. Annual summaries of the lists of the Legion of Decency are obtainable from 35 East 51st St., New York; and weekly lists are published in virtually all diocesan papers. See also "How Should Priests Direct People Regarding the Movies" by Francis J. Connell, *American Ecclesiastical Review,* April, 1946.
28. *Burstyn vs. Wilson,* 343 U. S. 495.
29. *New York Times,* January 14, 1956.
30. Brooklyn *Tablet,* June 1, 1957; *The Churchman,* May 15, 1955.
31. The background of federal government policy is outlined in the report of the Federal Communications Commission, March 7, 1946. See also the *Crozier Quarterly,* October, 1947, "Religious Radio in the United States," by Reverend Charles H. Schmitz.
32. *Catholic Almanac,* 1948, p. 737.
33. Brooklyn *Tablet,* March 20, 1948; other details are given in the *Catholic News,* February 14, 1948.
34. *New York Times,* August 24, 1948.
35. *The Commonweal,* April 23, 1948.
36. *Books on Trial,* June-July, 1956.

Chapter 10

Science, Scholarship, and Superstition

1. Martin J. Scott, S.J., *Science Helps the Church,* 1945, p. 8, Imprimatur Spellman.
2. *Five Encyclicals,* p. 53.
3. Bernhart, p. 417.

4. For this and much other valuable material I am indebted to Professor Conrad H. Moehlman of Rochester.
5. *Register*, July 7, 1957.
6. Schaff, p. 486. See also Kirby Page, *Jesus and Christianity*, p. 167.
7. Brooklyn *Tablet*, July 31, 1948.
8. Bernhart, pp. 424 ff.
9. Published by Macmillan, 1947.
10. See *Homiletic and Pastoral Review*, September, 1934, for rules concerning miracles and sainthood.
11. *Register*, August 3, 1947.
12. *New York Times*, July 7, 1946.
13. *Catholic News*, January 8, 1948.
14. Brooklyn *Tablet*, July 11, 1956.
15. *Catholic Almanac*, 1957, p. 57.
16. October, 1928.
17. Bouscaren, *Digest*, I, 596.
18. *Catholic Encyclopedic Dictionary*. See also *Lourdes and Modern Miracles* by Francis Woodlock, S.J., Paulist Press.
19. *Catholic Encyclopedia Supplement, Humani Generis*.
20. Article by Father Alfred C. Rush.
21. *Time*, March 22, 1954.
22. Sheen, p. 204.
23. Walsh, p. 213.
24. See *Vision of Fatima* by Thomas McGlynn, Little, Brown, 1948.
25. Brooklyn *Tablet*, September 4, 1948.
26. *New York Times*, June 10, 1948.
27. The Holy Office on April 26, 1947, forbade Catholics to participate or assist at any spiritualistic affair "even such as appear to be blameless." Bouscaren, *Digest*, I, 155.
28. P. viii.
29. *Register*, April 12, 1953.
30. August 13, 1953.
31. *National Catholic Educational Association Bulletin*, August, 1940.
32. Deferrari, *Vital*, p. 189.
33. P. 11 (Macmillan).
34. P. 28. (Permission for quotations granted by the National Catholic Welfare Conference.)
35. Husslein, I, 263.
36. Letter to the Archbishop of Munich, Gasparri, p. 332.
37. *Converted Catholic Magazine*, February, 1944.
38. P. 216.
39. Professor Sidney Hook wrote a candid description of this type of philosophical compromise in *The Humanist*, Autumn, 1942. The Catholic point of view of St. Thomas is set forth in Maritain.
40. *The Things That Are Not Caesar's*, p. 74.
41. P. 106.
42. P. 181.
43. *Register*, May 13, 1956.
44. *Catholic Traditions in American Democracy* by C. Smith, Jr., and Virginia Ryan, p. 6. See also Garrison, p. 167; and Father John C. Rager,

Political Philosophy of Blessed Cardinal Bellarmine, Catholic University of America, 1926.

45. Pp. 601 and 618. (Permission for quotations granted by Benziger Brothers.)
46. From *The Younger American Scholar,* quoted by Ellis, *American Catholics and the Intellectual Life,* p. 54.
47. *America,* August 3, 1946.

Chapter 11

Fascism, Communism, and Labor

1. *New York Herald-Tribune,* June 28, 1940.
2. *New York Times,* February 16 and 24, and March 11 and 14, 1948.
3. *Life,* April 19, 1948, showed a picture of this.
4. *America,* February 12, 1949.
5. Teeling, *Pius XI.*
6. *Five Encyclicals,* pp. 157-158. *The Catholic Encyclopedia Supplement,* p. 585, credits Pius XI with converting Mussolini from socialism "into a patriot and supporter of the House of Savoy."
7. Binchy, p. 85.
8. See pp. 61 to 70.
9. *Essays of a Catholic,* p. 242.
10. *Religion and the Modern State,* p. 134, Sheed and Ward, 1935.
11. Full text in T. E. Moore; portions and discussion in my *Communism, Democracy and Catholic Power.*
12. This quotation is taken from a valuable article by William Attwood, *The Nation,* August 28, 1948.
13. *New York Times,* June 6, 1936.
14. *Christian Crisis,* p. 87, by permission of The Macmillan Company. George N. Shuster, in describing the Vatican-Hitler Concordat in *The Commonweal,* September 1, 1933, said: "Accordingly we may sum up by saying that the Church has pledged itself not to interfere with the progress of Fascism in Germany."
15. *Five Encyclicals,* p. 151.
16. *New York Times,* August 10, 1947.
17. *The Secret Diary of Harold L. Ickes,* II, 390.
18. P. 75. (Copyright by Emmet John Hughes; permission for quotations granted by Henry Holt and Company.)
19. *Christian Crisis,* p. 101.
20. Pierre van Paassen, *Days of Our Years,* p. 470. See also pp. 425 ff. for an account of the Church and Franco in Spain's civil war.
21. P. 276.
22. II, 1424 and 1493; University of California Press, 1948.
23. Text in Bouscaren, *Digest,* II, 11 ff.
24. *Boston American,* April 24, 1941.
25. Brooklyn *Tablet,* October 23, 1948.
26. January 4, 1947.

27. Excerpts from M. Bérard's report were published in the *London Jewish Chronicle*, November 8, 1946, and later in *The Day* of New York, December 28, 1947. This material is available in a booklet, *Centuries of Intolerance*, by James M. Freeman, Agora Publishing Company, New York.
28. March, 1947.
29. Brooklyn *Tablet*, December 21, 1953.
30. *Crusade for Pan-Europe*, 1943, p. 173. (Permission for quotations granted by G. P. Putnam's Sons.)
31. *Reason, Social Myths and Democracy*, Day, 1940, p. 76.
32. *Christianity and Crisis*, November 1, 1948, from the Catholic weekly, *De Linie*.
33. *Five Encyclicals*, pp. 177 ff.
34. *New York Times*, November 6, 1947.
35. *Catholic News*, June 26, 1948.
36. See *Time*, December 20, 1954.
37. Brooklyn *Tablet*, May 18, 1957.
38. November 12, 1946. But see *Time*, July 8, 1957, for recent European Catholic anti-socialist policies, including the ruling by the Dutch hierarchy that Catholics may not even listen to socialist radio network programs regularly without risking the denial of the sacraments.
39. *Register*, June 16, 1957, and *New York Times*, April 4, 1957. The hierarchy's pastoral letters were later interpreted, in the *Times*, September 8, 1957, as "a clearcut signal to all Catholics to vote for Chancellor Adenauer's party."
40. *Catholic Almanac*, 1955, p. 728.
41. See *Moral Problems of Interracial Marriage* by Father John F. Doherty, Catholic University Press, 1949. *Osservatore Romano*, October 17, 1955, said that "racial exclusion is a sin against the nature of Catholicism."
42. See *Catholic Action of the South*, August 18, 1957; the Baton Rouge *State Times*, August 8, 1957; *New York Times*, August 9, 1957; *New Orleans States*, February 24, 1956.
43. An excellent description of A.C.T.U. and its work is contained in an unpublished M.A. thesis of Columbia University, 1947, by Harold L. Wattel. See also "Priests, Workers, and Communists," *Harper's Magazine*, November, 1948; and *No Friend of Labor* (pamphlet), an attack on A.C.T.U., by James Morton Freeman, The Fulfillment Press, 350 West 26th St., New York.

Chapter 12

The Catholic Plan for America

1. First Catholic Amendment: (1) Spanish Law of Succession, and Art. I, Vatican-Italy Concordat of 1929, hereinafter called Concordat, official text in T. E. Moore. (2) Leo XIII, *Immortale Dei*, Husslein I, 70; and Art. 7, Italian Constitution of 1947. (3) Canon Law 2341, and S. Woywod, *Homiletic and Pastoral Review*, November, 1935. (4) Con-

cordat, Art. IV. (5) Spanish Bill of Rights, Art. IV; *Time,* November 24, 1947. (6) An enabling clause.
Second Catholic Amendment: (1) *Five Encyclicals,* p. 40. (2) Canons 1381 and 1382, and *Five Encyclicals,* p. 43. (3) *Five Encyclicals,* p. 49. (4) *Ibid.,* p. 60. (5) *Ibid.,* p. 60. (6) *Ibid.,* p. 50. (7) *Ibid.,* p. 57. (8) *Ibid.,* pp 41 and 49.
Third Catholic Amendment: (1) Concordat, Art. 7, approved by Pius XI, *Five Encyclicals,* p. 116. (2) Canon Law 1021; and S. Woywod, *Practical Commentary on the Code,* I, 559. (3) Woywod, p. 563. (4) *Five Encyclicals,* pp. 102 ff. (5) *Ibid.,* p. 101. (6) *Ibid.,* p. 93. (7) *Ibid.,* p. 95. (8) *Ibid.,* p. 96.

2. Father James J. O'Toole, *What is Catholic Action?* Paulist Press, 1940. Imprimatur Bishop of Toledo.
3. *Ibid.,* p. 6.
4. *The Catholic Action Manual,* p. 116. (Permission for quotations granted by Sheed and Ward.)
5. The 1948 *Catholic Almanac* (p. 440) says that a recent survey "shows that the Young Christian Workers have more than 50 cells operating successfully in 30 major cities throughout the United States general [labor-union] membership: approximately 1,500 workers, 280 of them cell leaders."
6. Richard Pattee in *America,* April 12, 1947. "A citizen of Quebec may secure a divorce by a special act of the Canadian Parliament, but the province itself has no divorce laws or divorce courts."
7. *Annuaire Statistique,* Quebec, p. 117, according to Chamberlin, gives $1041 as the average salary for teachers in Protestant elementary schools in Quebec, as against $400 in Catholic schools, in 1937-38. Bovey, p. 158, cites 1934-35 figures showing a corresponding average in rural schools of $350 and less than $200 respectively. See also "French Canada—Can it Survive?" by Miriam Chapin in *Harper's Magazine,* November, 1948.
8. Mason Wade's *The French Canadian Outlook* is an admirably succinct and readable review of the whole problem. His reference to Papal flags is on p. 32.
9. *America,* April 22, 1944. Probably the Catholic proportion in the total Canadian population is now about 45 per cent.
10. *Social Thought of French Canada,* M. A. Gaudreau, pp. 103-104, Catholic University of America, 1946.
11. Riddell, p. 83.
12. *Harper's* article, *supra.*
13. Bovey, p. 158.
14. A detailed description of the system is contained in *The Separate School Question in Canada,* George M. Weir, Ryerson Press, Toronto, 1934. The methods of the Church in capturing northern Ontario are described in *The Separate School System in Ontario,* obtainable from the Inter-Church Committee, 574 Christie St., Toronto. Other valuable critical discussions are those of Claris E. Silcox, *Protestant-Catholic Relations in Canada,* 1938, United Church Publishing House, Toronto; *Canada Must Choose,* by the same author, Ryerson Press, Toronto, 1944; and *Maclean's Magazine,* May 28, 1955.

15. William Teeling, *American Stew*, London, 1933, p. 191.
16. *New York Times*, September 28, 1947.
17. Gaudreau, *supra*, p. 185. Seldes, *Crisis*, discusses fascism in Canada.
18. Pp. 135-136. (Permission for quotations granted by the Viking Press.)
19. Detailed discussions of this problem are contained in Howard, in Barclay and in Mecham.
20. Latin text in *Roccolta di Concordati*, 1919, Vatican Press, p. 937. Mecham, p. 734, describes the 1852 Concordat with Guatemala.
21. August 3, 1941.
22. January 24, 1947.
23. Parkes's history is probably the best. See also Carleton Beals's fascinating *Mexican Maze*, especially his chapter "Church and State"; *Renascent Mexico*, edited by Hubert Herring and Herbert Weinstock; *Official Catholic Year Book* of 1928 for "Pastoral Letter of American Bishops on Mexico"; Husslein, II, 278, for Pius XI, *The Mexican Persecution;* *America*, September 27, 1945, for current Catholic description of Mexican problem.
24. Text of pastoral letter of Mexican Archbishops, the *New York Times*, January 17, 1932.
25. *America*, February 8, 1947.
26. *Empire's Children: The People of Tzintzuntzan*, George M. Foster assisted by Gabriel Ospina.
27. Nathaniel and Sylvia Weyl, *The Reconquest of Mexico*, p. 166.
28. J. H. Moore, p. 12.
29. *America*, April 7, 1956.
30. *Bulletin of the National Catholic Educational Association*, XXXVII, 605.
31. *Courier-Journal*, Rochester, New York, February 12, 1948. Monsignor Matthew Smith declared in the *Catholic Register* of January 16, 1949, that a study "made in our own national advertising department" in 1945 showed that "we average 5.2 persons to the family in the nation, whereas the public average is 3.8."
32. *Register*, September 16, 1956.

Chapter 13

Tolerance, Appeasement, and Freedom

1. Boscaren, *Digest*, I, 607 ff., contains many official parts of this story from the Catholic point of view, as does the *Catholic Encyclopedia Supplement*, "Union of Christendom." Baron has much of the story from the non-Catholic point of view.
2. *Catholic News*, January 17, 1948.
3. *Ibid.*, June 12, 1948.
4. *Protestant Report*, July, 1954.
5. Bouscaren, *Digest*, II, 334.
6. April 2, 1948.
7. Bouscaren, *Digest*, I, 607.
8. January, 1946.

9. *Freedom of Worship,* Paulist Press, 1944, Imprimatur Spellman, pp. 5 and 13.
10. 1948, p. 235.
11. *The New Scholasticism,* April, 1947, Catholic University of America.
12. *The Christian Century,* June 23, 1948, partially reprinted in *Time,* June 28, 1948, under the heading "The Church Cannot Blush."
13. (1) Catholic advertisement: "You hear it said that Catholics believe all non-Catholics are headed for Hell."

   Actual Catholic teaching: *Non-Catholics who deliberately reject Catholicism are headed for Hell.*

   Monsignor Canon John Vaughan, *Is There Salvation Outside the Church?* (International Catholic Truth Society, Brooklyn), p. 14: "A man who deliberately remains outside the pale of the said Catholic Church through his own fault (such as through pride or willful ignorance, or through fear of loss of goods or of friends, or gross neglect or indifference) will most certainly be lost should he continue in this state to the end."

   (2) Catholic advertisement: "That they believe non-Catholic marriages are invalid."

   Actual Catholic teaching: *Non-Catholic marriages involving a Catholic are invalid.*

   Canon 1094; also Canons 1060, 1061, 1063, 1070; see Bouscaren and Ellis. *Catholic Almanac,* 1948, p. 577: "A Catholic who goes through a marriage ceremony before a minister or a Justice of the Peace contracts no marriage."

   (3) Catholic advertisement: "Some think Catholics believe the Pope is God."

   Actual Catholic teaching: *Catholics owe "complete submission and obedience of will to the Church and to the Roman Pontiff, as to God Himself."*

   Leo XIII in his encyclical *Chief Duties of Christian Citizens.*

   (4) Catholic advertisement: "That he can do no wrong."

   Actual Catholic teaching: *The Pope can do no wrong when he speaks as head of the Church in matters of faith and morals.*

   Pius IX, *Constitution Pastor Aeternus,* Cap iv, 1870. *Encyclopedia Brittanica,* article on infallibility. Martin J. Scott, S.J., *No Pope Can Be Wrong in Teaching Doctrine,* America Press, 70 East 45th St., New York.

   (5) Catholic advertisement: "That they owe him civil allegiance."

   Actual Catholic teaching: *They owe him civil allegiance in matters of morals, education, and priestly rights.*

   Leo XIII, *Christian Constitution of States,* Husslein, Vol. I, especially pp. 71, 72, 81, 83. Pius XI, *Christian Education of Youth,* Husslein, Vol. II, especially p. 92. *Catholic Almanac,* 1948, p. 94: "Under no circumstances may the Church be subjugated by the State." Pius XI, *Restoring the Christian Social Order,* Husslein, II, 192: "She [the Church] never can relinquish her God-given task of interposing her authority, not indeed in technical matters, for which she has neither the equipment nor the mission, but in

all those that have a bearing on moral conduct. For the deposit
of truth entrusted to Us by God, and our weighty office of declaring, interpreting and urging in season and out of season the entire
moral law, demand that both social and economic questions be
brought within Our supreme jurisdiction, in so far as they refer to
moral issues."

(6) Catholic advertisement: "And that he should have the political
    power to rule America."
    Actual Catholic teaching: *He should rule America in moral, edu-
    cational, and religious matters.*
    Same sources as No. 5.

(7) Catholic advertisement: "It is said that Catholics want religious
    freedom only for themselves."
    Actual Catholic teaching: *They advocate complete religious free-
    dom for non-Catholics only as a temporary concession in non-
    Catholic countries, but in Catholic countries they restrict other
    cults.*
    Francis J. Connell, C. SS R., *Freedom of Worship* (Paulist Press,
    401 West 59th St., New York), Imprimatur Cardinal Spellman:
    "In a country like the United States, where the religious affiliations
    of the citizens are so numerous and so diverse, and where no
    single denomination is predominant, complete equality of all reli-
    gions is undoubtedly the most commendable policy" (p. 15). "But
    it must ever be remembered that a Catholic cannot advocate such
    a plan [complete religious toleration] on the basis that all reli-
    gions have a genuine, God-given right to exist" (p. 13). "If the
    country is distinctively Catholic—that is, if the population is
    almost entirely Catholic, and the national life and institutions are
    permeated with the spirit of Catholicity—the civil rulers can con-
    sider themselves justified in restricting or preventing denomina-
    tional activities hostile to the Catholic religion" (p. 10).

(8) Catholic advertisement: "That they oppose public schools [as an
    evil which should be destroyed]"
    Actual Catholic teaching: *They oppose public schools for Catholic
    children as an evil which should be destroyed.*
    Canon 1374. Paul L. Blakely, S.J., *May an American Oppose the
    Public School?* Imprimatur Cardinal Hayes, America Press, p. 5:
    "The first duty of every Catholic father to the public school is to
    keep his children out of it."

(9) Catholic advertisement: "And separation of church and state as
    evils which should be destroyed."
    Actual Catholic teaching: *They condemn financial separation of
    church and state and advocate support of Catholic schools by
    public taxation.*
    Pius IX, *Syllabus,* Cap. vi: One of the "principal errors of our
    time" is the proposition that the "Church ought to be separated
    from the State, and the State from the Church." Monsignor
    George B. O'Toole (professor of philosophy, Catholic University
    of America) in *The Liberal Illusion* by Louis Veuillot, National

Catholic Welfare Conference: "It is clear, then, that no Catholic may *positively and unconditionally* approve of the policy of separation of Church and State." See also Chapter 5 of this book.

(10) Catholic advertisement: "The claim is made that Catholics pay the priest for the forgiveness of their sins."

Actual Catholic teaching: *They pay the priests for Masses and those Masses are recognized as factors in securing forgiveness of sins, granted by priests.*

Smith, II, 912: ". . . the propitiatory power of the Mass is a most efficacious agent for obtaining pardon of sin." *Catholic Encyclopedia:* X, 21: ". . . there exists in each diocese a fixed 'mass-tax' "; and "mass foundations" are allowed for perpetual Masses. Canon 824 permits stipends for Masses.

(11) Catholic advertisement: "That they must buy their departed relatives and friends out of Purgatory."

Actual Catholic teaching: *They pay established fees for priestly Masses for the dead, and the Church guarantees that these Masses will help departed souls in Purgatory.*

See above. A single Mass for a soul in Purgatory may be obtained for $1, and perpetual Masses for $10, from the following: (1) St. Francis Purgatorial Society, Loretto, Pa. (2) Shrine of Our Lady of the Snows, Belleville, Ill. (3) Purgatorial Society, Redemptorist Fathers, 387 East 150th St., New York.

(12) Catholic advertisement: "That they adore statues."

Actual Catholic teaching: *They venerate statues.*

Canons 1279 ff.

(13) Catholic advertisement: "Are forbidden to read the Bible."

Actual Catholic teaching: *They are forbidden to read any non-Catholic version of the Bible.*

Canon 1399.

(14) Catholic advertisement: "Use medals, candles, and holy water as sure-fire protection against the loss of a job, lightning, or being run down by an automobile."

Actual Catholic teaching: *They use scapulars, relics, and similar articles with written assurance of their priests that these articles will help to protect the faithful against disaster.*

St. Thomas Aquinas (Smith, II, 687): "God himself fittingly honors such relics of the saints by working miracles at their presence." Sample circular, *Whosoever Dies Clothed in This Scapular Shall Not Suffer Eternal Fire,* Imprimatur Cardinal Spellman, published by the Carmelite National Shrine, 338 East 29th St., New York. See also Chapter 10 of this book.

14. See my 1955 work, *The Right to Read.*

15. *Time,* January 10, 1955.

16. *Register,* August 1, 1954.

17. Letter from New York Chancery Office, quoted in full by the Very Reverend R. G. Handas in Brooklyn *Tablet,* March 27, 1954.

18. *Records of the American Catholic Historical Society of Philadelphia,* December, 1955.

19. June 12, 1953.
20. Father Murray's most discussed piece, from which I have quoted a phrase or two, was in the *Proceedings of the Catholic Theological Society,* 1948. A Murray bibliography of the controversy was in *Thought* (published at Fordham University), Autumn, 1951; and an anthology in *Thought,* Spring, 1952. See also *Thought,* Summer, 1954; *Theological Studies,* June-September, 1949; and *American Ecclesiastical Review,* May, 1951. The anti-Murray chorus is best represented in the *American Ecclesiastical Review,* June, 1952 (with Bibliography), and in many other issues from 1949 forward, particularly in 1950 (CXXIII), pp. 161-174; and May, 1953. For Cardinal Ottaviani's views see the *New York Times,* July 23, 1953; and for the Spanish hierarchy's views, *ibid.,* May 21, 1952.
21. The quoted words are from Father Paul Hallett's unflattering analysis in the *Register,* February 9, 1956.
22. Its journal, *The Church and State Review,* now has a circulation of more than 60,000. Literature can be obtained from 1633 Massachusetts Ave., N.W., Washington 6, D. C. The two most important Jewish organizations which are fighting to preserve the separation of church and state are the American Jewish Congress and the American Jewish Committee.

Index

Abortion, criminal, 143
Academic freedom, 98 ff.
Adenauer, Conrad, 297
Adultery, 206
Acton, Lord, 33
Adoption, 200
Agar, William, 263
Aiken, George, 118
Allport, Gordon, 337
Altman's, 7
Ambassador to Vatican, x, 57 ff.
America (weekly), 5, 8, 103, 106, 111, 217, 224, 273, 284, 291, 327, 345
American Association of Catholic Trade Unionists, 299 ff.
American Broadcasting Company, 240
American Civil Liberties Union, 100, 221, 348
American Ecclesiastical Review, 9, 135, 153, 218-219, 329
American Federation of Labor, 119
American Library Association, 226
American Medical Association, 169
American Protective Association, 12, 349
Americanism, 6, 36 f.
Anne, Saint, de Beaupré, 256
Anti-Catholic fanatics, 12 ff.
Anti-Semitism, 206, 289, 339
Appeasement movements, x, 337
Apostolic Delegates, 38, 56
Aquinas, Thomas, Saint, 101, 138, 163, 165, 267
Arizona, 15
Arnold, Melvin, 7
Atlantic Monthly, xi, 58
Austria, 287

Baby Doll, 237
Baltimore, Maryland, 37
Baptism, 138 ff.
Barth, Karl, 293

Beacon Press, 7
Beck, Sister Mary Berenice, 149
Belford, John L., 257
Belgium, 290
Bellarmine, Robert, 270
Belloc, Hilaire, 48, 71, 73, 85, 279
Benedict XV, Pope, 38, 261
Bérard, Leon, 290
Bergin, William J., 131
Berlin, Germany, 57
Bigotry, 79, 302
Binchy, D. A., 279
Binghamton, New York, 175
Bingo, 50
Birth Control, ix, 5, 164 ff., 228, 239, 343
Bishops (Catholic), 27, 39, 75, 120
Black, Hugo, 121
Blakely, Paul L., 103-104
Blum, Virgil C., 124
Books on Trial, 220
Boston, Massachusetts, 37, 44, 81, 105, 108, 200
Bowdern, William S., 138, 146
Boycotts, 7
Boy Scouts, 43
Bradfield vs. Roberts, 159
Bradfordsville, Kentucky, 128
Brazil, 11, 315
Brooklyn, New York, 213, 257
Brooklyn *Tablet,* 227
Brunini, John G., 187
Buchanan, James, 58
Buffalo, New York, 108, 164, 262
Bus transportation, 114 ff., 129
Butler, Pierce, 181

Cabrini, Mother, 253, 255
California, 15
Calles, President of Mexico, 318
Cambridge, Massachusetts, 44, 109
Campbell, Paul E., 90, 97
Canada, 309 ff.
Canon, George S. L., 173